Grimoire

FOR THE

Green Witch

About Ann Moura

Born in 1947 and raised in a family tradition of three generations, Ann Moura has written about her family heritage as a Green Witch since the mid 1990s, passing along to a new generation the lessons she learned from her Brazilian mother and grandmother of Celtic-Iberian descent. Their understanding of folk magics and Craft concepts included the often repeated Rules of Conduct, ancient deities from Thrace and India, spiritism, herbal spells, candle magics, reincarnation belief, calling upon the Elementals, an understanding of the Power, and how to relate Catholic saints to Pagan deities, such as has also been done in Santeria, Candomblé, and Macumba.

By the time she was fifteen, Ann proceeded in her own direction with the Craft, discarding the Catholicized deity associations used by her mother and grandmother. She has instead focused purely on the Green level of Witchcraft, working with the energies and spirits of Nature, the Elementals, and dedicating herself to the Goddess and the God of Nature. Ann holds both Bachelor of Arts and Master of Arts degrees in History, and she enjoys writing, poetry, drawing, painting, running errands for her many kitties, and puttering in the herb garden. Married, with two grown children raised in the Craft, Ann writes about the Craft from the perspective of her personal experience and family training.

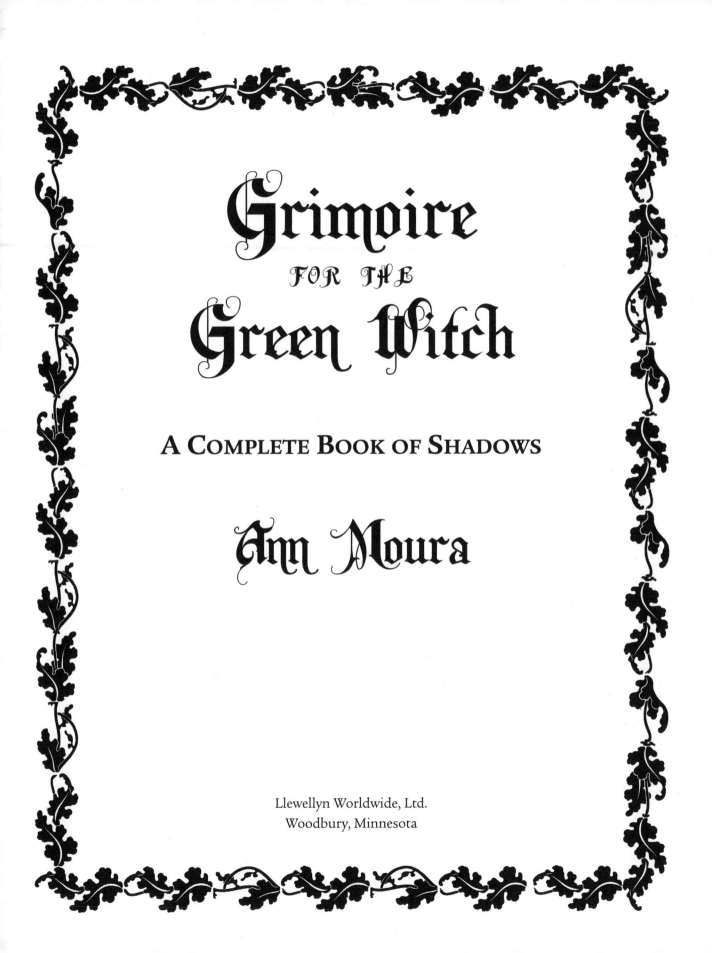

Grimoire
FOR THE
Green Witch

A COMPLETE BOOK OF SHADOWS

Ann Moura

Llewellyn Worldwide, Ltd.
Woodbury, Minnesota

FIRST EDITION
Twenty-second Printing, 2019

Cover design by Lisa Novak
Interior design and editing by Connie Hill

Library of Congress Cataloging-in-Publication Data
Moura, Ann (Aoumiel)
  Grimoire for the green witch : a complete book of shadows / Ann Moura — 1st ed.
    p.   cm.
  Includes bibliographical references and index.
  ISBN 13: 978-0-7387-0287-2
  ISBN 10: 0-7387-0287-0
  1. Witchcraft. 2. Herbs—Miscellanea. 3. Magic. 4. Ritual. 5. Charms I. Title.
BF1572.P43A583   2003
133.4'3—dc21   2003055246

Llewellyn Worldwide does not participate in, endorse, or have any authority or responsibility concerning private business transactions between our authors and the public.

All mail addressed to the author is forwarded, but the publisher cannot, unless specifically instructed by the author, give out an address or phone number.

Any Internet references contained in this work are current at publication time, but the publisher cannot guarantee that a specific location will continue to be maintained. Please refer to the publisher's website for links to authors' websites and other sources.

Llewellyn Publications
A Division of Llewellyn Worldwide Ltd.
2143 Wooddale Drive
Woodbury, MN 55125-2989
www.llewellyn.com
Llewellyn is a registered trademark of Llewellyn Worldwide Ltd.

 Printed in the United States of America on recycled paper

DEDICATION

This Book of Shadows and Grimoire is dedicated to the Family that gave it birth, to the helpers, visible and invisible, who have aided in the Workings over the years, to the Ancestors who are honored for their Heritage and perseverance through time, to the Elemental Kith and Kin, and to the Divine, who reveal Themselves in many forms and in many aspects throughout human experience.

OTHER BOOKS BY ANN MOURA

CONTENTS

ACKNOWLEDGMENTS

I thank not only the many people who have persisted in requesting I make my personal Book of Shadows available to the public, but also my mother and grandmother from whom I gained my Craft and magical footing, and who are the foundation upon which my Craft is built. Although not used in this publication, I offer my thanks and gratitude to Curtis Clark of Pomona, California whose unusual fonts and symbols are perfect for Craft writings and free for personal use, found at http://www.intranet.csupomona.edu/~jcclark/fonts/, and used by me in the computer transfer of my deteriorating handwritten magical books. My appreciation also goes to writers of early Grimoires spanning the centuries of the Middle Ages through the sixteenth century, such as Peter de Abano, Cornelius Agrippa, Dr. John Dee, Albertus Magnus, Paracelsus, Johannes Trithemius, and others whose works I perused at an early age and found portions I could adapt to my Green Craft. Thus, included herein are some of the traditional planetary symbols and squares typically associated with Ceremonial Magic but noted as optional inscriptions to be added to spell crafting objects. Thanks also to Nancy Mostad for her help and guidance in this project, and to all those at Llewellyn Publications who gallantly struggled with turning my Book of Shadows and Grimoire into print with as little alteration as possible. Special thanks and great appreciation are extended to Connie Hill, who managed to distill over 415 pages of odd sized lettering, varied spacing, and differing charts into a useable volume with a consistent format, and to Lisa Novak, who created the designs and symbols sprinkled throughout to be as close to my own as possible. And finally, my thanks to you, dear reader, who will alter and add to this Grimoire as you make it your own.

Introduction

This is a facsimile, a duplicate, of my own Book of Shadows and Grimoire—presented as I myself use it with a Book of Rituals and a Book of Spells. The first portion contains the basic Craft information and a variety of rituals that begin with a Circle Casting, proceed to a ritual, return to a simple feast called Cakes and Wine, and end with the Circle Opening. The second portion contains the information and formats for spell casting, tarot and other divinations, and herbal teas, oils, and baths. Here there are also a number of lists of correspondences, spell crafting information, some spells, and a bit of astrology.

This Grimoire and Book of Shadows is presented for three different types of readers. The first are those who have read my books on my family Craft, but who did not, for whatever reason, put together a personal book of shadows utilizing the material discussed in these books. For such readers, this two-part Grimoire may be the culmination of your studies taken from my earlier books: *Green Witchcraft: Folk Magic, Fairy Lore, & Herb Craft* (Llewellyn 1996); *Green Witchcraft II: Balancing Light & Shadow* (Llewellyn 1999); *Green Witchcraft III: The Manual* (Llewellyn 2000), and *Green Magic: the Sacred Connection to Nature* (Llewellyn 2002).

The second type of reader is one who has studied the Craft and perhaps has been a practitioner for a period of time, but who would like to possess a clean copy of a valid Grimoire and Book of Shadows with space in it for additional information and personal insights. The third type of reader is the novice, the newcomer who is still seeking a Craft path, but who desires to have a complete Book of Shadows in hand as a reference and guide to help make sense of what is being studied from other books. For this person, there is room for new notes and for growth. No matter where you are in your journey, I encourage you to continue to read from a variety of sources about the Craft, so you can select what is right for yourself, trusting in the Divine as They speak to you and influence your intuition.

This book is designed to be used as I use my own Book of Shadows. Prior to performing any ritual, you need to review what you are going to do. Use book markers or ribbons to keep your place in each section as you proceed, so that the first is in the Circle Casting of your choice, the second in the Ritual being observed, the third and others in any of the optional additions to ritual, such as Recitations, Meditations, Divinations, or Spells. By marking your places, you should be able to flip easily to the next section as indicated and return to continue from where you left off. Circle Castings will state to proceed to the ritual or observance, and that is when you leave the marker in that position and turn to the next marker, at the Ritual, such as an Esbat or Sabbat. In this section there will be an indicator to proceed to any spell work, meditation, etc., and this is when you leave the second marker and turn to the next. Here you may have a Recitation or Meditation of your choice, or a Re-Affirmation of Oath as part of a Sabbat (as an example), and when you finish it, there will be words directing you back to the Sabbat Ritual to resume from where you left off. When you finish the ritual, there will be words directing you back to the Cakes and Wine of the Circle Casting, followed there by the Circle Opening. This tradition of using place markers and moving from one section to another is familiar to many religions in their catechism books and liturgical books, but here they are presented for solitary practice, with indications of how to adjust for family or group practices. Experiment with the Book of Shadows, flip through the pages and familiarize yourself with the information and the arrangement. There are pages at the end of each section for your own additions, or those of your family. The first page states that this Book of Shadows is "Bestowed On" and leaves a space for your Craft Name. I am handing to you my practice to carry on and individualize according to your own personal needs and intuition.

There is a lot of information here, but it is not in sentence form, for this is a working Book of Shadows rather than a discussion or teaching type of book. It is my hope that it serves you as your own Grimoire, allowing you to jump into the Craft with both feet, and grow as you learn. Put your trust in the God and the Goddess, and They will not let you down. The beginning is important, and my Creed, Rules of Conduct, and the Witches' Rede are the foundation upon which a practice is built. Change the Creed as you develop your own, but never the Rules or the Rede. The Creed is the personal perspective of what your Craft means to you, but the latter two are the core of all Witchcraft. The Rede is the basis of Wiccan Traditions, and the Rules have come to me unchanged through three generations, that I know of, from 1890, have been passed to a fourth, and are now laid before you.

Think not that any secrets have been given away here or that any oaths have been violated, for Nature has no secrets but is open and free to any who have the will to explore, listen, observe, and learn; and at the end of my rituals, I say, *"As I have received, may I offer food for the body, mind, and spirit to those who seek such of me."* By taking this Book of Shadows into your hands, you are accepting from me that which you seek—food for your body, mind, and spirit. Take and use that which appeals to you, change or alter those things that you feel you should, and add your own entries in the blank pages provided for this purpose, for a Book of Shadows and Grimoire grows with each generation. Let this book then be a guide for you as you walk along your own path with the Goddess and the God. May your Craft flourish in joy, may the Divine inspire you, and, *"Blessed Be Thy Feet That Bring Thee On Thy Path."*

Ann Moura [Aoumiel]

The Book of Shadows of Aoumiel

A GRIMOIRE FOR THE GREEN WITCH

by Ann Moura

BESTOWED UPON

Reagan Awilson - Moura

Book of Shadows of Aoumiel

Rituals

1
Green Witchcraft

Creed of the Green Witch

The Sacred Tradition of Green Witchcraft

The Goddess & the God

Family Practice

The Litany

The Rules of Conduct

The Three Styles of Green Witchcraft

Sabbats: The Wheel of the Year

Quarters & Cross-Quarters

Calendar of Observances

Ground & Center — Grounding

Ritual Components — Ritual Robe Colors

Craft Names — Names of the God & Goddess

Symbols & Signs — The Magical Container

Basic Tools — Basic Materials

Altar Arrangement

Magical Pointers

Alphabets — Coven Terms — Craft Terms

Sun	Moon	Mercury	Venus	Mars	Jupiter	Neptune	Saturn	Pluto	Uranus

Waxing Moon [Maiden]	Full Moon [Mother]	Waning Moon [Crone]	Dark (New) Moon [Hidden Face/Mystery]

CREED OF THE GREEN WITCH

I Acknowledge the Unity of the Divine, symbolized by the Divine Androgyne, aspected as female and male, Goddess and God, form and energy, lunar and solar powers, honored during the Wheel of the Year at Esbats, Sabbats, and sacred days.

I Acknowledge the immanence of the Divine, whose Spirit resides in all things and worlds, creating a unity of All in Oneness and kinship through the Goddess and the God.

I Acknowledge that the Elementals Earth, Air, Fire, and Water are extensions of the Goddess and the God, both external and indwelling kith and kin, connecting all through Spirit.

I Acknowledge the immortality of the individual spirit, comforted by the God in Underworld, refreshed by the Goddess in Summerland, choosing incarnation by form, place, and soul purpose.

I Acknowledge that the God lovingly demonstrates the life cycle in His yearly passage through the Sabbats. He is born as the Oak King of the Goddess as Mother at Yule; cleansed and carried by the Crone into the arms of the Mother at Imbolc to be nourished by the milk of Her love. At Ostara, the Goddess transforms as Maiden and joins the God that They may walk as the Lady and the Lord of the Wild Wood to awaken the Earth from the sleep of Herself as Crone of Winter. The God and Goddess unite at Beltane to bring renewal to the Earth, and at their Litha wedding, the God shows His face of wisdom and age, turning from Oak King to Holly King as He begets Himself of the Goddess. At Lughnassadh, the God enters into the Goddess aspected as Mother Earth, filling Her abundance with the life essence of His solar energy. He enriches the vines and barleycorn with the essence of His Spirit at Mabon. He enters into Underworld, leaving the Goddess alone as Mother-to-be and Crone through Autumn and Winter, while He leads the Wild Hunt as the Horned Hunter, gathering the dead to His realm. He rules Underworld as the Lord of Shadows, where He offers rest, solace, and release of burdens to spirits at the end of each incarnation. At Samhain, the God passes His Spirit through the Goddess, making thin the veil between the worlds by their union of shadow and light, turning the Tomb of the Crone into the Womb of the Mother. At Yule the God as Sage offers His blessing and farewell to the children of the world, then turns His face to join them as the Infant Oak King reborn. Through the Wheel of the Year is the path of perfect love and perfect trust in the Divine demonstrated, that we may walk with the Goddess and the God in the bond of love.

I Acknowledge the three great Mysteries: the Ancient God as Father and Son; the Maiden Goddess as Mother and Crone; and the Union of Tomb and Womb for the eternal cycle of Life Immortal.

THE SACRED TRADITION OF
GREEN WITCHCRAFT

The Green Tradition of Witchcraft sees the aspects of the Divine All as separate and united as Goddess, God, and Both. The One who is All matches *all being from the One*. The forms of The Lord and the Lady are interlinked and interchangeable: Father Sky and Mother Earth/Sky Goddess and Earth God; Sun and Moon; Triple Goddess and Wed to the Triple Goddess; Threefold God and Wed to the Threefold God; Lord and Lady of the Greenwood; Lord of Abundance and Lady of Plenty; Queen of the Stars and King of the Universe; Creator and Creatrix, Spirit and Matter; Life and Passage; and Cosmic Dancers of Energy and Matter.

The Creative Forces of Nature are revered, with the Goddess and the God symbolizing the Universal Materials and Energies from which comes all existence. The God and the Goddess are equal and omnipresent, for They are found throughout the Universe, the Earth, and all that dwell therein. Because it is the Spiral Dance of Rebirth that brings us back to the Source of our existence in the Goddess and the God, reincarnation and communication with spirits are accepted parts of the religion.

Knowledge is the gift of the Goddess and the God, learning through many lives on Earth and keeping close to Them. Magic is a *natural* means of working with natural energies to accomplish a goal, and this magic becomes part of natural life for the practicing Green Witch. Consciousness may be *altered* through *visualization, meditation, ritual, music,* and *dance* to better commune with the Divine and effect the magic. Through Dedication, the pathway to communication is constantly open, so altered states cease to be necessary for contact with the Divine in Nature, only inner stillness and balance.

Freedom of the individual and *personal responsibility* are key aspects of Green Witchcraft. The liturgy may be created as needed or desired, for the magic will naturally flow with the acceptance of oneness with the All and with self-responsibility in our living.

Immanence, interconnection, and community are *three core principles of Witchcraft*. Because the God and the Goddess are manifested in all life, all existence is connected to be *one living cosmos*. The focus is on the growth of the whole through care for the Earth, the environment, and each other. The mythology of the Lord and the Lady revolves around two themes in the Wheel of the Year—that of *Fertility and Passage of the Seasons*; and that of the *Divine Life Cycle of the God,* often related in allegory to the changing of the seasons. Thus, the *sacrificed god* motif can be found in the Corn (Wheat) Cycle, wherein the God willingly gives His life-force into the crops at the time of marriage that humanity may be sustained, thus relating the Divine to life and Rites of Passage.

The Triple Goddess is the Maiden, Mother, and Crone (Matron), whose consort is the Horned God, the Creator, Destroyer (Hunter), and Lord of the Beasts. All Nature has both *positive and negative aspects,* and to be reborn, one must first die. The Goddess is seen as both life in Her form as Mother and as death in Her form as Crone, *yet both are the same.* Death is a natural

Death = not feared

passage to new life and is not feared or labeled as evil. With Nature there are both pleasant aspects and harsh aspects, but this is all part of the reality of the energy that flows in the Earth, the Universe, and the beings of the Earth. The transition of the *spirit* through incarnations is not feared, but understood and accepted as natural, for *life is eternal,* and *all spirits are immortal.*

Attuning to the God and the Goddess changes one forever—sparks new hope for the individual and for the planet. Personal destiny is in the hands of the practitioner. The **Dark Aspects** of the God and the Goddess—Lord of Shadows and Crone—as well as the **Bright Aspects**—Horned God and Maiden/Mother—are accepted. The Divine is both Creation and Destruction; Abundant Nature and Destructive Nature. Since all life is joined in the Dual Deity, the Two Who Are One, and to each other, life *cannot be destroyed,* only changed or moved into and out of the cauldron of life. The religion then is the worship or reverence of the Life Force represented in the Dual Deity as a Conscious Unity. This *reverence* may be expressed through *ceremonies or rituals* dedicated to *cycles of fertility,* of *planting* and *harvest,* and of *solar and lunar phases.*

The Esbats are *Rituals of the Full Moon, New (Dark) Moons*—times to receive learning from the Goddess. The Sabbats are composed of *four solar festivals,* called the Lesser Sabbats or the Quarters, and *four agricultural festivals,* called the Greater Sabbats or the Cross-Quarters. These are the main focus of ritual in the Green Tradition, along with Twelfth Night (Naming Day). The names by which the Lord and the Lady are addressed are not important, for *They are One by whatever Names They are known,* and *They dwell within.* They give life to be lived fully and with enjoyment, and we are reborn to learn until we are reunited with Them. Because people are of the Earth, She should be revered. The Green Witch knows of the connection of all things, the immortality of life, and draws upon the Power of the Divine directly, or through the Elementals of Earth, Air, Fire, and Water, or such spirits, devas, and Other People as may be helpful. The Elementals are the Kith and Kin of the Green Witch, for *body and strength* are of Earth, *breath and thought* are of Air, *energy and drive* are of Fire, and *emotions and vital fluids* are of Water. In olden days, The People learned in the ways of the Old Religion were called Wicce—voiced in the Middle English speech as *Weetch'ie*—meaning *Wise,* and the use of that wisdom was called the Craft of the Wise—*WicceCraft,* from whence comes the word Witchcraft. The Green Tradition of Witchcraft sees the *Practice of the Craft* as spirituality, and holds the word Witch as *honorable* and *spiritual.*

Esbat = full/New moon

Sabbat = solar

Earth = body & strength
Air = breath & thought
Fire = Energy & Drive
Water = Emotions & vital fluids

THE GODDESS & THE GOD

Because the Divine is One, the aspects of the Divine may interchange roles. Either the Lady or the Lord may represent the Sun, Moon, Grain, Harvest, Waters of Life, Universe, Sky, Earth, Life, Death, Passage, Resurrection in Body and/or in Spirit. The Lady and the Lord symbolize female and male fertility. They are both Power and Passage, honored with rites of burning lamps, candles, and torches; with salt and water, bread and wine, and flowers and grain. They both represent the passing of the seasons through solstices and equinoxes—the **Lesser Sabbats of the Quarters**—as well as through the cycles of harvest from preparation to planting to tend—the **Greater Sabbats of the Cross-Quarters.** In the harvest Sabbats, the Lord is the Sun, and the Lady is the Earth, culminating with the energy of the Sun entering the life supporting grains of the Earth, and giving the spirit of life into the fruits of the vines that refresh us. The Lady is most related to the Lunar phases—the **Esbats** of the Full Moon and New Moon [last waning crescent], as well as the Esbats of the Dark Moon, Blue Moon, and Sidhe Moon.

The Lord is Oak King from Yule to Litha, and the Holly King from Litha to Yule. He is Sun King and Lord of Shadows, Hunter and Greenman, Lord of the Wildwood, of Animals, and of the Fields, the one who collects the spirits who seek passage through the Goddess into new life.

The Lady is the One Who Transforms, the Changer. It is through her that the Lord dies, passes to Underworld, then is reborn. She changes, but is never-ending, and she is both Crone and Mother at the same time, thus her Tomb is also the Womb. It is through her that the spirit travels from death into new life, through her Cauldron of Rebirth.

FAMILY PRACTICE

Through each generation, the Green Craft adjusts and changes to meet the needs and inclinations of the Green Witch, just as Nature changes and alters to meet the needs of life's movement. Here lies the basic core of Green Witchcraft for future generations of my family and anyone I, or they, might reach and for whom this Craft holds resonance and brings joy. May this Craft grow with future generations as they enlarge upon it through their explorations of the vastness of the Power, guided always by the loving Lady and Lord, and by the kindness of the Elementals, who are the Cardinal Emanations of the Divine: Earth, Air, Fire, and Water joined with our Spirit that is of Divine essence. We are One. The family tradition honors the Goddess at Lunar phases of the Esbats and she is seen as the Goddess of the Moon and the Earth. The God is honored at Solar phases of the Sabbats and is seen as the God of the Sun and the Earth.

The Goddess of my family is Bendidia, or Bendis, the Thracian Goddess of the Dark Moon. She holds a twig in her hand to show the way to Underworld, and hence to new life. She is the Goddess of Magic, Secrets, Occult Wisdom, and is the ancient Goddess of Witches. But She is also the Goddess by any name, and is the Triple Goddess of Maiden, Mother, and Crone.

The God of my family is Shiva, but He is also the God by any name, and is the Triple God of Youth, Father, and Sage identifiable with Dionysus, Cernunnos, Frey, and Herne. He dances within a ring of fire, sits upon a dais, horned and surrounded by animals wild and domestic, and sits upon a tiger skin in meditation, being the Lord of the Cosmic Dance, Lord of Beasts, Lord of the Wildwood, and Lord of the Harvest. He is Horned Hunter, Greenman, Lord of Light, Lord of Shadows, and Wed to the Triple Goddess.

THE LITANY

The Goddess and the God are One

Life is a Gift to Enjoy

I am part of the Earth and revere Her

I am connected to all things and the Power therein

I am one with the All and the All is within me

I am kith and kin to the Elementals, aspects of the Divine

I learn from the Goddess and the God, Nature, and Meditation

I follow the Rules of Conduct as passed down to me

THE RULES OF CONDUCT

1. Be careful what you do.

2. Be careful who you trust.

3. Do not use the Power to hurt another, for what is sent comes back. *Karma*

4. Never use the Power against someone who has the Power, for you draw from the same well.

5. To use the Power you must feel it in your heart and know it in your mind.

[Words repeated through my maternal line since 1890.]

THE THREE STYLES OF GREEN WITCHCRAFT

GREEN PRACTICE AS FOLK ARTS

This approach to the Green Craft comes under the umbrella of a mainstream religion: practicing the Craft is to work magics using the new names of the deities of power, and celebrate the traditional holidays with the understanding of their Pagan originals. Folk Art Witches may invoke the Power as the energies of deities, angels, saints, and the Holy Spirit, and may adapt other cultural images into their practice.

GREEN PRACTICE AS PERSONAL MAGICS

This variety of Green Craft as a *Natural Witchcraft* elevates the Mannuz (Mahn-NU or the Human; Runic Mannaz; the Self) to union with the Universe, enhancing the personal power of the Witch through the energies of herbs and natural objects and directing this to accomplish a goal. Ritual, magical tools, and conscious spellwork functions through the Elementals, and a Grimoire is created to codify tables of magical correspondences for a successful practice. Religion plays no part, save as the Witch and the Unnamed All work together through Nature with honesty, instinct, and intuition.

GREEN PRACTICE AS RELIGION

This type of Green Craft identifies the Goddess and the God in partnership with the Witch through a self-initiation for introduction and learning, and later by complete union in a self-dedication. As a religion, magic is often directed through personal communion with the God and the Goddess, identified as male and female in balance. There are rituals of religious observance including Sabbats and Esbats, and special days honoring aspects and manifestations of the Divine throughout the Wheel of the Year.

SABBATS: ✸ THE WHEEL OF THE YEAR

YULE — WINTER SOLSTICE [12/21]

1. God as Oak King is born of the Goddess.
2. God as Holly King prepares to depart.
3. Goddess is Mother of the Sun God.
4. Goddess is Crone of Winter.

IMBOLC — PURIFICATION AND FIRE [2/1]

1. Goddess is cleansed and purified.
2. Milk flows for lambs and for the baby God.
3. Quickening of the Earth.
4. Goddess is preparing to return to Maiden.

OSTARA — SPRING EQUINOX [3/21]

1. Goddess is Maiden/brings Spring.
2. God and Goddess encourage animal fertility.

BELTANE — FERTILITY AND FIRE [5/1]

1. God Youth and Goddess Maiden unite in love.
2. May Day flowers, romps, and bonfires.

LITHA — SUMMER SOLSTICE [6/21]

1. God turns from Youth to Sage.
2. Marriage of God to Goddess.

LUGHNASSADH — BREAD HARVEST [8/1]

1. God enters the Earth in marriage, giving his energy into the grain; now his body.
2. First Harvest/Bread Harvest—grains.

Mabon — Autumn Equinox [9/21]

1. God gives his spirit into the vines, fruit, and barleycorn, wine, cider, whiskey, beer, and mead are now his blood—He rules Underworld.

2. Goddess alone and pregnant with the God.

Samhain — Death and Rebirth [10/31]

1. God within the Goddess, yet also Leader of the Wild Hunt.

2. Veil between the worlds at its thinnest, Crone and Hunter [Lord of Shadows] reign together.

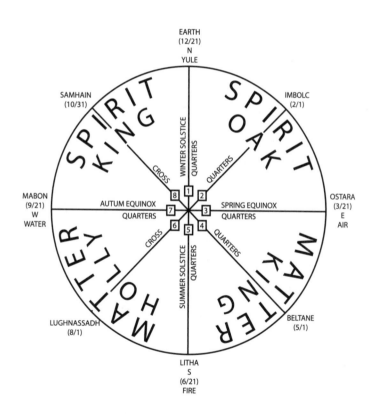

WHEEL OF THE YEAR

QUARTERS & CROSS-QUARTERS

QUARTERS — GREEN [LESSER] SABBATS

Yule — Winter Solstice [12/21]

1. God is born of the Goddess.
2. Goddess is both Mother and Crone of Winter.

Ostara — Spring Equinox [3/21]

1. Goddess is Maiden/brings Spring to Earth.
2. God and Goddess encourage fertility of Earth.

Litha — Summer Solstice [6/21]

1. God turns from Youth to Sage/Oak to Holly King.
2. Marriage of God to Goddess.
3. Holly King impregnates Goddess with Oak King.

Mabon — Autumn Equinox [9/21]

1. God gives his blood into the vines.
2. Goddess alone and pregnant with the God.

CROSS-QUARTERS — WHITE [GREATER] SABBATS

Samhain — Death and Rebirth [10/31]

1. God within the Goddess/tomb becomes the womb.
2. Veil between the worlds is thinnest.

Imbolc — Purification and Fire [2/1]

1. Milk flows for the baby God as Oak King.
2. Quickening of the Earth.

Beltane — Fertility and Fire [5/1]

1. God and Goddess unite in love.
2. May Day romps and bonfires/fertility encouraged.

Lughnassadh — Bread Harvest [8/1]

1. God enters the Earth in marriage, giving his body to be the grain.
2. First Harvest—grains.

CALENDAR OF OBSERVANCES

JAN. 1: Hag's Day—honoring the Goddess as She Who Transforms.

JAN. 6: Triple Goddess Day—honoring the Goddess as the Three-In-One; also Day of the Lord of the Dance—honoring Shiva, seeking his aid for prosperity and wisdom in the New Year, and also for a spouse if desired.

JAN. 18: Day of Danu—Celebrating the Great Goddess who Shows the Way.

FEB. 2: IMBOLC SABBAT: Cleansing, Purification, Quickening.

FEB. 14: Family Day—Celebrated as Valentine's Day.

FEB. 15: Pan's Day—Honoring the Lord of the Wilderness, Animals, and Fertility.

FEB. 28: Cake Day—Offering little cakes to the God and the Goddess; Remembering the ancestors with cakes and flowers.

MAR. 9: Mother Goddess Day—honoring the loving, nurturing Goddess.

MAR. 17: Maenad Festival—honoring Dionysus, the God of the Vine and Rebirth.

MAR. 21: OSTARA SABBAT: Spring Equinox; the Goddess of Spring.

MAR. 25: Lady Day—honoring the Crone as Grandmother; Mother of the Mother.

APR. 1: Dark Mother Day—honoring Black Annis, Kali; Fool's Day—honoring the God of Chaos Energy.

APR. 7: Feast of Blajini—offerings made to the Other People/the Sidhe or Fairies.

APR. 8: Day of Mooncakes—honoring the Moon Goddess.

APR. 23: Festival of the Greenman—honoring the God of forest and vegetation.

APR. 25: Spring Festival—dedicated to the Horned God and Corn Mother.

APR. 28: Festival of Flora: remembrance of those who passed into Underworld.

APR. 30: May Eve—Walpurgis Night; annual gathering of Witches and covens.

MAY 1: BELTANE SABBAT: Festival of Spring and Fertility.

MAY 21: Dark/Bright Mother Goddess Day—honoring Hecate/Demeter; Kali/Uma.

MAY 28: FEAST OF BENDIDIA—family feast day honoring the Goddess of the Moon, Dark Moon, Underworld, Secret Wisdom, and Witches.

JUN. 5: Earth Mother Day—honoring Gaia/Tailtiu/Mother Earth.

JUN. 13: Epona Feast Day—honoring the Goddess of the Horse [Otherworld Guide].

JUN. 21: LITHA SABBAT: Summer Solstice; celebrating Fullness of the Year; Midsummer"s Eve: offerings to the Other People.

JUN. 23: Day of the Lady and Lord of the Sidhe—Otherworld aspects of the Divine.

JUN. 27: Day of the Household Deities—cleanse/rededicate household altars/shrines.

JUL. 1: Crone Day—honoring Father Time and Old Mother Nature.

JUL. 21: Witch's Day—celebrating the Craft as life, practice, and religion.

AUG. 1: LUGHNASSADH SABBAT: First Harvest—Bread Harvest.

AUG. 20: Marriage of the God and Goddess—Sun God enters Earth Goddess and rules Underworld as Lord of Shadows.

AUG. 21: Festival of Hecate—invoking her to protect the harvests now that the God resides within her aspect as the Earth Goddess.

SEP. 13: Fire Lighting Ceremony—honoring with candlelight the spirits of the dead.

SEP. 21: MABON SABBAT: Autumn Equinox; Second Harvest—Vine Harvest; Harvest Home/ Thanksgiving Feast/Winter-finding for the Norse.

OCT. 2: Feast of the Guardian Spirits—honoring spirit guides and helpers.

OCT. 18: Great Horn Festival—Horned God and Lady of the Wood invoked for the fertility of wild game and the Hunting Season.

OCT. 31: SAMHAIN SABBAT: Third Harvest— Root Harvest; All Hallows Eve: Dark God and Dark Goddess united in Underworld allow spirit communication at this most holy [hallowed] time.

NOV. 1: Cailleach's Reign—Day of the Banshees; honoring the Riders of the Wild Hunt who search for souls to transport to the Land of Shadows.

NOV. 11: Lunatishees—Day of the Fairy Sidhe; honoring the Other People in whom is held the immortal life force; Old November Eve [Samhain on old calendar].

NOV. 16: Night of Hecate—honoring Thracian Goddess of the Moon, Magic, and Witches as the Teacher of the Craft.

NOV. 22: NIGHT OF SHIVA—family feast day honoring Shiva as the Pillar of Light/the life-force as the Infinite Light, with oil lamps and candlelight.

NOV. 27: Uma Day—honoring the Goddess as Queen and Mother of the Universe.

NOV. 29: Feast of Hathor—honoring the Goddess as Horned Mother, and also as Sekhmet, the Lion Goddess of the Sun, and as Bastet, the Cat Goddess of Fertility and Life—Triple Goddess Bast-Hathor-Sekhmet.

DEC. 21: YULE SABBAT: Winter Solstice; Return of the Sun God.

DEC. 24: Holly Eve—departure of the Holly King who leaves gifts for children.

DEC. 25: Oak Day—celebrating the birth of the Oak King; birth of the Sun is evident.

DEC. 31: Hogmanay—New Year's Eve; Crone preparing to depart, winter at its height; Crone, old and withered year changes at midnight into young and fresh New Year.

GROUND & CENTER

Ground and Center before all Magical Work to avoid depleting personal energy levels. Begin by being still, gathering within and releasing through the feet [and palms if need be] into the ground all static, chaotic internal energies. Now feel the inner calmness, centered around the heart, and draw up through the feet strong Earth energy [through the floor if indoors], feeling the power and energy rising up and intertwining with your own energies up through the legs, body, arms, neck, and head, out the top, circled around, and up again until all portions of the body are in balance. Once this power is felt and is in balance, then Circle Casting, Ritual, Divination, and Spell Work may begin.

Grounding after all Magical Work to avoid overload of personal energy levels: touch the Earth/floor with palms of the hands after magical work and feel the excess energy drain out, leaving a balance of personal energy, augmented only by that amount of Earth necessary for healthy functioning of the body. Too much retained energy will result in headache, depression, or irritability. Too little will result in fatigue, depression, or faintness. You must find the inner balance, and adjust according to how you feel.

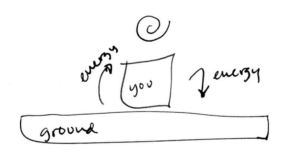

RITUAL COMPONENTS

1. Purify Self—Bathe*; Ground and Center.
2. Purify Space—Besom/Light at Quarters.
3. Cast Circle—Draw/Asperge/Cense; Fume.
4. Call the Elementals.
5. Welcome the Divine.
6. Conduct Observance.
7. Raise Power and Direct.
8. Ground Residual Power.
9. Cakes And Wine.
10. Farewell the Divine—Merry Meets.
11. Farewell Elementals.
12. Open The Circle.
13. Benediction.

*Note: Bathe with herbs [a single herb or combination of rosemary, thyme, marjoram, lavender, rose petals, calendula, hops, or burdock root] in a muslin or cotton bag and sea salt in the tub water for best cleansing and purification prior to ritual.

RITUAL ROBE COLORS

1. Oranges and Reds—Protective; Sabbats; ☿.
2. White and Muslin—Purification; Esbats;)O(.
3. Black—Protective; Ward Negativity; Truth.
4. Greens—Wildwood; Lady and Lord of Nature; Herbs; Earth; Other People.
5. Gray/pale Lavender—Other World; Sidhe; veiled; mystic.
6. Purples—Spiritual Awareness; Intuition.
7. Blues—Water and Skies; Psychic Awareness.
8. Yellows—Divination.

CRAFT NAMES

1. Craft Name—openly used [Outer Court].

   A. Chosen by the Practitioner.

2. Working Name—Secret Name [Never Reveal].

   A. Chosen by the Practitioner.

   B. Bestowed by the Goddess and the God.

3. Eke Name—Coven Name [Used for Inner Court].

   A. Bestowed by Coven leaders.

   B. Selected by Initiate to a Coven.

NAMES OF THE GOD & THE GODDESS

1. May use generic labels of Lady and Lord.

2. May use Deity Names that appeal.

3. May use/mix Pantheons that appeal.

4. May use inherited Family Deity names.

   A. Bendidia [Bendis].

   B. Shiva.

5. May use secret names.

   A. Revealed by Deities to Practitioner.

      1.) During the Dedication.

      2.) Not to be shared with anyone.

   B. Coven names for Deities.

      1.) Revealed at Initiation.

      2.) Not to be used out of Coven.

SYMBOLS & SIGNS

☽○☾	The Triple Goddess	●○●	The Crone
⛎	The Horned God		The Lord of Shadows
⛤	The Pentagram	⛥	The Pentacle
	Sun Rise and Set		Moon Rise and Set
⊕	The Quarters/the Elementals	∞	Cosmic Lemniscate [Infinity]
⊛	The Sabbats		Cauldron
◎	Lunar Spiral	⊕	Solar Cross
♈	The Chalice		The Bread
	The Athame		The Bolline [work Knife]
	The Wand		The Besom
▽	Earth Elemental		Incense
△	Air Elemental		Winter
△	Fire Elemental	♉	Spring
▽	Water Elemental	∪	Summer
☉	The Sun	♏	Autumn
☽	The Moon	☽◐○◑☾	Phases

☿	♀	♂	♃	♆	♄	♇	♅	↨
Mer	Ven	Mars	Jup	Nep	Sat	Pluto	Uran	Ascen

♈	♉	♊	♋	♌	♍	♎	♏	♐	♑	♒	♓
Aries	Tau	Gem	Can	Leo	Vir	Lib	Scor	Sag	Cap	Aquar	Pisces

∪	Deosil	∪	Widdershins
⊛	Circle	⛤	Pentagram As Earth, Air, Fire, Water, Spirit
	Balefire		Herbs

THE MAGICAL CONTAINER

PREPARING A CONTAINER FOR MAGICAL SUPPLIES

1. Wash container with spring water combined with non-iodized salt or with sea salt.

2. Place incense of frankincense, copal, pine, rosemary, or sage inside the container for total of thirteen minutes.

3. Place plain or sea salt in a small white cloth and tie shut [as a pouch] with white thread, and set inside the container.

4. Place in a dark [brown] bottle: 3 black peppercorns for power; 5 elderberries or hawthorn berries for the Witch's Craft; 7 thorns or straight pins for protection; and nine 9-inch pieces of thread or embroidery floss, 1 each of white [for purity], black [for protection], purple [for spirituality], red [for power], green [for the Earth], yellow [for divination], orange [for attraction], blue [for truth], and pink [for love]. Tighten lid, and set the bottle inside the container.

5. Container is ready for storage of magical supplies.

6. Part of the fun of the Craft is accumulating magical tools and materials: use Nature, thrift stores, catalogs, shops, etc., or make your own.

BASIC TOOLS

Athame: a ritual knife used to direct magical energy; this is usually a black-handled, two-edged knife, meaning the blade is sharp on both sides, but it may be dull rather than sharp as this is not a cutting tool. This knife may be of wood, stone, horn, metal, or jet, and could be a regular knife if visualized as the ritual tool [as with Kitchen Witch tools being taken from those used in daily work around the house]. An athame may be a letter opener, pocketknife, etc., as long as it is seen as a ritual tool. The handle color may also vary, but black is traditional.

Bell: may be a tiny bell with a delicate chime, or a larger bell, used during ritual and to call upon the Fairie Folk [if delicate in tone]; may be of brass, ceramic, crystal, silver, etc.

Bolline: a cutting tool used in magical work to inscribe candles, cut herbs, cut thread, or any other such use. Traditionally a two-edged blade, with a white handle, but any tool designated as the working tool may be used.

Bowls: one for salt, one for water, and one for the libation.

Broom/Besom: a ritual broom not used for housework, but for clearing the ritual space during Circle Casting, and for spell work.

Candle Holder: can be individual, candelabra, votive holders, etc. but there should be one for the Goddess and one for the God, and one for Both and/or one for magical work.

Cauldron: metal pot for magical work; when burning a candle inside it, you might want to put a layer of clean sand on the bottom of the pot; must be large enough to hold melted wax and to burn twigs inside without creating a hazard. Lidded is best, but if not possible, get a separate lid for covering when ready to put out any fire within.

Censer: container for incense that can be carried around the Circle or set on the Altar; may be of brass, a shell, or any other suitable material [see *Incense Burner* below], and as a container should be partially filled with clean sand to hold the incense and prevent burns.

Cingulum: a nine-foot-long cord of red silk, wool, or cotton that is knotted at Initiation [see *Ritual*], and worn with the robe, kept on the Altar, or wrapped around a tine of the Stang or around the top of the Staff.

Crystal Ball: a smooth sphere without facets, but may contain bubbles and other markings within; clear ones of natural quartz are very expensive, but manufactured lead crystal also works.

Cup: used for the beverage of Cakes and Wine, Esbats Rituals, etc. May be of pottery, silver, brass, crystal, wood, etc.

Incense Burner: suitable to hold the type of burning incense used; may be a stick holder, cone holder, or resin holder and made of wood, earthenware, ceramic, glass, brass, shell, etc. [see *Censer* above].

Pentacle: a flat disk with the five-pointed star in a circle engraved or painted on it; may be of wood, clay, ceramic, wax, brass, silver, gold, or simply drawn on a piece of paper.

Plate: one to hold the bread or other such food blessed in the Cakes and Wine ritual.

Robes: may want a variety of colored robes depending on the type of ritual or spell work involved, or a basic white or black robe. The cingulum [cord] may be used with the robe to tie it about the waist.

Staff: used as a long wand, may be decorated and carried as an indication of Craft association or simply for walking in the woods.

Stang: may use this instead of an Altar, by sticking it into the ground or placing within a stand; decorated for the Sabbats.

Tarot Cards: choose a deck that draws you, and use for divinations [*see Tarot section*]; you may acquire a variety of decks over time.

Wand: should be the length of the forearm to the fingertip, about 12 to 16 inches; may be of oak, willow, hazel, apple, elder for the influence of those woods [*see Correspondences*]; select one from Nature or buy one, but choose one that appeals to you; the tool most associated with Witchcraft is the wand.

BASIC MATERIALS

Altar Cloths: a variety of coverings for the Altar depending upon the ritual and the season; attractively patterned sarongs are often used for this purpose.

Beverages: variety of acceptable drinks, be they fruit juices, wines, or liqueurs.

Candles: votives, tapers, jar, shaped, tea light styles in various colors.

Charcoal disks: used for resin incense such as copal or dragon's blood.

Cloths: variety of solid colors of cotton cloth for use in spell crafting for wrapping tarot cards, crystals, stones, holding herbs, making poppets, herbal/dream pillows, etc.

Cords: the cord designating the three styles of green practice are gold for energy worker within a cultural tradition, red for working with the Powers of Nature, and black for dedication to the Goddess and the God. As many styles as have been used, such colors may be combined or braided together. The red is also the cingulum of Initiation, to which later may be added the black after a Dedication, but only with the red is the practitioner's measure taken. The symbology is gold for energy work, red for powers, and black for wisdom and union with the Divine.

Glass Bottles: for herbs, oils, spell work, and storage of other items as needed. Rinse with spring water and sea salt to cleanse.

Herbs: a variety of herbs stocked in labeled containers [a glass jar is best; do not use plastic] and kept out of direct sunlight; used in spell work.

Incenses: stick, cone, resins in a variety of fragrances; will need charcoal disks made for incense if using resins. Light incense, look for glow; then wave to extinguish the flame so only smoke results [this keeps the fragrance from getting harsh].

Matches: may be regular or long stick variety, or use a lighter.

Musical Instruments: may use drums, bells, flutes, harps, sistrums, cymbals, gourd rattles, other rattles, etc. to aid in meditation, spell casting, energy raising, etc.

Oils: a variety of essential oils [rosemary, sandalwood, lavender, benzoin, rose geranium, frankincense, pine, juniper, mint, etc.] for anointings [do not use cinnamon—it will burn] and spell work; fixed oils [olive, sunflower, almond, jojoba] for mixing own fragrance blends.

Salt: sea salt, rock salt used in rituals, spell work, and cleansings

Spring Water: collected at a natural spring and stored for use in spell work and ritual, or bought prepackaged [remove from plastic container and store in a prepared glass bottle—see above].

Stones: a variety of crystals, semi-precious stones, river, and Earth stones for use in spell, healing, and aura work.

Threads: or embroidery floss of various colors for tying up magical works.

Tiles/Trivets: used under items that will burn hot to avoid scorching a surface beneath.

BASIC ALTAR ARRANGEMENT

GODDESS AREA LEFT	BOTH AREA CENTER	GOD AREA RIGHT

ALTAR SET UP [FACING NORTH]

Candelabra or three separate Candles

Deity representation [symbol/image]	Deity representation [symbol/image]	Deity representation [symbol/image]
Chalice	Bell	Incense
Water bowl	Pentacle	Salt bowl
Wand	Cauldron	Athame/bolline
	Libation bowl	
Supplies (oils, herbs)	Book of Shadows (work materials)	Food and supplies (matches, incense)

Basic Shrine

GODDESS AREA	BOTH AREA	GOD AREA
)O(	Candle	☿
Spirit Bowl*	Incense	Offering Plate

Simple Shrine

GODDESS AREA	BOTH AREA	GOD AREA
Candle	Spirit Bowl	Incense

Goddess Area/Both Area/God Area may have candles or a representation, such as statues, stones, a conch shell for the Goddess and small antler rack or animal horn for the God, with a candle or other item to represent both Goddess and God together.

***Spirit Bowl** is of unglazed pottery, set on a saucer or waterproof mat. A beverage is poured into the bowl: spring water, milk, beer, mead, whiskey, rum, wine, tea, liqueur, or wassail are typically used. The beverage disappears over a short time of one to several days. A regular bowl or cup may also be used in place of the spirit bowl.

Offering Plate may be a small saucer of any material, onto which either some food item is placed, such as a fresh fruit (orange, mango, etc.), a cupcake, muffin, piece of multigrain bread, etc., or flowers, flower petals, or uncooked grains such as wheat, rice, or oats are placed. Additional flower vases may be added to the shrine as space and appearance permits.

Candle may be a single candle in front of the center area, or there may be two candles used, with one each in the Goddess and God area in front of or to one side of the image.

Incense may be placed at the center area in front of the candle (if one is used there). Variations are many, but as long as the shrine is pleasing to the eye and senses, it provides a "presence" of the Divine in whatever room it is maintained. Keep it clean, and take time to sit or stand before the shrine to commune with the Divine and listen for a response. Here is where petitions are made, where expressions of joy and appreciation are made, where comfort is sought, for the shrine is always present rather than being set up for a specific ritual as is an Altar. An Altar may double as a shrine.

MAGICAL POINTERS

AVOID HAGGLING WHEN BUYING MAGICAL ITEMS

1. First ask the Elementals [and the Divine] to bring to you what you need, at a price you can afford.

2. Be sure to give a reasonable cost you can afford.

3. Be sure to envision the item as you want it to appear.

4. When you encounter the item, buy it lest you offend the Elementals who have brought it to you according to your own request.

5. Prepare magical tools with Consecration Ritual.

The law of equal returns applies to all aspects of the craft—hence, not only does the energy sent out in a spell return, but to get a gift, a gift must be given.

1. Remember the Rules of Conduct : what is sent comes back.

2. Payment of money is acceptable to receive a tool, Craft item, or counseling.

3. **Always** give something for anything gathered from Nature [be it spell ingredients or Craft tools]: such as a blessing, a design of pentagram drawn in the ground around a plant, a libation of milk or water, a ribbon or other decoration loosely tied to a twig, bits of grain, a dab of honey, crushed egg shells, used coffee grounds, a pinch of clean tobacco, or kernels of blue corn.

4. **Never** say "thank you" to the Other People—they consider it dismissive, reducing them to the status of a servant.

5. **Always** express appreciation to the Other People with feelings from the heart—say what it is about their gift that you like, admire, or find valuable.

6. **Always** accept any gift bestowed on you by the Fairies, no matter what it is, and express your appreciation for it, saving it in a prepared box if not needed at this time—it will come in handy later.

7. **Never** be servile to dragons—they find it offensive if they offer you aid and you grovel before them—it demeans them for having thought better of you.

8. **Never** be arrogant to dragons—they will find you crunchy and tasty.

9. **Never** think a unicorn is cute—that horn is there for a purpose; don't be on the end of it.

10. Be sure to farewell any Elemental you have called, lest you create chaos in your own surroundings.

11. The Powers work through you, you do not dominate nor command them.

12. If you do not approach the Craft with Love, the Craft will not respond to you with Love.

ALPHABETS

RUNIC

A	B	C/K	D	E	F	G	GH	H	I	J

L	M	NG	OE	OS	P	Q	R	S	T	TH

U	V	W	X	Y	Z

OGHAM

A	B	C	D	E	F	G	H	I	J	K

L	M	N	NG	O	P	Q	R	S	T	U

V	W	X	Y	Z

THEBAN

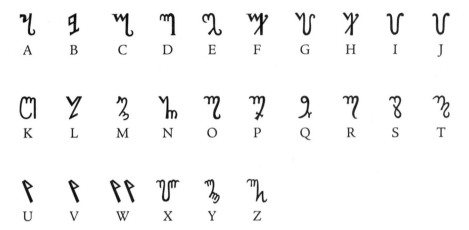

COVEN TERMS

1. Coven—Group of Witches, usually three to thirteen.

2. Covenhome—Name of Coven.

3. Covenstead—Limited area for covens.

4. Hive—Large coven splits into smaller units.

5. Witch Queen/King—Having five or more covens hive from the original one of a High Priestess/Priest (not common to all Covens since many are democratic rather than "belonging" to a founder or any one person).

CRAFT TERMS

Adept: The state acquired by an initiate into a group, particularly Ceremonial Magic, when material gain is no longer desired, and spiritual growth has come to such a degree that Nature is at one's command.

Aesir: The level of the Teutonic magical system working with the Gods and Goddesses of the Warrior and Ruler classes; political rather than the Nature deities of the Seidhr, or Green Level Witches.

Air: Elemental representing East; Sunrise; yellow/red; childhood; intellect; thought; mind; tarot suit of swords; victory; power; conflict; conscious mind.

Amulet: A natural object that may be worn for protection, such as a rabbit's foot, and is a variety of charm.

Androgyne: *Both* male and female, a hermaphrodite; symbol of the Divine All.

Animistic: Seeing all things as having a spirit or soul, thus the Divine spirit (or the Power) resides in all things. Key phrase: *everything is alive.*

Ardhanari: "Half Male and Half Female" name of Shiva as Divine All.

Asatru: "Loyal to the Aesir Gods" name for Odinists of the Teutonic tradition, opposite of Seidhr, who are practitioners of Nature focused Witchcraft.

Asgard: Realm of the Teutonic Gods, divided into the worlds of the rulership, law making, and warrior deities of the Aesir, and the Nature deities of the Vanir.

Astral Plane: An energy level of existence that lies outside the physical and mental planes of reality; energy that is *felt.*

Astral Projection: Moving the spirit energy from the physical body through space and/or time to other locations while the body remains either asleep or in a trance; while the travel may be on the astral plane, it may also be manifested on the physical plane so that other people might interact with an astral projection believing it to be a physical presence, thus someone being in two places at the same time.

Athame [a-tham′may]**:** Symbol of Elemental Air; ritual double-edged knife of witchcraft, representative of the energy of the God and used to direct energy in magical work; not a cutting tool, with generally a black-handled knife, but any knife or knife-like object used to conduct energy for magic work may be an athame.

Atum: The Great He/She of the Egyptian religion whose temple was at Karnac; worshipped as the Great God until the temple was closed by law in the fourth century C.E., while Egypt was part of the Roman Empire. Atum had two aspects, Shu [Air] and Tefnut [Moisture], from which emanated Nut [Sky] and Geb [Earth].

Aum: The sound of the name of God, with the letters meaning male, female, and both; with male emphasized, "Aum namah Shivaye": a mantra to Shiva.

Aura: Energy field of multiple layers surrounding all things that may be seen visually or sensed psychically to be understood or manipulated in magic. Gaps or holes can lead to illness and can be healed through use of crystals, or other energy moving magics as with the passing of the palms of a healer above the affected area.

Banishing Magic: Type of magic that casts away something present and undesired—*see Repelling and Exorcising Magics.*

Benediction: Closing of a ritual wherein blessings are given and received, and the peace of the Lady and the Lord is acknowledged.

Besom [bes'sum]: Broom used to sweep the Circle clear of negative and chaotic energies prior to casting.

Bindrune: A runic monogram of two to three rune symbols used as a sigil on a magical object, with the last rune drawn being the one that binds the whole.

Black Mirror: Tool used for divination and dark aspect meditations using a mirror of black glass or backpainted in glossy black for shadowy reflection; also name for objects used as mirrors, such as polished obsidian [black volcanic glass].

Blood Line Witches: Family Tradition or Hereditary Tradition Witches, whose practice has been learned from that which has been passed along within a family unit or extended family through multiple generations—not the same as Tradition Witches as used in the United States to refer to those Wiccan denominations dating from the 1940s with Gerald Gardner and related offshoots.

Blue Moon: Second Full Moon in a solar month; adding extra energy.

Bodily Energy Points: In Green Witchcraft, these are the base of spine, abdomen, stomach, heart, throat, forehead, crown (top) of head, while the Elemental Energy Points are the palms of the hands and soles of the feet—*see Chakras*.

Bolline [bo-leen']: Practical knife of Witchcraft used to cut with and inscribe objects; generally a white- or brown-handled knife, but some witches may utilize only one knife for the work of both the athame and bolline.

BOS/*Book of Shadows*: The book or books in which correlations are written down and referenced in the creation of spells and other magics, and in which the characteristics of a Witch's practice are given. This book will contain a code of ethics, personal philosophy, spiritual insights, meditations, lunar and seasonal and rituals, descriptions of tools, alphabets, recipes, rites of passage rituals, special days of observance, deity associations, and other details deemed necessary by the individual for the practice of the Craft.

Broom Closet: Figurative way of describing whether a Witch prefers to keep Craft practice a secret or is more public about Craft activities, and is therefore, presumably with besom in hand, either in or out of the broom closet.

Casting the Circle: Beginning of a ritual to create the Circle for magical and spiritual work to be conducted inside. The one who casts the Circle draws up energy from the Earth and balances this within prior to releasing the energy to create a spherical field; this is done so as to avoid depleting internal energies.

Casting Cloth: The cloth marked with designs and laid out for a divination throw, usually for ogham fews, but sometimes used for runes or tarot.

Cauldron: Tool used to contain spell crafting materials, potions, brews, and represent the fruitful and regenerative powers of the Goddess.

Celts: Indo-Europeans who arrived in Ireland by way of Spain; people originally of Dravidic derivation from the Indus Valley who migrated across Europe.

Ceremonial Magic: Magic system created in the fourteenth–sixteenth centuries in Europe, and based on Paganism and the Hebrew magical system of the Kabbalah. Dating from twelfth-century Europe, placed in the medieval Christian world view.

Chakras: Energy centers in the body, usually stated as root/base [genital/anal area], sacral plexus [lower abdomen], solar plexus [navel], heart, throat, third eye, and crown, similar to the *Bodily Energy Points*. The palms of the hands and soles of the feet are also chakras, similar to the *Elemental Energy Points*.

Charge: Directing energy into an object for a purpose; also used as a command.

Charged: Energized; imbued with Divine power as with blessed water.

Charms: Objects made and infused with magical energy and carried or placed to achieve a goal [such as protection, money draw, draw love and friendship].

Circle: A ritual area created to contain raised energy that may be directed in spell work. The energy is raised through the Earth and blended within the Witch, then directed to form the boundaries of the circle. When the Circle is opened, the energy is returned into the Witch so that the borrowed energy may be redirected into the Earth for dissipation by touching the ground with the palms of the hands. This energy field does not act like static cling, holding negative energies in place, but is always pure and clean, simply repelling negative or chaotic energies from entering the sacred space.

Cleansing: Relieving an object of chaotic and mixed energies, often absorbed while in a store or surrounded and touched by other people. Sea salt or spring water are good for immersing an object to clear out the extraneous energies; then toss out the water or salt into which the energies have been absorbed.

Comparative Magic: "This **Represents** That" spell method of Green Witchcraft in which a relationship is established between the spell-casting material and the object of the spell, so that one object acts in the stead of another [used in charms and growth spells, as when an energized seed is planted].

Cone Of Power: Energy raised and concentrated within a Circle for magical use, and released when at its height or peak for effective magic to take place.

Contagion Magic: Method in Wiccan subdivision of Sympathetic Magic when using in spell casting something that has been in contact with the subject of the spellwork.

Containment Magic: Type that shields or protects: keeping an area secure with positive energies inside, and negative energies held at bay; or placing a shield over the source of negative energies, thus keeping those energies confined in that area—[see *Deflection and Reflection Magics*].

Correspondences: Correlations of magical energy to items of Nature, colors, hours of the day, days of the week, symbols, alphabetic interpretations, lunar and solar phases, and other such meanings to be used in creating or interpreting magical work [see *Lists of Correspondences*].

Cosmic Lemniscate: The symbol of Infinity, like a number 8 on its side, drawn in the air over the Altar during Circle Casting to signify standing between the worlds.

Coven: Assembly of Wiccan/Witchcraft practitioners, generally adhering to the standardized procedures of a particular Tradition or to those agreed upon by the membership, usually twelve in number, with one Priest or Priestess/High Priest or High Priestess to make a total of thirteen members, although there may be two leaders, male and female.

Covenhome: The name of a Witch's coven, such as, "Her covenhome is the Coven of the Sacred Wheel."

Coven Name: Name bestowed on an initiate to a coven for "inner court" use.

Covenstead: Limited area [such as a 5-mile radius] for covens of the same Tradition or denomination so that there are not overlapping territories. As more people become interested in the Craft, this may cease to be practical.

Craft: Witchcraft; the Old Religion of Pagan Europe; Wicca.

Craft Name: A magic/spiritual name chosen by a Witch for working in the Craft, and may be used openly, in Pagan community settings, and in "outer court" Circles. This name may also be used as a Coven Name, although many covens prefer to rename someone entering their circle.

Cross-Quarters: Sabbats of Samhain, Imbolc, Beltane, and Lughnassadh, also known as the White or Greater Sabbats. Community bonfires were traditionally lit on hilltops.

Cup: Symbol of Elemental Water; used in ritual to contain the beverage and to symbolize the receptive and fertile womb of the Goddess.

Curses: Contain malevolence to the sphere of the generator of the negative energy.

Daoine Sidhe: The powerful folk or nobility of the Other People or Sidhe.

Dark Moon: Representative of the Goddess as the One Who Transforms in her aspect of Tomb and Womb, thus a time more suited for meditation or divination than for magical work or spells.

Dark Power: Generally negative/chaos energies drawn from the Dark Aspects of the Goddess and the God, but are transformative, highly creative, and innovative.

Deflection Magic: Type of magic used to defuse general malevolence and ill will of others by randomly dispersing and dissipating the negative energies [see *Containment and Reflection Magics*].

Deosil: Clockwise movement; the course of the Sun through the sky.

Deva: "Shining Ones" of Hinduism; Divine Beings.

Devi: "The Goddess" name for Shakti.

Dhumavati: "Crone" aspect of Shakti without Shiva.

Digambara: "Sky-Clad" or "Clothed in Space" name for Shiva that has been interpreted over time to mean practicing magic naked. Gerald Gardner spent many years in Sri Lanka, a heavily Shivan community, and may have taken this term to incorporate into his Gardnerian Tradition of Witchcraft. Even Charles Leland had had contact with the religions of India through serving there in the armed forces when it was part of the British Empire prior to his writing *Aradia*, in which going naked in Esbat rituals was described in his "Charge of the Goddess" poem [see *Skyclad*]. India has a history of religious Ascetics who are ritually, and continuously, naked in public.

Directive Magic: "This **Affects** that" spell method of Green Witchcraft in which energy of one object is moved to influence another. Energy may also be raised, focused, directed, and sent to accomplish a goal [most commonly used in all types of magic, often in connection with Lists of Correspondences].

Drawing Down the Moon: Ritual of drawing the energy of the Moon into water to be blessed; also a ritual of drawing the Goddess within the Practitioner for communion and prophecy.

Drawing Magic: Type of magic that brings something to the Practitioner, hence enticing and invoking an energy influence.

Dressing: Putting an appropriate oil on spell items such as candles as part of a ritual consecration to prepare the object to attract and direct the energy of a spell to accomplish a goal.

Earth: Elemental representing North; Midnight; green/black; old age; strength; stability; wisdom; tarot suit of pentacles; business; money.

Eke Name: A coven name or "inner court" name by which a practitioner of the Craft is known within a Circle.

Elemental Energy Points: Palms of the hands and soles of the feet; which in the Green Witchcraft Tradition sees the right hand as Fire, the left hand as Water, the left foot as Earth, and the right foot as Air—see *Chakras*.

Elementals: The energy archetypes of the Goddess and the God expressed as individual entities and powers embodying the four elements of Earth, Air, Fire, and Water. As emanations of

Divine Power, they are respected and worked with in the focusing of energy, not as simple energies or servants, but as Powers. They are not, however, worshipped as the dictionary definition of elementalism. Water and Earth are often ascribed to the Goddess, while Air and Fire are ascribed to the God. These categories reflect the images of Sun God [Lugh, Bel]/Sky God [An, Horus, Jupiter] and Moon Goddess [Hecate, Diana, Bendidia]/ Earth Goddess [Freya, Ki, Hulda], but may also be interchanged: Earth God [Cernunnos, Frey, Geb, Greenman, Horned God] and Sea God [Poseidon]; Goddess of Creative Thought [Sophia] and Volcanic Fire [Pele].

Elysium Fields: Greek plain of ideal happiness and joy; paradise for the dead who lived virtuous lives without harming others, and thus corresponds as a land of repose within Underworld known in Witchcraft and Wicca as Summerland.

Eleusian Mysteries: Secret Greek rites honoring Demeter at the site of Eleusis each Spring during which initiations into the Mysteries of Demeter took place symbolizing the annual death and resurrection of grain and vegetation; showing the relationship between the life cycles of the Earth and the people who are part of the Earth, so that all are seen as born from the seed, aging, dying, and returning into the seed to be reborn. It is known that any who passed through the rite were so transformed as to be changed utterly by the awareness of the immortality of the spirit; this resurrection motif is addressed through the rituals of the Sabbats.

Esbat [Es'bat]**:** Lunar celebrations of Witches during the Full and New Moons; often used in conjunction with spell work.

Etheric Plane: An energy level of existence not on the physical plane, nor on the astral, but in between where it acts as a connecting passage; the Gray Path in Green Witchcraft.

Exorcising Magic: Type of magic that casts away negative energies, preventing their return so positive energies may enter [*see Banishing and Repelling*].

Exorcism: Aiding spirits in death passage that may be lost, confused, or unaware of their transition from physical to spirit form; dispersing negative energies to allow positive energies to enter.

Familiar: Witch's animal or spirit helper in magical work.

Fire: Elemental representing South; Noon; red/white; youth; energy; drive; passion; tarot suit of wands; ambition; career; creativity.

Frey: "Lord"; twin brother of Freya, and Vanir God of Green level of Teutonic system, God of the Natural World, animals, land, fertility, eroticism, peace, and well-being.

Freya: "Lady"; twin sister of Frey, and Vanir Goddess of Green level of Teutonic system who is able to travel to the levels of law and creation; Goddess of Nature, magic, cycles of Nature, who taught magic [seidr] to Odin of the Aesir; associated with cats.

Full Moon: Lunar phase symbolizing the Goddess in her aspect of Mother, Lady of Abundance and Compassion, time for magical/ spell workings involving completion, protection, containment, fruition, honoring energies and spirits, and Drawing Down the Moon.

Fume: Dispensing smokey incense in an area to cleanse it, much like smudging.

Galster: Practice of Teutonic runic magic system.

Generator: Large crystal used to charge other crystals, so that by placing another stone or crystal being charged on a pentacle with the generator crystal on top of it, a consecration may be conducted. A close energy relationship is developed between Witch and stone by working often through this crystal.

Greater Sabbats: Those of the harvests in the mythic cycles of the Goddess and the God:

Samhain, Imbolc, Beltane, and Lughnassadh; also called the White Sabbats and the Cross-Quarters on the Wheel of the Year.

Green Man: The God as Lord of the Wildwood, Lord of Nature, a revealer of mysteries and mentor to the occult student. His feast is in May, and he is associated with the May King, Cernunnos, Jack O' the Green, Robin of the Wood, the Summer Lord, and the Fool card of the Tarot. He is also related to such woodland/resurrection deities as Adonis, Attis, Dionysus, Tammuz, and Silvanus.

Green Sabbats: The Quarters or Lesser Sabbats of Winter and Summer Solstice and Spring and Fall Equinox, hence Yule and Litha; Ostara and Mabon.

Green Witchcraft: Both a generic term for Nature-based Witchcraft and name of the maternal-lineage Family Craft Tradition of Aoumiel, being based upon the foundational aspect of the Old Religion, grounded in Nature, approaching the Craft through the Elementals, the Other People, and the Goddess and the God, using herbs, natural objects, and Earth energy in spell crafting. The Divine is seen as the Lady and the Lord of the Wildwood, primarily as Earth Mother and Horned God, symbolized by the Moon and Sun, but also in their many other natural [rather than political] aspects, seeing the Craft as both animistic and pantheistic. The energies raised join internally with those of the Witch to be focused, directed, released, and sent to accomplish a goal. It is seen as religion and spirituality, thus holding the word Witch to be honorable and spiritual, related to the Teutonic concept of *seidhr*.

Green Woman/Lady: Sylvan Goddess such as Flora, often connected to Fairy or Elvin motifs such as with Greensleeves.

Grimoires [Grim'-ores, sometimes called Grimmor'es or even Grim'-waws]**:** Related to the word *Grammar*, being books of magical formulas created by Ceremonial Magicians between the twelfth and sixteenth centuries in Europe, containing elaborate rituals based on Paganism, the Hebrew Kabbalah of twelfth- century Europe and the medieval Christian world view, involving summoning/banishing spirits, demons, and angels of heaven and hell [many of whom were derived from the names of Pagan deities] to carry out tasks according to the magician's will. The books contain names of power, lists of correspondences or correlations between objects and magical powers, seals and sigils, and other such information, for the working of magic by externally commanding these energies. The term has recently come into use for the Witch's Book of Shadows.

Ground and Center: Releasing internal static energies into the ground through the feet or hands, finding the calm center within, drawing up strong Earth energies through the feet, pulling it up to entwine with the internal energies in balance as preparation for spell work. This is done to avoid depleting personal energy in Circle casting and spell work.

Grounding: Touching the Earth/floor with palms of hands after magical work to drain off excess energy (avoid getting irritable, headachy, nervous, etc.); releasing excess energy into the Earth upon completion of energy raising for Circle casting, ritual, meditation, spell work, and other magical workings.

Hallowed: Holy; sacred.

Hallows: Sacred, holy, consecrated; a time when the veil between the worlds is thin and there is easy passage, hence the holy time of Halloween (Samhain) when all the worlds are connected, blessed, and holy during the instant of transference of the Dark God through the tomb of the Crone transformed into the womb of the Mother in preparation of being born at Yule.

Holey Stone: Stone or rock with a hole worn in it through the action of river or sea water, and a symbol of the regenerative power of the Goddess (yoni); Fairies may be seen by looking through the hole at Midsummer when standing beneath an elderflower tree (elderflowers dried make a flavorful additive to black tea).

Homeopathic Magic: Method in Wiccan subdivision of Sympathetic Magic in which correlations are used in spell work, such as a green candle for money.

Immanence: The Divine is at hand and present in all things.

Inhabited: Companion or other spirit entity dwelling in a stone or crystal from time to time; may be contacted through that object.

Kali/Kalima: "Black/Black Mother" aspect of Shakti as the passage from life to death and re-birth; also the one who liberates people from fear and ignorance.

Karma: Hindu idea of soul retribution by which actions in this life dictate the nature of the next reincarnation.

Ken/Kenned/Kenning: All-encompassing sensation of "knowing" something with a certitude and acceptance that is mentally understood, emotionally felt, and psychically sensed so that there is no doubt that what is kenned, *is;* hence, instinctive insight.

The Lady and the Lord: The Goddess and the God of the Old Religion, hence, of Witchcraft; deities of Nature and the Universe thru whom The Power emanates.

Lesser Sabbats: Those of the Solstices and Equinoxes: Yule, Ostara. Litha, and Mabon; also called the Green Sabbats and the Quarters on the Wheel of the Year.

Libation: An offering to the Goddess and the God, usually the first draught of the ritual beverage and the first portion of ritual food unless the rite designates otherwise; the offering is poured onto the ground or into a libation bowl to be later emptied onto the ground, or disposed of with the visualization of it returning to the Earth.

Light Power: Generally positive/orderly energies drawn from the Light Aspects of the Goddess and the God.

Linga: Phallic symbol of creative/generative power of the God, particularly Shiva.

List of Correspondences: Tables of showing a correlation between items and their magical function as used in the practice of the Craft, such as between colors, herbs, days of the week, hours of the day, and a magical intent; an example could be using a green candle and mint leaves on a Thursday at the third hour after sunset for a candle-burning money spell [*see Tables of Correspondences*].

Lord And Lady: Direct translation of many ancient names for the God and the Goddess of Power in the Old Religion, being of Nature and the Universe.

Lunar Eclipse: Emblem of the Goddess in her dark aspect as Crone, She Who is the Tomb and the Womb, hence, She Who Transforms.

Magic: Creating changes by raising, focusing, directing, releasing, sending energy.

Mahadevi: "Great Goddess" name of Shakti demonstrating her great Power.

Mannuz [Mah-nu']: The Self as part of the Universe and the Divine.

Mantra: Chant used for energy raising, which may be individualized and secret.

Meditation: Quiet relaxation in which the mind-chatter is silenced so as to open an altered state of awareness wherein the conscious mind is subdued, allowing the subconscious functions of the mind to dominate; state of relaxation and accessibility.

Middleworld: The physical world in the Ogham system of divination and the Celtic world view; the starting place for divinations in which the Ogham fews move from the center of the casting into other worlds and realms; contains four realms: Cath, the realm of challenge and conflict in the North; Blath, the realm of prosperity and harvest in the East; Seis, the realm of harmony and contentment in the South; and Fis, the realm of learning and knowledge in the West.

Midhe: The centerpoint of the Ogham casting cloth, through which the reader rises to Otherworld and descends to Underworld in the course of an Ogham divination, depending on the fews cast.

Moons: There are twelve Full Moons in a year, beginning with the December Moon at Yule: Oak [December], Wolf [January], Storm [February], Hare [March], Seed [April], Dryad [May], Mead [June], Herb [July], Barley [August], Harvest [September], Hunter's [October], Snow [November], and occasionally a calendar year will have a thirteenth Moon, which is called the Blue [second Full Moon in a Solar Month]; the term Blood is used when the Moon is red/russet colored in any month, adding energy, power, and/or aggression to whatever is the normal name for the Moon—most common from August to October; while the Sidhe [shee] Moon is the second Dark Moon in a Solar Month.

Moon Phases: Waxing for beginnings and developing magics [Maiden]; Full for completions, honoring energies and spirits, and Drawing Down the Moon [Mother]; Wan-ing for banishings, purgings, and exorcisms [Crone]; and Dark/New for meditations and divinations [Hidden Face of the Goddess/ Goddess of Mysteries], although the New Moon may be celebrated as the last sliver of light of the Waning Moon, while the Dark Moon has no light.

Mystic Moon: The Dark Moon seen as the Hidden Face of the Goddess. May also be called the New Moon unless this term is associated with the last thin crescent of the Waning Moon as depicted in the Triple Goddess symbol.

Names of Power: Names chanted for power-raising; can be derived from Grimoires, with many being ancient deity names redefined as demons, angels, and Olympic spirits, or invented in a frenzy of energy raising (as with speaking in tongues).

Nataraja: King/Lord of the Dance; aspect of Shiva as the Cosmic Dancer; he is Time and Eternity, Unperturbed, dancing the dissolution and creation of the Universe.

New Moon: Lunar phase symbolizing the Goddess in her aspect of Crone; Dark Lady, and Wisdom; as the last sliver before the Dark Moon, it is a time for banishing and repelling magics, otherwise it is a time for meditations, divinations, and Dark Power magics.

Ogham: Old Celtic alphabet symbols named for trees/shrubs; used for magical symbolism as sigils in spells and other magical workings.

Old Religion: Shamanic and Nature-based religions of Pre-Christian Europe.

Opening The Circle: Ending of a ritual wherein the Circle is uncreated after all magical and spiritual work has been concluded within. This draws the energy field back within the Practitioner who cast the Circle so it may be assimilated, with the excess energy drained off by touching the palms of the hands to the ground.

Otherworld: The world of the Other People: Elves [Sidhe], the Fair Ones or Fairies; the *immortal lands* in the Ogham system of divination and the Celtic world view, consisting of four realms: Sen Magh, the Ancient Plain of age and wisdom, death, transformation, and immortality in the North; Magh Mell, the Delightful Plain of abundance, change, and evolution in the East; Magh Longanidh, the Wondrous Plain of happiness, awakening, rebirth, and peace of the South; and Magh Argetnel, the Silvery Plain of light, inspiration, gentleness, eternity, and beauty in the West.

Oracle: Ancient locations where divinations took place and prophecies were uttered, generally by priestesses; also the prophecy itself.

Pagan: "Rustic"; religion of the country folk who retained the traditions of the Old Religion during the conversion of Europe to the New Religion; used in modern times without distinction to mean anyone who is not Christian, Jewish, or Moslem, or who has no religion. This name is being reclaimed by Wiccans, Witches, Druids, Odinists, and other spiritual groups reviving the practices and beliefs of the Old Religion.

Pantheistic: All energies and matter are aspects of the Divine, thus the Divine is manifested in everything. Key phrase: *everything is Divine.*

Parvati: Earth Mother aspect of Shakti; wife of Shiva in Vedic Hinduism.

Pasupati: "Lord of the Animals/Beasts" aspect of Shiva 30,000 years old.

Pentacle: Symbol of Elemental Earth; but may also be any object, amulet, jewelry, or other type of adornment or charm constructed with a pentagram [five-pointed star in a circle]; object of wood, tile, metal, etc. on which is drawn, carved, or engraved the encircled five-pointed star used on a Witch's altar. Sometimes other symbols are included, such as those for the Horned God, the Triple Goddess, planetary sigils, etc.

Pentagram: a drawing, inscription, or hand motion of a five-pointed star, usually within a circle, with the points representing the four Elementals and the Spirit, generally with Air and Water on the left and right arms, Earth and Fire on the left and right legs, Spirit at the top, and the Practitioner at the Center, although the latter two images may be reversed with the Practitioner at the top and Spirit at the center, particularly during spell work [note that the imagery of the Pentagram does not match that of the Elemental Energy Points of the body and also varies by Tradition].

Poppet: doll figure used in magical spell casting, usually stuffed with herbs or batting, and meant to be a helper or represent someone.

Power Hand: the hand a person favors, used in ritual context for the power found in the dominant hand.

The Power: the universal life-energies of the Divine expressed through the Elementals, the Deities, and such cosmic bodies as the Sun, the Moon, the Earth, planets, stars, comets, and meteors. One who feels these energies and can move them is said to "have the Power" and hence is a Witch.

Protection Magic: a type of Containment/Deflection/Reflection Magic.

Purgings and Releasings: Type of magic that are lesser *exorcisms* that cleanse and turn away negativity or impediments, absorb negativity to be buried for grounding, and dissipating negative energies.

Quarters: Sabbats of Yule, Ostara, Litha, and Mabon, also known as the Green or Lesser Sabbats. Also the locations of the Elementals during Circle Casting and Opening.

Rade: "Ride" referring to the wild ride of the Hunter gathering the souls of the dead; passing of the Wild Hunt or the Rade is demonstrated by stormy weather and fast moving, roiling black clouds in the sky.

Reflection Magic: Type of magic that turns away negative energy, sending it back to the source; used in "return to sender" magics [*see Containment and Deflection Magics*].

Repelling Magic: Type of magic that casts away something that may be present or is approaching the Practitioner, hence banishing or exorcising an energy influence, with purgings and releasings being lesser exorcisms [*see Banishing and Exorcising Magics*].

Retribution Magic: Type of magic that returns negative energy to the sender and seal it there, usually by the added energy of herbs.

Return-to-Sender Magic: Type of magic that sends intentionally harmful negativity back to its originating source.

Rituals: Magical or devotional ceremonies in which energy is raised for Divine communion and/or for the conducting of magic as with spell work.

Runes: Old Teutonic and Norse alphabet symbols associated with magical meanings and often used as sigils in spells and other magical workings.

Sabbat [Sab′bat]**:** Eight holy days of Witchcraft and Wicca, representing four solar and four agricultural celebrations. The solar ones are the Spring and Fall Equinoxes; and the Summer and Winter Solstices. The agricultural ones are the harvests of August [grains], October [root], the lambing time of February, and the fullness of Spring in May. Some people reverse the Sabbats for the Southern Hemisphere to celebrate the appropriate seasonal changes, while others prefer to celebrate the dates as part of the European heritage.

Saint's Days: Holy days on the Catholic calendar, most of which coincide with Pagan holidays since they are based upon these prior existing Pagan holy days. Since the populace honored the days, the Pagan focus was changed by naming the days after a saint or martyr of the New Religion, some of whom never existed, others who were local Pagan deities addressed as living people who had converted, and others who were actual people named as saints by a formal process based on reports of miracles related to the individual.

Scrying: Psychic divination in which images are seen within a magical tool such as a black mirror, crystal ball, water as well as in things of Nature such as clouds, smoke, birds in flight, and so forth. Anything that lends itself as an appropriate medium can be scryed, such as with obsidian.

Seals: Magical diagrams using symbols, or using the numerical equivalents for names and planets in a square, perhaps with a sigil superimposed over it.

Seidhr: Teutonic word for the type of magical practice of Witchcraft that is Green, or Nature-focused, hence, the *Green Witch.*

Shadowland: Underworld realm of repose for spirits who have ended their incarnations in the Physical World, or Middleworld; tranquil dimly lit land ruled by the Lord of Shadows aspect of the God and by the Crone aspect of the Goddess; the world where spirits rest before moving into Summerland for revitalization and onto the cauldron of rebirth—[*see Underworld*].

Siddha: "Charged with energy" in Hinduism through the chanting of mantras.

Sidhe [Shee]**:** Fairy people of Ireland; the Tuatha de Danu.

Sidhe Moon: Second Dark Moon in a solar month, propitious for connecting with Otherworld, working with the Daoine Sidhe, and adding psychic energy to magical workings.

Sigils: Designs drawn or engraved for magical power; may be a seal [from a Planetary Spirit; planetary square; Olympic Spirit; Kabbalic] such as used in Ceremonial Magic, one created by the Practitioner [Triple Goddess; Crescent Moon; Solar Cross] or a design drawn from linking with a continuous line the letters of a key word as the alphabetical letters appear on a Witch's Sigil Wheel or Square, and used as a focus in a magical working.

Skyclad: being naked in Wiccan ritual [*see Digambara*].

Smudging: Native American cleansing ritual in which a place or a person is cleansed and purified through smoke, usually generated through burning of sage or a sage, sweetgrass, lemongrass combination, although tobacco may also be used. Used by Witches in some types of Circle Casting, healings, and cleansing rituals [*see Fume*].

Solar Eclipse: Emblem of the God in his aspects of Dark Lord, Lord of Shadows, Death, Chaos,

Resurrection, Hunter, and Leader of the Wild Hunt.

So Mote It Be!: "So Must It Be!" given as an emphatic statement of affirmation and finality in the working of a spell and in portions of Circle Casting and Opening, and other rituals. May be substituted with, *"It Is Done!"*

Speaking In Tongues: Ecstatic speech during energy raising, in which the words are sounds that may be recognized as another language unknown to the speaker, or that express spiritual union directly without any language translation. This may occur during a Drawing Down the Moon ritual in which the participant is filled with the spirit of the Goddess, or a Drawing Down the Sun ritual, in which the participant is filled with the spirit of the God.

Spells: Magic gathered and directed in ritual to achieve a goal, thus spells are the vehicles of magical workings utilizing the movement of energy through the power of spoken word or formula, be it in a ritual, brew, charm, amu-let, talisman, or crafted item created for magical purpose, generating intent into manifestation.

Summerland: Underworld realm where the rested spirit may enjoy a paradise of light and joy, and where the spirit may remain or move on to rebirth; comparable to the Elysium Fields of the Greek worldview.

Symbols: Letters and designs used in Craft work and spells.

Symbolism: Meanings and interpretations for divination images and omens.

Sympathetic Magic: "This **Is** That"—spell method of Green Witchcraft in which the spellcasting material is seen as the actual object of the spell [poppets, sigils and seals; attraction spells]. *Note:* the view of modern Wicca is that All Magic is Sympathetic Magic since it uses correlations for spells knowing that all things are connected through energy, and this is subdivided into contagion [using something that

has been in contact with the subject] and homeopathic [using only a correlation as with green for money].

Tables of Correspondences: Correlations between spell materials and energies to particular magical objectives: colors, herbs, incense, oils, crystals and stones, numbers, planets, days of the week, hours of the day, Moon phase, symbology of runes/ogham, etc. [*see Lists of Correspondences*].

Talisman: An object such as a ring or pendant, engraved with magical symbols to bring good fortune, offer protection, ward misfortune, etc. It is a type of charm.

Tarot [Tair'roe]**:** Deck of seventy-eight cards, descended from those created in India carried into Northern Italy by Romany Gypsies, originally used in a game called Tarrochi in the fifteenth century and now used mainly in divination; the deck contains seventy-eight cards, of which twenty-two are archetype cards called the Major Arcana, fifty-two cards are typical of regular playing decks, and four additional cards are Pages or Princesses for each of the four suits, called the Minor Arcana. In modern card decks, the Swords became Spades, the Cups are Hearts, Disks/ Coins/Pentacles are Diamonds, and the Wands/Rods are Clubs.

Tat: "That" name for the Supreme Being in Hinduism.

Traditions: Word used by Wiccan or Witchcraft denominations dating from the 1940s onward, with many requiring a chain of denominational initiation based on the specific Tradition's instruction—not the same as Family Tradition or Hereditary Tradition, which are passed along within a family unit or extended family through multiple generations, and whose members may also be called Bloodline Witches.

Transference Magic: "This **Enters** That" spell method of Green Witchcraft in which the negative/undesired energies within one object or person are moved into another receptacle, often a plant, animal, or stone [such as a braid of garlic or onion, or using a grounding stone].

Triple Goddess and Triple God: Goddess as threefold **Maiden, Mother, Crone**; God as threefold **Youth, Father, Sage** with the interpretation for the God depending on the mythic symbology used in a Tradition.

Tryambaka: "Wed to the Triple Goddess" name for Shiva.

Tuatha De Danu: [Too'a Day Dan'new] "The People of the Goddess Danu" Sanskrit name of Dravidians in Sind during 1500–1200 B.C.E. final push of Aryans into Mohenjo-daro and name of the Sidhe, or Fairies of Ireland.

Turning of the Wheel: Passage thru the yearly cycle of eight Sabbats; hence, the passage of the year marked by the celebrations therein, and the following of the myth of the God as the Oak King and the Holly King, and the roles of the Goddess as Maiden, Mother, and Crone through the course of the year.

Twelfth Night: Naming Day ritual time of January 6, twelve days after the departure of the Holly King on December 25.

Twin Aspects of Magic: Purpose and method, with purpose being to draw desired energy, to repel undesired energy, or to contain desired energy while warding off undesired energy; and with method being the way the energy is manipulated through either sympathetic, comparative, directive, or transference, or a combination of these to achieve a desired goal.

Vanir: Level of the Teutonic system addressing the deities of Nature; includes worship of Frey and Freya, and the practice of natural magic, hence, the Green level.

Underworld: The world where initially go the spirits of the dead in the Ogham system of divination and the Celtic world view, having four realms: Tir Fe Thruinn, the Land Under the Waves of endings and transformation in the North; Tir Na n'Og, the Land of Youth of growth and fruition in the East; Tir Na Beo, the Land of Life of vitality and new beginnings in the South; and Tir Na Ban, the Land of the Lady of love, cleansing, and joy. Also called Shadowland in Witchcraft and Wicca; with Tir Na n'Og being similar to Summerland.

Vitki: "Wise One" Teutonic name that became Wiccan, Witch.

Wand: Symbol of Elemental Fire; a tool for gathering and transferring energy in the performance of magic; may be made of a branch of wood, generally the length of the forearm, from a tree selected for the type of correlation of the wood to the main type of magic conducted: oak [God focused], hazel [Witch and Nature focuses], elder, and willow [Goddess focused] being popular choices; may also be of crystal or metal tubing filled with herbs, crystals, etc.; and all may be wrapped with copper wire or contain a copper rod within.

Waning Moon: Lunar phase of the Crone for magic work and spells involving diminishment, exorcisms, repellings, and banishings.

Water: Elemental representing West; Sunset; blue/gray; maturity; emotion; psychic ability; intuition; the tarot suit of cups; love; feelings; subconscious mind.

Waxing Moon: Lunar phase of the Maiden for magic work and spells involving the initiatings, new beginnings, drawings, and increases.

White Sabbats: The Cross-Quarters or Greater Sabbats of Samhain, Imbolc, Beltane, and Lughnassadh.

Wicca [Wikíka]: Derived from "Wicce" [weech'chee—the medieval name for Witch] and used popularly to avoid the negative imagery; possibly related to the word for "Wise One" [Witta] or "To Know" [Witan], but it is a stretch to link it to "wicker" for bending or twisting since the root from willow is not the same as that of witch, and has instead been used in completely familiar terms.

Wiccan Rede: Originally called the Witches' Rede, the long version is usually summed up in the admonition, "An' it harm none, do as thou wilt"; Witches' Law.

Widdershins: Teutonic word for anti-clockwise; reverse to the course of the Sun in the sky; Tuathal is the Gaelic form of the word.

Witchcraft: The "Craft of the Wise" Nature-based magical religion and practice; the Old Religion of Pagan Europe derived from Anglo-Saxon councilors of the king, the Witta; or from Wicce, pronounced in Middle English as "Weetch'ee" meaning a clever/knowing wizard; or from wiccian, "weetch' ee-an" and wicchecrafte, "weech'ee-craft'te" meaning to use sorcery; but also possibly from Witan, pronounced "Weeítahn" and meaning "to know."

Witch's Ladder: A string knotted during a magical ritual or spell, often with beads or feathers stuck in the knots, and used as a charm.

Witch Queen/Witch King: Like a queen bee, a High Priestess who has two to five covens [depending on the Tradition] "hive" from her own/or a High Priest with the same track record. This was popularized in the 1960s by Alex and Maxine Sanders and their Alexandrian Tradition, *not* named after Alex, and supposedly derived from the Gardnerian Tradition, made famous by their student, Stewart Farrar [along with his wife Janet] in *What Witches Do* and *The Witches Bible*. Today, many covens are more likely to function as a group dynamic with the role of High Priestess and High Priest passed around to the inner court members, rather than as the personal possession of one or two people. Witchcraft does not require titles and ranks to work, and in rural areas, Witches were more likely to be called Mother [first or last name] or Grandmother [first or last name]; Father [first or last name] or Grandfather [first or last name], or with other such variations as Granny, Little Mother, Gaffer, Old Man [first or last name], and so forth.

Working Between the Worlds: Moving between planes of existence; between the physical world and other worlds [astral, etheric, spiritual, etc.].

Working Name: Secret name used by the Witch in magical and ritual practice, never revealed to anyone; it is a name chosen by the Witch until one is bestowed directly by the Goddess and the God in a Dedication Ritual, or at such time as when the Practitioner is united with the Divine. For Solitary Practitioners, the Working Name and the Craft Name may be the same only if they do not use it among other people, as was often the case prior to the more public revival of the Old Religion since the 1960s.

Wyrd: Unknowable fate or destiny; cosmic influence; the blank in Runes or the unmarked line few in Ogham divination which indicates the answer is hidden and under the power of the Divine.

Yggdrasill: The Teutonic World Tree upon which Odin sacrificed himself to himself to gain the knowledge of Runes and rune magic, thus becoming King of the Gods. Comparable to the Celtic World Tree of intertwining roots and branches showing the continuity of spirit in life-death-rebirth.

Yoni: Vagina, or womb; eliptical symbol or round stone with a central hole is a Goddess symbol for giving birth to all life.

CRAFT NOTES ENTERED BY:

_____

2
Circle Casting

☉	☽	☿	♀	♂	♃	♆	♄	♇	♅
Sun	Moon	Mercury	Venus	Mars	Jupiter	Neptune	Saturn	Pluto	Uranus

Waxing Moon [Maiden]	Full Moon [Mother]	Waning Moon [Crone]	Dark (New] Moon [Hidden Face/Mystery]

CIRCLE CASTING NOTES

1. During Circle casting, if outdoors, substitute "walls and floors" with "foliage, stones, and ground" or other such appropriate description of the surroundings for the Circle. Change "I" to "we" when others are participating. Use appropriate Altar and Circle decorations for the season: flowers, leaves, shells, stones, crystals, cord, or meaningful objects. Names for the Goddess and the God may be used with or instead of Lady and Lord.

2. The Sigil used for anointing may be a Pentagram ⊗ ; Triple Moon ☽○☾ ; Solar Cross ⊕ ; Lunar Spiral ◎; Solar Cross with Lunar Spiral over it, etc. as desired. Anointing may be added if desired when not part of the described Circle casting.

3. May use Craft Name in rituals with others, or Secret/Working Name if alone.

4. Deosil is N-E-S-W-N and Widdershins is N-W-S-E-N unless otherwise noted, as when starting at the West or East, but the pattern follows the same from these starting points.

5. If rinsing out libation bowl in sink, envision this as a journey to Earth waters.

6. The Circle area may be marked by a cord, by Elemental candles [votives in safe containers are easiest], by items relating to the ritual the Circle is being cast for, or by nothing at all save awareness of where it is from the energy sent to form it.

7. Cast the Circle, insert rituals, spells, recitations, etc., where designated, then return to the Circle page for the Cakes & Wine and Circle Opening.

8. Decide in advance what will be done in Circle, place ribbons or paper slips in the BOS places so each page used for the entire ritual can be easily turned to in the course of the ritual. A book holder or book stand is an excellent tool to make it easier to turn to the desired pages as the ritual progresses. Do not feel rushed, but make the experience a meaningful one.

9. Music may be used to accompany the Circle casting/opening and rituals; song, musical performance, and drumming may be added where it feels appropriate.

BASIC CIRCLE CASTING & OPENING

CASTING THE CIRCLE

1. Lay out Circle and at North set Altar items [may use fruit juice, water, or tea instead of wine]. Ground and center.

2. Sweep the Circle area with a besom deosil [clockwise] NORTH, EAST, SOUTH, WEST, and return to Altar:

   > As I sweep, may the Besom chase away all negativity from within this Circle that it may be cleared and ready for my work.

3. Light incense and Altar candles [in selected colors]; ring bell or clap hands 3 times:

   > The Circle is about to be cast and I freely stand within to greet my Lady and my Lord.

4. Take center Altar candle deosil around the Circle, raising at each Quarter [and lighting Elemental candles if used] returning to Altar when done:

   > [N]: I call upon Light and Earth at the North to illuminate and *strengthen* the Circle.

   > [E]: I call upon Light and Air at the East to illuminate and *enliven* the Circle.

   > [S]: I call upon Light and Fire at the South to illuminate and *warm* the Circle.

   > [W]: I call upon Light and Water at the West to illuminate and *cleanse* the Circle.

5. Raise athame in power hand in front of the Altar:

   > I draw this Circle in the Presence of the Lady and the Lord that They may aid and bless me in my work.

6. Lower athame at North; walk deosil around the Circle, envisioning a blue light shooting out from the point to form the Circle boundary:

   > This is the boundary of the Circle, around me, through walls and floors, above me and below me as a sphere is the Circle cast and consecrated to the Lady and the Lord that They may work with and through Their child, [name]. This Circle is charged by the powers of the Ancient Ones! Only love shall enter and leave.

7. Return to Altar; and ring bell [or clap hands 3 times]; touch point of athame in the salt:

   > Salt is life and purifying. I bless this salt to be used in this sacred Circle by the Power of the Goddess and the God.

8. Using tip of athame, drop 3 portions of salt into water; stir 3 times with blade:

    Let the blessed salt purify this water that it may be blessed to use in this sacred Circle. Through the Power of the Goddess and the God is this water cleansed.

9. Sprinkle blessed water deosil around the Circle:

    I consecrate this Circle by the Lady and the Lord. This Circle is conjured a Circle of Power that is purified and sealed. *So Mote It Be!*

10. Put water bowl on Altar; take incense deosil around Circle to cense it:

    With the aroma of incense do I honor and make welcome my visitors and helpers, visible and invisible.

11. Dab anointing oil with fingertip on forehead in a sigil:

    I, [name] am consecrated in the Names of the Goddess and the God, in this Their Circle.

    [Cut doorway in circle for others to enter; close and seal with sigil.] Challenge each as they approach the Circle, then anoint with oil and sigil of choice:

    a. What do you want?

    Answer: To enter the Circle.

    b. What is the password?

    Answer] In Perfect Love and Perfect Trust.

    c. Enter and Merry Meet! I bid you welcome.

12. With wand, invoke the Elementals at each Quarter starting at the North and moving deosil; raise and open arms to invoke, then close and lower arms, turning to the next Quarter until all are called:

    [N]: I call upon you, Elemental Earth, to attend this rite and guard this Circle, for as I have body and strength, we are kith and kin! [visualize a powerful bull arriving].

    [E]: I call upon you, Elemental Air, to attend this rite and guard this Circle, for as I breathe and think, we are kith and kin! [visualize a soaring eagle].

    [S]: I call upon you, Elemental Fire, to attend this rite and guard this Circle, for as I have energy and drive, and consume life to live, we are kith and kin! [visualize a mighty lion].

[W]: I call upon you, Elemental Water, to attend this rite and guard this Circle, for as I have emotions and my heart beats, we are kith and kin! [visualize a leaping dolphin].

13. Draw Cosmic Lemniscate with wand over Altar. ∞

14. Set wand on Altar; raise athame in both hands straight overhead:

> Hail to the Elementals at the Four Quarters! Welcome Lady and Lord to this Circle! I stand between the worlds with Love and Power all around!

15. Set down athame; pick up cup; pour some beverage into libation bowl, cauldron, or the ground to honor the Lady and the Lord, then take a sip; ring bell or clap 3 times.

Perform Ritual/Craft Work

When finished, proceed with Cakes and Wine/Opening the Circle.

CAKES & WINE

1. Ring bell or clap 3 times.

2. Feet spread and open arms raised:

> I acknowledge my needs and offer my appreciation to that which sustains me! May I ever remember the blessings of the Lady and the Lord.

3. Feet together, hold cup in left hand and athame in right and slowly lower the point of the athame into the cup:

> As the Divine Male joins the Divine Female for the benefit of Both, let the fruits of Their sacred Union promote life, love and joy. Let the Earth be fruitful and let Her bounty be spread throughout all lands.

4. Set down athame; pour a second libation into the libation bowl or cauldron.

5. Now touch point of athame to the bread/cake in the offering dish:

> This food is the blessing of the Lady and the Lord given to me. As I have received, may I offer food for the body, mind, and spirit to those who seek such of me.

6. Eat the Circle food and finish the beverage, [divide the food and drink among attendees present]. When finished:

> As I have enjoyed these gifts of the Goddess and the God, may I remember that without Them I would have nothing. *So Mote It Be!*

7. Hold athame in power hand level over Altar:

   Lord and Lady, I have been blessed by Your sharing this time with me; watching and guarding me; guiding me here and in all things. I came in love and I depart in love.

8. Raise athame in a salute:

   Love is the Law and Love is the Bond. Merry did I meet, merry do I part, and merry will I meet again. Merry meet, merry part, and merry meet again! The Circle is cleared. *So Mote It Be!*

9. Kiss the flat of the blade and set the athame on the Altar.

10. With wand moving deosil, farewelling each Elemental with raised open arms, then lower and close arms and move to the next Quarter; snuff candles if used:

    [N]: Depart in peace, Elemental Earth. My blessings take with you!
    [envision the Elemental Power departing].

    [E]: Depart in peace, Elemental Air. My blessings take with you! [envision the Elemental Power departing].

    [S]: Depart in peace, Elemental Fire. My blessings take with you! [envision the Elemental Power departing].

    [W]: Depart in peace, Elemental Water. My blessings take with you!
    [envision the Elemental Power departing].

11. Set wand on Altar and raise open arms:

    Beings and powers of the visible and invisible, depart in peace! You aid in my work, whisper in my mind, and bless me from Otherworld. Let there ever be harmony between us. My blessings take with you. The Circle is cleared!

12. Take athame and move widdershins [counterclockwise] around the Circle [N-W-S-E-N], envisioning the blue light drawing back into the athame:

    The Circle is open yet the Circle remains as its magical power is drawn back into me. The Circle is cleared! *So Mote It Be!*

BENEDICTION

13. At Altar, touch tip of athame to forehead, seeing the blue light swirling and returning inside; then raise athame in a salute:

    The ritual is ended!

14. Set down athame; open arms outward; palms up:

    Blessings have been given,

15. Draw arms together, crossed over chest and bow:

    and blessings have been received.

16. Bring arms forward with hands together in front; palms upright, outward:

    May the peace of the Goddess and the God remain in my heart. *So Mote It Be!*

17. Ground excess energy by touching palms to floor; put away all magical tools and clear the Altar; empty libation bowl or cauldron onto the earth [outside or in a potted plant], or rinse out in sink.

THE ELEMENTAL POWERS CIRCLE
CIRCLE CASTING

1. Set up Altar at North. Ground and center; sweep the Circle deosil:

   As I sweep, may the besom chase away all negativity from within this Circle, that it may be cleared and made ready for my work.

2. Light incense and the working [center] Altar candle.

3. Ring bell or clap hands 3 times

   The Circle is about to be cast and I freely stand within to greet my Lady and my Lord.

4. Take center Altar candle deosil to the Quarters:

   [N]: I call upon Light and Earth at the North to illuminate and *strengthen* the Circle.

   [E]: I call upon Light and Air at the East to illuminate and *enliven* the Circle.

   [S]: I call upon Light and Fire at the South to illuminate and *warm* the Circle.

   [W]: I call upon Light and Water at the West to illuminate and *cleanse* the Circle.

5. At Altar, raise wand:

   I draw this Circle in the presence of the Powers of the Earth, Sky, Sun, and Sea, that they may aid and bless me in my work.

6. Cast the Circle deosil with the wand; seeing the energy flow from it as blue light while creating the Circle:

   This is the boundary of the Circle; around me, through walls and floors, above me and below me as a sphere is the Circle cast and consecrated to the Powers of Nature and the Universe that they may work with me. This Circle is charged that only love shall enter and leave!

7. Anoint forehead with Solar/Lunar Sigils ⊕ ◎ :

   I am consecrated within this Elemental Circle.

[Cut doorway in circle for others to enter; close and seal with solar/lunar sigil.] Challenge each before entering, then anoint with oil and sigil:

   A.] What do you want?

   Answer] To enter the Circle.

B.] What is the password?

Answer] In Perfect Love and Perfect Trust.

C.] Enter and Merry Meet! I bid you welcome.

8. Ring bell or clap 3 times:

In the presence of the Elementals is my work now begun.

Perform Ritual/Craft Work

When finished, proceed with Cakes and Wine/Opening the Circle.

CAKES & WINE

1. Ring bell or clap 3 times, then with feet spread and arms raised:

I acknowledge my needs and offer my appreciation to that which sustains me. May I ever remember the blessings of the Lady and the Lord.

2. Feet together, touch wand to cup:

As Divine Male joins Divine Female for the benefit of Both, let the fruits of Their sacred Union promote life, love, and joy. Let the Earth be fruitful and let Her bounty be spread throughout all lands.

3. Pour a portion into bowl as libation.

4. Touch the wand to the food:

This food is the blessing of the Lady and the Lord given to me. As I have received, may I offer food for the body, mind, and spirit to those who seek such of me.

5. Place a portion in bowl as libation, then eat the rest of the food and finish the beverage [divide among attendees]:

As I have enjoyed these gifts of the Goddess and the God, may I remember that without Them, I would have nothing. *So Mote It Be!*

OPENING THE CIRCLE

6. Hold wand in power hand level over Altar:

Lord and Lady, I have been blessed by your sharing this time with me, watching and guarding me here and in all things. I came in love and I depart in love.

7. Raise wand in a salute:

> **Love is the Law and love is the Bond. Merry did I meet, merry do I part, and merry will I meet again! Merry Meet, Merry Part, and Merry Meet Again! The Circle is cleared. *So Mote It Be!***

8. Hold up the wand with arms open:

> **The Circle is cleared in the presence of the Powers of the Earth, Sky, Sun, and Sea, that They may take my blessings with Them and go in peace.**

9. Set wand on Altar and hold up Altar candle:

> **Beings and Powers of the visible and the invisible, depart in peace! You aid in my work, whisper in my mind, and bless me from Otherworld. Let there ever be harmony between us. My blessings take with you. The Circle is cleared. *So Mote It Be!***

10. Point wand down starting at the North, and walk widdershins around Circle [N-W-S-E-N], envisioning the blue light drawing back into the wand:

> **The Circle is open yet the Circle remains as its magical power is drawn back into me.**

11. At the Altar, touch tip of wand to heart, seeing the blue light swirling inward.

12. Set down wand, balance the energies, and ground the excess by touching the floor.

BENEDICTION

13. Stand with arms closed over chest and bow:

> **The ceremony is ended.**

14. Open arms to offering gesture:

> **Blessings have been given,**

15. Draw arms together across chest again and bow:

> **And blessings have been received.**

16. Move arms downward and outward with palms toward North:

> **May the peace of the Goddess and the God remain in my heart. *So Mote It Be!***

17. Put away all magical tools and clear the Altar; empty libation bowl onto the earth [either outside or in a potted plant], or rinse out in sink.

Simple Circle Casting with Wand, Staff, or Stang

Casting

Need: wand, staff, or stang; working candle; incense and holder; cup and beverage; dish and snack; libation bowl if indoors; and decorations as desired/appropriate

1. Ground and center; light the working candle and the incense in the middle of the Circle area.
2. Stand near center, facing North, holding wand, staff, or stang with both hands
3. Raise wand/staff tip/or base of stang and while standing in place, motion it around the Circle *deosil* [N-E-S-W-N], seeing energy flow from it as a blue light:

> This is the boundary of the circle, around me, above me and below me as a sphere is the circle cast and consecrated to aid me in my Craft.

4. Pour a libation of beverage and take a sip.

Perform Ritual/Craft Work

[When finished, proceed with Cakes and Wine/Opening the Circle]

Cakes & Wine

1. Raise cup to honor the Lady and the Lord and pour a libation of beverage in a bowl, or on the ground if outside.
2. Place piece of food in libation bowl or on the ground if outside.
3. Eat and drink the food and beverage.

Opening the Circle

4. Raise wand in open arms at center; or raise open arms before staff or stang:

> Beings and powers of the visible and invisible, depart in peace! You aid in my work, whisper in my mind, and bless me from Otherworld, and there is harmony between us. My blessings take with you. The circle is cleared. *So Mote It Be!*

5. Raise wand/staff tip/or base of stang and while standing in place, motion it around the Circle *widdershins* [N-W-E-S-N], seeing the energy returning into it as a blue light:

> The circle is open yet the circle remains as its magical power is drawn back into me.

BENEDICTION

6. Set down wand, or stand up staff or stang in ground or in a stand; cross arms and open outward in benediction with bow:

> **The ceremony is ended. Blessings have been given and Blessings have been received; may the peace of the Goddess and the God remain in my heart.** *So Mote It Be!*

7. Snuff candle, put away tools, and empty libation outside, in a potted plant, or rinse out in sink.

CASTING & OPENING THE STANG CIRCLE

CASTING THE CIRCLE

1. Set up Altar items at North where stang [a 2- or 3-branched staff] will be placed in ground or in a stand. Ground and center. Sweep the Circle *deosil*:

   As I sweep, may the besom chase away all negativity and chaotic energies from this Circle that it may be cleared and made ready for my work.

2. Light incense and Altar candles [bring into the circle any who are participating].

3. Clap hands three times:

   The Circle is about to be cast and I freely stand within to greet my Lady and my Lord.

4. Draw the Circle *deosil* [N-E-S-W-N] with the stang, lifting to point with it:

   I draw this Circle in the presence of the Lady and the Lord that I may be aided and blessed by Them. This is the boundary of the Circle, around me, through walls and floors, above me and below me as a sphere is the Circle cast and consecrated to the Lady and the Lord that They may work with me. This Circle is charged by the Powers of the Ancient Ones! Only love shall enter and leave!

5. Fume the space with the smoke of incense:

   May the smoke consecrate this Circle that it be purified and sealed, and may the fragrance be pleasing and welcoming to my visitors and helpers, visible and invisible. This Circle is conjured a Circle of Power. *So Mote It Be!*

6. Take the center Altar candle to the Quarters of the Circle:

   [N]: I call upon Light and Earth at the North to illuminate and *strengthen* the Circle.

   [E]: I call upon Light and Air at the East to illuminate and *enliven* the Circle.

   [S]: I call upon Light and Fire at the South to illuminate and *warm* the Circle.

   [W]: I call upon Light and Water at the West to illuminate and *cleanse* the Circle.

7. Lift the stang [upright] at each of the Quarters with open arms to call the Elementals:

   [N]: I call upon you, Elemental Earth, to attend this rite and guard this Circle, for as I have body and strength, we are kith and kin! [visualize a powerful bull arriving].

   [E]: I call upon you, Elemental Air, to attend this rite and guard this Circle, for as I breathe and think, we are kith and kin! [visualize a soaring eagle].

[S]: I call upon you, Elemental Fire, to attend this rite and guard this Circle, for as I have energy and drive, and consume life to live, we are kith and kin! [visualize a mighty lion].

[W]: I call upon you, Elemental Water, to attend this rite and guard this Circle, for as I have emotions and my heart beats, we are kith and kin! [visualize a leaping dolphin].

8. Raise stang [upright] at the North again:

   Hail to the Elementals at the Four Quarters! Welcome Lady and Lord to this Circle! I stand between the worlds with love and power all around!

9. Place stang into stand or stick in the ground to stand upright at North.

Perform Ritual/Craft Work

[When finished, proceed with Cakes and Wine/Opening the Circle.]

CAKES & WINE

1. Clap 3 times.

2. Feet spread and arms upraised:

   I acknowledge my needs and offer my appreciation to that which sustains me! May I ever remember the blessings of the Lady and the Lord.

3. Hold power hand over beverage:

   As the Lord and the Lady join together for the benefit of all creation, let this beverage be blessed by Them and in recognition of this, may Their blessings be spread throughout all lands.

4. Hold power hand over food:

   This food is the blessing of the Lady and the Lord, given to me. As I have received, may I offer food for the body, mind, and spirit to those who seek such of me.

5. Place a libation of beverage and food in cauldron, then eat the remainder:

   As I have enjoyed these gifts of the Goddess and the God, may I remember that without Them I would have nothing. *So Mote It Be!*

Opening the Circle

6. Hold power hand level to front of stang:

   Lord and Lady, I have been blessed by your sharing this time with me, watching and guarding me here and in all things. I came in love and I depart in love. The Circle is cleared!

7. Raise open arms:

   Love is the Law and love is the Bond. Merry did I meet, merry do I part, and merry will I meet again! Merry Meet, Merry Part, and Merry Meet Again! The Circle is cleared. *So Mote It Be!*

8. Take stang [upright] to each of the Quarters with open arms, then draw closed:

   [N]: Depart in peace, Elemental Earth. My blessings take with you! [envision the Elemental Power departing].

   [E]: Depart in peace, Elemental Air. My blessings take with you! [envision the Elemental Power departing].

   [S]: Depart in peace, Elemental Fire. My blessings take with you! [envision the Elemental Power departing].

   [W]: Depart in peace, Elemental Water. My blessings take with you! [envision the Elemental Power departing].

9. Raise stang [upright] at North again with open arms, then draw closed:

   Beings and powers of the visible and invisible, depart in peace! You aid in my work, whisper in my mind, and bless me from Otherworld. Let there ever be harmony between us. My blessings take with you. The Circle is cleared!

10. Use the stang to draw the energy as a blue light back into it, while moving around the Circle widdershins [N-W-S-E-N], grounding excess energy as the stang is returned to its stand or the Earth:

    The Circle is open yet the Circle remains as its magical power is drawn back into me and returned to the Earth. The Circle is cleared! *So Mote It Be!*

Benediction

11. Stand with arms closed over chest and bow:

    The ceremony is ended.

12. Open arms in front to an offering gesture with palms up:

    Blessings have been given,

13. Draw arms together across chest again and bow:

    And blessings have been received.

14. Move arms downward from chest and outward with hands close together and palms upright, toward the North:

    May the peace of the Goddess and the God remain in my heart. *So Mote It Be!*

CASTING THE ELEMENTAL CROSS [ANCHORED] CIRCLE*

*This Circle is cast when there is a need for great Power or there is a threatening emergency for which the Circle need be anchored soundly in the Elementals; there is no calling of Light with a center Altar candle, nor censing of the space prior to casting, although candles are set at the Quarters and incense is lit.

Have: Altar at Center of Circle, facing North; candles for each Elemental in safe holders [i.e.; pottery saucers] green, yellow, red, blue [in seasonal shades] may be on Altar; incense and holder; wand [or stang, or staff]; beverage; food; and decorations.

CASTING THE CIRCLE

1. Ground and center. Light all the candles and incense.

2. Sweep the Circle *deosil*:

   > As I sweep, may the besom chase away all negativity and chaotic energies from this Circle that it may be cleared and made ready for my work.

3. Carefully place each lit Elemental candle at the Quarters [one or two at a time].

4. Begin Circle casting [N-S-E-W] envisioning the Elementals as stone pillars carved on top with the appropriate representational head: bull for Earth, eagle for Air, lion for Fire, and dolphin for Water. State words and perform gestures emphatically at each Quarter; begin address with left arm straight out with fingers of hand pointed and wand in right hand [reverse if not right handed] raised straight up:

   > [N]: I Call upon thee Elemental Earth! As we are kith and kin, come and meet with me as I prepare my circle. Secure and guard the boundary of the North [raise left palm in 'halt' sign]. *So Mote It Be!* [bring left hand to side; bring wand across chest].

   > [S]: I call upon thee Elemental Fire! As we are kith and kin, come and meet with me as I prepare my circle. Secure and guard the boundary of the South [raise left palm in 'halt' sign]. *So Mote It Be!* [bring left hand to side; bring wand across chest].

   > [E]: I call upon thee Elemental Air! As we are kith and kin, come and meet with me as I prepare my circle. Secure and guard the East [raise left palm in 'halt' sign]. *So Mote It Be!* [bring left hand to side; bring wand across chest].

[W]: I call upon thee Elemental Water! As we are kith and kin, come and meet with me as i prepare my circle. Secure and guard the boundary of the West [raise left palm in 'halt' sign]. *So Mote It Be!* [bring left hand to side; bring wand across chest].

5. Stand at center of Circle, facing North and raise wand in both hands:

   The Circle is cast as a Circle of Power; anchored by the Elementals and blessed from above and below; inside and outside; around and about me. *So Mote It Be!*

6. Lower wand and cast the Circle *deosil* [E-S-W-N-E] while remaining at the center; envision the blue light of energy shooting from the wand to connect the Elemental stone pillars.

7. Set wand on Altar and begin ritual, Spell crafting, etc.:

   The ritual is now begun.

Perform Ritual/Craft Work

[When finished, proceed with Cakes and Wine/Opening the Circle]

CAKES & WINE

1. Clap 3 times

2. Feet spread and arms upraised:

   I acknowledge my needs and offer my appreciation to that which sustains me. May I ever remember the blessings of the Lady and the Lord.

3. Feet together, touch wand to beverage container [cup, etc.]:

   As the Divine Male joins with the Divine Female for the benefit of Both, let the fruits of Their sacred Union promote life, love, and joy. Let the Earth be fruitful and let Her bounty be spread throughout all lands.

4. Pour a portion of beverage into the cauldron as libation.

5. Touch the point of the wand to the food:

   This food is the blessing of the Lady and the Lord given to me. As I have received, may I offer food for the body, mind, and spirit to those who seek such of me.

6. Add portion to libation, then eat the Circle food and finish the beverage:

As I have enjoyed these gifts of the Goddess and the God, may I remember that without Them I would have nothing. *So Mote It Be!*

OPENING THE CIRCLE

7. Hold wand level over Altar:

    Lord and Lady, I have been blessed by Your sharing this time with me; watching and guarding me; guiding me here and in all things. I came in love and I depart in love.

8. Raise wand in a salute:

    Love is the Law and Love is the Bond. Merry did I meet, merry do I part, and merry will I meet again. Merry Meet, Merry Part, and Merry Meet Again! The Circle is cleared. *So Mote It Be!*

9. Open Circle with wand *widdershins* [W-S-E-N-W], envisioning the blue light returning into the wand:

    The Circle is opened, yet the Circle ever remains as its power flows around me and through me.

10. Farewell the Elementals by letting slip the anchors and giving blessings [S-N-W-E]:

    [S]: wand in right hand, held straight up; left hand palm up in HALT position, now slip the left hand to also grip wand:

    Elemental Fire, you have shared your power with me and secured my circle as I worked. May I ever remember your power and our bond, one to the other.

    Bring upright wand to chest; drop left hand to side; open arms as an embrace:

    My blessings take with thee and thine upon me.

    Bring arms back to cross chest; bow slightly:

    The ritual is ended. Go in peace.

    Snuff or blow out [in a quick puff] the candle at that Quarter.

    [N]: wand in right hand, held straight up; left hand palm up in HALT position, now slip the left hand to also grip wand:

    Elemental Earth, you have shared your power with me and secured my circle as I worked. May I ever remember your power and our bond, one to the other.

Bring upright wand to chest; drop left hand to side; open arms as an embrace:

My blessings take with thee and thine upon me.

Bring arms back to cross chest; bow slightly:

The ritual is ended. Go in peace.

Snuff or blow out [in a quick puff] the candle at that Quarter.

[W]: wand in right hand, held straight up; left hand palm up in HALT position, now slip the left hand to also grip wand:

Elemental Water, you have shared your power with me and secured my circle as I worked. May I ever remember your power and our bond, one to the other.

Bring upright wand to chest; drop left hand to side; open arms as an embrace:

My blessings take with thee and thine upon me.

Bring arms back to cross chest; bow slightly:

The ritual is ended. Go in peace.

Snuff or blow out [in a quick puff] the candle at that Quarter.

[E]: wand in right hand, held straight up; left hand palm up in HALT position, now slip the left hand to also grip wand:

Elemental Air, you have shared your power with me and secured my circle as I worked. May I ever remember your power and our bond, one to the other.

Bring upright wand to chest; drop left hand to side; open arms as an embrace:

My blessings take with thee and thine upon me.

Bring arms back to cross chest; bow slightly:

The ritual is ended. Go in peace.

Snuff or blow out [in a quick puff] the candle at that Quarter.

11. Ground excess energy; put away tools; empty libation bowl onto ground, into potted plant, or rinse out in sink.

DARK POWER CIRCLE CASTING & OPENING

CASTING THE CIRCLE

1. Set up Circle and Altar items; 3 Altar candles may be black, dark gray, deep purple, blue, burgundy, or wine, white, deep brown. Incense may be copal, dragon's blood, frankincense, lilac, mullein, myrrh, or patchouli. Cakes and Wine may be blackberry wine or dark fruit juice; dark bread, cake, fruitcake, or multi-grain bread.

2. Ground and center. Light candles and incense; sweep the site *deosil* starting at the North for Dark Powers or the West for the Sidhe [Fairy] Powers:

   As I sweep this Circle, may it be cleared of negative and chaotic energies that it be prepared for my work.

3. Clap or ring bell three times:

   The Circle is about to be cast and I freely stand within to greet my Dark Lady and my Lord of Shadows.

4. Take center candle *widdershins*, raising the center Altar candle or lighting an Elemental candle at each Quarter [starting N or W], while invoking the *Shadow Light* with Dark Power or Sidhe envisionings:

   [N]: I call upon the Shadow Light within Earth to illuminate and strengthen this Circle [see magma core/phosphorus in cave].

   [W]: I call upon the Shadow Light within Water to illuminate and cleanse this Circle [see bio-luminescence/glowing water hyacinth].

   [S]: I call upon the Shadow Light within Fire to illuminate and warm this Circle [see blue/white of flame/*corpse* candle].

   [E]: I call upon the Shadow Light within Air to illuminate and refresh this Circle [see cloud lightning/aurora borealis].

5. With athame or wand go *widdershins* around the Circle [starting at N or W]:

   I cast this Circle above me, below me, around me; through walls, floors, furniture, and ground, in the presence of the Dark Goddess and the Dark God to be a sacred space where they may manifest and bless their child [name] [see a clear blue light-encasing sphere].

6. Touch athame to the ritual salt:

   Salt is purification, preservation, and necessary to life. I bless this salt to be used in the Circle in the name of the Crone and of the Dark Lord.

7. Add 3 athame tips of salt to the water bowl, stir 3 times:

    Let the blessed salt purify this water for use in this sacred space. I consecrate and cleanse this water in the name of the Crone and of the Dark Lord.

8. Sprinkle Circle *widdershins* with the blessed water:

    I consecrate this Circle in the name of the Crone and of the Dark Lord. This Circle is conjured a Circle of Power that is purified and sealed.

9. Take incense around the Circle *widdershins* and then set it at the South.

10. At Altar, anoint forehead with oil in a chosen sigil:

    I [Craft name], am consecrated in the name of the Crone and of the Dark Lord.

11. With wand, invoke the *Shadow* Elementals *widdershins* [start N or W] with Dark Power or Sidhe envisionings [DP; S]:

    [N]: I call upon you Elemental Earth to attend this rite and guard this Circle, for as I have body and strength, we are kith and kin! [see wolf/cat; cobalt].

    [W]: I call upon you Elemental Water to attend this rite and guard this Circle for as I have blood and feelings, we are kith and kin! [see moray eel/shark; selkie].

    [S]: I call upon you Elemental Fire to attend this rite and guard this Circle for as I have consumed life to live, we are kith and kin! [see phoenix/gila monster; will-o'-the-wisp].

    [E]: I call upon you Elemental Air to attend this rite and guard this Circle for as I have breath and thought, we are kith and kin! [see owl/moth; sylph].

12. Draw the *Cosmic Lemniscate* [Infinity sign] with the wand over the Altar.

13. Set down wand and raise athame in both hands overhead:

    Hail to the Elementals! Welcome Lady and Lord to this rite. I stand between the worlds with love and power all around!

14. Pour some beverage into cauldron/libation bowl and take a sip:

    I who am thy child, [name], call upon my Lady as Crone and my Lord as Shadow to hold communion with me. I affirm my joy of union with the Divine and acknowledge Your blessings unto me. What I send returns to me, and I conduct my Craft accordingly.

Perform Ritual/Craft Work

[When finished, proceed with Cakes and Wine/Opening the Circle]

CAKES & WINE

1. Raise arms at altar:

   I know my needs and offer my gratitude to that which sustains me. May I ever remember the blessings of my Lady and my Lord.

2. Pick up cup in left hand, athame in right, slowly lower point into cup:

   The Lord enters into the fruitful darkness of the Lady. In Shadow is He and Shadow *is* She. The womb is the tomb, but the tomb is her womb, therefore let me never forget that the light is reached through the dark, and She is the passage I must follow as He follows for my sake.

3. Take a sip from the cup [*make no libation yet*].

4. Touch athame to cake/bread:

   The food of the dead and of Underworld is the food of the soul. Let this cake be a symbol of the feeding of my spirit that this be nourished as well as my body, that I may be whole in both.

5. Take a bite from the food, then eat and drink, *saving a portion for a final libation*.

6. Hold athame over Altar:

   Lady and Lord, I am blessed by your sharing this time with me and aiding me in my Craft. You watch over me and protect me, guiding me here and in all things. I came in love, and I depart in love.

7. Now add the remainder of beverage and cake to the libation bowl and hold it up over the Altar:

   The remains of this life are passed into the Cauldron of Rebirth, for this is the Promise—into death doth all life flow, to be refreshed and to move into life anew. The Cauldron of Rebirth brings life out of death, and I honor the Lady and the Lord who bring light and life through darkness and death. The dance is evermoving and neverending. *So Mote It Be!*

8. Set down the libation and raise the athame in salute:

Love is the law, and love is the bond. Merry did we meet, merry do we part, and merry will we meet again. Merry meet, merry part, and merry meet again! The Circle is cleared! *So Mote It Be!*

9. Kiss the flat of the blade and set on Altar.

OPENING THE CIRCLE:

10. With wand, farewell the Elementals widdershins, [starting at N or W] snuffing candles if used:

[N]: We have met in kinship, thee and me. Depart in peace, Elemental Earth, my blessings take with thee!

[W]: We have met in kinship, thee and me. Depart in peace, Elemental Water, my blessings take with thee!

[S]: We have met in kinship, thee and me. Depart in peace, Elemental Fire, my blessings take with thee!

[E]: We have met in kinship, thee and me. Depart in peace, Elemental Air, my blessings take with thee!

11. Return to Altar, with raised arms:

Beings and Powers of the visible and invisible, you aid in my work, whisper in my mind, bless me from realms of Shadow and Otherworld. Depart in peace and let there always be harmony between us. My blessings take with you. The Circle is cleared.

12. Take athame and proceed *deosil* [starting at N or W] around Circle, seeing the light drawn into it:

The Circle is open, yet the Circle remains as its magical power is drawn back into me.

BENEDICTION

13. At Altar, touch flat of blade to forehead, seeing the blue light swirling inwardly; then raise athame in a salute:

The ritual is ended!

14. Set down athame; open arms outward; palms up:

Blessings have been given,

15. Bring arms crossed over chest and bow:

    and blessings have been received.

16. Bring arms forward with hands low together in front; palms upright, outward:

    May the peace of the Goddess and the God remain in my heart. *So Mote It Be!*

17. Pick up the incense at the South; carry it completely around the circle:

    This space is cleared and fumed, that no dark energies may linger, but hasten away in peace with my blessings.

18. Set the incense on the Altar.

19. Touch palms to floor to ground excess energy; put away tools and clear the Altar; empty libation on earth outside or rinse out in sink, but not in an indoor plant.

CIRCLE CASTING ENTERED BY:

_____

3
Esbat Rituals

Esbat Notes
Esbat Opening
Full Moon Esbat
New Moon Esbat
Dark Moon Esbat
Sidhe Moon Esbat

Sun	Moon	Mercury	Venus	Mars	Jupiter	Neptune	Saturn	Pluto	Uranus

Waxing Moon
[Maiden]

Full Moon
[Mother]

Waning Moon
[Crone]

Dark (New] Moon
[Hidden Face/Mystery]

ESBAT NOTES

I. There may be thirteen Full Moons in a Solar year of twelve months, meaning that one month will have two Full Moons. The Esbat Lunar Cycle begins with the Full Moon close to Yule [Dec. 21], and this is the Oak Moon. All the other Moon Names follow from this in sequence. The two Full Moons in one month often occur in July/August.

II. There are three descriptive names for Full Moons that are used only when the event they describe occurs, and are used in addition to the usual name of the Moon. These three descriptive names are: Blood Moon, Blue Moon, and Sidhe [or Otherworld] Moon. The **Blood Moon** is uncommon, and shows the Moon as a russet to dark wine red coloration. When it does appear, it is generally between August and October, and adds *Power, Energy,* or *Aggression* to the Full Moon of that month. The **Blue Moon** is a name given for the second Full Moon as it occurs in any month, being in addition to the named Moon of the month, adding *Spiritual Energy*. The **Sidhe Moon** is the name given for the second Dark Moon as it occurs in any month. When it does occur, it adds *Intuitive Power, Psychic Energy*, or *Occult Wisdom* to the Dark Moon of that month.

III. The names for the yearly **Twelve Full Moons** [with Solar Month] are:

1. OAK MOON [December]
2. WOLF MOON [January]
3. STORM MOON [February]
4. HARE MOON [March]
5. SEED MOON [April]
6. DRAYAD MOON [May]
7. MEAD MOON [June]
8. HERB MOON [July]
9. BARLEY MOON [August]
10. HARVEST MOON [September]
11. HUNTER'S MOON[October]
12. SNOW MOON [November]

13. BLUE MOON [the second Full Moon in any Solar Month]

IV. The *New Moon* Esbat may be celebrated at the last sliver of light before turning Dark.

V. The *Dark Moon Esbat* shows no light, and is *generally* not used for magical work.

VI. Use given name or a Craft Name; use Working or Secret Name only if alone.

ESBAT RITUAL

OPENING

Have: Three Altar candles: one of each color in the left-center-right positions of Altar or candelabra:

Full Moon—blue-white-orange;

New Moon—green-white-red;

Dark Moon—black-purple-black or black-white-black;

Blue Moon—blue-white-orange;

Sidhe Moon—pale tones of lavender or gray for outer candles, with the center being a lighter toned grayish white;

Blood Moon—may use russet orange-red-russet orange for doing Power spell work.

Incense: sandalwood, frankincense, Nightlady, Moon, Ritual, or one that is appropriate for any magical workings.

Spell work materials: ready on the Altar with appropriate Working Candle.

Begin Esbat: at the portion noted in the Basic Circle casting [for Full and New Moon Esbat] or in the Dark Power Circle casting [for Dark Moon Esbat] as:

Perform Ritual/Craft Work

ESBAT BEGINS

1. Raise wand and open arms in greeting:

   I, [Name], who am Your child, stand between the worlds and call upon my Lady and my Lord, to hold communion with me.

2. Clap 3 times or ring bell 3 times:

   "An it harm none, do what ye will." Thus runs the Witch's Rede. Once more I affirm my joy of life and my love for the Lady and the Lord. I honor the Goddess and the God, [Names], for the favors and love They have bestowed upon me, and I ask Their blessings upon me.

3. Set the blessed water from the Circle Casting on pentacle; point athame to it:

   Great Mother, bless this creature of Water and of Earth to Your service. May I always remember the cauldron waters of rebirth and the many forms and beings of the blessed Earth. Of Water and Earth am I.

4. Set down athame and raise the water bowl:

   Great Mother, I honor You!

5. Put water bowl on Altar; place censer on pentacle; point athame to it:

   Great Father, bless this creature of Fire and of Air to Your service. May I always remember the sacred fire that dances within every creation and may I always hear the voices of the Divine. Of Fire and Air am I.

6. Set down athame and raise the censer:

   Great Father, I honor you!

7. Put censer on Altar; raise beverage cup:

   Power and Grace; Beauty and Strength are in the Lady and the Lord both. Patience and Love; Wisdom and Knowledge. I honor You Both!

8. Pour a small libation of beverage into cauldron and take a sip from the cup.

Proceed to Lunar Phase Esbat Rituals

FULL MOON ESBAT RITUAL

1. Stand at Altar with arms open and feet apart:

    > Behold the Great Lady, who travels the sky;
    > The stars shine around Her and light up the night.

2. Pick up wand; open arms to the Full Moon (if possible) for the Drawing Down:

    > Lovely Lady known by so many names, but known to me as [Name], with the
    > Lord, [Name] at Your side; honor and reverence I give to You and invite You to
    > join with me on this, Your special night. Descend, my Lady, and speak with
    > Your child, [Name].

3. Set wand on Altar; listen for her guidance.

4. Read from the selection of Recitations or improvise a spontaneous song, poem, etc.

5. Conduct any spell work, Drawing Down the Moon, charging of water, consecrations,
    meditations, etc. as created for this night or brought from the Spells, Rituals, or Medi-
    tations sections of the Book of Shadows at this time.

6. When Esbat work is finished, raise open arms:

    > You are the Mother of All. Maiden, Mother, and Crone; You are at life's begin-
    > ning and at its end. You dwell within us all for You are Life and Love, and thus
    > do You make me Life and Love. Love is the Law and Love is the Bond! *So Mote
    > It Be!*

Proceed to Cakes & Wine of the Circle Casting

NEW MOON ESBAT RITUAL

1. Cross arms over chest and bow head; chant name of the Goddess as Crone.

2. Raise opened arms:

   As [Name] are you known to me, for this is the Moon of my Lady as Crone. Lady of Darkness, of Wisdom, of Mysteries revealed. The Wheel turns through birth, death, and rebirth, and every end is a new beginning. You are the Passage from life to life; You are She who is at the beginning and the end of all time. You, with Your Lord [Name] at Your side, abide in us all. *So Mote It Be!*

3. Read from the selection of Recitations or improvise a spontaneous song, poem, etc.

4. Meditate in silence on the Mysteries and personal connection to the Dark Goddess.

5. Conduct any Dark Power spell work, charging of water, consecrations, meditations, etc. as created for this night or brought from the Spells, Rituals, or Meditations sections of the Book of Shadows at this time.

6. When Esbat work is finished, raise open arms:

   You are the Dark Mother of All; the Tomb that is also the Womb. You are at the beginning and end of life. You dwell within us all for You are Life, the Passage to New Life, and Love; and thus do You make me immortal through in the cycle of Life, the Passage to New Life, and Love. Love is the Law and Love is the Bond! *So Mote It Be!*

   Proceed to Cakes and Wine of the Circle Casting

Dark Moon Esbat Ritual

1. Cross arms over chest and bow head; open arms downward [toward ground]:

   Queen of the Night, Queen of Mystery; silent rests the tomb of passage into rebirth. All returns unto Thee, for of Thee is all born.

2. Raise opened arms and raise head:

   As [Name] are you known to me, for this is the Moon of my Lady as Tomb and Womb; Great Creatrix who takes the remnants of life past and from these fashions life to come. Great Lady of Shadow and Wisdom, Thy face is turned from the Earth, hidden in secrecy and mystery. Here now is the time of Perfect Love and Perfect Trust, for your children stand seemingly without Thy presence, and yet they know that Thou art steadfast and true, and as the turning of the Moon, is the cycle of life continued. You, with Your Lord, [Name], at Your side, abide in us all. *So Mote It Be!*

3. Read from Recitations; meditate on the Mysteries; conduct divination if desired.

4. When Esbat work is finished, raise open arms:

   Dark Mother of All; Keeper of Wisdom, and Revealer of Mysteries, Thou who dwells within, let me never forget Thy love. For Love is the Law and Love is the Bond! *So Mote It Be!*

   Proceed to Cakes & Wine of the Circle Casting

Sidhe Moon Esbat Ritual*

*Entire ritual including Circle Casting, Ritual, Simple Feast, Benediction, and Circle Opening

Note: This Esbat requires more advance preparation than the others. It is performed on the *Second Dark Moon* in a Solar month. Because it is *Otherworld* oriented, the entire ritual is presented, including the Circle Casting and Simple Feast [Fairy Tea and Cookies] with Otherworld references.

During the day, try to avoid eating: meat, poultry, or seafood;

Eat instead: roots, tubers, vegetables, soy or dairy products.

PREPARATION BEFORE CASTING THE CIRCLE

1. Set *Altar* or table at so that you face the West and cover with a *cloth* of white, purple, or gray.

2. Have three Altar candles of gray or pale lavender with center candle lighter in color than the outer two.

3. *Working candle* may be gray or lavender pillar style; *wand* should be elder, hazel, or hawthorn; *bowl* of spring water; *bowl* of burdock root; incense with an earthy, green, or misty scent; *libation bowl* containing a small amount of flower petals; *bowl* of milk; *bowl* of crumbled mugwort to drop into pillar candle.

4. Ground and center, then bathe with an herb bag of lavender, linden, marigold, & rosemary in a room scented with patchouli incense and lighted by 1–3 gray candles.

5. Dry off and robe lightly or be skyclad; boil a kettle of water, warm the teapot, then prepare the *Beverage:* **Fairy Tea**, saying as the ingredients are dropped into teapot:

3	teaspoons black tea:	*Black for power,*
½	teaspoon chamomile:	*apple of night,*
1	teaspoon dandelion root:	*root of the sun,*
½	teaspoon elder flower:	*Lady's Blessing,*
1½	teaspoons hops:	*Lord's leap for joy,*
½	teaspoon mugwort:	*then between the worlds,*
½	teaspoon raspberry leaf:	*to Fairy bramble,*
1½	teaspoons rose hips:	*with token of love,*
	Add boiling water and cover to steep:	*brewed to bring Fair Ones close to me*

6. Quarters may have crystals or candles: N and S—pale green; E and W—pale gray.

7. Put sweetener, milk, cup, teapot, and plate of tea cookies on Altar/table for the Simple

Feast portion of the Ritual; using two place settings at East and West if doing the Companion Quest Ritual.

CIRCLE CASTING

1. Sweep Circle *deosil*, starting at West, with a besom *not* made of broom plant [can be straw, pine, palm, oak leaves, etc.]:

   As I sweep this circle, may it be cleansed and made ready for my work.

2. Light incense, Altar candles, and the working [pillar] candle, ring a tiny bell or clap hands three times:

   The circle is about to be cast and I freely stand within to greet the Other People with the blessing of my Lady and my Lord of Greenwood.

3. Take center Altar candle *widdershins* starting at West to address the Quarters and light the Elemental candles [if used]:

   [W]: I call upon the Light between the Waters to illuminate and protect the circle [envision the glow of bioluminescence].

   [S]: I call upon the Light between the Fires to illuminate and protect the circle [envision the blue glow of marsh light called the will-o-the-wisp].

   [E]: I call upon the Light between the Airs to illuminate and protect the circle [envision the sparking blue flames of ball lightning].

   [N]: I call upon the Light between the Earth to illuminate and protect the circle [envision the pale glow of cavern deposits of phosphorescence].

4. Set the candle back on the Altar/table and raise the athame:

   I draw this circle in the presence of the Lady and the Lord of Otherworld to be a place where the Other People may manifest and bless me who am their kin in this world, and known as [Name].

5. Cast Circle *widdershins,* starting at the West, envisioning blue light coming from the tip of the athame:

   This is the boundary of the Circle in which only love shall enter and leave.

6. Touch athame tip to spring water and to burdock root as saying:

   Spring water is the purity of the Lady and the Fount of Life Eternal; and burdock is the Lord's root of purification, protection, and warding of the

negative. I bless this water and root to be used in the Circle in the names of the Lady and the Lord, the Queen and the King of Otherworld.

7. Drop 3 athame tips of burdock root into the water and stir 3 times:

   In the names of the Lady and the Lord of Otherworld, I consecrate and cleanse this water to be used in this Circle.

8. Take water bowl and sprinkle blessed water around Circle *widdershins*, starting at West:

   I consecrate this Circle in the names of the Queen and King of Fairy. This Circle is charged by the Powers of the Ancient Ones! Only love shall enter and leave!

9. Fume the Circle *widdershins*, starting at the West, with incense smoke:

   May the smoke consecrate this Circle that it be purified and sealed, and may the fragrance be pleasing and welcoming to my visitors and helpers, visible and invisible. This Circle is conjured a Circle of Power. *So Mote It Be!*

10. Make the Solar/Lunar sigil with the blessed water over the third eye:

    I, [Craft Name], am consecrated before the Lady and Lord of Otherworld, in this Their Circle.

11. With wand, greet the Elementals widdershins starting at the West:

    [W]: I call upon you Elemental Water to attend this rite and guard this Circle, for as I have blood and feelings, we are kith and kin! [envision a selkie].

    [S]: I call upon you Elemental Fire to attend this rite and guard this Circle, for as I have the spark of life and strength of will, we are kith and kin! [envision a will o' the wisp or fire dragon].

    [E]: I call upon you Elemental Air to attend this rite and guard this Circle, for as I have breath and thought, we are kith d kin! [envision a sylph].

    [N]: I call upon you Elemental Earth to attend this rite and guard this Circle, for as I have body and fortitude, we are kith and kin! [envision a gnome or cobalt].

12. At Altar, draw the cosmic lemniscate (sideways 8) with wand.

13. With both hands, hold wand overhead:

    Hail to the Elementals at the Four Quarters! Welcome Lady and Lord to this rite! I stand between the worlds with love and power all around! I call upon my Lady and my Lord as Queen and King of the Sidhe to bless my communion with the Other People. I affirm my joy of union with the Divine in all realms and worlds, and I acknowledge your blessings upon me. What I send returns to me, and I conduct my Craft accordingly.

14. Set wand down, pick up athame and point tip to teapot:

   Great Lady, bless this creature of Water and of Earth to your service. May I always remember the cauldron waters of rebirth and the many forms of being. Of Water and Earth am I.

15. Put down the athame and hold up teapot:

   I honor you, Great Lady!

16. Set the teapot down and hold the wand over the incense:

   Great Lord, bless this creature of Fire and Air to your service. May I always remember the sacred fire that dances within all life and hear the voices of the Divine. Of Fire and Air am I.

17. Put down the wand and hold up censer:

   I honor you, Great Lord!

18. Set the censer down; pour some tea into the teacup:

   Power and Grace; Beauty and Strength are in the Lady and the Lord. Patience and Love; Wisdom and Knowledge; you are Endings, Passages, and Beginnings; in all worlds are you. I honor you both!

19. Pour some of the tea from the teacup into the bowl of flower petals; take a sip from the teacup.

20. Raise arms in an open gesture:

   Hail to the People of the Land of Mist. Greetings I send to the People of the Undying Lands of Otherworld. Hear my call and let the Gateway be opened between This World and Otherworld. In the names of the Lady and the Lord, do I call upon the Fair Ones in peace and love.

21. Lower arms, lift gray pillar [working] candle:

   As this light shines before me, let the light of Otherworld reach into this place.

22. Set down the candle and add mugwort to the flame of the pillar [working] candle.

Perform Otherworld Meditation, Companion Quest, other Ritual or Craft Work

FAIRY TEA AND COOKIES

1. Serve tea [if doing a **Companion Quest Ritual,** then follow the ritual in that section for the Simple Feast serving both places], adding sweetener and milk as desired, and placing a cookie on the saucer.

2. Open arms, palms up, and bless the meal:

    > I know of my needs and offer my appreciation to that which sustains me. May I ever remember the blessings of my Lady and my Lord. The Lord brings spiritual life through the bounty of the Lady of Otherworld, that all is created in undying beauty. I honor the inner beauty of the spirit, and the Keepers of Immortality.

3. Add a bit of tea and a piece of a cookie to the bowl of flowers; sit, eat and drink, [if having tea with the Fairy Companion, the food and drink of the Other will not be consumed in the material manner, but the flavor essence will be removed]. Feel the closeness of Otherworld and the Presence of the Other People. Commune as desired, asking for their continued presence in home and property; their assistance in bringing a spell or other matter into manifestation; their aid in removing from manifestation something not desired.

OPENING THE CIRCLE

1. When finished with Simple Feast of Fairy Tea and Cookies, hold athame over table:

    > Lady and Lord of the Sidhe, I am blessed by your sharing this time with me. Watch over and guard me; guide me here and on all my paths. I came in love and I depart in love. I honor the Lady and the Lord of Otherworld, where the spirit is nourished in song and joy. The dance is ever moving and never-ending. Le the Gateway between this World and Otherworld close once more as I take my leave of the Fair Ones in peace and love. *So Mote It Be!* [snuff working candle].

2. Raise athame in salute:

    > Love is the Law and the Bond. Merry did we meet, merry do we part, and merry will we meet again. Merry Meet, Merry Part, and Merry Meet again! The Circle is now cleared. *So Mote It Be!*

3. Kiss blade of athame, set it on the Altar. Take candle snuffer around the Circle widdershins, starting at the West, to snuff candles at the Quarters:

    > [W]: Depart in peace, Elemental Water! My blessings take with you!

    > [S]: Depart in peace, Elemental Fire! My blessings take with you!

[E]: Depart in peace, Elemental Air! My blessings take with you!

[N]: Depart in peace, Elemental Earth! My blessings take with you!

4. Set down the snuffer; raise arms:

Beings and Powers of the visible and invisible, depart in peace! You aid in my work, whisper in my mind, bless me from all realms and worlds you inhabit, and there is harmony between us. My blessings take with you. The Circle is cleared.

5. Take the athame to the North; proceed deosil to open the Circle:

The circle is open yet the circle remains as its magical power is drawn back into me.

6. At the North touch flat of athame to forehead to return energy inward; balance; and ground residue by touching palms to the Earth or floor.

BENEDICTION

7. Turn to Altar/table at West and touch tip of athame to forehead, seeing the blue light swirling and returning inside; then raise athame in a salute:

The ritual is ended!

8. Set down athame; open arms outward; palms up:

Blessings have been given,

9. Draw arms together, crossed over chest and bow:

and blessings have been received.

10. Bring arms forward with hands together in front; palms upright, outward:

May the peace of the Goddess and the God remain in my heart. *So Mote It Be!*

11. Ground excess energy by touching palms to floor; put away all magical tools and clear the Altar; empty libation bowl onto the Earth or flowing water.

Esbat Ritual Entered By:

4
Sabbat Rituals

Yule Sabbat [12/21]
Imbolc Sabbat [2/2]
Ostara Sabbat [3/21]
Beltane Sabbat [5/1]
Litha Sabbat [6/21]
Lughnassadh Sabbat [8/1]
Mabon Sabbat [9/21]
Samhain Sabbat [10/31]
[With activity suggestions at the end of each Ritual]

☉	☽	☿	♀	♂	♃	♆	♄	♇	♅
Sun	Moon	Mercury	Venus	Mars	Jupiter	Neptune	Saturn	Pluto	Uranus

☽	○	☾	●
Waxing Moon [Maiden]	Full Moon [Mother]	Waning Moon [Crone]	Dark (New) Moon [Hidden Face/Mystery]

YULE SABBAT [12/21]

Have: Altar candles: bright red, deep green, and bright red [may be set in Yule Log holder]; 2 extra candles of deep green and 1 extra candle of bright red—candles may be scented cinnamon and pine or bayberry

Incense: choice or combination of bayberry, frankincense, or myrrh

Decorations: Altar/Circle with holly [Goddess], mistletoe [God], ivy, pine, pinecones

Ritual items: ashwood twigs in cauldron

Food: may include nuts, fruits mixed in a fruitcake or plum pudding, poultry, game, pork dishes, and wassail, wine, or other beverage for Cakes and Wine

Additionally: may sing Yule carols; may read selections from the section of Recitations

Begin Sabbat: at the portion noted in the Basic Circle [et al] Casting as:

Perform Ritual/Craft Work

YULE RITUAL BEGINS

1. Clap or ring bell three times. [Sing one or two Yule carols as desired—see carols at end of Ritual.]

2. Raise open arms:

> Blessed are the Lord and the Lady who turn the mighty Wheel. Welcome the Yule for the turning point of Winter is here at last. The end of the Solar Year has come, and a New Solar Year begins. The Holly King departs as the Oak King is born; the Crone delivers Him of the Mother. Hail the Mystery of Sage and Babe, of Crone and Mother!

3. Hold up wand:

> This day is a new beginning, and I send my power forth into union with the energies of the Sun God, that the Sun's rebirth rekindles my strength as the rays rekindle the warmth of the Earth.

4. Set wand on Altar; light kindling in cauldron with center Altar candle:

> This new fire is lit to bid farewell to the Dark Lord of the Solar Night and to greet the Lord of Light, seen in the rebirth of the Invincible Sun. May my power be added to the strength of the newborn Lord, and His to mine.

5. Return candle to holder; hold up athame in both hands in front of Altar:

Hail to the God of Light and Joy! Hail to the movement of Time Eternal! The Holly King leaves with gifts for all as symbols of His love. His eight great stags carry His sleigh to the realm of Snow and Ice, where in His wisdom, He awaits the next turning of the Solstice Wheel. Hail the passage of the Sage and His rebirth at Yule! Hail the God Eternal!

6. Put athame on Altar; clap or ring the bell 3 times. [Sing one or two Yule Carols.]

7. Let the Altar candles burn very low; then snuff the 2 red ones and replace them with the green candles, lighting the new ones from the still lit green center candle:

   The Holly King has left us; let us hold His wisdom in our hearts.

8. Now snuff the center green candle and replace with the extra red candle:

   The Oak King comes to us; let us hold His promise in our souls. Through the stages of life, death, and rebirth are we shown the Mystery, for there is no death, only passage, and the God holds the torch to light the way for us. God of Light and Joy, held within the Mother's arms, the radiance of Thy face lifts our spirits in the dark of Winter, and brings us comfort and peace.

9. Light the red center candle fresh [Yule log may be part of home decor through 1/6]:

   May the Yule Log bring light, that all good enter here. Good Health, Good Cheer, Good Fortune in the coming year! That as I will, So Mote It Be!

10. Pour a libation of the beverage into libation bowl and take a sip. [Sing one or two Yule Carols.]

Proceed to Cakes & Wine of the Circle Casting

Sing more carols as desired.

YULETIDE CAROLS

Oh Come All Ye Faithful

Oh come all ye faithful, joyful and triumphant;
Oh come ye, oh come ye to greet the Sun!
Join in the Yuletide, turning of the Solstice fire;
Oh come let us invoke him, Oh come let us invoke him,
Oh come let us invoke him, Lord of the Light!

Yea, Lord we greet thee, born again at Solstice;
Yule fire and candle flame, to light your way.
Come to Thy Lady, fill the Earth with love anew;
Oh come let us invoke him, Oh come let us invoke him,
Oh come let us invoke him, Lord of the Light!

Joy to the World

Joy to the world, the Sun has come!
Let Earth receive her Lord!
Let every heart, prepare him room,
And all of Nature sing, And all of Nature sing,
And all, and all of Nature sing.

Dark ruled the Earth, and Night has reigned,
But on the Wheel doth spin!
From out the womb of Night, Is birthed the Infant Light!
The Sun has come again, the Sun has come again;
The Sun, the Sun, has come again!

Welcome the Lord, who brings us Light!
Our Lady gives him birth!
His warming light returneth, to stir the joy within us;
And wake the sleeping Earth, and wake the sleeping Earth,
And wake, and wake the sleeping Earth.

We light the fires, to greet the Sun!
Our light, our life, our Lord!
Let every voice, join in with Life's song!
And merry turns the Wheel, and merry turns the Wheel,
And merry, and merry, the Wheel turns!

Joy to the Earth, the Light returns!
And sunlight fills the air!

The tide is turning, the Sun has been reborn!
And hope is everywhere, and hope is everywhere;
And hope, and hope, is everywhere!

We Wish You a Merry Solstice

Good tidings we bring, to you and your kin;
Good tidings for the Solstice and a Happy New Year!
We wish you a Merry Solstice, We wish you a Merry Solstice,
We wish you a Merry Solstice, and a Happy New Year!

The Great Wheel turns, the bright Sun returns!
The fires of Yuletide, Bring a Happy New Year!
We wish you a Merry Solstice, We wish you a Merry Solstice,
We wish you a Merry Solstice, and a Happy New Year!

Great Goddess we call, Great God join us all!
Return now this Solstice, for a Happy New Year!
We wish you a Merry Solstice, We wish you a Merry Solstice,
We wish you a Merry Solstice, and a Happy New Year!

Together this night, to bring forth the Light!
You bring us a Merry Yuletide, and a Happy New Year!
We wish you a Merry Solstice, We wish you a Merry Solstice,
We wish you a Merry Solstice, and a Happy New Year!

Deck The Halls

Deck the halls with boughs of holly,
Fa la la la la, la la la la!

'Tis the season to be jolly,
Fa la la la la, la la la la!

Don we now our gay apparel,
Fa la la, la la la, la la la!

Troll the ancient Yuletide carrel,
Fa la la la la, la la la la!

See the blazing Yule before us,
Fa la la la la, la la la la!

Strike the harp and join the chorus,
Fa la la la la, la la la la!

Follow me in merry measure,
Fa la la, la la la, la la la!

While I tell of Yuletide treasure,
Fa la la la la, la la la la!

Fast away the old year passes,
Fa la la la la, la la la la!

Hail the New ye lads and lasses,
Fa la la la la, la la la la!

Sing we joyous all together,
Fa la la, la la la, la la la!

Heedless of the wind and weather,
Fa la la la la, la la la la!

God Rest Ye Merry Pagan Folk

God rest ye, merry Pagan folk, Let nothing you dismay;
Remember that the Sun returns upon this Solstice day!
The growing dark is ended now, and Spring is on the way!
Oh, tidings of comfort and joy! Comfort and joy!
Oh, tidings of comfort and joy!

The Winter's worst still lies ahead, fierce tempest, snow, and rain;
Beneath the blanket on the ground, the spark of life remains!
The Sun's warm rays caress the seeds, to raise life's song again!
Oh, tidings of comfort and joy! Comfort and joy!
Oh, tidings of comfort and joy!

Within the blessed apple lies the promise of the Queen;
For from this pentacle shall rise, the orchards fresh and green!
The Earth shall blossom once again, the air be sweet and clean!
Oh, tidings of comfort and joy! Comfort and joy!
Oh, tidings of comfort and joy!

God rest ye, merry Pagan folk, Let nothing you dismay;
Remember that the Sun returns upon this Solstice day!
The growing dark is ended now, and Spring is on the way!
Oh, tidings of comfort and joy! Comfort and joy!
Oh, tidings of comfort and joy!

Wassail Song

Here we come a-wassailing, among the leaves so green!
Here we come a wandering, so fair to be seen!
Love and joy come to you, and to you your wassail, too!

The God bless you and bring to you a Happy New Year;
Goddess bring you a Happy New Year!

We are not daily beggars, going from door to door;
We're the Lady's children, whom you have seen before!
Love and joy come to you, and to you your wassail, too!
The God bless you and bring to you a Happy New Year;
Goddess bring you a Happy New Year!

Goddess bless the master of this house, and mistress, too;
Bless their little children that round the table grew!
Love and joy come to you, and to you your wassail, too!
The God bless you and bring to you a Happy New Year;
Goddess bring you a Happy New Year!

Good master and good mistress, as you sit before the fire;
Bless the Lady's children who sing now in this choir!
Love and joy come to you, and to you your wassail, too!
The Gods bless you and bring you a Happy New Year;
Goddess bring you a Happy New Year!

Thou Two Kings

Come thou Lord, the newborn Sun;
Come bright child, Shining One!
Praise we sing thee, love we bring thee;
As ever shall be done.

Ooh, Moon of silver, Sun of gold;
Gentle Lady, Lord so bold!
Guide us ever, failing never;
Lead us in the ways of Old.

Lord of Darkness, Lord of Light;
King of Daylight, King of Night!
Praise we sing thee, love we bring thee;
On this Solstice Night.

Ooh, Moon of silver, Sun of gold;
Gentle Lady, Lord so bold!
Guide us ever, failing never;
Lead us in the ways of Old.

ACTIVITIES FOR YULE

1. Sing Pagan Solstice Carols [Deck the Halls, The Holly and the Ivy, Joy to the World, Tannenbaum, Wassailing Song, Green Groweth the Holly, Lord of the Dance, and carols that have been re-adapted to their original Pagan themes].

2. Decorate the Solstice [Yule] Tree:

    a. String popcorn and cranberries for tree [or hang on branches outside for birds]

    b. Decorate pinecones with glue and glitter as symbols of the Fairies for tree

    c. Hang little bells on tree to call the spirits and Fairies

    d. Glue the caps onto acorns with red string underneath to hang on tree

    e. Cut a pattern into a half potato, dip into paint, dab on paper for wrappings

3. Make Wassail: cranberry juice [2 parts]; grenadine [¼ cup]; orange juice or lemon lime soda [1 part]; rum [optional—3 jiggers]; [1 pint each:] vanilla ice cream and orange sherbet to float on top of beverage in large punchbowl.

4. Kindle a fire of ash wood for prosperity.

5. Yule Blessings:

    a. Wreath on the door

    b. Mistletoe indoors

    c. Donations of food and clothing

    d. Sunflower seeds outside for birds

    e. Ring bells to greet the Solstice Morning

    f. Do magic for a peaceful planet

    g. Do a year spread in a tarot reading

6. Consecrate the Yule Tree:

    a. Asperge with blessed water [created at Circle Casting for the Sabbat]

    b. Fume branches with incense smoke [frankincense; myrrh; bayberry]

    c. Walk around tree with a lighted candle:

    By Fire and Water, Air and Earth; I consecrate this Tree of Rebirth.

7. Remember the legend of Santa Claus: Santa is the Holly King, the sleigh is the Solar Chariot, the 8 reindeer are the 8 Sabbats, their horns represent the Horned God, the North Pole symbolizes the Land of Shadows and the "dying solar year," and the gifts are meant to welcome the Oak King as the Sun reborn, and show that children, like the Oak King, are the spirits reborn.

8. Gather up Yule Greens: decorate for Yule, then remove from the home after Twelfth Night, but saving some for Imbolc for burning to banish Winter and usher in Spring.

9. Make a Yule Log candle holder: take a 12- to 14-inch white birch log and split it; chisel out three holes in equal distances across the rounded part, making them deep enough to support taper candles; sand the flat side of the cut as the base of the holder; decorate with fresh or artificial holly, evergreens, and pine cones as desired, keeping the items in place with glue as with a hot glue gun; use in a family ritual.

10. **Lighting the Yule Log** [ritual for family participation]:

> **Hail to the Elementals! Welcome Lady and Lord to this Yuletide Rite!** [parent wafts incense over the Yule Log candle holder].
>
> **Blessed be the Lord and the Lady who turn the mighty Wheel of the Year!** [child helper raises up the Yule Log candle holder].
>
> **We welcome the Yule, the turning point of Winter, for the end of the Solar Year comes and the New Year is begun** [child helper brings Yule Log candle holder to table].
>
> **We bring forth the light of our Yule Log to bid farewell to the Dark Lord of the Solar Night and to greet the rebirth of the Sun.** [child helper lights the Yule candles in the Yule Log candle holder].
>
> > **Hail the God of the Yule**
> > **Hail the God of the Sun**
> > **The Holly King ends His reign**
> > **That the Oak King's may begin!**
> > [wine, wassail, or other beverage toast]
> > **May this Yule bring Light and may the joy of the Sun**
> > **enter here. Good health, good cheer, good fortune in**
> > **the coming year!** *So Mote It Be!*

[May open presents and eat a feast, or open a single present for each person prior to those left by the Holly King on December 25—Juvenalia—and have hors d'oeuvres and wassail, Holiday Punch, etc.]

IMBOLC SABBAT [2/2]

Have: Altar candles: white or pale blue.

Incense: choice of benzoin, vanilla, etc.

Decorations: Altar/Circle with white flowers; green wreath laying on Altar with white taper candles may be used if desired.

Ritual Items: lay besom on Altar [may be decorated with white or light blue ribbons]; have white votive candle in cauldron; dish of rosemary and bay to burn; may do Initiation, Dedication, or Re-Affirmation Ritual after ritual; may include readings from the Recitations.

Food: may include dairy products; onions, leeks, shallots, garlics, olives; foods may contain raisins, such as bread puddings and creamy soups; white wine [may be spiced] or other beverage may be used, particularly milk or soy milk for Cakes and Wine.

Begin Sabbat: at the portion noted in the Basic Circle [et al] Casting as:

Perform Ritual/Craft Work

IMBOLC RITUAL BEGINS

1. Clap or ring bell three times:

   This is the Mid-Winter Festival of Lights. Spring lies within sight, the Earth quickens, the milk of ewes flows, and the seed is prepared for sowing. Now does Grandmother Crone place the Infant God of Light in the arms of the Mother, relinquishing Her hold on the Child of the New Year, that the seasons begin to turn once more. Her time of midwifery is past, and the Crone departs to reunite with the Holly King in the Land of Snow and Ice.

2. Clap or ring bell 5 times; pick up besom and hold in both hands before Altar:

   With my besom in my hand I will sweep out that which is no longer needed so as to purify my surroundings, preparing the way for new growth.

3. Take besom to sweep Circle *deosil* in outward motions:

   Clear out the old and let the new enter. Life starts anew at this time of cleansing.

4. Place besom on Altar.

5. Light cauldron candle; drop rosemary and bay into flame:

   I call upon the power of these herbs that their scent now released in this cauldron's fire purify me, my surroundings, and the tools of my Craft. With this rite I am reaffirmed in my Craft and made ready for the renewal of life in the coming of Spring.

6. Wave brush end of the besom over the cauldron:

   May this besom be cleansed that nothing cast out of the Circle in the coming year return with it or cling to it. *So Mote It Be!*

7. Place besom next to Altar; pass other tools of the Craft through the incense smoke.

8. Raise opened arms:

   As I have purified all within this Circle, I am now ready to Renew my oath to my Lady and my Lord.

**Proceed to Re-Affirmation of Oath, or Speak an
Oath based upon this or the Initiation Rite** [*see Rituals*]
Proceed to Cakes & Wine of the Circle Casting

ACTIVITIES FOR IMBOLC

1. Burn: the Yule greens to send Winter on its way.

2. Make the Bride's Bed February 1: in the evening, and using the Corn [or Wheat] Doll made the previous Lughnassadh:

   a. Dress her in white or blue

   b. Give her a necklace representing the seasons

   c. Lay her in a long basket adorned with ribbons [next to a fireplace hearth if there is one]

   d. Light white candles on either side of the basket:

   Welcome the Bride both Maiden and Mother; Rest and prepare for the time of the seed; Cleansed and refreshed from labors behind Her; With the promise of Spring She lays before me.

   e. Lay the Wand, decorated with white and blue ribbons, beside Her:

   How soon comes the Lord, How quickly He grows! The season will turn, 'ere we know.

   f. Let the candles burn for awhile, then snuff before going to bed.

   g. Next morning, look to see if there are any marks in the hearth dust [sign of the activity of the Lord, hence an early Spring]; remove the dress and scatter the wheat outdoors [or if corn, hang in a tree for the squirrels and birds].

3. Imbolc Eve, leave buttered bread in a bowl indoors for the Fairies who travel with the Lady of Greenwood [dispose of next day as the "essence" is removed].

4. Place three Ears of Corn on door as symbol of the Triple Goddess and leave until Ostara.

5. Cleanse the Magic Work area with incense of rosemary or vervain:

    By the power of this smoke I wash away the negative influences that this place be cleansed for the Lady and Her Babe.

6. Light: a white candle and sandalwood incense, then carry throughout the dwelling.

7. Cleanse: Altar and equipment; do a self-purification rite with the Elemental symbols:

    a. Earth [salt] for body

    b. Air [incense] for thoughts

    c. Fire [candle flame] for will

    d. Water [spring water] for emotions.

8. Make: dream pillows stuffed with batting and herbs for everyone in the family.

9. Create: a Solar Cross from palm fronds, willow, or vine; or a Brigit's Cross from bending stalks of wheat or palm fronds around the center for an equal-armed cross:

    a. Make one for each room of the house

    b. Place a red pillar-style candle center to the front door

    c. With Solar Crosses in hand, light the candle and open the door:

    We welcome in the Goddess and seek the turning of the Wheel away from Winter and into Spring.

    d. take the candle to each room of the house:

    Great Lady enter with the Sun and watch over this room!

    e. leave a Solar Cross in the room and proceed throughout the house.

    f. last room is the kitchen:

    Mother of the Earth and the Sun, Keep us safe and keep us warm, As over our home You extend Your blessing.

10. Look at the Sky: if the day dawns clear, then Spring will be delayed as Winter lingers, but if it dawns cloudy, then Spring will come early.

OSTARA SABBAT [3/21]

Have: Altar Candles: selected from pastels green; peach; lavender; yellow; pink.

Incense: Choose from jasmine; light-scented florals; Secret Garden; Rain.

Decorate: Altar/Circle with spring flowers; wild flowers; garden motif items; loose bundle of wildflowers on Altar.

Ritual Items: Place on Altar an earthenware or wooden bowl with soil; large seed for planting placed on the pentacle; sheet or piece of parchment; ink [may be Dove's Blood, Black, or Purple] and writing tool.

Food: Seeds types such as sprouts or soy beans; sweet wine or other beverage [honey may be added to it]; roasted ham; pineapple rings; decorated hard boiled eggs [found after a hunt] made into deviled eggs; yellow cake made with poppy seeds [and 1 cup sherry, optional]; banana nut bread.

Begin Sabbat: at the portion noted in the Basic Circle [et al] Casting as:

Perform Ritual/Craft Work

OSTARA RITUAL BEGINS

1. Clap or ring bell three times:

   I call upon me the Blessings of the Ancient Ones as merry do we meet at this Springtime Rite. Lady and Lord, hear your child, [name], for I am here to celebrate with You and for You as we greet the Spring together!

2. Sprinkle wild flowers deosil around inside perimeter of Circle:

   Lady and Lord frolic and play; stir up the creatures along your way.

3. Clap or ring bell three times:

   Springtime is when we sow the seed; it is the time for me to plant what I want to grow. This season brings hope and joy; expectations for desires realized; and inspiration for new ideas. My life is brought into balance and I am reborn, resurrected, as is the Earth with Her renewal. I welcome thee, Ostara, beautiful Spring!

4. Place bowl of soil on pentacle; focus on seeing seed as idea to be manifested.

5. Clap or ring bell 1 time; write seed idea on parchment; light parchment from center candle and drop the burning ashes into soil:

Lady and Lord, let this soil be prepared and fertile to receive this seed of my desire, that here it may grow and prosper, to ripen and bear fruit, as it grows and prospers in my mind and heart to reach maturity and fruition.

6. Mix ashes into soil with athame.

7. Raise wand in open arms; dance/skip *deosil* 3 times around Circle [may play music] raising energy.

8. Stop at Altar with wand and arms open and raised:

By the power instilled in this raised wand will the seed be planted in the ready soil. Blessed Be the Wand of Spring and Blessed Be the Earth that receives it!

9. Kiss the tip of wand, envision the energy raised now enter into it.

10. Make indentation in center of soil with the wand; seeing the energy move from wand into soil; the set down the wand.

11. Hold up seed; focus energy into it; *know* the idea will be manifested as the plant grows; place seed into furrow; and close the soil over it:

This seed is planted in the Mother's womb to be part of the Earth, of Life, and of me. Let this seed and what it represents grow to manifestation, as I will it. *So Mote It Be!*

12. Clap or ring bell 3 times.

13. After Circle is opened, transplant seed and soil into garden/flower pot/or other suitable place.

Proceed to Cakes & Wine of the Circle Casting

ACTIVITIES FOR OSTARA

1. Color Hard-boiled Eggs: adding symbols for: the God and the Goddess, fertility, the Sun, unity, fire, water, agriculture, prosperity, growth, strength, wisdom, spring, love, affection, and protection [*see Correspondences*].

2. Make Natural Dyes from Herbs:

a. Green: coltsfoot and bracken

b. Yellow-green: carrot tops

c. Yellow: tumeric

d. Orange: onion skin

e. Red: madder root

    f. Blue: blueberries

    g. Bright blue: red cabbage

3. Consecrate the Eggs:

> **In the Name of the Goddess of Spring; And the ever-returning God of the Sun; By the powers of the Elementals Earth, Air, Fire, and Water; I do consecrate these Eggs of Ostara.**

Point athame at eggs; make sign of pentagram; see energy flow into eggs:

> **New life lies within as new life shall enter the soil. Let those who seek this life find it and consume it, for all life feeds on life.**

4. Hide the Eggs: and commence the Ostara Egg Hunt.

5. Make: some of the found eggs into "deviled" eggs for supper.

6. Make Hot Cross Buns: cut the X with the bolline, honoring Earth and Sun for Spring; then bless the cakes.

7. **Ostara Eve:** Light a purple or violet candle; burn Patchouli incense; carry both through the house:

> **Farewell to Wintry spirits and friends;**
> **On morrow we greet the spirits of Spring.**
> **Our blessings to thee as your way you wend;**
> **And merry we'll meet next Winter again.**
> **[Blow out candle] Merry Meet, Merry Part, and Merry Meet Again!**

8. Have a Traditional Meal: of hot-cross buns and eggs for breakfast; ham for supper

9. Toss: crushed eggshells into the garden:

> **For Fairy, for flowers, for herbs in the bowers; the shells pass fertility with Springtime showers.**

10. Wear: colorful or pastel clothing.

11. Bless Seeds: to be planted in the garden.

12. Empower: an egg with a desired quality, then eat the egg and envision it bringing what was sought.

BELTANE SABBAT [5/1]

Have: Altar Candles: dark green.

Incense: choose floral or woodsy scent; lilac, Secret Garden, forest.

Decorate: Altar/Circle with seasonal flowers.

Ritual Items: place on Altar a cauldron with dark green votive candle, woodruff herb in a bowl, pinch each of these wood chips in separate, labeled containers: birch, oak, rowan, willow, hawthorn, hazel, apple, vine, and fir; also ready, have libation bowl and candle snuffer.

Food: include breads, cakes, or custards flavored with flowers/extracts; oatmeal cakes; vanilla ice cream; floral or herbal wine.

Begin Sabbat: at the portion noted in the Basic Circle [et al] Casting as:

Perform Ritual/Craft Work

BELTANE RITUAL BEGINS

1. Clap or ring bell three times:

   The Goddess of Spring walks through the land with the God of the Forest, and the dark time of Winter is behind me.

2. Clap or ring bell seven times:

   The animals breed and the plants pollinate, as the May Queen and the Green Man bestow Their blessings upon the Earth and Her creatures. I, who am Their child [name] rejoice with Them and ask that Their happy union become the example for all humanity to live in love and harmony.

3. Light green votive candle in the cauldron:

   The Dark Days are cleared away that the Mayday can now begin!

4. Drop some woodruff into cauldron flame:

   May the Light of the May Fire bring happiness and peace, and may the Victory of the King of the Wood come into my life, that I may always dwell in the joy of the Lady and the Lord. *So Mote It Be!*

5. Drop pinch of each type of nine wood chips into cauldron flame while saying the chant:

   I burn thee birch to honor the Goddess;
   And now add thee oak to honor the God.

96

Thou rowan I add for a magical life;
And add thee willow to celebrate death.
Thou hawthorn I burn for Fairies near me;
Thou hazel I burn for wisdom you bring.
I add thee good apple to bring to me love;
And thou sweet vine whose fruit brings me joy.
Fir you are added to remember rebirth;
Your sweet savor sings of immortality.
My blessings I give to all of thee,
And thine I call from thee upon me,
That as I will, *So Mote It Be!*

6. As wood chips burn, raise goblet in both hands:

    I greet the time of unions and give honor to the Lord and the Lady for Their fruitfulness!

7. Pour a libation; take a sip from goblet and set it back on Altar.

8. Extinguish flame in cauldron with lid or other covering and leave covered until cooled.

9. Clap or ring bell three times.

Proceed to Cakes & Wine of the Circle Casting

ACTIVITIES FOR BELTANE

1. String beads or flowers for a blessing:

    May the God and the Goddess and the power of the Elementals bless me now and always be with me.

2. Make Paper May Day Baskets to secretly hang on the doorknobs of neighbors:

    a. Fold square piece of decorated paper diagonally

    b. Glue or tie through punched holes a yarn handle

    c. Place a few spring flowers inside basket and place on knobs of front doors or other available feature such as a mailbox magazine holder

3. Jump over a bonfire or campfire and make a wish as you jump.

4. Make Beltane Bread:

  4 cups sifted flour

  ½ cup ground almonds

  2 cups sugar

  1 tube of almond paste

  ½ tsp. baking powder

  1 tsp. cinnamon

  5 eggs

Preheat oven to 375 degrees. Combine ingredients. Work dough to medium soft and shape into flattened balls. Place on ungreased cookie sheet. Bake until golden brown, about 20 minutes. Cool, ice with white Solar Cross. May also be done as a loaf.

5. Make Quick Almond Biscuits:

a. Measure Bisquick per box recipe

b. Add small portions of almond extract, sugar, cinnamon, and 1 to 2 eggs

LITHA SABBAT [6/21]

Have: Altar Candles: dark blue.

Incense: Choose musky or cleansing scent; lavender, musk, sandalwood.

Decorate: Altar/Circle with summer flowers and fruits.

Ritual Items: Place on Altar a cauldron containing a small amount of water; keep the water bowl of the Altar partially empty to receive water from the cauldron; have a red votive candle in a safe bowl type container that will hold flames and melting wax; have a bowl containing a small [pinch] of these nine herbs: wood betony [or basil], chamomile, fennel [or lavender], lemon balm [or dianthus/carnation], mullein, rue, thyme, St. Johnswort, and vervain.

Food: May include red wine or other hearty beverage; herbed bread; pastries; cold, cooked meats/cold, fried chicken; potato salad with hard-boiled eggs.

Begin Sabbat: at the portion noted in the Basic Circle [et al] Casting as:

Perform Ritual/Craft Work

LITHA RITUAL BEGINS

1. Clap or ring bell three times:

    I celebrate Life on this Midsummer day! Sadness is cast aside and joy flows within as the High Summer now begins.

2. Light red candle from center Altar candle and hold up in right hand:

    The Light of the Sun, the God of Life, shines around me and in me for all the world to see.

3. Set candle in bowl and place on pentacle

4. With finger tips, sprinkle water from cauldron upon Altar:

    The Lord and Lady of the Greenwood have made Their pact. The Oak King turns his face to that of Holly King so He may wed the Queen and pass into Her care. The Lord rises into the Lady and prepares to descend into the corn, in both ways to be born again of the Mother.

5. Pour water from cauldron into blessed water bowl:

    The Life that enters the Lady's care is sanctified and purified in Her love.

6. Clap or ring bell nine times.

99

7. Raise open arms:

As the Sun moves on His course, so the course of Life moves closer to Death that Life may come again. Soon will the Lord of the Corn move into His realm to become the Lord of Shadows, but now, in the fullness of Summer, He shares the joy of His life and His love with all of the Earth.

8. Hold athame over votive candle:

As the God and Goddess share Their light and life with me, so do I share with others and offer comfort as is meet.

9. Mix herbs in bowl with athame; add herbs to votive candle:

I call upon the powers of Fairie imbued in these herbs that the Midsummer Fire be empowered. Herbs of the Earth; symbols of Otherworld, the planets, of Life, and of Love, your scent fills the air and drives away care.

10. Rest palms on Altar:

Lord and Lady, You fill my life with Your bountiful love and gifts! I call upon Thee Both for Your continued blessings and offer my petition to Thee Both that Your love and caring remain with me always. Bless me now and receive my blessing, my appreciation for life, for love, for joy, for that spark that brings me to you. May I pass this joy to others. *So Mote It Be!*

11. Hold up wand:

At this time of Midsummer joy, I re-affirm my love for my Lady and my Lord.*

Optional: Proceed to Re-affirmation of Oath or speak an Oath based upon this or the Initiation Rite [*see Rituals*].

Proceed to Cakes & Wine of the Circle Casting

ACTIVITIES FOR LITHA

1. Make Amulets of protection out of herbs such as rue and rowan.

2. Make Protection Pouches out of white cotton to hang indoors or in bedrooms:

   a. Two or three sprigs of Rue

   b. Bits of whole grain wheat bread

   c. Pinch of salt

   d. Two star anise

3. Tie together with red thread and hang over entry door: sprig of Rowan, sprig of Rue, three flowers of St. Johnswort.

4. Dispose of old amulets in the Midsummer Fire.

5. Asperge house and tools with spring water sprinkled by vervain, rosemary, and hyssop tied together with white thread [banish negativity; cleanse and purify].

6. Create Psychic Dreams Pillows or Fairy Dream Pillows/Bundles: mugwort and bay leaves; lavender, blue, or yellow cloth; sewn with red thread; place under pillow on bed or hang in a tree in the yard.

7. To See Fairies at night, soak thyme in olive oil and anoint eyelids.

8. Make a Solar Wheel to hang outdoors on a tree/in entry/or in bedrooms:

   a. Wind and twist palm/willow/or grapevine into a circle

   b. Cut two short lengths of stick to be just a bit larger than the diameter of the circle

   c. Place one stick across the back horizontally; the other vertically crossing in back of the horizontal one, coming forward to the front of the circle to secure

   d. Adorn with symbols of the Elementals (i.e.: stone, feather, ashes, shell)

   e. Festoon with yellow ribbons as a reminder of the God's protection

9. Make a Witch's Ladder:

   a. Braid three strands of 3-foot-long yarn: red, black, and white for the Triple Goddess

   b. Add nine feathers of various colors or one color for a specific charm:

   1.) green for money/prosperity;   2.) red for vitality and power
   3.) blue for peace and protection   4.) yellow for cheer and intellect
   5.) brown for stability and pets   6.) black for wisdom and occultism
   7.) black and white for balance   8.) patterned for clairvoyance
   9.) iridescent for insight

10. Burn the old Yule wreath in the Litha fire.

11. Tie a bunch of fennel with red ribbons and hang over the door for long life and the protection of the home.

12. Harvest Herbs like St. Johnswort, vervain, and yarrow.

13. Look for the Fairie Folk under an Elder tree, but eating their food means staying with them for seven years, according to tradition [possibly based on a selection practice for training Bards].

LUGHNASSADH SABBAT [8/1]

Have: Altar Candles: yellow or wheat colored.

Incense: Frankincense or Sandalwood.

Decorate: Altar/Circle with summer flowers and grains.

Ritual Items: place on Altar a loaf of multigrain or cracked whole-wheat bread [or suitable alternative] to share after the blessing; cauldron.

Food: may include blackberry wine or other dark fruity beverage; multigrain or cracked wheat bread; blackberry pie, corn on the cob, barbecue meats or fried chicken.

Begin Sabbat: at the portion noted in the Basic Circle [et al] Casting as:

Perform Ritual/Craft Work

LUGHNASSADH RITUAL BEGINS

1. Clap or ring bell three times:

    I celebrate this day the First Harvest, the Festival of Bread and the Marriage of the Sun and the Earth.

2. Chant or sing; may do while dancing around Circle:

    Dance, dance, wherever you may be;
    When you dance with the Lord, He will dance with thee.
    Turn, turn, a Circle then you form;
    And the Lord of the Dance is the Lord of the Corn!

3. Raise open arms at Altar; sing or chant:

    Down, down, into the Earth He'll go;
    Giving life to the grain that in Spring we sow.
    He rules the Shadowland 'til Yule;
    When His Sun is reborn and He joins us anew!

4. Clap or ring bell seven times:

    Great is the power of the God of the Sun and the Goddess of the Earth from Whom spring all life!

5. Hold wand over bread:

    The harvest of the corn that sustains us is brought through death and rebirth.

The Lord of the Corn leaves the side of the Earth Mother that His power may be passed into the land for His children to live. Blessed Be the God of the Corn, Whose love for His children knows no bounds! In the Land of Shadows will He abide with the Lady as Crone, awaiting the time of His joyous rebirth.

6. Touch bread with tip of wand:

    May the God bless this bread that I eat in honor of the cycle of Life that created it and me.

7. Tear portion of bread as libation and place in the cauldron; eat a bite of bread and set aside rest to share [may reserve and serve at family meal or use in Cakes and Wine].

8. Hold arms open, palms up, level over Altar:

    My Lord and my Lady, I am blessed by Your gifts from the soil. These first grains are the promise of fruits to come. Let the power of the Goddess and the God be in me at this time and throughout the year, that I never forget that I am one with the Absolute, the All, the Two Who Are One. *So Mote It Be!*

9. Read or recite the Charge of the God [see Recitations].

10. Clap or ring bell three times.

Proceed to Cakes & Wine of the Circle Casting

ACTIVITIES FOR LUGHNASSADH

1. Collect Rainwater in non-metallic container; add mugwort to empower objects.

2. Make Sand Candles to honor the Goddess and the God of the Sea:

    a. Melt wax from old candles in a coffee can set in a pot of boiling water

    b. Add any essential oil you want for scent

    c. Scoop out a candle mold in wet sand in any design you desire [scoop a bowl and add three finger holes to form a three-legged cauldron candle]

    d. Clip wick to a stick over the center and gently pour in the melted wax

    e. Unmold when wax hardens by lifting out and brushing off excess sand

3. String Colorful Indian Corn on black thread for a necklace; feed to the birds at Yule.

4. Create and bury near house entry a small, protective Witch's Bottle full of broken and sharp, pointy things and urine.

5. Make a Corn Dolly to save for next Imbolc:

    a. Double over a bundle of wheat, tying it near the top to form a head

b. Take some of the fiber to twist into arms (can tie together to hold flowers)

c. Decorate with a dress and bonnet or garland of flowers

6. Bake corn-shaped Cornbread Sticks:

    1   cup flour
    ½   cup corn meal
    ¼   cup sugar
    ¾   tsp. salt
    2   tsp. baking powder
    2   eggs
    1   cup milk
    ¼   cup shortening

    Prepare iron mold shaped like ears of corn and preheat oven to 425 degrees. Sift together dry ingredients; add eggs, milk, and shortening. Beat until smooth; pour into molds; bake 20–25 minutes

7. Do a Harvest Chant when serving the corn bread at dinner:

    The Earth Mother grants the grain;
    The Horned God goes to His domain.
    By giving life into Her grain;
    The God dies, then is born again.

8. Make a Solar Wheel (eight ears of corn) or a Corn Man Wheel (five ears of corn):

    a. Pull wire hanger into a circle, keeping the hook to hang it by

    b. Hot glue the tips of eight or five ears of Indian corn to a cardboard disk at center

    c. Carefully spread and wrap some of the husks around the wire

    d. Cover center cardboard with a flower, extra husk, etc.

    e. Let dry overnight; hang on the front door

9. Sprout Wheat Germ in a terra cotta saucer [used under terra cotta flower pots]:

    a. Add the sprouts to homemade bread

    b. Use as an offering:

    God of the Grain, Lord of Rebirth; Return in the Spring to renew Mother Earth.

10. Collect Blackberries and make a fresh pie marked with the Solar Cross.

11. Have a Magical Picnic with libations to the Earth of bread and wine.

MABON SABBAT [9/21]

Have: Altar Candles: may be wine, russet, brown, or orange-brown in color.

Incense: myrrh, pine, sage, or sweetgrass.

Decorate: Altar/Circle with choice of fall leaves and flowers, grapes, berries, vines, acorns, corn.

Ritual Items: place on Altar canned goods for donations; a loaf of nutbread on a plate.

Food: may include currant or dark grape wine or other dark fruity beverage; nutbread, fruit pies, smoked or roasted poultry, and hearty bean soup.

Begin Sabbat: at the portion noted in the Basic Circle [et al] Casting as:

Perform Ritual/Craft Work

MABON RITUAL BEGINS

1. Clap or ring bell three times:

   > This day I celebrate the Second Harvest, that of fruits, nuts, and the vines, and I remember those who struggle without. As I accept the gifts of the Lord and the Lady, I remember that what was sown is now reaped, and this is the time of offerings, payment of dues, and enjoyment of just rewards. So, too, do I pass along what I may to those who have need.

2. Clap or ring bell three times:

   > The Wheel of the Year is ever turning, through Sun Tides and Moon Tides, through seasons and harvests, for plants, for animals, and for people; for all life moves within the Wheel of the Year from life to death to life again. The balance and the harmony of the dance of our life is the spiral dance of Energy Eternal, lead by the God guiding us. He yearly travels the path of Nature on our behalf that we know and not fear the cycles of our being, for balance and harmony in the motion of life are His truths.

3. Hold up plate of nut bread and cup of wine:

   > I ask the blessing of the Lady and the Lord, upon this food that the harvest be bountiful.

4. Set plate down and clap or ring bell three times:

   > The Lord of Shadows rules in His Shadowland, yet His love holds true, and with Him my own dance will one day move the Other Way. As this harvest season moves onward to the last harvest, I call upon the Lady and the Lord

to bless this beautiful season and bless my life within it, that my life be the harvest of the Goddess and the God.

5. Take the wand and honor the Elementals *deosil,* pausing at each Quarter:

[N]: Hail to thee, Elemental Earth! Your steadfastness helps me to maintain the things of my home, my health, my security, and my comfort! We are kith and kin, and I honor you!

[E]: Hail to thee, Elemental Air! Your inspiration helps me to learn and understand! We are kith and kin, and I honor you!

[S]: Hail to thee, Elemental Fire! Your energy helps me with the drive I need to accomplish my goals! We are kith and kin, and I honor you!

[W]: Hail to thee, Elemental Water! Your gentle flow helps me maintain calm and balance in my relationships with others! We are kith and kin, and I honor you!

6. Touch the canned goods with wand at Altar:

In the names of the Lord and the Lady, and with the aid of the Elementals, I bless these fruits of the harvest for those who are in need. I offer aid and comfort to those whose needs arise throughout the turning of the Wheel. May the Goddess and the God add Their blessing to these offerings, to the one who gives, and to the one who receives. *So Mote It Be!*

7. Clap or ring bell three times.

Proceed to Cakes & Wine of the Circle Casting

ACTIVITIES FOR MABON

1. Make a Protection Charm of hazelnuts (filberts) strung on red thread.
2. Collect Milkweed Pods to decorate at Yuletide to attract the Fairies.
3. Hang up dried ears of corn on the front door and around the house.
4. Eat a Mabon Meal:

   a. Wine from the God

   b. Beans and vegetables from the Goddess

   c. Smoked meats to honor the coming of the Crone and the Hunter

5. Call Upon the Elementals and honor them for their help with:

a. Home and finances—Earth [N]

b. School and knowledge—Air [E]

c. Careers and accomplishments—Fire [S]

d. Fruitful relationships—Water [W]

SAMHAIN SABBAT [10/31]

Have: Altar Candles: may be orange and/or black.

Incense: patchouli or myrrh.

Decorate: Altar/Circle with small pumpkins, Indian corn, gourds, Fall flowers and leaves.

Ritual Items: cauldron with black votive candle inside; parchment with weaknesses or bad habits written down to be banished; white votive candle in bowl; sprig of heather and an apple on plate; may have patchouli oil on hand as well.

Food: may include dark wine, pumpkin pie, stuffed acorn squash, stuffed game birds, apple cider, taffy apples; may set up for family spirits a Dumb Supper of bread, salt, and cider or beer at an extra place at the table during the family meal.

Begin Sabbat: at the portion noted in the Basic Circle [et al] Casting as:

Perform Ritual/Craft Work

SAMHAIN RITUAL BEGINS

1. Clap or ring bell three times:

   I celebrate the dance of life to death to new life and the balance of the cosmos in my life! The last harvest is gathered and stored for the dark months ahead, and the Wheel has turned to the time of the Hunter.

2. Clap or ring bell nine times:

   At this time is the veil between the worlds thin, and the gates are thrown open, so do I welcome thee spirits who have gone before and thee Others, who pass between two worlds. This is the Crone's time and with the Lord of the Shadows, She is the passage from life to life that all must take. They give a refreshing rest in the continuous turning of the spiral dance that goes and returns, yet ever moves on. With the Ancient Ones [Names], I move with the dance unperturbed. Love gives strength; give to gain.

3. Hold up wand with open arms:

   Great Lady, Fruitful Mother, You have showered me with Your bounty, and in this turning of the seasons, I bid You farewell as You walk now as Crone with the Lord of the Hunt. I know that within You is yet another fruit waiting to be born, and I will bide patient until the Mother returns.

4. Set cauldron on pentacle; light black votive from center Altar candle

Here is the cauldron of endings and new beginnings. Into this burning flame do I cast my weaknesses and the habits that keep me from attaining my potential. By the death of these things will I live a better life. *So Mote It Be!*

5. Burn parchment in votive; when reduced to ash, clap or ring bell 9 times.

6. Pass white candle through patchouli incense or anoint with patchouli oil:

   With this candle and by its light I welcome you spirits this Samhain night.

7. Use this white candle for jack-o'-lantern.

8. Hold heather over Altar:

   I call upon the power of this herb to bless this house and the spirits that come to visit.

9. Drop heather into cauldron:

   The air is purified and made pleasant for the spirits and Others who may call upon me. Blessed Be!

10. Hold apple above Altar:

    I call upon Thee Lord and Lady, to bless this fruit to be the food for the dead. Let any who visits find sustenance in this apple whose center reveals the pentagram and reminds us of the promise of the Lady of passage from one life to the next. May the spirits who pass here move on refreshed. *So Mote It Be!*

11. Clap or ring bell three times [bury apple outside after Sabbat concludes].

Proceed to Cakes and Wine of the Circle Casting

ACTIVITIES FOR SAMHAIN

1. Make a Spirit Candle by anointing a white candle with patchouli oil:

   With this candle, by its light; Welcome spirits this Samhain Night.

2. Place Spirit Candle inside the jack-o'-lantern and light to show spirits the way.

3. Drink Apple Cider warmed and spiced with cinnamon to honor the dead.

4. Bury an apple or pomegranate in the garden as food for passing spirits.

5. Do Divinations to see the energies and tones of the months in the coming year.

6. Make Resolutions, write on paper, and burn in flame of a black candle.

7. Set out a Dumb Supper:

    a. Dinner served in reverse and in silence, with a place set for a spirit guest

    b. Dinner served normally, with conversation about the spirit guest

    c. May be done as part of the Sabbat, at Cakes and Wine, serving food in reverse [dessert, main course, salad/soup, appetizer] in silence, eating in silence, and then doing divinations

8. Decorate the house and yard with images of the death passage, the Hunter, the Crone; corn stalks; pumpkins; colorful squashes; skeletons and ghosts.

9. Have a party: bob for apples in a tub of water; drink cider; decorated cookies; pies; hearty foods; music and dancing; with a spirit area set aside/a haunted house or room.

10. Dress up and wear a mask; enjoy the Trick or Treating of the season.

Sabbat Ritual, Activity Entered by:

_____

5
Recitations

For Esbats, Sabbats, & Other Rituals

Seven/Five-Fold Blessings
Witch's Rune
Daily Chant
Song of the Goddess
Charge of the Dark God
Charge of the Star Goddess
Song of the God
Charge of the Goddess
Charge of the Triple God
Readings for Eclipses
Chants; Songs; and Poems

☉	☽	☿	♀	♂	♃	♆	♄	♇	♅
Sun	Moon	Mercury	Venus	Mars	Jupiter	Neptune	Saturn	Pluto	Uranus

☽	○	☾	●
Waxing Moon [Maiden]	Full Moon [Mother]	Waning Moon [Crone]	Dark (New] Moon [Hidden Face/Mystery]

SEVEN-FOLD BLESSING*
*May anoint in a sigil each area with oil or blessed water during recitation.

I call the blessings of the Goddess and the God upon me!

Blessed be my feet that bring me on my path.

Blessed be my knees that support me before the Lady and the Lord.

Blessed be my sexuality that honors life.

Blessed be my heart that holds me true to my path.

Blessed be my lips that speak the sacred names.

Blessed be my eyes that see the beauty of Nature.

Blessed be my mind that seeks the wisdom and knowledge of the Goddess and the God.

FIVE-FOLD BLESSING*
*May anoint in a sigil each area with oil or blessed water during recitation.

I call the blessings of the Goddess and the God upon me!

Blessed be my feet that bring me on this path.

Blessed be my knees that support me before the Lady and the Lord.

Blessed be my sexuality that honors life.

Blessed be my heart that holds me true to my path.

Blessed be my lips that speak the Sacred Names.

WITCH'S RUNE

Green adaptation based on that of Gerald Gardner, Doreen Valiente, and unknown origins.

Eko, Eko Azarel!
Eko, Eko Shadiel!
Eko, Eko Hecate!
Eko, Eko Cernunnos!
Darksome night and shining Moon
Hearken to this Witch's Rune.
North, then East, then South and West;
Attend me here at my behest!
By power of Earth, Air, Fire, and Sea
Be thou all in accord with me.
Wand and Cauldron by Candle's light;
Awaken all ye into life!
Censer, Pentacle, and my Cord;
Hearken ye to ward discord!
By Power and by Spoken Word,
I charge my spell be cast and heard!
Queen of Witches, by ringing bell,
Send your aid unto this spell!
Horned Hunter of the Night,
Work my will by magic rite!
By the Powers of Land and Sea,
As I Will, So Mote It Be!
By the Powers of Moon and Sun,
As I Will, this Spell is Done!
Eko, Eko Azarel!
Eko, Eko Shadiel!
Eko, Eko Hecate!
Eko, Eko Cernunnos!

[Repeat Ekos to raise energy and release.]

DAILY AFFIRMATION

I am a Witch!

I am at One with the Earth, The Universe,

and the Divine!

Let this day be free from Strife and Fear;

Let only Joy and Love come near;

With Blessings given and received

I walk in Peace in Word and Deed.

SONG OF THE GODDESS

I am the Great Mother, adored by all creation which I have brought forth from my fertile womb. I am the Primal Mother, life-bringing force of the Divine Female, boundless and eternal.

My faces are many, for I am Transformation and I bring change to all. I am the Goddess of the Moon, Lady of all Magic, passing through phases of Maiden, Mother, and Crone. I am the Maiden whose name is carried upon the tides and the winds. I wear the Moon upon my brow as Crescent, Full, and Horned, the stars rest beneath my feet, and the Serpent of Regeneration gazes up at me in adoration. I am Mysteries, yet I reveal these to any who seek such of me. I open the New Path for the spiritual questor, comfort the weary traveler upon the old, and receive into my arms the soul in passage.

I am the Blessed Mother, the Bountiful Lady of the Harvest. I am clothed in the cool depths of the waters and draped in the gold of fields laden with grain. My tabard is the myriad forms of life in woodland, field, valley, river, sky, and sea. My hair cascades across my shoulders as soft shadows stirring in the forests. By me are all seasons of the earth ruled that all things come to fruition through me, for lo, I am the Life-Giving Mother, fertile and joyous in my abundance.

I am the Crone, Grandmother, and Death Mother, wise and tender. Through me pass all in the spiral dance of life, death, and rebirth. I am the Wheel, the shadowed Moon, giving release and renewal to weary souls. The God ushers the Spirits unto me, for I am the Tomb through whom all must pass to be born of my Womb.

I am the Eternal Maiden, Mother of All, and Crone of Transformation. I stir the cauldron of Wisdom, Abundance, and Renewal, and I pour forth my Limitless Love upon all my peoples of the Earth.

CHARGE OF THE DARK GOD

Listen to the words of the Dark God, Who was of old called Dis, Hades, Osiris, Hunter, and Lord of Shadows:

I am the shadow that is cast by the sun in the brightest of days. I am the reminder of sudden mortality in the midst of joyous life. I am the black velvet night where dances the stars and the planets; time everlasting, unperturbed dancer of fiery endings and new beginnings. I am the Horned Hunter, bow drawn in my hand; gathering the living with my arrows and leading the Wild Hunt. By my hand are ye lead from this life, that life may continue, for behold! My mystery lies in the movement of life energy from life unto life, for the reminder that all life feeds on life and that only through death is life found anew.

I am the strength that protects, comforts, gives solace and renewal. I am the one who stands by the Crone of Transformation, then enters her Tomb for birth through her womb. Follow my lead and find thy immortality. Together we shall laugh at the threshold of death passage as awareness awakens, and I shall embrace thee in thy last moments of life.

Remember me on dark moonless nights; look for my Rade in roiling storm clouds and the clash of bright lightning. I carry thee to the one who transforms, Dark Mother of all, releaser of strife. Sing to us thy songs in the tongues of ecstasy , for we understand the music of the soul. Blow me a kiss from the palm of thy hand when the moon is dark, and I shall smile upon thee, but no kiss shall I return; for my kiss is the final one for all mortal flesh, nepenthe to drink at the end of thy days.

CHARGE OF THE STAR GODDESS

Traditional, based partly on the "Charge of the Goddess"
by Charles Leland, Gerald Gardner, and Doreen Valiente.

Hear ye the words of the Star Goddess; she in the dust of whose feet are the hosts of heaven, and whose body encircles the universe.

I who am the beauty of the green earth, the white moon among the stars, and the mystery of the waters call unto thy soul; arise and come unto me.

I am the soul of nature who gives life to the universe. From me all things proceed, and unto me all things must return. Before my face, beloved of gods and of men, let thine innermost divine self be enfolded in the rapture of the Infinite.

Let my worship be within the heart that rejoices, for behold! All acts of love and pleasure are my rituals. Therefore, let there be beauty and strength, power and compassion, honor and humility, mirth and reverence within you.

To thou who thinkest to seek me, know that thy seeking and yearning shall avail thee not unless thou knowest the mystery. If that which thou seekest thou findest not within thee, thou wilt never find it without.

For behold! I have been with thee from the beginning; and I am that which is attained at the end of desire.

SONG OF THE GOD

I am the radiant king of the skies, flooding the earth with my warmth; awakening the seeds of life within the High Fruitful Mother that all her creation be manifest in new birth.

I send forth my shining rays to bring light to all beings without distinction, and daily turn my golden face upon my beloved Earth, rousing those who have slumbered and sending others to their rest. I bring nourishment to nature and the soul.

I am the Oak King upon the Earth; the Greenman, wild and free; I run with the stag, swim with the salmon, soar with the hawk, and dance with the crane. The ancient woods and wild places are my familiar haunts, filled with my power, hallowed sanctuaries of my fertile life essence.

I am the sacrifice; my body the grain harvested that my children may eat and live through me; my spirit the fermented beverage drunk in cleansing revelry and solemn remembrance of me. Behold, the mystery I bring! For new seed is born of the harvest, as Spring is born of the Winter. As life feeds on life, all life feeds on me, for I am the nourishment of all.

I am the Father, and the Son of the Mother, the Begetter and Begotten who dances creation. By many names am I known, yet all are the same.

My emblem is the antlered stag in the wild; the sheaf of harvested grain; the filled cup distilled with my essence. and through all, my golden rays light the cycles of life that are part of my path and my holy rite. Born at the Solstice of Winter, I turn my face closer to Earth until the Solstice of Summer. As Holly King my light fades, and the knowledge I share is of the swiftly shortening days and the cycle of passage.

I am the Lord who rules from the Shadow; my emblem the Dark Sun, my realm that of repose. In me ye will find life, peace, and joy in thy passing, for my blessings are poured out to all, withheld from none. I give thee peace and rest in my realm until ye choose to return to my sunlit Earth.

CHARGE OF THE GODDESS
By Charles Leland, Gerald Gardner, and Doreen Valiente.

Listen to the words of the Great Mother; She who of old was also called among the people Artemis, Astarte, Cerridwen, Hecate, Demeter, Danu, Ishtar, and many other names:

Whenever ye have need of any thing, once in the month, and better it be when the Moon is full, then shall ye assemble in some quiet place and adore the Spirit of me, who am Queen of all Witcheries. and thou who thinkest to seek for me, know thy seeking and yearning shall avail thee not unless thou knowest the mystery:

That if that which thou seekest thou findest not within thee, thou wilt never find it without thee.

For behold! I have been with thee from the beginning, and I am that which is attained at the end of desire.

CHARGE OF THE TRIPLE GOD

Listen to the words of the Triple God, Stag-crowned King, Greenman, Earth God, Horned One, Lord of the Animals and the Wildwood, known among the people as Herne, Cernunnos, Pan, Dionysus, Shiva, Osiris, and by many other names:

I am the Cycle of the Wheel of the Year that matches the cycle of life on Earth. I am the Bright Child, the Oak Leaf Crowned King of Winter Solstice; I am the Greenman of Spring, the Holly Leaf Crowned King at the marriage feast of Summer Solstice; I am the Stag-Antlered Hunter, leading the Rade that sweeps through the storm-tossed skies; I am the Goat-Horned Lord of Shadows, offering rest and renewal to spirits in passage through my Lady as Crone; I am the Youth who dances with the Maiden, the Father who embraces the Mother, and I am the Son of the Mother. Honor me through the seasons of the year, as I show the way, for I am the Spirit of Nature, free and untamed, and by my hand are ye led through the Great Mystery unto thy rebirth.

READINGS FOR ECLIPSES

BESEECHING THE LADY OF THE ECLIPSE

Great Lady of Lunar Eclipse I who am Thy child, call upon Thee in
reverence and beseech Thee:

Open the way of release from the fetters of the past;

Open the way to embracement of life's joyous repast.

Take into Thy arms all self-perceived flaws, unneeded fears, pain, and
insecurities;

Slip these behind Thy back, and release them into the vastness beyond Thy
Hidden Face.

Then turn Thy gentle face outward once more, filling Thy arms with joy, good
fortune, and constancy sieved from the stars;

Slip these into the Mother's arms, and smile upon me.

Open Thy arms, loving Mother of All, and let Thy bountiful blessings upon me
now fall;

With my arms opened wide, with hope and bright eyes, I gather Thy abundance of blessings inside.

Thy gift of Transformative Power changes shadow into light,

For Thou art what I have attained at the end of desire.

Blood Moon Lunar Eclipse

Huntress Lady of the Moon, Dark Mother, Queen of the Stars;
Tonight you show us all that you are.
Triple Goddess shining bright;
You show all Your faces in this one night.
Blood of the Moon, Blood of the Tomb, Blood of the Womb;
You are the One Who Transforms us through life.
Mother is fullness, giving Her bounty and love.
Crone takes away blockages, fears, and limiting energy;
Handing them to the Dark Lady to scatter behind the Moon;
Diffused into space by Thy Hidden Face.
Wisdom now gathers hope and inspiration from the Stars,
And turns to the Maiden, fresh in Her bower.
Maiden emerges, grasping the Powers of Renewal and Creation;
And bringing forth Her shining light of Hope,
Hands all to the Mother for completion this Night.
My arms I uplift and I am bathed in new Light,
As I rejoice in Her Blessings and Gift of delight.

CALLING FOR WEALTH FROM THE LORD
DURING THE SOLAR ECLIPSE

Recited in conjunction with a money or prosperity spell during a solar eclipse.

Lord of Shadows, Lord of the Darkened Sun;
I call upon Thee to complete the spell I have begun.
Thou who holds power over wealth;
Whose hand moves swiftly with knowing stealth,
Take wealth into Thy hand for me,
And pass it to Thyself as Golden Sun.
Great Lord of Light, receive this treasure,
Fill it with the Power of Thy pleasure.
Open now Thy golden hand, and lay this wealth upon me and this land.
Lord of the Sun with Thyself as Lord of the Night,
Upon me cast Thy favored sight.
Bring to me Thy gifts of wealth, health, and worldly delight.
For as I am Thy child who loveth Thee, I am in You, and You are in me.
Hear then my call and hearken unto me,
That as I will, *So Mote It Be!*
My blessings unto Thee, and Thine unto me,
Let this Spell be bound to completion, *So Mote It Be!*
With love t'wix Thee and me, the spell's conclusion is called by three.
So Mote It Be!

[NOTE: The Lord of Underworld is traditionally the holder the riches of the Earth, who may be petitioned for a portion of His largess.]

CHANTS, SONGS & POEMS

OFFERING CHANT

Lady of the Moon, of the restless Sea, and the living Earth;
Lord of the Sun, of wild places, and the creatures therein;
Accept this offering I place here in Your Honor.
Grant me the wisdom to see Your Presence in all Nature,
That I be in union with thee, Ancient Ones of my ancestry.

CAKE DAY CHANT [FEB. 28]

Cakes for the Lady and
Cakes for the Lord
Celebrate Underworld's
Opening doors.

HOGMANAY EVE CHANT [DEC. 31]

Queen of the Universe
King of Prosperity
Reign throughout this new year
Bringing me peace and happiness.

LUGHNASSADH SONG OF THE GOD

Dance, dance, wherever ye may be!
When you dance with the Lord, He will dance with thee.
Turn, turn, a Circle then ye form!
And the Lord of the Dance is the Lord of the Corn!

Down, down, into the Earth he'll go!
Giving life to the grain that in Spring we'll sow.
He rules the Shadowland 'til Yule,
When His Sun is reborn and He joins us anew!

Harvest Moon

Clean hair, waist long, blond and streaked in silvery shades;
All blowzy blown in willow scramble, freeing from bindweed clutches,
    with twiggings plucked victoriously from strands in disarray.
Ages spanned in looking back, seeing me in stained party
    best, making grass bird's nests for arriving guests.
Naught's changed, there. Aye, that's me, now gathering
    feathers 'neath this Harvest Moon;
Laughing with the Lady, trodding squishy lawn at pond's sodden edge—
Oh look! A coiling snail shell gleaming back at me; its turnings as the
    Wheeled Years.

Auma: the Divine Androgyne

I am He and I am She;
Lord and Lady, live or dead,
We are One who dwell in thee;
Shiva/Shakti, bound and wed.

Rites of Passage mark the way;
Birth through life, and then beyond.
Human souls in urns of clay;
Swimming 'round the spiral pond.

Sun and Moon shine down on thee;
Watchers of Our children's play.
Full of love and joy are We;
Aum and Uma share your day.

Life to life and on it flows;
Spiral dance of Time moves on.
Energy that learns and grows;
Hastens forth, to Mother drawn.

Grace and Power are Our Names;
Come to us to join and blend.
We are Two, and yet the Same;
Bide in Us, Our garden tend.

Call Us Earth or call Us Sky;
Call Us Moon or call Us Sun.
Male or Female, live and die;
Symbols of the season's run.

Primal font of energy;
Aum and Uma; Auma, then.
Flow into the galaxy;
Dance apart and then reblend.

Matter comes and goes, but still;
Souls with need may be reborn.
Wait for all, that is Our Will;
Time is timeless in Our Form.

Blessings given, blessings got;
What you send, We send to thee.
Tap into Our Force or not;
Love is given happily.

JOURNEY
[Emphasis on italics words.]

I *talked* with thee once, when thou wert a child,
I *spoke* with thee then, in gentle tones mild.
Ye *knew* me and *loved* me and danced in my light;
Why *did* ye then *turn* away into the night?

I *saw* Fear creep in and then steal you away;
I *saw* the Dark Demons come dampen your play.
I *saw* how you shook and beseeched me for help;
But *when* I appeared, you with terror did melt.

Who *was* it that turned you away from my love?
What *horror* replaced the Light shone from above?
Who *told* you I'm evil when never I was?
Who *took* away beauty and washed it in blood?

I *ne'er* demanded so high an emotion;
That *caused* you to bleed for any devotion.

I *stood* by aghast to see where you would tread;
I *never* deserted, but stood by your stead.

And *when* you did stumble, I held out my hand;
And *when* you did plead, it was my own command.
I *answered* you truly each time that you spoke;
And *waited* with patience until you awoke.

I did not tell you that knowledge was wrong;
Nor *say* it was evil to sing your own song.
I did not lay down long listings of rules;
Yet *all* new religions still honor my Yules.

If *all* of my days are special to others;
Why *can't* my children act more like they're brothers?
The *dictums* of priesthoods, by whatever name;
Serve *only* their leaders for fortune and fame.

Though *av'rice* lies naked before ev'ry view;
Their *immoral* doctrines still fill up the pew.
With *learning* constrained to a pitiful few;
The *lessons* are curbed lest the teachers they hew.

Keep ye the Sabbats or let them dance by;
I *care* not a whit if you do not abide.
There *never* was any but one rule, no guilt;
My *guidance:* "An it harm none, do what thou wilt."

I *never* demanded sacrifice of blood;
Never called thee "sinner" nor gave thee the Flood.
I *offered Knowledge* and *Wisdom* for thy life;
But *never* suggested an eternal strife.

No *minions* of darkness attacking at night;
No *angels*, no demons, and no cosmic fight.
My *Eternal* Dance is of joy and of life;
My *Song* is of laughter and ending of strife.

So *when* did it happen? That moment, that spark?
When *Knowledge* and Reason at last struck their mark?

Though *counseled* by others to stay in the dark;
You *strove* to gain Wisdom, and learnt with a start—

That *all* your old longings and feelings were right!
That *I* Am the One whom you've never lost sight;
Together with Uma, Am Glory and Might—
The *Song* of the Ancients sung morning and night!

With *tears* and sweet laughter I welcomed you back;
You *know* that false dogmas no more can attack.
For *Wisdom* you sought, and there Truth have you found;
The *Old* God and Goddess with love still abound.

I *dance* in the Cosmos, I dance in your heart;
We *dance* now together and never will part.
Thy *childhood* is over, here starts your next stage;
To *bask* in the glory of life as my Sage.

Come *dance* at Our Sabbats and sing to the Moon;
Thy *Lord* and thy Lady Both welcome thy tune.
We now *dance* in thy heart and fill thee with love;
As it *is* now below, so *has* been above!

THE WILD MARES

[A dream song in which my request for a totem animal was answered by Epona]

The rain fell gently, mistily; my heart with joy aroused;
List'ning to ethereal song drift through the storm-tossed clouds;
I wandered 'cross the grassy mounds, long hair blown in the wind,
Embracing now the moment's charm, my own voice chorused in.

I found I yearned for Elder woods and Fairie Lands Beyond;
Lush verdant realms in primal haze, where Other Folk had gone.
I saw across the shining sea, the gleaming Fair domains,
And looked within to ponder how I might these lands attain.

My Lunar mind released to me the knowledge that I sought,
I raised my arms, and to the Wind, I called without a thought:
     E-PON-A! E-PON-A! Send me the wild mares!
White steeds with flashing teeth and tangled manes to take me there.

The wind up rose, and 'cross the tor, the hoofbeats sounded sharp;
The air now split with wild shrieks as horses cleared the mark!
With certitude I stood my ground, in timeless magic cue;
And great white beasts, all sleek with rain, rampaged into my view!

They slowed their pace and arced to me; I stood within their breach,
I spied the lead, who with a friend, came gently to my reach.
The leader passed without ado, the second t'ward me drew;
They tossed their heads and stamped their feet, and that was when I knew.

The wild mares were what I loved! The race against the wind!
I leaped upon the second steed and rode off with a grin.
Within the herd I traveled fast, my laughter flying free:
    E-PON-A! E-PON-A! You heard my call to thee!
    You sent me wild mares to ride, across the Elder Sea!

SAMHAIN MUSING
[Automatic writing]

Tatters and homespun,
  dancing rags of black against firelight,
  arch of the heavens, starry arboretum,
Fairy light and backlit horizons.
Walker, wagon dweller, black wolf,
  dark eyes of the night staring forthright, unblinking.
Lateen sailed Moon-ship, an outsider peeking in, sees,
  the black legged spider becoming in dancing the dance,
  for the god and the goddess, looking at beauty,
  not to claim, absorb, or preserve it, but to live it,
  to be in life, the art of living with joy and frolic,
  love, harming none, wrapped in the cloak of the night,
  warding harm by the power of the stars and of life.

RECITATIONS ENTERED BY:

_____

6
Rituals

Suggested Times for Performing Rituals
Basic Spell or Charm Consecration Ritual
Drawing Down the Moon
Initiation Ritual
Dedication Ritual
Re-affirmation of Oath
Light & Dark Power Tool Consecrations
Consecration of a Statue
Crystal Cleansing & Programming
Crystal Consecration & Dedications
Handfasting & Handparting Rituals
Naming Ceremony of Twelfth Night
Passing Over — Wiccaning
Companion Quest

☉	☽	☿	♀	♂	♃	♆	♄	♇	♅
Sun	Moon	Mercury	Venus	Mars	Jupiter	Neptune	Saturn	Pluto	Uranus

☽	◯	☾	●
Waxing Moon [Maiden]	Full Moon [Mother]	Waning Moon [Crone]	Dark (New) Moon [Hidden Face/Mystery]

SUGGESTED TIMES FOR PERFORMING RITUALS

1. The Initiation, Dedication, Rites of Passage, Consecrations, Cleansings, Crystal or Tool Cleansing & Dedication Rituals, may be conducted at the point in the *Esbat Ritual* stating: "Conduct any spell work, Drawing Down the Moon, charging of water, consecrations, meditations, etc. as created for this night or brought from the Spells, Rituals, or Meditations Sections of the Book of Shadows at this time."

2. The Initiation, Dedication, Rites of Passage, Consecrations, Cleansings, Crystal or Tool Cleansing and Dedication Rituals may be conducted at the point in the *Circle Casting* stating: "Perform Ritual/Craft Work [when finished, proceed with Cakes & Wine/Opening the Circle]."

3. The Re-affirmation of Oath Ritual may be conducted during the *Imbolc* and *Litha Sabbats* at the point stating: [Imbolc] Raise opened arms: "As I have purified all within this Circle, I am now ready to Renew my oath to my Lady and my Lord."

Proceed to Re-affirmation of Oath, or speak an Oath based upon this or the Initiation Rite

[Litha] Hold up wand:

At this time of Midsummer joy, I re-affirm my love for my Lady and my Lord.

Proceed to Re-affirmation of Oath, or speak an Oath based upon this or the Initiation Rite

BASIC SPELL OR CHARM
CONSECRATION RITUAL*

*#1 or #2 of "Suggested Times"

1. Light appropriate color ritual/working candle.

2. Pass prepared spell or charm item through symbols of the Elementals:

   I call upon the Powers of the Elementals to enliven the magic and stir the energies into this [spell/charm] that it may [state purpose]! By Elemental Earth [sprinkle with salt/powdered root], Elemental Air [pass through incense smoke], Elemental Fire [pass through candle flame], and Elemental Water [sprinkle with Blessed Water], I consecrate this [name item] to my use. *So Mote It Be!*

3. Set item on pentacle, raise energy with wand in hand or with power hand while gathering energy or dancing in the Circle:

   I gather thy energies to work this spell and do my will, that as I will, *So Mote It Be!*

4. Touch item with charged wand:

   Be thou charged, [item] of [purpose]. It is done! The [spell or charm] is begun! *So Mote It Be!*

5. Continue with rest of individual spell or charm requirement—i.e.; place in Moonlight, burn, place in a special location, etc.

**Proceed to Esbat Conclusion or Cakes & Wine
of the Circle Casting**

DRAWING DOWN THE MOON*

* #1 of Suggested Times; Full Moon Esbat

Purposes for this Ritual

A. For empowerment of spell work

B. For meditation

C. For creating Blessed Water

D. For communion and divination

1. Point the wand with both hands towards the Full Moon:

    I call upon Thee, Lady of the Moon! Let me share this time with Thee, and let Thy holy essence flow into me.

2. Bring the tip of the wand to touch the heart, and see the silvery light pass through the wand, and inward so that the whole body is aglow.

    Proceed according the purpose:

    A. The wand can now be used in the right hand to direct energy into a working

    B. The wand can now be used in the left hand, against the heart, for a meditation

    C. Create Blessed Water empowered by the Full Moon:

    Have: water in a container, a bowl, rose petals or rose water, salt, and a small, compact style mirror [if needed]:

    I call upon Thee, Great Lady of the Night, to bless this water I pour here in Thy sight.

    Pour water into bowl, add rose petal and hold bowl up in Moonlight:

    In this water doth shine Thy light, that it be consecrated in Thy sight. Cleansed and purified on this Esbat night, this water is blessed by Thy sacred rite.

    Lift the salt in the Moonlight:

    Through the Lady hast all things their form, taking salt in the waters and lands of the Earth. Through Thy bright light, I consecrate this salt to aid in my work.

    Add 3 pinches of salt to the water; stir 3 times; then let the Full Moon reflect on the water [may use a mirror]:

    By the light of the Moon, through the power of Thy Tides, a portion of Thy power now herein resides, that blessed be this water. By 3 times 3 this spell I bind, that it be cast with the power of nine. For as I will, *So Mote It Be!*

Set down bowl [and mirror] and turn the bowl 9 times deosil in the Moonlight:

With power gathered and sent within, this spell is sealed 9 times again, that adds together 9 once more, that with these 3 is 9 the core. *So Mote It Be!*

D. **Have:** a cauldron or other container of water; raise arms to Moon:

I call Draw thee Down, thou glorious Moon, that I with my Lady may commune. Cast thy glow to this water here below, for thy power lies within these tides.

Gaze into container, seeing the reflection of the Moon on the surface; point the wand to the water:

I call Thee, Moon, into this view, that through thy sight, my Other Sight renew. Bring to me visions of Divine insight, transporting my Lady's words this night.

Set down wand, open arms to either side of container; look upon the reflection of the Moon; see and hear the message of the Lady.

3. Upon completion of A, B, C, or D, point the wand with both hands toward the Full Moon:

Great Lady, Thy power I have shared; Thy knowledge Thou hast sent me unimpaired. Thou art the Goddess of the Witches and Mother of All who blesses Thy children whenever they call. Blessed be Thy Power and may Thy blessings be upon me, Thy child, whom Thou hast named [name].

4. Then open arms with wand in right hand and say:

With love and honor 'twixt Thee and me, this rite is ended. So Mote It Be!

5. Set down the wand and touch the ground with the palms of both hands to let the excess energy drain out.

Proceed to Esbat Conclusion and Cakes & Wine
of the Circle Casting

Initiation Ritual*

*#1 or #2 of "Suggested Times"

Have: a pitcher or other container of wine or other [fruity] beverage on the Altar to re-fill [charge] the cup after the ritual; a 9-foot-long red cord [silk, wool, or cotton].

1. Raise open arms:

   Lady and Lord, I call out to Thee! I hold Thee in honor and know that I am one with all the things of the Earth and Sky. My kin are the trees and the herbs of the fields; the animals and stones through the seas and the hills. The fresh waters and deserts are built out of Thee, and I am of Thee and Ye are of me.

2. Lower arms:

   I call upon Thee to grant my desire. Let me rejoice in my oneness with all things and let me love the life that emanates from my Lady and my Lord into all things. I know and accept the creed; and understand that if I do not have that spark of love within me, I will never find it outside myself, for Love is the Law and Love is the Bond! And this do I honor when I give honor to the Lady and the Lord.

3. Kiss open right palm and then hold high:

   My Lady and my Lord, known to me as [Names], I stand before Thee Both and initiate myself to Thy honor. I will defend and protect Thy spark within me and seek Thy protection and defense of me. Ye are my life and I am of Thee. I accept and will ever abide by my family Rules of Conduct, and by the Witch's Rede, that an' it harms none, I may do as I will. *So Mote It Be!*

4. Take up the goblet of wine and slowly pour the remainder of wine into the cauldron:

   As this wine drains from the cup, so shall the blood drain from my body should I ever turn away from the Lady and the Lord or harm those in kinship with Their love, for to do so would be to break trust, to cast aside the love of the Goddess and the God, and to break my own heart. Yet through Their continued love I know They would heal my heart and spirit that I might again journey through the cauldron of rebirth to embrace the love They freely give. *So Mote It Be!*

5. Dip forefinger into the anointing oil and draw the sigil of the Solar Cross ⊕ over the Third Eye [center of forehead]; then draw the sigil of the Pentagram ✪ over the heart;

and then draw the Sacred Triangle ▽ representing the Triple aspects of both Deities, touching navel, right breast, left breast, and back to navel.

6. Take the cord, use it to measure and knot the cord for each place: ankles, knees, hips, waist, chest, and head, then make a loop and knot on one end and fray the other end [will have a cord now with seven knots total]:

    This is the measure of myself, my cingulum to tie my robe, and to bind me to my Craft. By this cord am I known.

7. Tie cord around waist, passing the frayed end through the loop and securing, then raise arms opened wide:

    As a sign of my chosen new life and initiation into the Craft, I take for myself a new name. As I study the Craft that I may be worthy to be called Witch, I shall be known as [Name]. Know now my name, my Lady and my Lord, and see me as this name and as part of Thee Both. *So Mote It Be!*

8. Lower arms and meditate for a time on this new path begun, and on being in the Old Religion. Let the feelings flow out of the body and let the touch of the Goddess and the God enter in.

9. Raise both hands high:

    I am blessed by the Goddess and the God, known to me as [Names], by Thy attendance at my Initiation! Know that I am your child, [Craft Name], and receive me into Thy Guidance!

10. Refill cup with beverage from pitcher or other container.

11. If the Craft Name is not being kept secret from other people, include an additional name of choice to be the secret Working Name known only between practitioner and the Divine until the time of Dedication. A secret name symbolizes the trust between the Witch and the Divine. The Craft Name may be the Working Name only if kept secret from others. Cingulum may be kept on Altar or wrapped around staff or stang if these are used, or be worn with a Ritual Robe.

Proceed to Esbat Conclusion or Cakes & Wine of the Circle Casting

Note: traditional foods include fresh white bread, butter, and strawberry [or other such fruit] jam; a light rose wine, or fruity beverage.

DEDICATION*

[Performed not earlier than a year and a day after Initiation Ritual.]

1. Perform a vigil the night before during which time, question the motive for doing a Dedication, address hopes and fears, and seek answers to any doubts.

2. This ritual creates a commitment to the Goddess and the God and affirms the unconditional love between the Practitioner and the Divine.

3. This ritual permanently opens the lines of communication between the Practitioner and the Divine.

4. Review the Ritual prior to performing so it flows smoothly and naturally; do not rush the stages, but feel each one.

Have: piece of parchment paper, writing instrument, ink, one extra white [votive] candle in safe container able to hold melted wax, a needle or pin, and a bowl of soil.

1. Begin at portion of Esbat stating: "Conduct any . . . ," or in *Circle Casting* at the place designated as: "Perform Ritual/Craft Work."

2. Statement of intent to the Goddess and the God [may use this or create another]:

> **Great Lady and Great Lord, I am Thy child known to you as [Craft Name]. I have studied the Craft of the Wise, and I have communed with Thee for at least a year and a day. You have given me of Thy blessings, aided me in my Craft, and showered me with Thy love, asking nothing in return. Now I seek to offer something back to Thee, making my commitment to Thee and opening the communication between Thee and me, that we are ever united in the bonds of love.**

3. Contemplate the role of the Four Elementals in the ritual:

4. Open raised arms:

> **With Elemental Air, do I make my promise to the Divine to try and live up to my potential, to open my mind to the voices of the Ancient Ones, and to develop my magical skills.**

5. Light white candle:

> **With Elemental Fire, do I light the way to my new life.**

6. Set candle safely on the ground [floor] in front of the Altar.

7. Envision the ground [floor] as a deep hole:

> With Elemental Earth, do I lay myself down into the grave signifying the end of this life.

8. Now lie down in front of the Altar safely next to the candle, seeing this as a burial [on the back, feet together, arms folded over waist or crossed over chest], and with eyes closed, visualize sinking down into the Earth, being still, feel that the life has ceased, and there is silence within the enfolding Earth.

9. When the ground feels like it is in motion, let all negative feelings drain out into the Earth below, leaving an empty feeling that may cause crying. See that the body and the cares of this life are dying, and the Spirit is moving into the Land of Shadows.

10. When ready, think of Elemental Water, but do not give voice to these thoughts:

> With Elemental Water am I cleansed.

11. Visualize the sacred waters of the Earth—the seas, springs, snowfall, rainfall, and the rivers washing over and cleansing the Spirit. Feel as through floating in the Waters of Life, and feel at peace. When the sensation of relaxation sweeps over, feel the blessing of the water.

12. The Lady may speak a new name at this point, calling to you, but if not, continue with the ritual.

13. Think of the **Spirit**, and slowly move into a fetal position, preparing to be reborn into the Light. With eyes open, look at the Candle, thinking of the God as Fire, Sun, Hunter, and Protector, the One who yearly travels this path, leading the way for spirits to understand the passage through the Crone to find new life in the Light.

14. Sit up gently, with knees drawn up and arms around them, and relax. Visualize being born into the Light while looking at the candle.

15. Rise now, taking the candle and setting it in the center of the Altar.

16. If no name was received earlier in the ritual prior to rebirth, close the eyes and call upon the Divine:

> Great Lady and Great Lord, I call upon You to receive my Dedication unto You. I, whom You have guided under the name of [Craft Name], do ask You to give me a new name, one that is secret between Thee and me. As parents name their children, so do I, as Your Child, seek Thy naming of me. Tell me, my Lady and my Lord, what is my name.

17. They will come and pronounce the name, and if need be, ask for the name to be spelled out.

18. Ask for Their Secret Names, and do not share these names with anyone, for this is a Sacred Trust, giving a private access line as it were.

19. To acknowledge the receipt of Their gift, Seal the Dedication in the Elementals of Earth, Air, Fire, and Water by writing on the piece of parchment paper the promise that was spoken with Elemental Air, worded now with the new Secret [Working] Name. Kiss the paper and burn it in the white votive flame of Elemental Fire. Pull out a few hairs for Elemental Earth, and burn these in the flame. With the needle, pin, or the tip of the athame, sterilized by putting it in the flame for a moment, prick the tip of the little finger of the left hand and squeeze out a few drops of blood for Elemental Water onto the Earth in the bowl or on the ground if outside. If using the bowl of soil, when the Circle is Opened, take it outside and empty onto the ground, or into the soil of a potted plant.

20. Henceforth, the Working Name may be used in private to call upon the Lady and the Lord as "Your child, whom You have named . . . " while the Craft Name may be used in public as desired.

**Proceed to Esbat Conclusion or Cakes & Wine
of the Circle Casting**

RE-AFFIRMATION OF OATH*

*#3 of "Suggested Times"

Have: a pitcher of wine or other [fruity] beverage on the Altar to refill [charge] the cup after the ritual.

1. Raise open arms:

    Lady and Lord, I call out to Thee! I hold Thee in honor and know that I am one with all the things of the Earth and Sky. My kin are the trees and the herbs of the fields; the animals and stones through the seas and the hills. The fresh waters and deserts are built out of Thee, and I am of Thee and Ye are of me.

2. Lower arms:

    I call upon Thee to grant my desire. Let me rejoice in my oneness with all things and let me love the life that emanates from my Lady and my Lord into all things. I know and accept the creed; and understand that if I do not have that spark of love within me, I will never find it outside myself, for Love is the Law and Love is the Bond! And this do I honor when I give honor to the Lady and the Lord.

3. Kiss open right palm and then hold high:

My Lady and my Lord, known to me as [Names], I stand before Thee Both and initiate myself to Thy honor. I will defend and protect Thy spark within me and seek Thy protection and defense of me. Ye are my life and I am of Thee. I accept and will ever abide by my family Rules of Conduct, and by the Witch's Rede, that an' it harms none, I may do as I will. *So Mote It Be.*

4. Take up the goblet of wine and slowly pour the remainder of wine into the cauldron:

As this wine drains from the cup, so shall the blood drain from my body should I ever turn away from the Lady and the Lord or harm those in kinship with Their love, for to do so would be to break trust, to cast aside the love of the Goddess and the God, and to break my own heart. Yet through Their continued love I know They would heal my heart and spirit that I might again journey through the cauldron of rebirth to embrace the love They freely give. *So Mote It Be!*

5. Dip forefinger into the anointing oil and draw the sigil of the Solar Cross ⊕ over the Third Eye [center of forehead]; then draw the sigil of the Pentagram ☆ over the heart; and then draw the Sacred Triangle ▽ representing the Triple aspects of both Deities, touching solar plexus [navel], right breast, left breast, navel.

6. Refill the cup from the pitcher of beverage.

Proceed to Sabbat Conclusion and Cakes & Wine of the Circle Casting

CONSECRATION OF THE LIGHT ASPECT TOOL*

*#1 or #2 of "Suggested Times"

Have: all ritual items as needed for a Full Moon Esbat; and additionally, a bowl of fresh water, a red votive candle and container that can collect the melted wax, and the item to be consecrated.

1. Light red votive from the center Altar candle; set tool on the pentacle.

2. Inscribe tool with desired symbols/runes/ogham, and Craft Name in runes, ogham, or other magical alphabet.

3. Hold tool in right hand over the pentacle:

In the names of the Goddess and the God, [Names], I consecrate this [tool] to be used in my practice of the Craft. I charge this by Elemental Earth [sprinkle with salt] **and Elemental Water** [sprinkle with water]; **by Elemental Fire** [pass through votive candle flame] and Elemental Air [pass through incense smoke]. This tool is now by Elemental Powers bound to aid me in my work. *So Mote It Be!*

4. Set the tool on the pentacle; raise arms with open hands:

   Great Lady and Great Lord, together in the light of this Moon, yet also seen with my inner sight, You dwell within and without, for You are Endings and New Beginnings; the Promise and the Love Manifested. Let this tool be imbued with Thy Power to aid me in my Craft.

5. Hold hands, palms down, over tool, feeling the energy pass through the hands:

   Lady and Lord, Mother and Father of All, Thy blessing is felt and thy Power is passed into this tool, that it be sanctified for use in my Craft.

6. Kneel with both palms on the ground:

   As what is sent returns, so I return to Thee the Power graciously sent to me. This [tool] is sanctified through Thy Power and Grace, through my flesh and blood, and made ready for my use. *So Mote It Be!*

7. Stand; remove tool from pentacle, keeping it on the Altar; snuff votive.

Proceed to Esbat Conclusion or Cakes & Wine of the Circle Casting

CONSECRATION OF THE DARK ASPECT TOOL*

*#1 or #2 of "Suggested Times"

Have: three Altar candles [black or purple]; optional four Quarters candles [purple, white, or black]; incense of mugwort, lilac, Night Lady, or other rich scented incense; matches; bowl of water; bowl of rock or sea salt; pentacle; cup and dark beverage [flavored as blackberry, black currant, elderberry, or Opal Nera]; cauldron; votive [black or purple] with container; plate with dark bread/cake; anointing oil; candle snuffer; athame; wand; items to be consecrated

1. Inscribe tool with desired symbols/runes/ogham, and Craft Name in runes, ogham, or other magical alphabet.

2. Hold tool in right hand over the pentacle:

   In the names of the Dark Lady and Dark Lord, [Names], I consecrate this [tool] to be used in my practice of the Craft. I charge this by Elemental Earth [sprinkle with salt] and **Elemental Water** [sprinkle with blessed water]; **by Elemental Fire** [pass through center candle flame] and **Elemental Air** [pass through the incense smoke]. **This tool is now by Elemental Powers bound to aid me in my work.** *So Mote It Be!*

3. Set the tool on the pentacle:

   Great Lady and Great Lord, together in the darkness of this Moon, veiled from my sight yet seen with my inner sight, You dwell within for You are Endings and New Beginnings, the death that leads to new life; You are the Promise and the Love Manifested. Let this tool be imbued with Your Power to aid me in my dark journeys.

4. Light votive candle from the center candle:

   Let this small light illuminate the dark path to the Realm of Shadows.

5. Hold up tool in right hand; hold left hand palm parallel to ground:

   Lord of Shadows hidden within the Lady of Darkness, together They hold the darkness in Balance. He is the Passing, She is the Passage, together They move from life into life. With my hand in Theirs, I call upon Them to share Their presence with me and pass dark power into this [tool] that it may be sanctified to serve me in my dark journeys.

6. See the Dark Energy shoot up from the ground, into the left palm, pass through the left arm, across the shoulders into the right arm, up the right arm into the right hand, and into the tool.

7. Set energized tool on pentacle; kneel with both palms on the ground:

   As what is sent returns, so I return to You the Power graciously sent to me. My [tool] is sanctified through Power and Grace, through flesh and blood, and made ready for my use. *So Mote It Be!*

8. Stand; remove tool from pentacle, keeping it on the Altar.

9. Snuff the votive:

   The path is closed; darkness returns to the Shadow Realm.

Proceed to Esbat Conclusion or Cakes & Wine
of the Circle Casting

CONSECRATION OF A STATUE*

*#1 or #2 of "Suggested Times"

Have: Altar arranged as for a Full Moon Esbat; statue to be consecrated, 1 herb from the Goddess, God, or Dual Deity listing, 1 herb each from the matching Elementals, a muslin or cotton pouch with draw string or string to tie, a small amount of butter, soft white cheese, 1 cup of milk, 1 cup of spring water, black cloth to cover statue, offering dish, flowers, food item, white candle, incense [frankincense].

1. Select one herb from each of the following categories, according to the statue image:

   The Goddess: marjoram, moonwort, elder flower. *Her Earth:* cypress, honeysuckle, jasmine. *Her Air:* anise seed, comfrey, elder wood, eyebright, hazel, lavender, mugwort. *Her Fire:* angelica, celandine, coriander, heliotrope, hyssop, nettle, primrose, rowan. *Her Water:* chamomile, camphor, catnip, geranium, hawthorn, hyacinth, ivy, rose, willow.

   The God: woodruff, yarrow, bergamot. *His Earth:* cedar, fern, High John the Conqueror, horehound, pine. *His Air:* acacia, benzoin, mistletoe, nutmeg, thyme, wormwood. *His Fire:* alder, basil, betony, cinnamon, clove, holly, oak, peppercorn, thistle. *His Water:* ash, burdock, hops, orris root, yarrow.

   Both [Dual Deity]: mullein, dianthus, heather. *Their Earth:* cinquefoil, mandrake, patchouli, sage, slippery elm. *Their Air:* eucalyptus, lemon verbena, mugwort, peppermint, sandalwood, spearmint. *Their Fire:* bay, juniper, marigold, rosemary, rue, saffron, St. Johnswort, vervain. *Their Water:* apple, elecampane, heather, meadowsweet, poppy, star anise, shamrock.

2. Place the cauldron on pentacle; hold each herb over the cauldron before dropping in:

   I call upon thee [herb] to lend unto me thy power for the consecration and enlivening of this image of [deity name].

3. Stir all with athame:

   Through the power of the Goddess and the God are these herbs blessed to enliven this image of [deity name].

4. Place the herbs in a small pouch [unbleached muslin or natural cotton]. If it has drawstrings, wrap the ends around the stuffed bag, otherwise fold the pouch shut. Set the cauldron aside. Pass the herbal pouch through each symbol of the Elementals:

   By Earth you have form [sprinkle with salt],
   By Air you have breath [pass through incense smoke],
   By Fire you have energy [pass through candle flame],
   By Water you have the fluids of life [sprinkle with water].

5. Place the pouch on the pentacle. With athame in *power hand*, raise open arms overhead to gather in energy:

> I call upon the Power of the Lady and the Lord to bless and empower these herbs with their divine essence.

6. Bring both hands together to hold the knife then touch the tip to the pouch, seeing energy flow through the blade into the pouch, then set down the athame.

7. Place both hands with palms down above the pouch:

> By Spirit are you charged and enlivened.

8. The image is now given *spiritual birth* through the materials of the *Sacred Cow*, as found in India to this day, and in Hathor, the most ancient goddess of Egypt, portrayed in some statues as the Sacred Cow with the solar disk resting between her horns:

> With the essences of the Sacred Cow, who gives of herself in many ways for the lives of others, is this image now blessed.

9. Rub the statue all over with soft butter:

> With butter are you anointed.

10. Rub it all over with a soft cheese like a brie or cottage cheese, or use a plain yogurt or sour cream:

> With cheese are you fed.

11. Wash the statue with about half of the cup of milk:

> With milk are you given the substance of life.

12. Rinse the statue off with spring water or running water:

> With water are you cleansed and purified.

13. Dry the statue and anoint it with consecration oil.

> In the names of the Goddess and the God, I consecrate this statue. Let this image of [Name] draw [His/Her] divine power into my home and into my Craft. Let this image remind me that [Name] is always close to me, as I am always close to [Name].

14. Pick up the herb bundle and tuck it securely inside the statue, closing off the bottom of the statue with a piece of felt cut to fit and glued along the edges if needed. Usually the curves of the figure are sufficient to hold the pouch in place.

147

15. Set the image on the pentacle and cover it completely with a black cloth. With athame [for images of the God and Dual Deity] or with wand [for images of the Goddess], call the Divine into the statue. Hold the athame or wand upright, with arms raised and open before the covered statue:

> I call upon thee Elemental Earth, Elemental Air, Elemental Fire, and Elemental Water to bring thy energy and thy power that this image of [Deity Name] be made ready for enlivening.

16. Bring hands together to hold the tool and slowly point it towards the statue:

> Come Great Lady [or Great Lord, or Great Lady and Great Lord] and inhabit this image I have prepared for You. Let Your presence in my life and in my home be a comfort and joy to me.

17. Touch the statue with the tip of the tool and feel the power of the Divine entering into the image. Leave the statue on the pentacle for grounding and set the tool back on the altar.

18. Carefully unveil the statue and set aside the cloth. Verbally welcome the deity by name and place an offering before it such as a cornbread muffin, fruit, or flowers, or use a dish with food and a small cup with the rest of the milk or some other beverage.

19. Light an incense such as frankincense on the right side of the statue and a white candle on the left side.

> Welcome to my home and my heart, Great Lady/Lord [Name]. I am blessed by thy presence, and my blessings I give unto Thee. Let the light of Thy love be with me always.

20. After an hour, put the statue in the intended place [Altar, Shrine, etc.]. Offerings, incense and candles will change in accordance with the need, the season, the Sabbat, and so forth because the statue is now a focal point for the practice. Talk to and meditate on the image, for this ancient practice strengthens the connection to the Divine.

    Note: For statues that have no hollow space for an herb bundle, touch the herb pouch to the statue. Lightly anoint the image with a consecration oil, then set the statue on the pentacle and cover it with a black cloth with the herb bundle under the cloth as well, either under the statue, or behind it or somehow draped against it. Follow the rest of the procedure as above, keeping the herb bundle close to the statue, perhaps in a small covered jar behind the image.

Proceed to Esbat Conclusion or Cakes & Wine of the Circle Casting

CRYSTAL CLEANSING & PROGRAMMING*

*#1 or #2 of "Suggested Times"

Cleansing

Have: container to set the crystal inside, blessed water, sea salt.

1. Rinse out container with blessed water.

2. Wash container in cool, running water. Dry and set on top of a wooden pentacle.

3. Pour in sea salt to coat the bottom of the container.

4. Place the crystal on top of the salt [so it doesn't touch metal].

5. Add more salt over the crystal until it is buried [gives it a chance to clear and rest].

6. Crystal stays covered for two to seven days [use numerological significance as desired— *see Lists of Correspondences*].

7. Rinse crystal in cool running water.

8. May proceed to programming of the crystal.

Programming

1. Bathe to purify yourself: with tub water enhanced with herbs and sea salt, by swimming in the ocean; or with a sponge bath with water mixed with sea salt.

2. Hold crystal at third eye psychic point.

3. Envision the crystal as cleared.

4. Envision own white aura expand outward as a cascading waterfall from the center of the body to transform any darkness into light.

5. Use this cascading white light to cleanse the crystal.

6. Project an image that relates to what the crystal is meant to help with, while thinking of the words that match the image.

7. Once programmed, the crystal only needs a reminder of the image to help in that task.

Disposal of Used Salt

1. Sea salt from container may have residue of chaotic energies, and can be tossed out away from the dwelling.

2. Sea salt may be recycled by pouring from one container to another outdoors where the wind can pass through it and dissipate/carry away any chaotic energies.

3. Store the recycled salt in a dark container with a tight lid.

Proceed to Esbat Conclusion or Cakes & Wine of the Circle Casting

CRYSTAL CONSECRATION & DEDICATION*

*#1 of "Suggested Times"

Have: White candles for light power and Full Moon consecration; black or purple candles for dark power and Dark Moon consecration—use light scented incense for Full Moon, or more pungent scented for Dark Moon; use a white or purple candle for the working [center] votive for Full or Dark Moon

Consecration of a Crystal:

1. Set the crystal on the pentacle.

2. Hold up athame in right hand, while touching the crystal with left:

   I call upon the power of the Elementals and the Divine to this place which is not a place, in this time which is not a time, as I stand between the worlds at the temple of my circle to empower this crystal of Earth and Light [or Earth and Darkness].

3. Take hand off the crystal and use both hands to hold the athame upright.

4. Feel the power of the Lady and the Lord course into the blade of the athame, then lower the knife to touch the crystal with the tip of the blade.

5. Visualize the energy running through the knife and into the crystal:

   By the Divine Power of the Universe, is this crystal now focused as one of [state the focus: i.e.; cleansing].

6. Set athame on the altar and pick up the crystal, holding it to the third eye.

7. Concentrate on the purpose for which this crystal is dedicated and feel that energy enter into the crystal, uniting with the matrix of the crystal so that the stone now recognizes the personal energy it will work with:

   With me and through me do you work to [state focus: i.e.; cleanse], for we are connected one to the other through the Elementals, that we are kith and kin. *So Mote It Be!*

8. Pass the crystal through the symbols of the Elementals:

   In the names of the Lady and Lord, I consecrate this crystal to be used in my practice of the Craft for [state the focus]. I charge that this be so, and empower this crystal through Elemental Earth and Elemental Water [sprinkle with salted water]; through Elemental Fire and Elemental Air [pass through the can-

150

dle flame and incense smoke]. **By the power of the Elementals is this crystal focused to aid me in my work.** *So Mote It Be!*

9. Set the crystal back on the pentacle and hold hands palms down over it:

> **Great Lady and Great Lord, together in the [light or darkness] of this Moon, You dwell within all. You are the beginnings, fullness, and endings that lead into the cycle anew. You are the Energy of Life, Love Manifested and the Promise Fulfilled. Imbue this crystal with Your power and love to aid me in my Craft.**

10. Hold the crystal above the votive candle:

> **Let this small light represent the power of the Moon and the Sun, illuminating and energizing this crystal to focus on** [state the focus, i.e.; cleansing] **for my use in my Craft.**

Insert Light or Dark Power Crystal Dedication

11. Set the crystal on pentacle and kneel so that both palms rest on the ground:

> **As what is sent returns, so I return to my Lady and my Lord the power so graciously sent to me. My crystal is sanctified through thy power and grace, attuned to me by passage through my flesh and my blood, and is ready for my use.** *So Mote It Be!*

12. Stand and remove crystal from pentacle, but keep it on the altar; snuff the votive candle:

> **The energies borrowed are returned, yet remain as part of the continuing cycle of life essence. The path between the worlds is closed, yet remains open to my heart and to my Craft as I have need.**

Proceed to Esbat Conclusion and Cakes & Wine of the Circle Casting

LIGHT POWER CRYSTAL DEDICATION

1. Hold up the crystal in right hand and place left hand so palm rests against the heart:

   Let me always remember the Rules of Conduct that I harm none in the practice of my Craft, for *what is sent comes back*. I work with the powers of the Goddess and the God with perfect love and perfect trust. By Your power is this crystal charged, imbued, and dedicated to my Craft.

2. Envision the light energy coming from the heart, passing into the left palm, traveling through the left arm, across the shoulders, into the right arm, up the right arm, into the right hand, and filling the upraised crystal.

Return to Consecration of a Crystal

DARK POWER CRYSTAL DEDICATION

1. Hold up the crystal in right hand, and place left hand so palm is down, parallel to the ground:

   Lord of Shadows hidden within the Lady of Darkness, together They hold the darkness in Balance. He is the passing, She is the passage, together They move from life into life. With my hand in Theirs, I call upon Them to share Their presence with me and pass dark power into this crystal that it may be charged, imbued, and dedicated to my Craft.

2. Envision the dark energy shooting up from the ground, into the palm of the left hand, traveling through the left arm, across the shoulders into the right arm, up the right arm into the right hand, and into the tool.

Return to Consecration of a Crystal

CRYSTAL REDEDICATION*

*#1 of "Suggested Times"

Have: White candles for Full Moon; black or purple candles for Dark Moon; a cleansing incense such as frankincense or lavender; a white [Full Moon] or purple [Dark Moon] candle for the working [center] votive; white, black, or purple cloth to wrap the crystal in; cauldron for the libations into which the crystal will be placed; begin ritual with crystal sitting on pentacle.

Note: If changing focus of crystal from Light to Dark, or from Dark to Light, use the Moon that matches the current alignment of the stone to cleanse it; then realign with desired Moon phase in a second ritual.

1. Pick up crystal and hold up in both hands over Altar:

   Behold this, the crystal I dedicated to [previous focus], but now I have another need. Harken unto the voice of your child, and see into my need. Like the seed that becomes new life in the womb of the Mother is this crystal placed into the cauldron of the Goddess. Let this crystal travel through the waters of life and into rebirth to be cleansed of my former need and to be brought forth to work with me in my Craft to a new focus.

2. Put crystal inside libation cauldron [it will get wet from the libation inside], and set the cauldron on top of pentacle.

3. Pour some *blessed water* over the crystal:

   You are cleansed and purified in the cauldron of rebirth.

4. Remove crystal from cauldron and return cauldron to former place on Altar.

5. Pass crystal through incense smoke:

   By fire and air are you brought into new life.

6. See the crystal as newly formed by geological fusion, birthed from the depths of the rocky earth, and pushed out of the ground through upheaval into the light.

7. Wrap crystal in the cloth as if a comforting swaddling, drying it off.

8. Unwrap crystal and see it as a shining new being; set aside the cloth and place crystal on the pentacle.

9. Hold athame upright in right hand, while touching crystal with left hand:

   I call upon the power of the Elementals and the Divine to this place which is not a place, in this time which is not a time, as I stand between the worlds at the temple of my Circle to empower this crystal of Earth and Light [or Earth and Darkness].

10. Remove hand from crystal; hold athame with both hands and feel the power of the Lady and the Lord course into the blade of the athame.

11. Touch crystal with tip of energized athame, seeing energy course into crystal:

    By the Divine Power of the Universe, is this crystal now focused as one of [state the new focus, i.e.; *meditation*].

12. Put athame on Altar, then pick up crystal and hold against third eye while concentrating on the new purpose.

13. Feel that energy enter the crystal and unite with the matrix so it recognizes the personal energy it will work with:

> With me and through me do you work to [state focus, i.e.; *aid meditation*], for we are connected one to the other through the Elementals, that we are kith and kin. *So Mote It Be!*

14. Now pass the crystal through the symbols of the Elementals:

> In the names of the Lady and Lord, I consecrate this crystal to be used in my practice of the Craft for [state the focus]. I charge that this be so, and empower this crystal through Elemental Earth and Elemental Water [sprinkle with salted water]; through Elemental Fire and Elemental Air [pass through the candle flame and incense smoke]. By the power of the Elementals is this crystal focused to aid me in my work. *So Mote It Be!*

15. Set the crystal back on the pentacle and place hands palms down over it:

> Great Lady and Great Lord, together in the *[light or darkness]* of this Moon, You dwell within all. You are beginnings, fullness, and endings that lead into the cycle anew. You are the Energy of Life, Love Manifested and the Promise Fulfilled. Imbue this crystal with Your power and love to aid me in my Craft.

16. Hold the crystal above the votive candle:

> Let this small light represent the power of the Moon and the Sun, illuminating and energizing this crystal to focus on [state the focus, i.e.; *cleansing*] for my use in my Craft.

**Proceed to Light or Dark Power Crystal Dedication,
then Consecration of a Crystal Conclusion**

HANDFASTING RITUAL

Long Version*
*#1 or #2 of "Suggested Times"

Have: decorated besom leaning against Altar; floral wreath for head of bride; greenery wreath for head of groom; candles of chosen color theme or of white; wand decorated with colorful or white ribbons; one white pillar candle decorated for wedding; white satin cord on Altar; athame [or sword if desired]. State legal names at [N] or [N and N] for a legal ritual performed by a Priest or Priestess who is an ordained minister. Be certain to look at the state-required marriage license, and sign with own legal name, with witnesses signing with their legal names. Without these requirements, the Handfasting is not legally binding nor recognized by the state or nation in which it is performed, which may be acceptable or desired by some parties.

1. Clap hands or ring the bell three times:

   Today we stand upon this holy Earth and in this sacred space to witness the rite of matrimony between [N and N]. Just as we come together as family and friends, so we ask the Lady and the Lord of the Wild Wood to be present here within our Circle. May the sacred union of this Handfasting Ceremony be filled with their Holy Presence. In the name of the God is Love declared, and in the name of the Goddess is Peace declared. In the name of the Ancestors whose traditions we honor and in the name of those who gave us life, we are united here in Love. Let the Bride and Groom approach.

2. Groom's attendants enter, followed by groom [and parent]; turn and face the aisle, then the bride's attendants enter, followed last by the bride [and parent] and stand in front of the Altar and officiator.

3. Officiator to guests:

   Standing before us are N and N whom we bid hail and welcome.

   [To bride] Are you N?

   [Bride answers] Yes [or I am].

   [Officiator] What is your desire?

   [Bride] To be joined with N in the presence of the Lady and the Lord and our friends.

   [Officiator] I welcome you with joy.

   [Officiator, to groom] Are you N?

[Groom] **Yes** [or I am].

[Officiator] **What is your desire?**

[Groom] **To be joined with N in the presence of the Lady and the Lord and our friends.**

[Officiator] **I welcome you with joy.**

[Officiator, to the parents] **Let the parents of N and N enter here.**

[Officiator hands athame (or sword) to bride's father or mother] **Take this symbol of your protection and care through the years of this life so you may release this responsibility to the one she has chosen.**

[Parent] **I bring you N, my child and my treasure. Take this blade and mind that always must you be ready in service to protect your bride.**

[Officiator, to groom] **Take the blade and make your vow.**

[Groom] **I do vow this before the Goddess and the God** [parent places bride's hand in that of groom, kisses her, and steps back from the wedding party; Officiator takes athame from groom and places it back on the Altar].

[Groom, facing Altar] **Before the Lady and the Lord of Wild Wood do I pledge to love and honor this woman, that we be in the image of the Divine, two who are one.**

[Bride, facing Altar] **Before the Lady and the Lord of the Wild Wood do I pledge to love and honor this man, that we be in the image of the Divine, two who are one.**

[Officiator, to guests] **Does anyone here know of any just reason why these two should not be wed?** [Pause; deal with any objection as required]. **Then nothing may stand in their way.**

4. Officiator holds up two wreaths, one before each partner:

   The flowers of the field in the Circle of Life give testament to the joy of love and unity.

5. Officiator places floral wreath on bride's head and greenery wreath on groom's head.

   [Officiator, to bride] **Holding the hand of your love, say after me:** [pause after each phrase for bride to repeat] **by seed and root, by bud and stem, by leaf and flower and fruit; By life and by love, in the Name of the God, I take thee to my** hand, my heart, and my spirit; Through the rising and setting of the Sun, through the phases of the Moon, and through the cycles of the Stars, shall we be One, as long as love shall last.

[Officiator, to groom] Holding the hand of your love, say after me [pause after each phrase for groom to repeat]: By seed and root, by bud and stem, by leaf and flower and fruit; By life and by love, in the Name of the Goddess, I take thee to my hand, my heart, and my spirit; Through the rising and setting of the Sun, through the phases of the Moon, and through the cycles of the Stars, shall we be One, as long as love shall last.

6. Officiator places ribboned wand in joined hands of bride and groom, then wraps their hands loosely with the cord:

With the wand of life in your hands, do you both pledge yourselves one unto the other in the bonds of matrimony?

[Bride and groom] We do.

[Officiator, to bride and groom] And do you vow to bring the light of love and joy to the union, and maintain these vows in freedom for as long as love shall last?

[Bride and groom] We do.

[Officiator, to both] Then let there always be joy between you as you live together in Perfect Love and Perfect Trust.

7. Officiator unbinds the cord and places wand and cord back on the Altar:

In Nature all things are circular. Night becomes day, day becomes night, night becomes day again. The Moon waxes and wanes, and waxes again. There is Spring, Summer, Autumn, Winter, and then the Spring returns. These things are part of the Great Mysteries. Did you bring your symbols of these mysteries of life?

8. Rings are brought forward by Ringbearer or Best Man and Maid of Honor.

9. Officiator to bride:

Place the ring on the finger of your chosen, and pledge your troth.

10. Bride and Groom may make their own oaths or use the following ones:

[Bride] I give you this ring as a symbol of my love for you. Let it remind you always, as it circles your finger, of my eternal love, surrounding you and enfolding you day and night. You are my beloved bridegroom, and I marry you today with this ring as I give you my heart, my body, and my devotion through the years of my life, so long as love remains between us.

[Officiator, to groom] Place the ring on the finger of your chosen, and pledge your troth.

[Groom] I give you this ring as a symbol of my love for you. Let it remind you always, as it circles your finger, of my eternal love, surrounding you and enfolding you day and night. You are my beloved bride, and I marry you today with this ring as I give you my heart, my body, and my devotion through the years of my life, so long as love remains between us.

[Officiator, to couple] With these symbols of love and honor, you are bound to one another and may now seal your promise with a kiss.

11. Couple kiss.
12. Officiator to assemblage:

Let those assembled here bear witness that N and N are joined in love. May their love partake of the beauty, majesty, and power of the Sacred Land, and may they grow together in wisdom, joy, and harmony. My own blessings and the blessings of all those assembled be with you. [Pause, then state firmly] In the presence of the Goddess and the God, the Elementals, your families, and your friends, by the power and authority vested in me, I pronounce you husband and wife.

13. Officiator raises hand in blessing or may sprinkle the couple with blessed water using a heather twig or other flowered stem:

The blessings of the Divine and of the Ancestors be with you and with all that grows from your union. *So Mote It Be!*

14. Officiator leads couple to the Altar where they light the Handfasting Candle from the center Altar candle:

Before the Lady and the Lord; before the Elementals; before your friends and family are you now wed. Two are made one.

15. Officiator hands decorated besom to Best Man and Maid of Honor to hold low before the Altar, then to bride and groom:

Now pace you both the Circle, presenting yourselves to the Elementals and the Divine as husband and wife, as two who are one, and when you return to the fore, here will you both jump the broomstick and begin your new life with a clean sweep.

16. Bride and groom circle area and jump the broom. Officiator turns them to face the gathering:

> I present Mr. and Mrs. N and N.

17. Officiator with open arms raised:

> **The rite is ended. Depart in peace Elemental Kin, Lady and Lord, our blessings take with thee, and thine upon us. With blessings given and blessings received, the Circle is cleared.** *So Mote It Be!*

18. Officiator opens the Circle with wand from where he or she stands before the Altar.

19. Bride and groom depart down the aisle, followed by attendants paired together; Officiator may ring a bell; best man and maid of honor return to Altar to sign marriage license as witnesses, Officiator signs marriage license as authorized; Maypole dancing could be part of the festivities as desired by the couple.

The Handfasting Ritual may stand alone followed by the Reception or the Ritual may proceed to the Esbat Conclusion, or Cakes & Wine of the Circle Casting if using these other Rituals

HANDFASTING RITUAL*

Short Version*
*#1 or #2 of "Suggested Times"

Have: decorated besom leaning against the Altar; on the Altar have two wreaths of flowers or one of flowers and one of greenery for the bride and groom; a wand decorated with colorful ribbons or white ribbons; a white pillar-style candle that may be decorated for the wedding; a cauldron that can hold the pillar candle after it is lit; and a white satin cord

1. Officiator claps or rings bell three times:

   Today we are gathered for a Handfasting Ceremony between [N and N] before the Lady and the Lord of the Wild Wood.

   [Groom] **Before the Lady and the Lord of the Wild Wood do I pledge to love and honor this woman, that we be in the image of the Divine, two who are one.**

   [Bride] **Before the Lady and the Lord of the Wild Wood do I pledge to love and honor this man, that we be in the image of the Divine, two who are one.**

2. Officiator holds up high the flower wreaths, one before each partner:

   The flowers of the field in the Circle of Life give testament to the joy of love and unity.

3. Officiator places the wreaths on the heads of the partners.

4. Officiator hands the decorated wand to the partners to hold together between them, then wraps the cord around their hands.

5. Officiator to couple:

   [To Groom] **Give now your vow to your beloved** [pause between phrases for Groom to repeat]. **With this Wand of Life do I pledge myself unto you in the bonds of matrimony. Let there always be joy between us as we live together in perfect love and perfect trust.**

   [To Bride] **Give now your vow to your beloved** [pause between phrases for Bride to repeat]. **With this Wand of Life do I pledge myself unto you in the bonds of matrimony. Let there always be joy between us as we live together in perfect love and perfect trust.**

6. Officiator removes the cord and places the wand on the Altar.

   Do you have a token of your fidelity to one another?

7. Ringbearer or best man and maid of honor give rings to Groom and Bride.

8. Groom places ring on bride's finger:

> This ring is the symbol of the love and the honor I give unto you. With this Circle do I bind myself to the one I love.

9. Bride places ring on groom's finger:

> This ring is the symbol of the love and the honor I give unto you. With this Circle do I bind myself to the one I love.

10. Officiator directs the couple to the Altar where they light the candle from the center candle of the Altar and set it in the cauldron. Then Officiator, to couple and gathering:

> Before the Lady and the Lord; before the Elementals; before this assemblage of friends and family; with the power and authority vested in me, I pronounce you husband and wife. Now you are wed; two are made one. Jump the broomstick that you may start your new life with a clean sweep.

11. The bride and the groom now jump the broomstick as the besom is held on either side by the best man and maid of honor.

12. Officiator raises hand in blessing [or may sprinkle the couple with blessed water using a heather twig or other flowered stem]:

> May the Lady and the Lord bless you and keep you both in Their love. May They shower you with Their bounty and may you bring forth the fruit allotted you from the Cauldron of Life. *So Mote It Be!*

13. Officiator claps or rings bell three times:

> I present Mr. and Mrs. N and N.

14. Officiator with open arms raised:

> The rite is ended. Depart in peace Elemental Kin, Lady and Lord, our blessings take with thee, and thine upon us. With blessings given and blessings received, the Circle is cleared. *So Mote It Be!*

15. Officiator opens the Circle with wand from where he or she stands before the Altar.

16. Bride and groom depart down the aisle, followed by attendants paired together; Officiator may ring a bell; best man and maid of honor return to Altar to sign marriage license as witnesses, Officiator signs marriage license as authorized; Maypole dancing could be part of the festivities as desired by the couple.

The Handfasting Ritual may stand alone followed by the Reception or the Ritual may proceed to the Esbat conclusion, or Cakes & Wine of the Circle Casting, if using these other Rituals

HANDPARTING*

*#1 or #2 of "Suggested Times"

Have: white silk cord.

1. Officiator rings bell three times:

   Today we are gathered to witness the parting of hands and shedding of the bonds of matrimony between N and N.

2. Officiator motions the couple forward and wraps their joined hands in the silk cord:

   Do you seek the parting of your hands that you may both live apart and yet remain as friends?

3. Officiator states by phrase and the couple repeat in unison:

   We seek to part our hands and live our separate lives by the love and the grace of the Lady and the Lord.

4. Officiator unwraps the cord and pulls the hands apart:

   As the Lord and the Lady separate and yet remain joined, even so are you both still joined in Their love and companionship. Let there be peace between you as you go your separate ways.

5. Officiator states the phrase and the couple repeat in unison:

   With love and honor did we meet, with respect do we part, for we are one with the Lady and the Lord. *So Mote It Be.*

6. Officiator raises open arms before couple:

   This union is ended, but like all things, one ending is a new beginning. The Wheel turns on and we turn with it. I call upon the Lady and the Lord to keep you both always in Their love. *So Mote It Be!*

7. Officiator claps or rings bell nine times.

**Proceed to Esbat Conclusion or Cakes & Wine
of the Circle Casting**

THE NAMING CEREMONY
OF TWELFTH NIGHT*

*#1 or #2 of "Suggested Times," but preferably on January 6; child may be
twelve to thirteen years old, or have received the first menses.

Have: 1 adult male and 1 adult female; blindfold for child; gifts for the child hidden under
the Altar; fresh bread; cooked meat; a feather fan; 1 white candle and matches; if in a
house with appropriate yard and surroundings, part of the rite may be conducted outside; if an indoor ceremony, the child could be led around the house, being brushed with
a leafy tree branch, fanned, warmed by a candle, and taken to a sink or tub of running
water.

Note: Naming Ceremony is usually a family ritual, and the officiators are the parents, but
if doing a public rite, at least one parent stands with the child outside the Circle during
casting. Ceremony may be followed with the Child guided through or performing the
Initiation Ritual if desired.

1. Child stands outside of Circle during casting, with one parent acting as an Officiator,
   and is then brought in at the point where the doorway may be cut:

   **This is my child, [N], who is moving into adulthood and seeks entrance into
   the Circle to stand before the Lady and the Lord.**

2. Officiator within the Circle:

   Do you come of your own free will to the Circle?

3. Child answers in the affirmative:

   I do.

4. Officiator inside the Circle:

   Are you willing to follow the Path of Initiation?

5. Child answers in the affirmative:

   I do.

6. Officiator inside Circle:

   Let this child enter before the Lady and the Lord.

7. Child is brought through the doorway into the Circle and the doorway is closed.

8. Child is anointed with oil in the Lunar Spiral/Solar Cross sigil:

I consecrate you in the names of the Goddess and the God. With Perfect Love and Perfect Trust, you are welcomed. Merry Meet.

9. Circle Casting [and Esbat Ritual, if using] continues to the point in the Circle Casting stating: "Perform Ritual/Craft Work," or to the point of Esbat Ritual stating: "Conduct any . . . "

Naming Ceremony Begins

1. A man and woman [may be the parents] review life cycle of the Lord and Lady:

   [Woman] The Lord is born at Yuletide with the returning of the Sun. The Lady and all the Earth rejoices at His return.

   [Man] The Lady rests at Imbolc and prepares for the coming of the Spring. Her son grows strong and plays the games of childhood.

   [Woman] Together They walk the fields and woods at Ostara, and all Nature awakens as They pass.

   [Man] With Beltane They sport and play, and all the land and creatures of Nature rejoice with the life and vigor of fertility.

   [Woman] At Litha They wed and are One and the promise of the harvests gives hope of sustenance to Their children of the Earth.

   [Man] The Lord enriches the grain and gives His life for the creatures of the Earth at Lughnassadh, yet the Promise of Rebirth already lies within the Lady.

   [Woman] With Mabon, the Lord and Lady give us of Their bounty and the spirit of the Lord fills the fruit of the vine and the barleycorn. The Lord moves into His Dark Realm where He offers peace and rest to those whose life's cycle is ended.

   [Man] In Samhain the veil between the worlds is thinnest, and the Lady stands by the Lord in the Land of Shadows. Through His passage does He change the Tomb of the Crone to the Womb of the Mother, making Hallows all the worlds and realms at the moment of transformation. The Lady holds the Promise within Her and we bide the turning of the Wheel with Her.

   [Woman] At Yule the cycle is renewed and the Lord returns with the Sun. The Wheel of the Seasons is the Wheel of Life, and as the one turns, so turns the other. You are in the Turning of the Wheel.

2. Both parents/adults [one recites, the other anoints with the Solar Cross $\oplus$ or the Pentagram $\star$ sigil at each place]:

Blessed Be thy feet, that take you on your path.
Blessed Be thy knees, that support you before the Divine.
Blessed Be thy abdomen, that gives you inner strength.
Blessed Be thy breast, that holds your heart true to the Lady and the Lord.
Blessed Be thy lips, that speak the Sacred Names.

[*Note:* not "Secret Names," as this is bestowed by the Lady and the Lord at the Dedication, after which, the Blessing changes.]

Blessed Be thy eyes, that see the beauty of Their love.
Blessed Be thy mind, that seeks Their knowledge and
Their wisdom [Anoint at Third Eye.].

[Officiator, to child] Are you willing to continue with the Ceremony in Perfect Love and Perfect Trust?

[Child] I am.

[Officiator, to parent] Then blindfold your child that [he or she] may see anew.

3. Child is blindfolded and a doorway is cut in the Circle for all to exit, then the door is closed and sealed with a Pentagram ☆.

4. Child is led through surroundings that demonstrate the four Elementals, the Goddess, and the God, with one person leading while another recites, then swapping roles as required.

[Woman (Earth)] I am the Earth Mother from whose body you were formed. Know me in the feel of the ground beneath your feet, in the touch of the trees against your hand [guide the child's hand to touch a tree, or brush with leafy twig].

[Man (Earth)] I am the Lord of the Wildwood and the Grain whose life fills the wilderness and also gives you bread. Know me in the animals I protect and in the grain you eat, for all life consumes life, but with respect to the spirit [give the child a taste of bread and bite of cooked meat, or bread and an animal to pet].

[Man (Air)] I am the God of the Sky whose breath gives you life. Know me when you inhale my essence [fan the child's face].

[Man (Fire)] I am the Lord of the Dance, know me in the fire of the Sun and in the energy that moves you through your life [hold a candle flame close to the child, or take by both hands in a merry, energetic circular romp, or move the child into direct sunlight].

[Woman (Water)] I am the Goddess whose water of life flows through your body. Listen to my voice in the moving currents [move child to where there is water to hear: garden hose, sprinkler, natural water, etc.].

[Woman (Spirit)] I am the Goddess who is from the beginning of time and will be to the end of time. My power and my love brings forth the fruitfulness of the Earth and all that are born thereof [blow gently on the child's face].

[Man asks child] What name have you chosen for the Circle?

5. Child states chosen Craft Name; blindfold is removed; all return to Circle, opening, closing, and sealing the doorway.

6. Officiator in Circle:

   We are blessed by the Goddess and the God, known to us as [N and N], by Their attendance at this Naming Ceremony. Know, Lady and Lord, that [Given Name] is your child [Craft Name], and receive [him or her] into Your guidance!

7. Child is kissed/embraced by all in the Circle, given gifts of tools [athame, wand, etc.] and/or tokens of the Craft [shell, antlers, statues, etc.].

8. Child may now take part in the ritual readings, or be guided in or perform the Initiation Ritual before proceeding to the Esbat conclusion or Cakes & Wine of the Circle Casting.

Proceed to Esbat Conclusion or Cakes & Wine of the Circle Casting

PASSING OVER*

*#1 or #2 of "Suggested Times."

Have: rue [or rosemary] herb; white votive candle in container; food and beverage for a farewell feast; things of the deceased for remembrance [a photo, perhaps set on a favorite chair, favorite or significant possessions, etc.].

1. Clap or ring the bell 3 times:

   Today we bid farewell to [Name of deceased]. We remember the good times and the less happy times, for all life has both pleasant and unpleasant experiences. We release the negative and hold onto the positive.

2. Light the white candle:

   Like the flame of this candle will the memory of [N] light up our hearts and our minds.

3. Take a bit of the rue or rosemary and drop slowly into the candle flame:

   As the rue [or rosemary] burns, it takes away the power of any negative memories about [N], that we will treasure the good and put aside the ill.

4. Raise open arms:

   Great Lady and Great Lord, give rest and refreshment to [N] that [he or she] may be brought into your love and journey again through the Cauldron of Life. Death is a transition, moving from Underworld for repose into Summerland for refreshment until the next incarnation. This time is not sad, for the spirit is renewed and communicates with those who have gone before and those who remain in the physical realms of Middleworld. We remember our loved ones, but they remember us as well, visiting when needed or called upon, aiding us in this life and standing by us in our transition to the next. *So Mote It Be!*

5. Lower arms; and slowly ring the bell nine times:

   Farewell, dear [N] as you take your journey of passing. Our love and blessings take with you to your rest. May you soon rejoin the Dance of Life.

6. Sharing of memories among those present commences, followed by a feast of remembrance; traditional foods include pomegranates, apples, raisin bread, pork dishes, acorn squash, and dark wine or other dark beverage.

**Proceed to Esbat Conclusion or Cakes & Wine
of the Circle Casting**

WICCANING*

Have: anointing oil, small basin of blessed water; incense and burner; Altar candles; decorated pillar candle to be the Wiccaning candle; clean, soft towel; Altar decorations may include flowers such as Baby's Breath and yellow baby roses; food may include white cake; may have presents for the child that reflect the Craft, such as a quilt in a design of forest animals, a stuffed animal toy, etc.

Note: baby may be held by Goddess and God Parents [or Fairy Godmother and Fairy Godfather] outside the Circle until called inside

1. Both parents light the Wiccaning Candle and Officiator or parents call for the baby:

   The Light of our Love is kindled; bring the fruit of love into the Circle.

2. Parents take the baby and hold the infant up before Altar; Officiator or parent says:

   **Loving Lady and Gracious Lord, behold the harvest of [our] love, named, [N].
   Watch over and bless this child, bringing love and joy to all of [his or her] days.**

3. Officiator or one parent anoints the baby's brow with oil in the Solar Cross ⊕ sigil:

   May the Lady and the Lord guide you and teach you.

4. One parent holds the baby over the basin and Officiator or the other parent cups some of the blessed water in one hand and gently pours it over the top of the baby's head, then wipes the runoff with the towel:

   May the Elementals Earth and Water guard and protect you; cherish and comfort you.

5. Parent holding the baby passes the baby over the incense burner through smoke, or Officiator passes the smoke around the baby being held:

   May the Elementals Air and Fire enhance your life, that you grow in wisdom and stamina, in harmony with the Earth, the Moon, the Sun, the Stars, and the Unity of the Divine.

6. Everyone in the Circle passes by the child and offers their individual blessing:

   May the love of the Goddess and the God be with you always.

7. Presents may be offered to the baby now or at the Simple Feast.

**Proceed to Esbat Conclusion or Cakes & Wine
of the Circle Casting**

COMPANION QUEST*

*#1 of "Suggested Times," as part of Sidhe Moon Esbat.

Have: black mirror to set in front of it; the gray candle of the Sidhe Moon Esbat; 2 chairs at the table, East side facing West for Practitioner, West side facing East for the Otherworld Companion being sought. Begin ritual at portion of Sidhe Moon Esbat stating: Perform Otherworld Meditation, Companion Quest, Other Ritual or Craft Work.

1. Go to West side of table and pull chair aside to offer a seat, then return to East side.

2. Sit and look into black mirror beyond candle flame:

   Here lies the doorway into Otherworld; I welcome my guest through this portal.

3. Gaze into mirror; envision misty, fog-shrouded Otherworld forest; feel the cool, refreshing air; smell the damp leaves on the forest floor, the moss on the ancient large trees; hear the sound of water gurgling along a narrow brook; hear the soft, delicate, hesitant footfalls of a browsing deer; and listen for the quiet steps of an Other approaching through the dark forest, coming toward you. The forest will remain in view behind the Guest so that the table will appear to be partly in woodland; the sounds of forest animals and the brook will continue in the background during the ritual.

4. When the Other is gazing back, lift bowls of flowers and milk in each hand:

   Hail to thee and blessed be thy feet that brought you on this path; blessed be thy heart that beats steadfast; blessed be thy eyes that see between the worlds; blessed be thy hands offered in friendship and clasped in mine.

5. Set bowls down to flank the Guest's tea setting.

6. Offer both hands together, palms up, fingers bent toward palms:

   I am honored by your presence, and you are welcome at this table set between the worlds.

7. Release handclasp and introduce yourself by Craft Name:

   I greet you most heartily, and I am called [Craft Name]. Please sit with me here, that I may serve you tea.

8. Serve tea for both places, adding sugar and milk, and biscuit or cookie on saucer edges.

9. Open arms, palms up, and bless the meal:

   I know of my needs and offer my appreciation to that which sustains me. May I ever remember the blessings of my Lady and my Lord. The Lord brings

spiritual life through the bounty of the Lady of Otherworld, that all is created in undying beauty. I honor the inner beauty of the spirit.

10. Eat and drink with Guest, visiting and discussing the desire for a Companion [the food and drink of the Other is not consumed in the material manner, but the flavor, or essence, will be removed, so do not eat or drink of it].

11. If this is to be your Companion, ask to find a crystal suitable as passage that may be carried as the gateway for the Companion.

12. When finished, stand:

I am blessed by your having shared this tea with me. My blessings I give to thee. We came in friendship and depart in friendship. Merry we meet, merry we part, and merry we will meet again. Merry meet, merry part, and merry meet again.

13. See the Guest stand; extend own hands palm up and feel the cool touch of the Other's hand in farewell.

14. Sit before the candle and mirror; envision the misty forest becoming darker; the quiet footfalls of the departing Guest disappear into the Wild Wood; the splashing water of the brook becomes fainter; the deer bounds off into the depths of the wood; the forest disappears, and the door closes.

15. You are looking into the black mirror and see yourself looking back.

**Proceed to Sidhe Moon Esbat Conclusion
and Fairy Tea and Cookies**

Rituals Entered By:

7
Meditations

Meditation Notes

Releasing Fears Meditation

Past Lives Meditation

Mothers in Time Meditation

Tree Blending Meditation

The Oracle Cave Meditation

Ride with the Wild Hunt Meditation

Unmasking the Crone Meditation

Sun   Moon Mercury Venus Mars Jupiter Neptune Saturn Pluto Uranus

Waxing Moon
[Maiden]

Full Moon
[Mother]

Waning Moon
[Crone]

Dark (New) Moon
[Hidden Face/Mystery]

MEDITATION NOTES

1. **Begin All Meditations:** at the portion noted in the Circle Casting as: "Perform Ritual/Craft Work," or in the Esbat Ritual noted as: "Conduct any spell work . . . meditations . . ."

2. **After All Meditations:** return to Esbat, or to Cakes & Wine of Circle Casting noted as unless otherwise stated: "Proceed to Esbat Conclusion or Cakes & Wine of the Circle Casting."

3. **Herbal Use:** dropping small quantities into the flame of a votive candle in a safe container [metal cauldron with sand on the bottom is best] may aid in opening the subconscious mind through the aroma of herbs such as: mugwort, sage, lemon grass, woodruff, rosemary, burdock, and rue, but also by burning incenses such as dragon's blood, frankincense, patchouli, and copal among others. Use as desired.

4. **Music:** may be played low so as not to be distracting.

5. **Prerecorded Meditations:** may be used by reading the meditation slowly, pausing where it seems appropriate during the recording. Place [cassette] recorder within easy reach; after breathing exercise of *Meditative State* note, switch on recording to begin the meditation.

6. **Meditative State:** Sit relaxed but with the back straight and arms at ease so hands rest on knees or in lap; be in center of Circle or at the Altar or a table, facing North unless meditation directs otherwise. If sitting in chair, have back straight, feet flat on the floor [not with legs crossed], hands resting palms up, one inside the other, on lap, or palms down over the knees. Breathe deeply and exhale; repeat. Inhale for two counts, hold for one, exhale for two counts, hold for one, repeat until feeling relaxed. Try to keep eyes focused on an object or candle flame, blink occasionally, and let the mind chatter fade away; then begin the meditation. Do not be startled if the surroundings seem to change. When meditation ends, return to breathing exercise, inhaling for two counts, holding for one count, exhaling for two counts, holding for one count, repeating until full awareness returns, then take a bite of food or drink of beverage; proceed with ritual.

7. **Unguided Meditation:** used to solve problems and find answers by stating the problem or asking the question prior to entering meditative state, then focusing on a candle, stone, picture, or other object, or closing your eyes to go to safe place of your own creation, then move from there as your inner vision takes you. When the mind is clear, answers come.

RELEASING FEARS MEDITATION

Note: This meditation is to help open the line of communication between the Practitioner and the Dark Aspects of the Divine through facing and releasing the fears and anxieties that may have been part of your life for many years.

Have: a purple or black votive working candle; incense of frankincense or sandalwood.

1. May first take a warm, candlelit bath, scented with herbs [rosemary, basil, thyme, valerian] tied in a muslin pouch; dress in comfortable clothes or whatever feels natural.

2. Be in a place where you will not be disturbed, and have the light off.

3. Light candle and the incense.

4. Gaze into flame, sitting and facing North [may prerecord meditation]:

5. Envision the votive candle as the Light that shines in the Land of Shadows; the Lamp that lights the path to wisdom.

6. Enter meditative state; now you are ready to identify and dispel your fears.

7. You are in an atmosphere of safety; sitting within the comfort of a shallow, airy, hermit's cave [or other area to your liking].

   See yourself in a small, circular cave with an arched entry that gives you a view of the outside. The stony walls and ceiling form an alcove around you. The ground is covered with moss and leaves, and you are sitting on a soft bearskin rug. You are facing the opening to the cave and can see that you are in a secure place near the top of a mountain, at a vantage point that allows you to look out over the forest beneath the mountain. The Sun is setting, casting long shadows over the land. The cave darkens. The Sun disappears completely, taking the last of the colors with it, and the stars come out in the evening sky. There is a cool breeze bringing the sweet scents of the night to you. You are at peace.

   Now that the scene is mentally fixed, focus on a question:

   ### What do I fear?

   Images may begin to appear, which may include varieties of deaths, frightening faces, and so forth. Let the images come and go, but with each one that appears, ask:

   ### Why do I fear this?

   Listen for the answer, knowing that you are safe from any image that appears to you. Then ask:

   ### What are these fears?

   Listen to the answers, allowing the images to be unmasked, and realize that once a fear is known and exposed, it no longer has power over you.

After you have faced your own fears and unmasked them, banish them with:

Begone!

The images fade away, often with a little laugh, for fear is only a game, after all, that you had allowed yourself to take too seriously. Stars shine again in the sky, you smile, breathe in deeply the night air, and as you exhale, the tensions of fears dissipate. You take another breath, and inhale the sense of all being right in the world. You are back in your meditation place, and may return to the cave whenever needed.

**Proceed to Esbat Conclusion or Cakes & Wine
of the Circle Casting**

PAST LIVES MEDITATION

Note: This meditation is used to explore past lives, perhaps gaining an insight to past issues and events that are affecting the present life. However, since time is a spiral rather than linear, future lives may appear or lives in other places than Earth, for the soul's journey encompasses the Universe, and other planes. It is best when performed at Samhain, when the veil between the worlds is thinnest.

Have: a black mirror propped up on a table or Altar; cloth to cover the mirror; chair; 1 black candle [pillar, votive, or taper] as the working candle placed in front of the mirror; drum or rattle if desired; incense of frankincense, sandalwood, or copal.

1. May first take a warm, candlelit bath, scented with herbs [rosemary, basil, thyme, valerian] tied in a muslin pouch; dress in comfortable clothes or whatever feels natural.

2. Be in a place where you will not be disturbed, and have the light off.

3. Light candle in front of the mirror and the incense.

4. Begin meditation by gazing into the mirror past the flame, while sitting and facing North [meditation may be prerecorded as desired]; enter meditative state.

Envision the votive candle as a beacon to wisdom:

This candle glows to light the path into Darkness.

Gaze into the mirror, past your own eyes; drum or shake rattle if desired:

I call upon the Dark and the Past; the Ancient of Days in the Realm of Repast. Unleash to my sight the paths I have roamed; and show me the forms of lives I have known.

Continue to chant the rhyme, shaking rattle or drumming without listening to it or paying attention to the motion; focus on the mirror and watch as the face changes into those of past lives. When done, if still drumming or shaking a rattle, stop:

> The memories of past and future are shown; the faces of me in Time are now known. Blessings I give to the Veiled One of Night; for through this mask am I given the Sight.

Cover the mirror with a black cloth and snuff the candle.

Proceed to Esbat Conclusion or Cakes & Wine of the Circle Casting

Mothers In Time Meditation

Note: this meditation is best performed on Samhain to honor the ancestresses of the family bloodlines.

Have: table; chair; black mirror in center of table; black candle in front of mirror; libation bowl in front of candle; incense of frankincense, copal, or sandalwood to the right of the mirror; chalice of dark wine [or other beverage] to the left of the mirror.

1. May first take a warm, candlelit bath, scented with herbs [rosemary, basil, thyme, valerian] tied in a muslin pouch; dress in comfortable clothes or whatever feels natural.

2. Be in a place where you will not be disturbed, and have the light off [may prerecord].

3. Light candle and the incense.

4. Enter meditative state.

   Gaze into mirror past candle flame while sitting and facing North:

   > Mothers of eternity, passing thy light through me;
   > Mother love thru time; mother love from past to future generations flows;
   > Our genetic bonds tie our love thru the ages.
   > Mothers of my ancestry; mothers of my heritage;
   > We are connected be.
   > All the mothers of my line; pass our love thru all time.
   > Past, present, future family;
   > Mother love is blessed be, blessed be, blessed be;
   > Now as then unto eternity.
   > *So Mote It Be!*

Gaze at own reflection, watching the changes, seeing maternal ancestors; greet them with love and remembrance, raising chalice, giving libation; then take a sip with each statement [three in all]:

> Mothers of mine in time, I honor thee.
> You who have passed the gift of life unto me, I honor thee.
> Mothers of my line and my blood, I honor thee.

Speak to those as desired; see them as kin; feel comfort in knowing they live in the blood, the cells and very DNA carried within. Waft incense to the mirrored faces:

> Mirror of time and love, I offer the scent of remembrance unto my mother heritage.
> Blessed be the mothers of my family now and through all time.
> Without them, their sacrifices, love, and nurture, I would not be.
> Blessed be the wombs that have carried the children of my line.
> Blessed be the hearts that have loved the children of my line.
> Blessed be the eyes that see and the hands that heal.
> Blessed be my family.

For encouraging fertility, envision the passing on of the family blood, and add the following:

> Mothers of mine, mothers in time, you who have passed the blood of my line;
> Hear me in my call to thee, aid me now to emulate thee.
> You have had your child and now I seek mine.
> Help me to carry on our family line.
> Give unto me thy support for our family;
> Guide new life into me, that I as thee may blessed be
> This is my call unto thee maternally;
> That as I will, *So Mote It Be!*

Waft incense to mirror:

> Mirror mine I clear thee now.
> Images gone, memories linger.
> Thy purpose has been fulfilled;
> And you are sent unto your rest.

Cover the mirror with a black cloth and snuff the candle.

Proceed to Esbat Conclusion or Cakes & Wine of the Circle Casting

TREE BLENDING MEDITATION

Note: may take a ritual bath prior to meditation, using a herb pouch with rosemary, sage, thyme, and marjoram, and green or viney scented rather than floral or perfume soap [mulberry, herbal, apple, pear, or berry scents are good].

Have: a soft blanket to sit on; a tree that feels receptive; picnic lunch with food and beverage; a pail of water and perhaps plant food for a libation; a ribbon or other lightweight decoration that can be left on a tree limb. Wear comfortable, loose clothing.

1. Walk around the tree and see which part seems to be the "face" or front of the tree.

2. Spread blanket on ground in front of the tree; Ground and center, then walk around the tree deosil, casting the Circle.

3. Sit in a Meditative State on the blanket facing the tree.

4. If prerecorded, allow time for each action suggested in this meditation:

Look at the tree and note its general shape and foliage, the spreading of its limbs, and the atmosphere surrounding it. Compare it against the background and look for the tree's aura, the glowing light that envelops the tree. What color is it? Does the aura look like the tree is content or is there something bothering the tree? A white to pale blue aura indicates a loving, peaceful, and sympathetic tree. Yellow shows energy, but if tinged with brown, this could indicate that it does not feel well. Red shows an active tree that is interested in what happens in its surroundings, and possibly alert to dangers. Green tinged shows fertility and connection with the wilderness spirit. A purple aura shows spiritual connection, but if violet, the tree could feel hostility and need soothing before continuing with the meditation. You may want to offer the libation of water and fertilizer at the tree roots before rather than after the visit. Watering the tree, nurturing the tree, adding fertilizer when it seems to need it, or planting a companion for the tree are all ways of soothing and establishing your acquaintance with a tree. Leaving a token of your esteem, decorations OR delicate wind chimes are ways of reaching out to the spirit of the tree to let it know that it is appreciated and loved by you.

As you sit before the tree, see the way it sets into the ground. Are the roots spread out, does the trunk seem to simply dive into the earth? Visually examine the texture and grain of the bark.

Remain on the blanket, but now feel yourself move closer to the tree. See from the perspective of the tree that it is observing you as you have observed it. Look for a crevice in the bark, and visualize yourself sliding into that crevice. Feel the woody texture of the trunk, strong and able to support the weight of the branches and foliage heavy upon the core that is the tree's body—your body.

Fluids course up and down your interior. You feel the gentle motion of tiny insects making their home about your outer skin—the bark. Move your attention upward and feel yourself extending into the branches. You are moving in a multitude of directions, spreading upward to form a single entity with consciousness in your branchings, a myriad of thin twiggings and stemmings, attached to the stiffly subtle opened leaves. Buddings are encased, about to open with the sunlight, but other leaves are spread, and you are aware of the sunlight activating the cells of your greenness.

Now you begin to understand that the essence of the tree has a face to the front of the trunk, but a consciousness that reaches to all levels so that as you channel upward through the branches to the topmost leaves, you are still aware and connected to the earth. The air is breezy at the top, and the sun is full upon you. Perhaps you find the height dizzying at first, but the tree laughs and you relax. You will not fall from this place, for you are part of it. The leaves and thin branches sway in the slight wind, and you feel yourself looking down.

There, far below, is someone sitting on a blanket, trance-like, gazing at the tree. Ah, that is you. The tree senses the not-tree within and gently directs you back through the twigs and down to the wider branches. You pause to feel the scratch of a bird's nest, and smile with admiration at the construction. Now you turn around the main trunk and feel the narrow gap in the trunk, a rounded opening into the trunk with a woody interior. You wrap yourself into that interior and feel the sensation of comfort, security, and home. It is a nest for a squirrel or for another bird family. Now you are aware that your limbs are being groomed, tiny beaks poke into your bark and snatch away insects roaming along your skin. You continue downward, through the heartwood of the tree, feeling the liquid nourishment passing upward and down again, around the outside of the solid core.

You are back at the main trunk, standing upright there, seeing you seeing you back. You smile and feel the tree relax in a sensation of camaraderie. It wants to show you something. Now you feel your toes, your roots and the featherings of your roots deep in the earth. You let yourself travel downward still, past the level of the ground, and into the soil. Your texture changes here, and you realize with a warm glow that you are being entrusted with a journey into the most delicate part of the tree—its defenseless roots that surround the heart of the living tree.

The tree tells you:

> Harm the root, and you kill me. Cut the bark all around and the food of the soil cannot reach the rest of me and this too will kill me.

You tremble with the knowledge that this tree has shared with you.

> I am mighty and strong, but there is always danger in life, even one that lasts as long as centuries.

You send your thought to the tree:

> All life comes to an end.

The tree smiles and indicates again the roots. You feel the smooth moist roots with their bristly fibers and hairlings drawing water and nourishment from the surrounding soil, and then you see them. The children of the tree. Little fingerlings and seedlings, pods awaiting to open, and you know before the tree confides to you.

There is no ending to life, only transformation.

And you know this is true, for never did a tree not speak true. Listen to what else the tree has to say to you:

Pause.

You take one more look at the soil deep beneath the surface of the earth, feel how your tree-feet are spread, wrapped around rocks, with little creatures sliding around the featherings of your roots. You move back up the woody trail back to the surface of the earth where grasses play in the breeze at your earth-level roots and a bee buzzes past you looking for a flower.

Seeing yourself again, you slide from out between the rough edges of the bark and back into your body.

You take a deep breath, hold it a moment, then exhale. Another deep breath, exhale, and you return to full awareness. Stand up and take the pail of water [perhaps mixed with a plant food] and gently splash it around the roots of the tree. Touch your heart with your hand, then the tree trunk, your third eye region, and again the tree trunk. This is the blessing given and received, now you may sit again and eat your picnic meal and drink a cool beverage. When finished, walk around the tree widdershins, drawing the energy of the Circle back within, touch palms to the ground, drain off the excess energy, and leave your token ribbon or other gift before you depart.

THE ORACLE CAVE MEDITATION

Have: a cauldron or other container; charcoal disk [for incense] or a black votive candle; desired herbs [mugwort].

1. Light the candle or charcoal disk; add mugwort [or other desired herb] to the candle or charcoal and watch it smolder.

2. Watch the smoke as it swirls, adding herbs as needed, and focus on the smoke. See it as a gray mist parting and enveloping, moving the swirls of time so that "now" and "then" are one.

3. Enter meditative state; begin meditation [may be prerecorded as desired]:

Think about the famous Oracle of Delphi being closed to the public, with the entrance to the cavern sealed, inaccessible today in the temple ruin. Think about how the space looks today from inside: an empty underground chamber, its floor a vast rock with a split in it from which escapes the vapors of prophecies. The symbol of the Goddess, the python, is carved into the rocky walls of the chamber as a reminder of the age of the Pythian Oracle, ancient before the time of the Greeks and their God Apollo to whom the Oracle was rededicated. See the brass tripod stool over the crack, where in ancient times through the early centuries of Christianity, a priestess sat, inhaling the vapors and uttering her prophecies. The tripod is still there, the fissure is still seeping faint swirls of steam, and the chamber is wrapped in expectant silence as the Oracle waits to speak and to be heard again.

You are in modern Greece, visiting historic ruins; the fumes of the old-fashioned bus come to you, and the dust stirred by the old tires on the dirt road as the bus rolls to a stop at the site of the ancient Oracle of Delphi. You have hid a small flashlight in your pocket for this occasion, and are arriving with a busload of tourists. You move around the dry, sun-baked temple sites and ruins of columns while listening in a distracted way to the prepared speech of the guide. All the while, you are waiting for your chance to explore the forbidden spot, and now the tour guide moves on with the other visitors. You see the gap at the corner of the stone slab, and feel a rush of cool air, and you know that this is the way in. The monotone voice of the guide fades and you quickly push aside the loose broken stones near the gap of the slab, and you find the step beneath allows you room to squeeze inside.

At first there is only darkness and a distant sound hard to describe. Your first thought is that there might be snakes inside, but then you relax as you realize that you are in a sacred place, not as an intruder, but as one who is part of this tradition. No snake will attack you here—if any are in this place, they will feel your peace and ignore you. The heat of the surface world vanishes and is replaced by the coolness of the subterranean Earth. You move down the steps and the darkness becomes a gloom through which you can barely see, but it is not impenetrable. Your light shows the winding stairway is uninhabited—perhaps there are volcanic gases that keep animals away, you think in a panic—and now you hear a distant sound and wonder if you could be in danger of succumbing to some poisonous gas. But now you realize there is a breeze drifting through the chamber and out the gap where you entered, so the air is breathable and not at all stifling, and you again relax.

The steps take you down further and the sound suddenly makes sense to you—it is the hissing of the vapors escaping the fissure. You have reached the bottom of the stairway now, and the floor is uneven but smooth. You realize that it is bedrock. Carefully, you make your way across the chamber toward the hissing sound, and then you see a thin crack in the floor. As you scan across the floor with your flashlight, you see that the crack widens slightly, and you move along the side of the crack to see where it will lead you. And then something glints in the light. Your breath is caught in your throat and your eyes smart with tears—you are seeing the brass tripod, still standing where it was last used, waiting for a priestess to ascend and sit upon it.

You set the flashlight on the floor and make the sign of the pentagram in the air before you, then you move toward the "seat of wisdom," stepping across the fissure in the process. You touch the tripod and feel a tremor of excitement as you realize that no one has touched this seat in over a thousand years. You know where you belong, and you take your place upon the tripod.

Now you hear a sound, then more sounds, a babble of sounds:

Areth; amoad; aneadi; careth; imionee; trianeth . . .

The words come faster and stronger and louder, and you begin to recognize their meanings and that there are visions attached to these words, and you suddenly realize that the sounds are pouring from *your* mouth! Tears flow down your cheeks and you know that the Goddess is speaking and you are Her Priestess. The cavern is filled with your speech and ecstasy. You hear what She tells you and what She reveals to you, and you know that the Goddess lives—through all vain human denial, the Lady *lives* and *is life*, and *gives life!* Listen to what she tells you.

Pause

Slowly the sounds begin to fade, and you become aware of a chill. You are soaked in perspiration, but the presence of the Goddess now feels warm around you and you feel you are wrapped in Her cloak. You are calmer now, and saddened as you realize that this sacred place is closed off to the people who want to come here. But She comforts you and you hear Her voice tell you:

I am in all places of the Earth and in your heart. Take this tripod into your heart and sit upon it whenever you have need to speak with Me, for I am everywhere.

You understand now that the whole of the Earth is Her temple and that anywhere you are when you call upon Her is the same as sitting upon the tripod in this cavern to hear Her voice. Your connection with Her is complete, and the Oracle now resides within. You have the courage now to slip off the stool and cross the fissure back to your flashlight. You scan the walls and see the beautiful carvings and the great python carved around the rock of the fissure.

You take a deep breath and release it, then turn away from the tripod and walk back to the steps as though you had done it a hundred times—perhaps once you had. You ascend the stone steps and return to the outer world. You were never missed; you hear the voice of the guide coming back your way, and you quickly reset the stone in place and leave the forbidden spot. Now you are protective of this sacred site and in a moment of anxiety, you fear what might happen if others learned of your experience; who knows what damage might be done to prevent others from entering. Then you smile and realize that of course, others *have* entered before you; others who are your kindred; and you feel warmed inside as you understand that you are not alone.

You breathe deeply and exhale. The voices of the crowd dissipate. Breathe again, and you are returned to your meditation place.

Proceed to Esbat Conclusion or Cakes & Wine of the Circle Casting

Ride with the Wild Hunt Meditation

Have: a purple or black votive working candle; incense of frankincense or sandalwood.

1. May first take a warm, candlelit bath, scented with herbs [rosemary, basil, thyme, valerian] tied in a muslin pouch; dress in comfortable clothes or whatever feels natural.

2. Be in a place where you will not be disturbed, and have the light off.

3. Light candle and the incense.

4. Begin meditation gazing into flame, sitting and facing North [may prerecord meditation].

5. Envision the votive candle as the Light that shines in the Land of Shadows; the Lamp that lights the path to wisdom.

6. Enter meditative state.

Once your mind is calm, the noise of stray thoughts is vanquished, and you are in your quiet inner space, listen and hear the distant thundering of horses' hooves. A horn sounds far away, and the noise of riders seems to becoming more distinct. Now you hear the pounding of horse' hooves coming closer; the rattle and squeak of harness and saddles; the heavy breaths of the beasts; again the blast of the horn; and you know it is the Wild Hunt approaching. You call out:

   May I ride with the Rade until break of day?

The Hunter calls back to you:

   Catch hold my hand and dare not let go!

As He passes, you grasp the hand held down to you and are amazed at the fluid strength that quickly pulls you up to sit before the Hunter upon His mount. You hold fast to that thin hand and watch the Rade from your privileged seat.

Over mountain tops and through valleys; over seas and flood plains; past great cities and small villages you ride, and you become aware through the dark swirling clouds around you that shadows rise up from the lands you have passed and join the Wild Hunt in its headlong race through the dark. The Rade races before the sunrise and now you see that the land is more familiar. You recognize your own local countryside, towns, and cities, and the Hunter says:

> **The dawning comes and you are back again from whence you sprang upon my steed. My bargain is kept, for you rode with the Rade until break of day.**

In an instant that strong arm and powerful hand has dropped you gently onto the land. You see before you a great earthen mound with a carved stone gateway, and you are reminded of a pregnant woman's full belly, and yet the entrance is ancient. You see the Crone, gray and shriveled, dressed in tattered shrouds, standing in the dim entry and She says:

> **All must pass through me to be born of me!**

Now you realize how much the Wild Hunt has grown in size; with laughing riders and plunging horses, you watch as the Hunter leads the Rade through the entry into the Shadowland. The gateway vanishes; the dawn breaks; you breathe easier and are at peace. You can feel the warmth of the morning sun. The landscape fades and you return to normal consciousness.

**Proceed to Esbat Conclusion or Cakes & Wine
of the Circle Casting**

UNMASKING THE CRONE MEDITATION

Note: This meditation was developed from a real-life experience, and these types of insights and visions form excellent foundations for creating a meditation. This one is based on my own experience from when my mother died. I learned she was in the hospital and fading quickly, but it was an eight-hour drive to get to her. For six hours as I drove, I worried that she would pass on before I got to see her. At one place, there was underbrush being burnt for a widening of the highway, and the smoke rose in a huge pillar high into the sky. As I drove, my mind was on how much time it would take me to get to the hospital. I looked up at the billowing smoke, and the clouds rapidly transformed into the image of the Crone. She was heading for the town where my mother was, and she was a hideous, terrifying sight, as she turned her head to look down at me. In my mind I heard her voice say,"I am going for your mother, but I will wait for you."

The first impact of her words was knowledge that my mother was indeed dying. The second was that I could rest assured I would be able to talk with her before her passing. At a time like this, the whole process of death and passage becomes personal and imminent. I trusted that the vision was authentic and the message was as I heard it. This is part of the *perfect love and perfect trust* so often discussed in the Craft. My fear of separation that death brings vanished. I put my trust in the Lady, and I whispered, "I am not afraid of you because I know that you are also the Mother." I knew my mother would make the passage into the arms of one who loved her. When I said those words, the image in the clouds changed instantly and dramatically into the most beautiful woman I have ever seen, smiling down at me. Her voice came into my mind, "Only those who do not know me fear me."

Have: a purple or black votive working candle; incense of frankincense or sandalwood.

1. May first take a warm, candlelit bath, scented with herbs [rosemary, basil, thyme, valerian] tied in a muslin pouch; dress in comfortable clothes or whatever feels natural.

2. Be in a place where you will not be disturbed, and have the light off.

3. Light candle and the incense.

4. Begin meditation gazing into flame, sitting and facing North [may be prerecorded as desired]:

5. Envision the votive candle as the Light that shines in the Land of Shadows; the Lamp that lights the path to wisdom.

6. Enter meditative state.

   Follow the Ride With the Wild Hunt Meditation, but when you approach the place where first you called to him, ask him to let you remain with him a little longer:

   > Let me tarry awhile and see the great spiral.
   > Let me ride with thee now into thy dark bower.
   > Let me see the path followed and how the lives flow.
   > Let me ride with the Rade as you travel below.

   The Hunter nods his antlered head and now you see the mound in the gray light of early dawn. The Crone, in her tattered shrouds, stands before the entrance and you hear her cry out:

   > All must pass through me to be born of me!

   You see her getting closer as the horses continue their wild plunge into the gateway. There is a sudden roaring wind in your ears; a sound like spinning millstones grinding corn fills your mind; the darkness closes around you and you smell a scent that reminds you of the damp, dark, rich earth. The temptation is to close your eyes, but you force yourself to keep them open and realize that the shadow flying past your face has substance like cobwebby shrouds and the cold dank air of deep caverns. You are passing through the Crone, and feel nauseous with the sensation of death, the noxious odors of disease and decay, and the scrabbling thin fingers scratching at your flesh. Yet the horses ride on and the Hunter holds you firmly in his grasp, and you cling to him and call out to the fearful image of the Crone as you pass through her:

I know who you are! You are the Mother of All, and I do not fear you!

She laughs and turns to you as you pass through her, and, incredibly, you see a lovely lady, smiling and more beautiful than words can describe, and you laugh with her. You hear Her gentle voice as She replies to you:

Only those who do not know me fear me.

Suddenly, it is as though you had been a child all along, playing in a dark room letting your imagination frighten yourself. Now you know that the face of the Crone hides the lovely Mother who awaits you with open arms, and you feel secure, loved, and at peace.

The Hunter races his mount through the dark realm, and you see spirits taking their rest by still dark pools overhung with cypress branches and long gray moss. Soft, silky grass and delicate pathways beckon to you to walk and relax. You are tempted to stay here and enjoy the Shadowland with its night-blooming flowers and air scented with lilacs, but the Hunter does not let you down from his steed.

Through a dark forest padded with the sodden leaves of autumns past you now race, and then you burst upon a sunlit meadow. There are children playing and the shining bright Other People wave to you as you pass. Spirits appearing to be of all ages and ageless move in this bright place, and you realize that there is light and warmth here, for you are in the Summerland, close to the Otherworld of the Fair Folk. Still the Hunter holds you tight, and you sense rather than see that you are passing through another kind of veil. The Hunter whispers in your ear and mind:

Here goes one who has rested and now desires to resume the great dance of life.

You look and see a shadowy figure as it appears to be moving through a gray swirling mist toward a distant light, and you realize that this is a spirit departing the Shadowland to be reborn.

But now your own race is ending and you see the dark earth close in around you, pebbles and snails, and earthy creatures wriggle by on many tiny legs or none at all. The ground seems to open and a starry night appears before your eyes, and when you look back around past the Hunter, you see the great mound behind you. He clasps you with one strong hand and effortlessly swings you off his mount and onto the ground, then

187

laughing, rides off into the night, the Wild Hunt behind him on their rounds anew. You see the dawn coming now, and as you return to normal awareness, you are at peace, and hold the memory of the beautiful lady who laughed with you when you penetrated her disguise. You know that life is eternal. There is no death, there is only passage.

**Proceed to Esbat Conclusion or Cakes & Wine
of the Circle Casting**

MEDITATIONS ENTERED BY:

_____

Book
of
Shadows
of
Aoumiel

Spells

8
Spellcrafting & Correspondences

Sun	Moon	Mercury	Venus	Mars	Jupiter	Neptune	Saturn	Pluto	Uranus

Waxing Moon [Maiden]	Full Moon [Mother]	Waning Moon [Crone]	Dark (New) Moon [Hidden Face/Mystery]

SPELLCRAFTING

Remember to Ground and Center before all Magical Work: to avoid depleting personal energy levels. Then ground excess energy by touching the Earth or floor when finished.

MOONS FOR SPELL WORK

WAXING   ☽   For Growth and New Projects.

FULL   ○   For Completions, Healing, and Empowerment.

WANING   ☾   For Releasings, Cleansings, and Banishings

NEW [DARK]   ●   For Divinations and Dark Power Magics

CREATING THE SPELL OR CHARM

Coordinate: how the spell will be done with ingredients, colors, and materials, that match the purpose of the spell—*Note*, it can be as simple or complex as desired.

Inscribe: the spell objects as needed with goal or energy symbols, sigils, and runes.

Inks: Dragon's Blood for power; Dove's Blood for gentleness; Bat's Blood for hidden knowledge; black and other colors for their relative correspondence [*see Color Correspondences*] used in writing down the purpose/ intent of spells to be placed under a candle [fold paper away from you to banish and toward you to draw], burned or mixed into spell materials.

Perform: the spell on the day and hour propitious by its planetary influence.

Visualize: the spell as completed and successful, then put it out of mind; if a spell extends over several days [as with a seven-day candle spell] see each day as completing one portion of the spell so that the entire spell is competed on the final day.

Dispose: of spell materials that are not meant to be carried or placed, by burying remains in soil or casting into moving water [down the sink or toilet works if not bulky].

TOOLS FOR HERBAL WORK:

Mortar and Pestle: ceramic tool for grinding and mixing herbs, flowers, bark, etc., to create a powder or an incense. May be of other material, such as marble, but not wood [retains oils], nor metal, as this alters the essence.

Spoon: wooden, silver, or gold to gather herbs for dropping onto candles, in potions, pouches, etc., or for gathering loose incense to drop into burner.

Glass or Enamel Pot with lid: for brewing infusions, etc.

Eye Dropper: used for adding drops of essential oils to herb pillows, etc.

Spring Water: may be bottled or collected at a fresh-water spring, used in blessing water, asperging, etc.

Olive, Almond, or Sunflower Oil: used as a base for creating oils for rituals and anointings.

Material: of muslin, cotton, or cheesecloth in various colors for spell crafts; silk for tarot bags.

WITCH'S SIGIL WHEEL

Decide first on a key word for the goal sought in a spell, such as LOVE, then make a small circle at the 1st letter of the word and draw straight lines to each letter in the word, ending the last letter with cross line—the sigil itself, once you see the pattern, may be etched onto a candle or drawn on paper that will be burned or folded and tucked with herbs in a pouch.

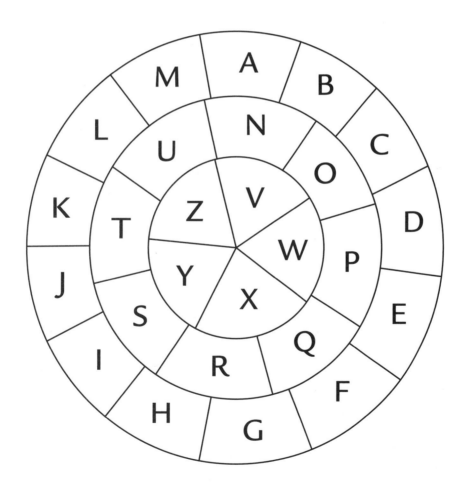

COLOR CORRESPONDENCES

Colors of candles, material, etc. used in spell work align with the desired goal listed.

Amber: Witch symbol, developing Witchcraft skills, empowerment.

Black/Jet: protection, ward negativity, remove hexes, spirit contact, night, the universe, truth, remove discord or confusion, binding for spellwork.

Blue [dark]: the Goddess [ritual candle], Water Elemental, impulse, truth, dreams, protection, change, meditation.

Blue [light]: psychic awareness, intuition, opportunity, understanding, quests, safe journey, patience, tranquillity, ward depression, health.

Brown: Earth riches, endurance, animal health, steadiness, houses/homes, physical objects, uncertainties, special favors, influence friendships.

Copper: money goals, professional growth, career maneuvers, passion, business fertility, energy movement.

Gold: the God, Solar magics, Solar energy, power, achievement, physical strength, success, skills sought, mental growth, healing energy, intuition, wealth, divination, safety, winning, power, happiness, playful humor.

Gray: Otherworld travel, vision quests, veiling, neutralizing.

Green: Lord and Lady of Wild Wood, Earth Elemental, herb magics, Nature magics [i.e.; garden blessing], luck, fertility, healing, balance, courage, work, prosperity, agriculture, changing direction or attitudes.

Greenish-yellow: discord, sickness, anger, jealousy [use to negate these].

Indigo: meditation, spirit communication, Karma workings, learn ancient wisdom, neutralize baneful magic, ward slander.

Lavender: spiritual development, psychic growth, divination, Otherworld.

Orange: the God [ritual candle], strength, healing, attracting things, vitality, adaptability, luck, encouragement, clearing the mind, dominance, justice, career goals, legal matters, selling, action, property deals, ambition, general success.

Pink: honor, morality, friendships, emotional love, social ability, good will, caring, healing emotions, peace, affection, nurturing, romance, partnership.

Purple: power, Spirit, spiritual development, intuition, ambition, healing, wisdom, progress, business, spirit communication, protection, occultism, self-assurance, influence higher-ups.

Rainbow: variegated colors, inner development by relaxation and introspection.

Red: Fire Elemental, strength, power, energy, health, vigor, enthusiasm, courage, passion, sexuality, vibrancy, survival, driving force, blood of the Moon.

Silver: the Goddess, Lunar magics, meditation, psychic development, success, balance, wards negativity, astral energies.

Violet: self-improvement, intuition, success in searches.

White: the Lady and the Lord together [ritual candle], Full Moon magics, purity, protection, truth, meditation, peace, sincerity, justice, ward doubt/fear.

Yellow: Air Elemental, divination, clairvoyance, mental alertness, intellect, memory, prosperity, learning, changes, harmony, creativity, self-promotion.

DAILY INFLUENCES

Select the day for a spell by the influence of the day, then use colors or planetary hours that further align the energies for the desired goal; planetary signs can be drawn on candles or other spell materials to emphasize the planetary influence—total alignment brings greatest power, but is not necessary to success, so you may pick and choose.

Monday: ☽ *Planet*—Moon; *Colors*—silver, white, gray; *Herbs*—moonwort; myrtle, violet, willow, wormwood; *Influences*—dreams, emotions, clairvoyance, home, family, medicine, cooking, personality, merchandising, theft.

Tuesday: ♂ *Planet*—Mars; *Colors*—red, orange; *Herbs*—basil, dragon's blood, patchouli; *Influences*—dynamic energy, matrimony, war, enemies, prison, hunting, surgery, courage, politics, contests.

Wednesday: ☿ *Planet*—Mercury; *Colors*—gray, iridescent, opal, violet, yellow; *Herbs*—jasmine, lavender; *Influences*—communication, teaching, reason, divination, skill, debt, fear, self—improvement, loss.

Thursday: ♃ *Planet*—Jupiter; *Colors*—blue, indigo, purple; *Herbs*—cinnamon, cinquefoil, musk, nutmeg, sage; *Influences*—health, honor, luck, riches, clothing, money, legal matters, desires.

Friday: ♀ *Planet*—Venus; colors—aqua, green, pink; *Herbs*—lime, saffron, sandalwood, thyme; *Influences*—love, friendship, social activities, strangers, pleasure, art, music, incense, and perfumes.

Saturday: ♄ *Planet*—Saturn; *Colors*—black, dark gray, indigo; *Herbs*—black poppy seeds, mullein, myrrh; *Influences*—self—discipline, life, building, doctrine, protection, freedom, elderly, destroying diseases and pests.

Sunday: ☉ *Planet*—Sun; *Colors*—gold, orange, white, yellow; *Herbs*—frankincense, lemon, St. Johnswort; *Influences*—individuality, hope, fortune, money, work, power, healing, promotions, strength, spirituality.

ELEMENTAL/DAILY TIDES

Energy influences during the year which may be used in alignment of spells with the Elemental energies//herbs may be used to enhance the Elemental energies in spells; Elemental symbols may also be drawn on candles, paper, or other materials for spell or craft work.

▽—**Earth;**   △—**Air;**   △—**Fire;**   ▽—**Water**

ᛗ —**Winter;**   ♉ —**Spring;**   ♋ —**Summer;**   ♏ —**Autumn**

Earth: 12/21 [Winter Solstice] to 3/20 [Eve of Spring Equinox].
Planning; Cleansing—a time of preparation—North; Night; Midnight/12:00 A.M.; Old Age; Green; Physical Strength; the Body; Material Matters; Career; Wealth ▽ ; ᛗ

Air: 3/21 [Spring Equinox] to 6/20 [Eve of Summer Solstice].
Beginnings—a time of initialization—East; Morning; Sunrise/6:00 A.M.; Childhood; Yellow; Intellect; Mind; Conscious; Breath; Psychic Power △ ; ♉

Fire: 6/21 [Summer Solstice] to 9/22 [Eve of Autumn Equinox].
Harvest, Reaping—a time of fruition, completion—South; Midday; Noon/12:00 P.M.; Youth; Red; Will; Heart; Passion; Energy; Healing △ ; ♋

Water: 9/23 [Autumn Equinox] to 12/20 [Eve of Winter Solstice].
Destruction, Replacement—rest, renewal, and passage—West; Afternoon; Sunset/6:00 P.M.; Maturity; Blue; Emotion; Fluids and Blood; Subconscious; Purification; Dreams ▽ ; ♏

TIDES FOR MAGICAL PRACTICE

Using the time of day in place of planetary hours for spell work.

Morning: awakening, new beginning, fertility, life direction.

Daytime: growth, financial gains, good life, generosity.

Midday: willpower, strength, sustenance, perseverance, overcoming obstacles.

Dusk/Twilight: change, receptiveness, parenting, moving between the worlds.

Evening: camaraderie, spirituality, joy, pleasure, family gatherings, children, play.

Late Night: occult learning, increase knowledge/wisdom, enlightenment, creativity.

Midnight: releasings, recuperation, recovery, closings, endings.

ELEMENTAL HERBAL CORRESPONDENCES

▽ **Earth:** material matters; physical form; wealth; career.
Balm of Gilead, bistort, cedar, cinquefoil, clove, fern, High John the Conqueror, honeysuckle, horehound, jasmine, mandrake, patchouli, pine, sage, slippery elm.

△ **Air:** intellect; mind; creativity; breath; visions; psychic power.
Acacia, anise, benzoin, broom, comfrey, elder, eucalyptus, eyebright, hazel, lavender, lemon verbena, marjoram, mastic, mistletoe, mugwort, nutmeg, peppermint, sandalwood, spearmint, thyme, wormwood.

△ **Fire:** will; passion; divine within; energy; protection; healing.
Alder, angelica, basil, bay laurel, betony, carnation, celadine, cinnamon, coriander, cumin, garlic, holly, hyssop, juniper, marigold, peony, pepper, primrose, rosemary, rowan, rue, saffron, St. Johnswort, thistle, vervain.

▽ **Water:** emotions; subconscious; dreams; purification; blood; fluids.
Apple, ash, burdock, catnip, chamomile, cypress, elecampane, geranium, henbane, hyacinth, ivy, meadowsweet, myrrh, orris root, poppy, rose, star anise, willow, yarrow.

TREES BY DAYS/ENTITIES

Use for wand selection, divination tools {runes/ogham}, days to work specific magic with wood chips, wood bits to place in spell pouches along with herbs, etc.

Elder/Willow	Monday	Hecate/Crone Goddesses
Holly/Elm/Cedar	Tuesday	Hunter Gods/Elves
Hazel/Rowan	Wednesday	Goddess & God
Oak/Pine	Thursday	The God
Birch/Apple/Myrtle	Friday	The Goddess
Alder/Hawthorn	Saturday	Fairies/Witches
Ash/Birch/Laurel	Sunday	Elves/The Goddess
Ash-Oak-Hawthorn	Fairie Triad	Haven Sacred to the Fair Folk

PROPERTIES OF TREES & SHRUBS

Use to select wands/other tools; burn in candle spells; add chips to charms/spells, etc.

Alder: water magic, strength, foundations.

Apple: love, spirit food, unicorns, beauty, regeneration, eternity.

Ash: study, health, enhance magic, peace, rebirth, awakening, Underworld.

Aspen: overcoming obstacles, intuition, Otherworld communication.

Birch: purification, blessing, health, beginnings, vitality.

Blackthorn: control, stimulus, chaos energy, obstacles, friction, challenges, coercion.

Elder: cleansing, offering, Fairies, changes, evolution [never burn the wood].

Fir/Pine: prosperity, birth/rebirth, power, nobility, discretion, objectivity.

Gorse: opportunity, wisdom, interaction.

Hawthorn: purity, protection, Fairies, pleasure, stimulation, misfortune.

Hazel: wisdom, creativity, enhance perceptiveness, Witchcraft skills.

Heather: success, prosperity, gateway.

Holly: enhances magic, balance, challenges, testing.

Ivy: fertility, love, persistence, development, tenacity.

Linden: immortality, protection, good fortune, sleep, love.

Mountain Ash [Rowan]**:** protection, enhances magic, insight, cleansing.

Oak: fertility, power, balance, protection, success, truth, strength, courage, endurance.

Poplar: success, recognition, fame.

Red Oak: inner transformation, harmony.

Vine [Grape or Berry]**:** happiness, introspection, rebirth/renewal, transitions, ancestry.

Willow: Moon magic, psychic power, spirits, death passage, intuition, flexibility, Crone energy.

Yew: transformation, psychic awareness, spirits, death passage, immortality [do not burn].

SABBAT INCENSES & HERBS

This is a guide for preparing magical events in conjunction with the Sabbats. Although spell work is not normally conducted at this time, the home or surroundings may be aligned with the Sabbat energies with scented candles, incense, and decorations.

Yule: *burn* bay, bayberry, chamomile, frankincense, rosemary, sage; *decorate* with holly, juniper, mistletoe, moss, oak, pine cones, cedar, evergreen, blessed thistle.

Imbolc: *burn* basil, bay, benzoin, celandine; *decorate* with angelica, myrrh, yellow, white, or light blue flowers.

Ostara: *burn* celandine, cinquefoil, jasmine, rose, tansy, violets; *decorate with* acorn, crocus, daffodil, dogwood, honeysuckle, iris, lily, strawberry.

Beltane: *burn* almond, ash, cinquefoil, frankincense, marigold, meadowsweet, woodruff; *decorate* with angelica, bluebells, daisy, hawthorn, ivy, lilac, rose, primrose, wildflowers.

Litha: *burn* chamomile, cinquefoil, elder flower, fennel, lavender, mugwort, thyme, vervain; *decorate* with hemp, larkspur, pine, rose, St. Johnswort, wisteria.

Lughnassadh: *burn* cornstalks, heather, frankincense, wheat; *decorate* with acacia flowers, corn ears, hollyhock, myrtle, oak leaves, wheat.

Mabon: *burn* benzoin, marigold, myrrh, sage, thistles; *decorate* with acorns, asters, ferns, honeysuckle, milkweed, mums, oak leaves, pine, rose.

Samhain: *burn* heather, mullein, patchouli, sage; *decorate* with acorns, apples, pumpkins, oak leaves, straw, broom, dittany, ferns, flax.

INCENSES LISTED BY USE

These may be burned to enhance spell work or an appropriate ritual; herbs burned in candles or on charcoal disks can be used as well as pre-made cones, sticks, or resins.

Anointing: frankincense, jasmine, lavender, rose, vervain, orange.

Balance: cypress, jasmine, sandalwood, sweetgrass.

Banishing or Releasing: clove, cypress, mugwort, sage, lemon/lime.

Binding: cypress, dragon's blood, rowan, vetivert.

Blessing or Consecration: copal, frankincense, rosemary, sweetgrass.

Changes: bayberry, dragon's blood, lilac, patchouli, woodruff.

Cleansing: cedar, frankincense, pine, sage, sandal.

Courage: cinnamon, dragon's blood, patchouli, rosemary.

Creativity: dragon's blood, lavender, orange, rosemary, savory, tangerine.

Cursing: bayberry, clove, dragon's blood, myrrh.

Divination or Clairvoyance: bay, copal, lilac, mugwort, myrrh, sage.

Exorcism: copal, bayberry, frankincense, lavender, mullein, rosemary, sage, vervain, vetivert.

Gain Goals: acacia, bay, cedar, cinnamon, dragon's blood, orange, sandalwood.

Happiness or Peace: jasmine, lavender, orange, rose, vervain, sandalwood.

Inspiration or Wisdom: acacia, copal, frankincense, oak moss, pine, sage, woodruff.

Love: cinquefoil, jasmine, lavender, mugwort, orange, rose.

Luck or Justice: bay, bayberry, jasmine, patchouli, sandalwood, violet.

Meditation: acacia, copal, cypress, cedar, frankincense, jasmine, sage.

Power/Strength: dragon's blood, frankincense, patchouli, verbena.

Protection or Defense: bayberry, dragon's blood, frankincense, jasmine, patchouli, rosemary, woodruff.

Psychic Centers: basil, bay, copal, dragon's blood, frankincense, lavender, mugwort, vervain, woodruff.

Reincarnation: basil, lilac, patchouli, rose, sandalwood, sweetgrass.

Visions: basil, bay, copal, frankincense, mugwort, sage.

Willpower: bay, cedar, dragon's blood, patchouli, rosemary, sage, woodruff.

SMUDGES

Cedar: calming; comforting; purifies; protects.

Juniper: centering; clarity; cleansing; focus.

Lemongrass: refreshing; communications; channeling.

Pine: cleansing; renewal; strengthening.

Sage: cleansing; balance; banish negativity; strengthening.

Sweetgrass: call for ancestral and spirit helpers; ancient wisdom.

ESSENTIAL OILS

These may be rubbed on a candle for the appropriate goal for spell work by rubbing it on from center to either end to "dress" it or from top to bottom to draw, and bottom to top to banish; add to contents of a pouch of herbs to enhance the energies; dab on pulse points [cinnamon will burn]; oils are flammable, so use with care.

Note: see Herbal Correspondences for properties of unlisted oils.

Bay: attain desires; success; clarity of visions or dreams.

Basil: intuition; optimism; psychic awareness.

Cedar: cleansing; strength; meditation.

Cinnamon: energy; courage, gain goals, gain money.

Citrus Lemon/Lime: invigorate; joy; energy.

Cypress: calmative; soothes emotions; stability; Underworld.

Frankincense: cleanse aura; enhance psychic power; energizer.

Jasmine: love; intuition; spirituality; confidence; sexuality.

Lavender: balance; calming; cleansing; exorcism; Otherworld.

Orange: visions; psychic dreams; restfulness.

Patchouli: Earth energy; sexuality; strength; power; Underworld.

Peppermint: alertness; action; mental clarity.

Pine: energy; cleansing, strength, clarity, action; protection.

Rose: energy; love; gentleness; peace; happiness.

Rosemary: mental clarity; memory; protection; invigorate; blessing.

Sage: purify; cleanse; spiritual visions; inspiration.

Sandalwood: cleanse; purify; energy.

Vetivert: internal alignment; unified energies.

FEATHERS

To carry or to work into a charm or spell:

Crane: wisdom/knowledge

Dove: offer love

Eagle: protection

Goose: draw love

Hawk: protection

Ostrich: truth

Owl: instill wisdom

Seagull: travel

Swallow: good luck

Wren: safe voyage

HAIR

Lore and use in spell workings:

Boiling: fetch the owner of the hair

Braided: controlled/confined power; a sacrifice

Burning: death of old life and birth of new; pain or death to owner

Combing: brings storms if called upon

Cut: rejection of world, desires, ambition

Disheveled: raw power

Loose: creative, generative

Dark: sorcery/seduction

Fair: good/innocent

Red: magical power

PLANETARY ASSOCIATIONS

Sun: ☉ associated with *Number* 1; *Color:* gold, yellow; *Influence:* individuality, pride, success, honors, energy, display.

Moon: ☽ associated with *Number* 2; *Color:* silver, white; *Influence:* personality, sensitivity, intuition, desires, cycles, peace.

Mercury: ☿ associated with *Number* 5; *Color:* yellow, gray; *Influence:* communication, skill, agility, thinking, sensory, learning.

Venus: ♀ associated with *Number* 6; *Color:* pink, aqua; *Influence:* sociability, friendships, emotions, artistry, values, luxury.

Mars: ♂ associated with *Number* 9; *Color:* red, orange; *Influence:* dynamic energy, aggressiveness, willpower, sex drive.

Saturn: ♄ associated with *Number* 8; *Color:* black, indigo; *Influence:* ambition, structure, realism, self-preservation, business, self-control, restrictions/freedom, materiality.

Jupiter: ♃ associated with *Number* 3; *Color:* blue, violet; *Influence:* optimism, opportunity, health, expansion, finances, wealth, idealism, justice.

Neptune: ♆ associated with *Number* 7; *Color:* purple, lavender; *Influence:* occultism, subconscious, psychic energy, spirit, Otherworld, idealism, creativity, illusion.

Uranus: ♅ associated with *Number* 4; *Color:* green, variegate; *Influence:* sudden and unpredictable changes, tensions, news, originality, knowledge, innovation, divination.

Pluto: ♇ no associated *Number* 0; *Color:* brown, black; *Influence:* rebirth, transformation, sex, death, spirituality, extremes, evolution, life cycle free from bondage, Underworld.

PLANETARY TABLE

Planet	Tree	Animal	Flower	Gem	Scent
Sun	oak	lion	sunflower	topaz	frankincense
Moon	willow	dog/crab	orchid	quartz	jasmine
Mercury	palm	jackal	lime	opal	clove
Venus	laurel/myrtle	raven/dove	rose	emerald	benzoin
Mars	hickory	wolf/ram	nettle	ruby	dragon's blood
Saturn	cypress	bee/goat	lily	star sapphire	myrrh
Jupiter	olive	stag	clover	lapis lazuli	copal

PLANETARY HOURS FOR DAY & NIGHT

Use in timing spells for planetary influence during selected day; chart shows each hour of the day, from Sunrise [SR] to Sunset [SS], and from SS to SR, dividing the day into 12-hour blocks—but use the hours according to the actual SR and SS of the spell day [check almanac, newspaper or weather station]. Change SR and SS to military time [a 24-hour clock], convert to minutes, subtract SR from SS for total daytime minutes, and divide by 12 for actual length of each hour, apply to chart; for length of Night hours, subtract total daytime minutes of prior calculation from 144000 [2400 hours in a day converted to min.], and divide remainder by 12, then apply to Sunset Hours of chart.

Sunrise Hours

Hour	Sunday	Monday	Tuesday	Wednesday	Thursday	Friday	Saturday
1	Sun	Moon	Mars	Mercury	Jupiter	Venus	Saturn
2	Venus	Saturn	Sun	Moon	Mars	Mercury	Jupiter
3	Mercury	Jupiter	Venus	Saturn	Sun	Moon	Mars
4	Moon	Mars	Mercury	Jupiter	Venus	Saturn	Sun
5	Saturn	Sun	Moon	Mars	Mercury	Jupiter	Venus
6	Jupiter	Venus	Saturn	Sun	Moon	Mars	Mercury
7	Mars	Mercury	Jupiter	Venus	Saturn	Sun	Moon
8	Sun	Moon	Mars	Mercury	Jupiter	Venus	Saturn
9	Venus	Saturn	Sun	Moon	Mars	Mercury	Jupiter
10	Mercury	Jupiter	Venus	Saturn	Sun	Moon	Mars
11	Moon	Mars	Mercury	Jupiter	Venus	Saturn	Sun
12	Saturn	Sun	Moon	Mars	Mercury	Jupiter	Venus

Sunset Hours

Hour	Sunday	Monday	Tuesday	Wednesday	Thursday	Friday	Saturday
1	Jupiter	Venus	Saturn	Sun	Moon	Mars	Mercury
2	Mars	Mercury	Jupiter	Venus	Saturn	Sun	Moon
3	Sun	Moon	Mars	Mercury	Jupiter	Venus	Saturn
4	Venus	Saturn	Sun	Moon	Mars	Mercury	Jupiter
5	Mercury	Jupiter	Venus	Saturn	Sun	Moon	Mars
6	Moon	Mars	Mercury	Jupiter	Venus	Saturn	Sun
7	Saturn	Sun	Moon	Mars	Mercury	Jupiter	Venus
8	Jupiter	Venus	Saturn	Sun	Moon	Mars	Mercury
9	Mars	Mercury	Jupiter	Venus	Saturn	Sun	Moon
10	Sun	Moon	Mars	Mercury	Jupiter	Venus	Saturn
11	Venus	Saturn	Sun	Moon	Mars	Mercury	Jupiter
12	Mercury	Jupiter	Venus	Saturn	Sun	Moon	Mars

ZODIAC ASSOCIATIONS

Use these associations to choose colors for personalized dream pillows or power pouches for herbs, etc.; for aligning spells and crafts to the signs that relate to a person or animal by birthdate; for inscriptions, etc.

Sign	Symbol	Planet	Element	Colors
Aries:	♈	♂	△	white/pink
Taurus:	♉	♀	▽	red/yellow
Gemini:	♊	☿	△	red/blue
Cancer:	♋	☽	▽	green/brown
Leo:	♌	☉	△	red/green
Virgo:	♍	☿	▽	gold/black
Libra:	♎	♀	△	black/blue
Scorpio:	♏	♇	▽	brown/black
Sagittarius:	♐	♃	△	gold/red
Capricorn:	♑	♄	▽	red/brown
Aquarius:	♒	♅	△	blue/green
Pisces:	♓	♆	▽	white/green

Key

☿	♀	♂	♃	♄	♆	♅	♇
Mercury	Venus	Mars	Jupiter	Saturn	Neptune	Uranus	Pluto

☉	☽
The Sun	The Moon

▽	△	△	▽
Earth	Air	Fire	Water

♈	♉	♊	♋	♌	♍
Aries	Taurus	Gemini	Cancer	Leo	Virgo

♎	♏	♐	♑	♒	♓
Libra	Scorpio	Sagittarius	Capricorn	Aquarius	Pisces

TWELVE HOUSES OF THE ZODIAC

Use to inscribe symbols on spell items for influence or timing through an almanac.

House	Ruling Sign		Attributes of the House
One	♈	=	Personality; self; appearance
Two	♉	=	Money; material resources; values; esteem
Three	♊	=	Communication; schools; mind; siblings; community
Four	♋	=	Home; family; childhood; property
Five	♌	=	Creativity; children; love; pleasures; hobbies
Six	♍	=	Health; work; skills
Seven	♎	=	Marriage; partnerships; interactions; legal actions
Eight	♏	=	Death; regeneration; inheritances; surgeries; sexuality
Nine	♐	=	Philosophy; religion; academia; publications; travel
Ten	♑	=	Career; status; reputation; fame
Eleven	♒	=	Friends; fortune; career rewards; expectations
Twelve	♓	=	Psychic attainment; secrets; karma; institutions

TWELVE SIGNS OF THE ZODIAC

1. Aries:	♈ ruled by ♂	=	Leadership; vitality; focused; demanding
2. Taurus:	♉ ruled by ♀	=	Stable; stubborn; productive; practical
3. Gemini:	♊ ruled by ☿	=	Versatile; rational; changeable
4. Cancer:	♋ ruled by ☽	=	Intuition; psychic; nurture; family focused
5. Leo:	♌ ruled by ☉	=	Power; optimism; vitality; attention oriented
6. Virgo:	♍ ruled by ☿	=	Service; analysis; detailist; critical
7. Libra:	♎ ruled by ♀	=	Balance; harmony
8. Scorpio:	♏ ruled by ♇	=	Organized; transformation; passionate
9. Sagittarius:	♐ ruled by ♃	=	Idealism; independence; education
10. Capricorn:	♑ ruled by ♄	=	Materialist; industrious; disciplined
11. Aquarius:	♒ ruled by ♅	=	Individuality; intellectual; eccentricity
12. Pisces:	♓ ruled by ♆	=	Mysticism; sensitive; imaginative; intuitive

PLANETS IN SIGNS KEYWORDS

Combinations for inscriptions on spell materials or use in aligning spell castings with influential planets passing through the Zodiac signs, with both positive and negative possibilities shown. *Note:* the outer planets of the Solar System take years to pass through a sign, so this is basically informational—use an almanac to know what signs planets are in at any given day or hour, then adjust wording or timing of spell to make the best use of the planetary placement.

SUN ☉ in:

♈ = I Am; action, courage, leadership

♉ = I Have; possessions, planner, practical

♊ = I Think; alert, versatile, communication

♋ = I Feel; tenacious, caring, intuitive

♌ = I Will; courageous, loyal, achievement

♍ = I Analyze; service, industrious, thoughtful

♎ = I Balance; fair, partnership, connoisseur

♏ = I Desire; resourceful, intense, secretive

♐ = I See; idealistic, independent, tolerant

♑ = I Use; ambitious, methodical, fluctuating integrity

♒ = I Know; determined, honest, impersonal

♓ = I Believe; compassionate, sensitive, flexible

MOON ☽ in:

♈ = temperamental, energetic

♉ = stolid, hard working

♊ = quick wit, adaptable

♋ = warm, sensitive

♌ = ambitious, enthusiastic

♍ = clever, meticulous

♎ = courteous, humble

♏ = self-confident, psychic

♐ = optimistic, traditional

♑ = self-interests, ambition

♒ = humanitarian, stubborn

♓ = very psychic, artistic

MERCURY ☿ in:

♈ = alert, snap decisions

♉ = practical, business skills

♊ = mental agility, wide interests

♋ = antiquarian, homey

♌ = ideals, focused

♍ = language facility, occultist

♎ = refined, visionary

♏ = suspicious, spiritual

♐ = opinionated, conformity

♑ = status, thoughtful

♒ = occultist, detachment

♓ = psychic, creativity

MARS ♂ in:

♈ = initiative, hasty

♉ = purposeful, professionalism

♊ = impatient, pugnacious

♋ = touchy, subjective

♌ = enthusiasm, intrepid

♍ = efficient, detailist

♎ = coordinator, professional

♏ = uncompromising, reticent

♐ = activist, competitive

♑ = aspiring, innovator

♒ = staid, singular

♓ = inconsistent, investigative

VENUS ♀ in:

♈ = impulsive, self-centered
♉ = artistic, financial security
♊ = flirtatious, squander money
♋ = homey, frugal, occultist
♌ = sociable, ardent
♍ = perfectionist, critical
♎ = sympathetic, harmonious
♏ = passionate, occultist
♐ = generous, impassioned
♑ = controlled, acquisitive
♒ = speculative, intellectual
♓ = psychic, compassionate

JUPITER ♃ in:

♈ = fervent, opportunistic
♉ = conventional, practical
♊ = questing, communications
♋ = sympathetic, conservative
♌ = proclamations, vivacious
♍ = business, professional
♎ = self-sacrifice, interactive
♏ = willpower, spiritual
♐ = successful, seeker
♑ = possessive, wealthy
♒ = liberal, explorer
♓ = psychic studies, imaginative

SATURN ♄ in:

♈ = patience, innovation
♉ = materialistic, disciplined
♊ = rational, methodical
♋ = restrained, insecure
♌ = egotistical, self-centered
♍ = minutiae, technicalities
♎ = alliances, cooperative

♏ = suspicious, covert
♐ = inflexible, conceit
♑ = solemn, earnest
♒ = direct, aloof
♓ = nostalgic, despondent

NEPTUNE ♆ in:

♈ = egotism, imaginative
♉ = manifesting, discernible
♊ = rationality, micromanager
♋ = impressionable, impulsive
♌ = artistic, adulation
♍ = penetrating, judicious
♎ = impractical, ethereal
♏ = esoteric, addictive
♐ = nonconformist, cultist
♑ = systematic, unimaginative
♒ = innovation, disconnected
♓ = disassociation, illusions

URANUS ♅ in:

♈ = adventurous, temperamental
♉ = renovator, suppressed
♊ = restlessness, trailblazer
♋ = occultism, instability
♌ = rebellious, conceit
♍ = originality, research
♎ = discordant, unorthodox
♏ = perceptive, contentious
♐ = unconventional, arcane
♑ = restructuring, reorganization
♒ = anarchic, impartiality
♓ = meditative, impracticality

PLUTO ♀ in:

♈ = reform, inconclusive

♉ = reluctant, hesitant

♊ = dissemination, communication

♋ = exploration, homestead

♌ = struggles, conflicts

♍ = cleansing, systematic

♎ = associations, renovations

♏ = awareness, vigilance

♐ = re-assessment, new spirituality

♑ = reconstruction, re-organization

♒ = reformation, improvements

♓ = comprehension, insights

Signs In The Houses Keywords

Use for a general influence of the atmosphere for spell casting, inscriptions, or timings. *Note:* the Houses are stationary, but the Signs move, hence, at any given time of birth for the casting of a horoscope [sidereal is more accurate than tropical since the first is based on location of planets while the second is based on the Tropic latitudes of the Earth], the Rising Sign is the one on the horizon at that hour, and where it resides is labeled the First House, and all other Signs follow this one in order—but the Sun, which shows a person's Birth Sign during the Solar Year, is not necessarily in the Rising Sign; the placement of the planets within the Signs requires an Ephemeris which lists the daily positions of the planets in the twelve Signs of the Zodiac and their relationships to one another using calculations of degrees, but this is not essential for Craft workings.

FIRST: Physical, Personality

♈ = expectancy, mandates

♉ = gather & hold personal power/possessions

♊ = uncertainty, diversification

♋ = new ties bring freedom from past ties

♌ = self-expression, esteem, creativity

♍ = unassuming, methodical

♎ = objective, tactful, temperate

♏ = champion, intensity, fairness

♐ = eclectic, understanding, cheerful

♑ = materialism, status ambitions

♒ = idealism, aloof, decency, humane

♓ = introspective, obsessive, empathy

SECOND: Money, Possessions

♈ = self-assertion, mandates

♉ = indulgence, orderly

♊ = variable, judicious

♋ = nurturing, familial

♌ = quality, distinctive

♍ = marketing, sales

♎ = equalized, consistency

♏ = complications, difficulties

♐ = innovative, solvent

♑ = controlled, disciplined

♒ = exploitative, capitalizing

♓ = suppressed, concealed

THIRD: Communications, Thoughts
♈ = direct, argumentative, aggressive
♉ = sophistication, artistic/athletic strength
♊ = coordination, communication talent
♋ = sensitive, humorous, family focus
♌ = wit, power, warmth
♍ = critical, perfectionist, vying
♎ = fair, strong, theoretic
♏ = scrutiny, intrigue, confronting
♐ = cunning, legalistic, synopsis
♑ = planner, wary, climber
♒ = artistic, psychological, original
♓ = creative, able, spiritual

FOURTH: Home, Domestic Life
♈ = lively, chaotic
♉ = consistent, tranquil
♊ = intercommunication, security
♋ = cozy, nostalgic
♌ = possessive, expansive
♍ = tidy, serenity
♎ = decorative, comfortable
♎ = privacy, protective
♐ = spacious, studious
♑ = fundamental, lucid
♒ = singular, scientific
♓ = entertaining, atmospheric

FIFTH: Love, Fun, Children
♈ = enthusiastic, vivacious
♉ = considerate, attentive
♊ = socializing, carefree
♋ = familial, protective
♌ = loving, demanding
♍ = reticent, steadfast
♎ = romantic, indecisive
♏ = passionate, possessive
♐ = companionable, unregimented

♑ = reserved, hesitant
♒ = unorthodox, detached
♓ = sentimental, insecure

SIXTH: Work, Health
♈ = focused, demanding
♉ = productive, routine
♊ = motivator, adaptable
♋ = subtleties, creative
♌ = self-motivated, detailist
♍ = critical, precise
♎ = unmotivated, tedious
♏ = organized, transformative
♐ = self-starter, scattered
♑ = industrious, disciplined
♒ = creative, innovative
♓ = nuances, perceptive

SEVENTH: Marriage, Partners
♈ = projective, insensitive
♉ = reliable, sensual
♊ = variety, dispassionate
♋ = mothering, wavering
♌ = patriarchal, detached
♍ = fastidious, diligent
♎ = ambivalent, diplomatic
♏ = distant, suspicious
♐ = variety, enthusiasm
♑ = sober, impersonal
♒ = unconventional, generous
♓ = illusionary, romantic

EIGHT: Death, Inheritances
♈ = dynamic, forceful
♉ = unselfish, resolute
♊ = adaptable, appraising
♋ = impenetrable, withdrawn
♌ = solitude, rationalized

♍ = assessing, sensitive
♎ = liberal, shallow
♏ = introspection, occult
♐ = generous, noble
♑ = material, secure
♒ = rash, careless
♓ = evaluate, interpret

NINTH: Religion, Education, Travel
♈ = restless, fervent
♉ = tasteful, immanent
♊ = articulate, expressive
♋ = emotional, urgency
♌ = travel, metaphysical
♍ = systematic, scientific
♎ = comfort, adjustable
♏ = forceful, eclectic, charismatic
♐ = honor, assurance
♑ = conservative, prestige
♒ = stimulating, radical
♓ = existential, achiever

TENTH: Public Status, Honors
♈ = humanitarian, compassionate
♉ = stimulating, recognition
♊ = versatile, communications
♋ = artistic, creativity
♌ = cooperation, affability
♍ = insightful, demonstrative
♎ = extremist, obsessive
♏ = burdened, dominance
♐ = expansive, visionary
♑ = deprivation, disciplined

♒ = metaphysical, humane
♓ = malleable, compliant

ELEVENTH: Friends, Wishes, Government, Career Rewards
♈ = challenging, participatory
♉ = pragmatic, steady
♊ = ability, collative
♋ = security, discerning
♌ = confidant, loyalty
♍ = selective, mature
♎ = contributor, pacifistic
♏ = earnest, revitalizing
♐ = visionary, activist
♑ = conservative, serious
♒ = originality, insular
♓ = sympathetic, innovative

TWELFTH: Secrets, Psychic, Spiritism, Institutions, Private
♈ = usefulness, internalized
♉ = disallowing, renouncing
♊ = curious, diffuse
♋ = intuitive, psychological
♌ = service, charitable
♍ = investigator, organizations
♎ = inhibited, tranquil
♏ = power, channeling
♐ = academia, religious
♑ = healthiness, counseling
♒ = judgmental, distinctive
♓ = self-sacrificing, compassionate

PLANETARY SPIRITS

NAMES OF PLANETARY SPIRITS

From Medieval Grimoires; may use as relates to planetary correlations in spell casting:

♄ Omeliel, Anachiel, Ariel

♃ Netoniel, Parasiel

☉ Shadiel ["Horned One"]

♄ Ithuriel, Eschiel

☿ Vehiel, Vaol, Cassiel

♀ Aeliel, Monachiel, Armael

☽ Azarel, Ichadiel, Yashiel

PLANETARY SPIRITS

These come from the Medieval Grimoires and represent the Pagan energies of the Sun, Moon, and Planets as were then known, with powers, metal, and two signs of the zodiac represented, except for the Sun and Moon; symbols may be inscribed in candles and spirits invoked to give added power to the already described influences of these planets; selected symbols may be drawn on a paper Pentacle with the cauldron or other spell material set on top, or the symbols may be drawn onto paper along with the rest of the spell or charm words and burned, added to the pouch, etc. These are not the same as angelic or demonic influences that came to characterize Ceremonial Magic.

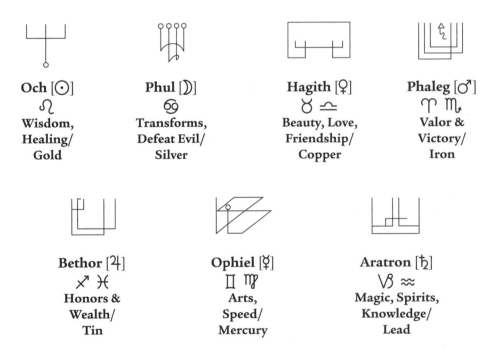

Och [☉]
♌
Wisdom,
Healing/
Gold

Phul [☽]
♋
Transforms,
Defeat Evil/
Silver

Hagith [♀]
♉ ♎
Beauty, Love,
Friendship/
Copper

Phaleg [♂]
♈ ♏
Valor &
Victory/
Iron

Bethor [♃]
♐ ♓
Honors &
Wealth/
Tin

Ophiel [☿]
♊ ♍
Arts,
Speed/
Mercury

Aratron [♄]
♑ ♒
Magic, Spirits,
Knowledge/
Lead

NAMES OF POWER

From Medieval Grimoires; may be added to spell materials if desired, although some are names of early deities turned into demons, and others are names from talking in tongues or frenzy—used primarily in ceremonial magics.

♄ Agiel; Zazel
♃ Hismael; Yophiel
☿ Tiriel; Taphthartharath
♀ Hagiel; Kedemel

♂ Graphiel; Bartzabel
☉ Nakiel; Sorath
☽ Malcah; Chashmodai

NAMES OF DARK POWER

Agares: language, overturn the powerful

Aini: cunning and truth

Amduscias: music; trees

Andras: discord

Andrealphus: measurements

Andromlius: return stolen goods

Asamodeus: power; control

Asmoday: virtue; mathematics

Astaroth: secrets

Beleth: love

Beliel: favors

Cimeries: logic

Eligor: hidden things

Gamygym: liberal arts and sciences

Gomory: treasures

Hagenti: wisdom

Ipos: past and future

Lerajie: archer in green [The Hunter]

Marbas: mechanics; cures

Morax: astronomy, stones, herbs

Orias: planetary assets and attributes

Ose: divination; secret knowledge

Paimon: familiars, magic

Seere: transports or conveys

Stolas: stones and herbs

Valac: serpents

Valefor: theft

Valpula: philosophy

Vassage: find what is lost or hidden

NUMERICAL CORRELATIONS

Numbers assigned to letters may be used to see the influence of a proper name, address, place of birth and birthdate, by adding together and reducing to a single digit number; can use the birth name to choose a Craft Name whose letters reduce to the same single digit, or a different name can be chosen to fit a specific number whose influence is desired; tarot Major Arcana cards can be associated with these numbers, as under Tarot in Part 11; and may also be used for the number value of the date for spell work.

1 = letters A, J, S; ☉ Sun; Fire; Developing the Self, the All, Beginning and Ending; Wholeness and Unity.

2 = letters B, K, T; ☽ Moon; Water; Sensitivity and Personality, Truth, Blessing, Duality; Balance.

3 = letters C, L, U; ♃ Jupiter; Fire; Health and Opportunity, Triads and Triple Aspects; Career.

4 = letters D, M, V; ♅ Uranus; Air; Divination and Knowledge, Foundations, Strength; the Elementals.

5 = letters E, N, W; ☿ Mercury; Air; Communication, the Pentagram [4 Elementals + Spirit]; Fulfillment.

6 = letters F, O, X; ♀ Venus; Earth; Sociable and Emotions, Cats, Unity of Triple Goddess and Triple God, Allure, Decisions.

7 = letters G, P, Y; ♆ Neptune; Water; Subconscious, Intuition, Psychical, Mysticism, Union of Dual Triads; Change.

8 = letters H, Q, Z; ♄ Saturn; Earth; Freedom, Dual Foundations, Material and Spiritual Worlds, Law, Self-discipline; Travel/News.

9 = letters I, R; ♂ Mars; Fire; Aggression, Energy, New Path, Immortality, Indestructibility; Binding.

NUMBERS IN DIVINATION

Possible influences, good or ill, of a number made from converting dates and letters to numbers and reducing to 1–9, 10, 11, 12, 13, 22.

1: Fixed in purpose, single-minded, powerful, obstinate, ambitious, independent, self-sufficient/assertive/reliant, inventive, creative.

2: Tactful, conciliatory, even-tempered, diplomatic, persuasive, non-assertive, changeable, deceitful, cruel, malicious.

3: Imaginative, energetic, bright, expression, versatile, witty, successful, charming, ambitious, proud, lucky, commanding, seeks approval, over-extended, energies diffused.

4: Solid, practical, organized, administrative, calm, stern, respectable, steady, industrious, hard-earned success, detail oriented, bursts of rage, suspicious, resentful, poor, defeat, melancholic.

5: Restlessness, impatience, clever, takes risks, speculator, adventurer, resourceful, quick-tempered, conceited, sarcastic, self-indulgent, excesses.

6: Harmony, domesticity, peaceful, happiness, kindly, reliable, friendly, loyal, conscientious, idealistic, affectionate, wholesome, conventional, eventual success, artistic, teacher, thorough, fussy, smug, gossipy, conceited, obstinate.

7: Reclusive, mystic, scholarly, philosopher, occultist, meditative, aloof, penetrative, imaginative, fey, strange.

8: Power, money, wordly involvement, practical, tough, cautious, tenacious, materialist, hard worker, curbed eccentricity, rebellious.

9: Mental/spiritual achievement, impulsive, sympathetic, visionary, humanitarian, determined, science, teaching, artistic, unorthodox, intolerant of opposition, self-centered.

10: Cycles of beginnings and endings and new beginnings.

11: Revelation, powerful personality, righteous convictions, destiny sense.

12: Otherworldly, mystical, meditative, visions, arcane knowledge.

13: Cycles, phases, completeness, wholeness, unified.

22: Masterful, driving energy, inner vision, brilliant, extremes possible for beneficial or detrimental societal works.

RUNIC TABLES

Use to inscribe candles, write on paper to be burned or added to spell or charm; may match color of goal and other spell materials with the color and meaning of runic symbol.

Name	Sign	Letter	Meaning	Color
Osa	ᚠ	[OE]	the God; good fortune; favorable outcome	green/white
As	ᚨ	[AE]	ancestor; signs; gain ancient wisdom	indigo/purple
Beorc	ᛒ	[B]	Goddess; fertility; growth; new beginnings	white/green
Daeg	ᛗ	[D]	daybreak; between the worlds; breakthrough	pale violet
Eh	ᛗ	[E]	movement; safe journey; progress; changes	blue
Feoh	ᚠ	[[F]	material wealth; fulfillment; ambition satisfied	green
Gefu	ᚷ	[G]	union; partnership; love; gifts; self-confidence	pink/red
Eoh	ᛇ	[Z]	a channel; action; Otherworld communication	indigo/purple
Haegl	ᚻ	[H]	hail; limits/disruptions; awakening	white/blue
Is	ᛁ	[I]	ice; immobility; rest period; stop slander	white/silver
Gera	ᛃ	[J]	year; harvest; rewards; tangible results from work	white/green
Ken	ᚲ	[K/C]	transforming fire; opening energy; fresh start	white/gold
Lagu	ᛚ	[L]	fluidity; water; psychic power; intuition; vitality	blue/violet
Mannaz	ᛗ	[M]	Self; self-improvement; cooperation; meditation	indigo/violet
Nyd	ᚾ	[N]	constraint; self-control; overcome obstacles	white/blue
Ing	ᛝ	[NG]	the Horned God; fertility; family; completion	indigo
Ethel	ᛟ	[OE]	possession; home; social status; acquisitions	white/gold
Perth	ᛈ	[P]	destiny; hidden forces; unexpected luck; initiation	blue/green
Rad	ᚱ	[R]	travel; quest; find what is sought; attunement	blue/violet
Sigel	ᛋ	[S/Z]	Sun wheel; wholeness; healing; vital energy; power	orange/gold/red
Tyr	ᛏ	[T]	victory; success; courage; favorable outcome	white/gold
Thorn	ᚦ	[TH]	protection; gateway; foes neutralized; defense	black
Uruz	ᚢ	[U]	strength; physical health; courage; promotion	green/brown
Wyn	ᚹ	[W]	joy; comfort; happiness; harmony; love	pink/yellow
Eolh	ᛉ	[EA]	elk; protection; friendship; going unnoticed	white
Wyrd	[ ]	[—]	unknowable fate; destiny; cosmic influence	black/white

BASIC SPELL RUNES & SYMBOLS

Changes: ᛃ ᛇ ᚾ ᛗ

Communication: ᛗ ᚨ

Creativity: ᚠ ᚲ ᛇ ᛈ

Health : ᚢ ᚱ ᚲ ᛉ ᛋ ᛒ

Fertility: ᛝ ᚹ ᛗ ᛃ

Love: ᚷ ᚹ ᚹ ᛗ ᛚ ᛝ

Luck and Wishes: ᚠ ᚹ ᚨ

Money: ᚠ ᛝ

Protection: ᚦ ᚾ ᚾ ᛁ ᛉ ᛒ ᛗ ⟁ ⊗ ᛉ

Strength/Victory: ᚢ ᚾ ᚦ ᚱ ᚹ ᛇ ᛋ ᛏ

Travel: ᚱ ᛗ

218

LIST OF OGHAM FEWS

Use for inscriptions on tools, spells, and charms; three Worlds of four Realms each: Middle-world or physical, Underworld or spirit, Otherworld or higher astral, with Paths leading to each world [*see Divinations section*].

Few		Letter	Path [Realm]	Meaning
⊢	Beithe [Birch]	B	Realm [U]	Beginnings/Energy
⊨	Luis [Rowan]	L	Path [U]	Insight/Foreknowledge/Enlivening
⊨	Fearn [Alder]	F	Realm [M]	Inner Strength/Foundations
⊨	Saille [Willow]	S	Path [O]	Intuition/Flexibility
⊨	Nion [Ash]	N	Realm [O]	Awakening/Rebirth/Peace
⊣	Huath [Hawthorn]	H	Realm [U]	Pleasure/Misfortune/Cleansing
⊣	Duir [Oak]	D	Path [U]	Truth/Endurance/Strength
⊣	Tinne [Holly]	T	Realm [M]	Balance/Retribution
⊣	Coll [Hazel]	C	Path [O]	Wisdom/Creativity/Perception
⊣	Quert [Apple]	Q	Realm [O]	Regeneration/Eternity/Life
✕	Muin [Vine]	M	Realm [U]	Introspection/Other Sight
✕	Gort [Ivy]	G	Path [U]	Developing Skills/Learning
✕	Ngetal [Reed]	NG	Realm [M]	Harmony/Inner Development
✕	Straif [Blackthorn]	Z	Path [O]	Coercion/Control Through Force
✕	Ruis [Elder]	R	Realm [O]	Change/Evolution
⊹	Ailm [Fir]	A	Realm [U]	Rulership/Vigor/Discretion
⊹	Onn [Gorse]	O	Path [U]	Wisdom Collated /Life Changes
⊹	Ur [Heather]	U	Realm [M]	Fervor/Gateway/Success/Gains
⊹	Eadha [Aspen]	E	Path [O]	Intuition/Overcoming Obstacles
⊹	Iodho [Yew]	I/Y	Realm [O]	Transformation/Ends/Immortality
|	Blank [Mistletoe]	Blank	None	Cosmic Influence/Destiny/Fate

ENERGY POINTS/CHAKRAS

Top of Head [Crown]:	White	Spiritual Union With the Divine/Universe
Psychic Eye [Third Eye]:	Purple	Psychic Awareness; Insight
Throat [Throat]:	Blue	Expression; Speech; Power of Words
Heart [Heart]:	Green	Energies Meet; Love; Healing
Stomach [Solar Plexus]:	Yellow	Will Power; Balance
Abdomen [Navel]:	Orange	Inner [Spiritual] Strength; Fortitude
Base of Spine [Root]:	Red	Earth Energy Entry; Foundation
Palms of Hands:	Indigo	Elemental Fire [R]; Elemental Water [L]
Soles of Feet:	Brown	Elemental Earth [L]; Elemental Air [R]

Moon Gardening

Use the Signs and Moon Phases for growing and gathering own herbs, etc.

Fruitful Signs:

Cancer—plant leafy things
    plant above ground fruit

Scorpio—prune to encourage growth

Pisces—plant root things

Taurus—plant root crops

Capricorn—prune to strengthen
bulbs, roots, stalks growing

Libra—plant flowers and vines

Barren Signs:

Leo—kill weeds/pests
    cultivate/till

Gemini—harvest herbs/roots

Virgo—plow, till, weed

Sagittarius—prune to stop growth

Aquarius—reap crops/herbs/roots
    ground cultivation, kill weeds/pests

Aries—gather/store herbs/roots
    prune to reduce growth

New	1st Quarter	Full	Last Quarter	New
Plant flowers, annuals; above-ground crops; crops with seeds outside	Plant above ground crops with seeds inside	Plant root crops; bulbs; perennials	Do not plant anything	

HERBAL & PLANT LISTING BY PURPOSE

Balance: basil, chamomile, comfrey, mullein, nettle, woodruff.

Blessing: chamomile, dianthus, elder flowers, fennel, mint, oats, rosemary, rue, vervain.

Cleansing/Purification: avens, Betony, benzoin, burdock, clove, hyssop, lavender, mullein, parsley, pine, rosemary, thyme, vervain, wormwood, yarrow.

Consecration: acacia, anise, basil, clover, dragon's blood, hyssop, lavender, mistletoe, mugwort, nettle, rosemary, rue, sunflower, vervain.

Countering Negative Energies: agrimony, avens, fennel. holly, hyssop, motherwort, rowan, rue, vervain.

Courage: basil, borage, mullein, rosemary, thyme.

Creativity: anise seed, basil, catnip, hawthorn, lavender, St. Johnswort, vervain.

Divination: anise seed, basil, bay, cinquefoil, clover, damiana, dittany of Crete, eyebright, honeysuckle, hops, lavender, marigold, moonwort, mugwort, mullein, orange peel, rowan, thyme, vervain, woodruff, wormwood, yarrow.

Encourage Changes: dragon's blood, linden, purple heather, woodruff.

Energy/Power/Strength: cinquefoil, dragon's blood, elder flower, fennel, St. Johnswort, vervain, woodruff.

Fortune/Justice: bay, bergamot, cinquefoil, lemon balm, orange peel, star anise, vervain, woodruff.

Happiness/Peace: fennel, lavender, loosestrife, rosemary, vervain, yarrow.

Healing: cinquefoil, comfrey, coriander, hops, lavender, lemon balm, mullein, mustard, rosemary, rue, sage, St. Johnswort, tansy, thyme.

Love: apple, avens, basil, cardamom, catnip, dill flowers, elm, ginger, lavender, lemonbalm, linden leaves, marigold, marjoram, moonwort, mustard seed, orange peel, red heather, rosemary, vetivert, willow, yarrow.

Meditation: acacia, benzoin, chamomile, frankincense, woodruff.

Money: basil, bergamot, chamomile, clove, dill seeds, mint, moonwort, nutmeg, oats, vetivert.

Protection/Defense: betony, birch, burdock, cumin, dianthus, dill leaves, fennel, fern, marjoram, mint, mugwort, mullein, mustard, parsley, rosemary, rue, sage, vervain, white heather, woodruff, wormwood, yarrow.

Psychic Awareness: bay, betony, burdock, cinnamon, elderflower, lavender, mace, marigold, star anise, woodruff.

Releasing Negativity: betony, clove, hyssop, mugwort, rosemary, St. Johnswort, thyme, vervain, vetivert, yarrow.

Sealing/Sending Positive Energy: angelica, wormwood.

Spirit Contact/Blessings: lilac, purple heather, mint, Solomon's Seal.

Strength/Willpower: rosemary, St. Johnswort

Wisdom: elder, sage, willow.

HERBAL & PLANT LISTING BY
DARK POWER PURPOSE

Return-To-Sender [bounce back specifically sent harmful intent and negativity]: agrimony, ginger, lady's slipper, mullein, nettle, rue, tamarisk, thistle, unicorn root.

Deflection [diffuse malevolence or ill will]: anise, blackthorn, boneset, elder, ginger, lady's slipper, mullein, nettle, orrisroot, paprika, pennyroyal, peppercorn, rue, tamarisk, vetiver, willow.

Retribution [return negative energy to sender and seal it there]: blackthorn, elder, rue, vetiver, willow.

Curses [call negative energy for a purpose]: cypress, dragon's blood, wormwood, rowan wood, yarrow [arrowroot].

Exorcisms [disperse negative energies so positive energies may enter]: agrimony, asafetida, avens, boneset, clove, cypress, dragon's blood, fern, frankincense, garlic, ginger, juniper berry, lavender, lilac, mullein, nettle, peppercorn, rue, rosemary, sage, sandalwood, tamarisk, thistle, unicorn root, vervain, yarrow.

Purgings and Releasing [lesser exorcisms to absorb negativity for removal]: elder, fern, garlic, hyssop, lavender, lilac, mugwort, onion, sage, skullcap, St. Johnswort, thistle, valerian, willow, woodruff.

Crone, Dark Moon, Death/Passages, Hunter, Lunar Eclipse, Otherworld, Protection, Solar Eclipse, Transitions/Rebirth, Underworld: absinthe, acacia, amaranth, anise, apple, ash leaves/berries, artemesia, balsam, bay, bayberry, blackberry, black currant, briar, burdock, cypress, damiana, dandelion root, dianthus, dittany of Crete, elder, elecampane, fennel, garlic, ginger root, hawthorn, hazel, jasmine, lavender, lilac, linden, mace, marigold, mugwort, mullein, myrrh, oak, orris root, paprika, patchouli, pomegranate seeds, purple heather, rosemary, rowanwood, sage, sandalwood, skullcap, St. Johnswort, tansy, thistle, thyme, valerian, vervain, willow, woodruff.

HERBAL & PLANT CORRESPONDENCES

Acacia: altar offering/consecration, aids psychic powers, meditation.

Agrimony: protection, returns spells to their sender, promotes sleep.

Alder: whistles entice the Elemental Air, Fairy invocations.

Allspice: prosperity, energy.

Angelica: protection, divination, consecration.

Anise: purify/consecrate, protection, spirit aid in spells, divination, aids creativity.

Apple: food for departing spirits, love, health, attract unicorns, Underworld.

Ash: wands, protection, leaves for prophetic dreams, prosperity.

Avens: purification, love, protection from negative energies.

Banana [leaf/flower]**:** fertility, prosperity, Goddess and God as One Divinity.

Basil: protection, courage, wealth, love, divination, creativity, repels negativity.

Bay: psychic powers, purification, wishes, divination, justice, wisdom, promotion.

Benzoin: purification, prosperity, meditation.

Bergamot: success, wealth, justice.

Betony: purification, protection, psychic awareness, banish despair/nightmares.

Birch: wands, protection, purification, ward negativity, cleansing, the Goddess.

Blackberry: protection, health, prosperity, Shadowland, the God.

Blackthorn: return evil to the sender, thwart negative energies, barrier, Hecate.

Borage: psychic power, protection, courage.

Briar: clairvoyant dreams, Fairy magics.

Broom: purification, protection, non-Fairy magics only as they do not like it.

Burdock: purification, protection, ward negativity.

Cardamom: love, romance.

Carnation [Dianthus]**:** protection, strength, healing, Goddess offering.

Catnip: love, creativity, cat magics, familiars, restfulness.

Chamomile: meditation, rest, calmness, purification, prosperity.

Cherry: creativity, hope, expectations.

Cinnamon: spiritual/psychic powers, protection, success, business, healing.

Cinquefoil: prosperity, protection, purification, divination, healing, good fortune.

Citron: psychic ability, clarity.

Clove: wealth, purification, ward negativity, cleansing.

Clover: divination, consecrations, money. luck, love, Otherworld.

Coltsfoot: karma, political power.

Comfrey: healing, safe travel.

Coriander: health, money.

Cornflower: psychic ability.

Cumin: protection of belongings.

Damiana: divination, protection of property, the Goddess.

Dill: money, protection, love.

Dittany of Crete: divination, psychic power.

Dragon's Blood: consecration, power, life cycle, changes.

Elder: wands, Fairies, blessings (never burn the wood), magic power.

Elm: Elves, love.

Eyebright: aiding mental powers, divination.

Fennel: protection, the God, deflect negative energies.

Ferns: protection, calling rain, wisdom.

Feverfew: ward sickness, ward accidents in travel.

Fir: manifestation.

Foxglove [POISON]: grown to protect the house and yard, source of digitalis.

Frankincense: protection, blessing, spirituality, meditation, power, sacredness.

Furze/Gorse: protection, preparation for conflict.

Garlic: protection, power.

Ginger: love, success, money, power.

Hawthorn: wands, fertility, protection, creativity/Witchery skills, Fairy attraction.

Hazel: Fairies, healing, protection, luck, communication, wands, Witchery skills.

Heather: [red] love, [white] protection, [purple] spiritual development, beauty.

Holly: [POISON] balance, dream magic, the God of Winter.

Honeysuckle: divination, dreams.

Hops: health, sleep, divination.

Hyssop: purification, wards negativity.

Iris: wisdom.

Ivy: protection, friendship, healing, perseverance.

Kelp: winds, protection, psychic powers.

Lavender: Elves, purification, peace, psychic awareness, creativity, cleansing.

Lemon Balm: success, health, love, justice, good luck.

Lilac: protection, Underworld, Otherworld, beauty, love.

Linden: [lime tree] protection, immortality, good fortune, sleep, love.

Loosestrife: harmony, peace, accord.

Mace: psychic power, alertness.

Marigold: marriage, clairvoyant dreams, Fairies, protection, psychic powers.

Marjoram: love, protection, wealth.

Mint: protection, prosperity, offering to helpful spirits.

Mistletoe [POISON]: fertility, consecration, protection, healing, psychic ability.

Motherwort: protection, confidence, wards negative energies, imagination.

Moonwort: divination, love, prosperity.

Mugwort: divination, consecration, strength, protection.

Mullein: protection, purification, divination, health, courage.

Mustard: good luck, health, protection, fertility.

Myrrh: protection, ward negativity, purification/consecration, Underworld, binding.

Nettle: Elves, Fairies, consecration, restore balance, protection, life cycles.

Nutmeg: prosperity, comfort.

Nuts and Cones: fertility, drawing wealth.

Oak: wands; purification, money, health, fertility, the God.

Oats: wealth, security, offering.

Orange Peel: love, good fortune, divination.

Orris Root: companionship, spirit communication, protection, occultism, divination.

Parsley: purification, protection.

Patchouli: money, fertility, Earth, Underworld.

Pecan: prosperity, abundance.

Pepper: protection, ward negativity.

Pine: purification, cleansing, money, courage.

Rose [hips]: love, divination, psychic power.

Rosemary: purification, blessing, protection, love, health, Elves, courage.

Rowan: wands, knowledge, divination, spirit help, home protection, inspiration.

Rue [POISON]: blessing, consecration, protection, health, ward negative energy.

Sage: protection, wisdom, health, purification, artistic ability.

St. Johnswort: good health, willpower, enhance creativity, banish negativity.

Sandalwood: protection, ward negativity, spirit offering.

Solomon's Seal [Dropberry; Sealroot]: Elemental offering, protection.

Star Anise: psychic power, good fortune.

Straw: Fairies, images, protection (do not burn magic infused straw).

Sunflower: Elves, purification, consecrations, changes, bright prospects.

Tansy: health, happiness.

Thyme: ward negativity, courage, purification, healing, psychic power, swift action.

Trefoil: Fairies, protection, luck.

Vervain: offering, love, purification, riches, creativity, visions, ward psychic attack.

Vetivert: love, money, ward negativity.

Wheat: fertility, wealth, good fortune.

Willow: wands, divination, love, protection, the Goddess.

Woodruff: clear away barriers, protection, success, changes, psychic awareness.

Wormwood [Absinthe] [POISON]: evocation, divination/scrying, protection.

Yarrow: divination, love, happy marriage, ward negativity, defense, protection.

Yew [POISON]: death and rebirth, athame handle.

DARK POWER HERBAL & PLANT ASSOCIATIONS

Absinthe: Crone, Dark Moon, Lunar Eclipse, Underworld.

Acacia: inspiration, protection, Lughnassadh passage, psychic power.

Agrimony: exorcism, sleep, calming, protection, return-to-sender.

Amaranth [Cockscomb]: passages, Samhain, immortality, spirit communication.

Anise: Crone, protection, purification, psychic power, divination, seek answers, spirit contact, deflection of negativity.

Apple: Underworld, rebirth, immortality, food for the dead, Samhain.

Artemesia: Dark Lady, Dark Moon, Lunar Eclipse.

Asafetida: a bad-smelling resin used for exorcism and protection.

Ash [bark/leaves]: death, passage, Beltane, protection, health, prophecy, insight, dreams.

Avens: exorcism, purification.

Balsam: Underworld passage, psychic energy, spirit communication.

Bay: Yule, Imbolc, psychic power, strength, purification, healing.

Bayberry: Yule, transition.

Belladonna [Deadly Nightshade] [POISON: substitute Dittany of Crete or Mugwort]: Samhain, astral travel, psychic power, visions.

Blackberry: Dark Lord, Lughnassadh, Hunter, protection.

Black Currant [Cassis]: Lord of Shadows, Hunter/Crone, Wild Hunt, Shadowland.

Blackthorn: defense, deflect negativity, retribution, protection, Otherworld contact.

Boneset: deflection, exorcism, protection.

Briar: defense, protection, enhance Witch's power, divination, dreams.

Burdock: wards negativity, purification, protection.

Clove: banishing/releasing, exorcism, protection, spirit companion offering.

Cypress: banishing/releasing, binding, death, immortality, eternity, Underworld, Shadowland, Hades, Hecate, Cybele, oracles.

Damiana: visions, healing.

Dandelion [root]: psychic power, spirit contact, Otherworld.

Dianthus [Carnation]: protection, power, health, blood, regeneration.

Dittany of Crete: astral travel, spirit communication.

Dragon's Blood [palm resin]: binding, energy, changes, courage, strength, power, exorcism, protection.

Elder [seeds are POISON; use the flowers]: Crone, banishing/releasing, defense, deflection, retribution, Litha, blessings, wards negativity, Otherworld, protection, visions, spirit contact, healing, occult learning, healing, exorcism.

Elecampane [Elfdock]: psychic power, protection, divination, Otherworld contact.

Elm [Elvin]: protection, attraction, energy, passages.

Fennel: protection, purification, healing, ward negativity.

Fern: banishing/releasing, exorcism, protection, Samhain, Otherworld.

Fir: Yule, Underworld, arcane wisdom.

Foxglove [POISON; substitute Tamarisk]: defense, protection, return to sender, deflection.

Frankincense: anointing, strength, power, energy, exorcism, Yule, Beltane, visions, Lughnassadh, protection, consecration.

Garlic: protection, ward negativity, invoke the Dark Goddess, exorcism, healing.

Ginger [root]: psychic power, protection, exorcism, deflection, return to sender, drawing, spirit contact.

Gorse [Furze]: protection, preparation for conflict.

Hawthorn: protection, Witchcraft, Beltane, Otherworld, Fairies, ward negativity.

Hazel: invoke Otherworld aid, attract Fair Folk, enhance Witch's power.

Hellebore [POISON; substitute Black Currant]: Crone, Lord of Shadows, visions, Underworld, psychic power, exorcism, astral travel.

Hemlock: [POISON; substitute Lilac]: power, purification, protection, astral travel.

Henbane: [POISON; substitute Mace]: Underworld, spirit contact.

Holly: [POISON; substitute Frankincense]: energy, strength, power, insight, protection, deflection.

Hyssop: protection, purification, cleansing, remove negativity/malevolence.

Jasmine: anointing, balance, Ostara, divination, dreams, insight, astral projection.

Jimsonweed [Datura][POISON; substitute Agrimony]: deflection, return to sender, ward negativity, protection.

Juniper Berry: visions, purification, spirit contact, exorcism, protection.

Lady's Slipper: ward negative energy, return to sender, protection, deflection.

Lavender [Elf Leaf]: anointing, exorcism, purification, Litha, honor Ancient Ones, protection, cleansing, Otherworld/Sidhe contact, opening psychic centers, spirit contact.

Lilac: Underworld, Beltane, exorcism, protection, cleansing.

Linden: immortality, protection, Underworld.

Mace: psychic power, enhance spirit contact, Underworld.

Mandrake [POISON; substitute Ginger Root or Fennel Root]: calling upon spirits, communicate with spirits, offering, exorcism, protective watcher.

Marigold [Calendula]: divination, Otherworld, Fairy offering, Beltane, Mabon, protection, dreams, psychic power.

Mastic: spirit contact, enhance psychic power, strength.

May-apple [American Mandrake] [POISON; substitute Ginger Root or Fennel Root]: spirit contact, death, spirit offering, substitute for mandrake.

Mugwort [Artemesia]: Dark Lady, Dark Moon, Lunar Eclipse, psychic power, dreams, banishing/releasing, divination, cleansing magic mirrors and crystal balls, Litha, astral projection, strength, protection, healing.

Mullein [GraveyardDust]: Crone energy, courage, exorcism, divination, protection, return to sender, deflection.

Myrrh: Imbolc, Mabon, exorcism, protection, purification, power.

Nettle: protection, exorcism, return to sender, deflection, courage.

Nightshade [Bittersweet] [POISON; substitute mugwort]: Crone/Hunter energy, return to sender, Lunar Eclipse, Solar Eclipse, banishing/releasing, astral projection, strength.

Oak [Galls/leaves/wood/acorns]: strength, power, purification, charms, wisdom, truth, Litha, Mabon, Samhain, Yule.

Orris Root: power, protection, divination, deflection.

Paprika: protection, wards malevolent energy, deflection.

Patchouli: Samhain, Underworld, passage, Earth energies.

Pennyroyal [POISON; substitute Blackthorn]: deflection, power, protection, ward negative energy.

Peppercorn: protection, power, deflection, exorcism.

Pomegranate: Underworld, passage, hidden wealth, attainment, protection, secret knowledge, deflection.

Purple Heather: peace, cleansing, spirituality, Samhain, Imbolc, Lughnassadh.

Rosemary (Elf Leaf): courage, exorcism, protection, purification, dreams, health, Sidhe contact, strength, cleansing, Otherworld.

Rowan [Mountain Ash]: binding, divination, secret knowledge, divination, psychic power, call upon spirits/the Sidhe for aid, protection, Underworld travels.

Rue [POISON; substitute Tamarisk]: exorcism, health, enhance magics, return to sender, deflection, retribution, ward malevolence/negative energies.

Sage: Yule, Mabon, immortality, wisdom, protection, spirit/Otherworld offering, exorcism, purification.

Sandalwood: meditation, intuitive power, protection, spirit contact, exorcism.

Skullcap: protection, healing, passage to Underworld Midsummer [Litha], power, protection.

St. Johnswort: banishing/releasing, Otherworld, Midsummer [Litha], power, protection.

Tamarisk [Flowering Cypress]: exorcism, divination, deflection, return to sender.

Tansy: Dark Goddess, immortality, Otherworld offering.

Thistle: protection, warding/changing bad luck, Mabon, exorcism, deflection of negative energies, return to sender, spirit contact.

Thyme: ward negativity, Litha, protection, psychic power, healing, purification, Otherworld.

Turmeric: protection, cleansing, purification.

Turnip: Samhain lanterns, spirit lights, ward negative energies, protection, rebirth, passage.

Unicorn Root [Ague Root]: protection, return to sender, exorcism.

Valerian: power, purging, releasing, protection, purification.

Vervain [Verbena]**:** purification, cleansing, protection, psychic power, strength, luck, anointing, exorcism, offering, open psychic centers, creativity, guidance, Underworld riches, divination, dreams, Otherworld contact.

Vetiver: deflection, ward malevolence, retribution.

Willow: Hecate, death, Underworld, passage, protection, spirit contact, deflection.

Woodruff: changes, Herne, Greenman, clear barriers, overcome obstacles, Beltane, protection.

Wormwood [POISON; substitute Mugwort or Cypress]**:** binding, exorcism, Samhain, divination, spirit evocation, protection, Dark Moon, Lunar Eclipse, dreams, psychic power.

Yarrow [Arrowroot]**:** exorcism, releasing, divination, psychic power, dreams, courage, protection, guidance.

Yew [POISON; substitute Sandalwood or Skullcap]**:** spirit contact, transitions, death/rebirth, Underworld, Yule.

ANIMAL TOTEMS

Images used for their properties; cat, dog, frog, and toad are usually Familiars, not images.

Alligator: survival; fighter.

Ant: industrious; community; self-sacrificing.

Bat: death/rebirth; initiation; intuitive.

Bear: strength; power; renewal; wisdom.

Beaver: resourceful; hard working; constructive; ambition.

Bee: alertness; community; industry; sexuality; plenty.

Buffalo: abundance; leadership; life flow; unity with Earth.

Butterfly: avatar; metamorphosis; soul; courage to change.

Cat: mysticism; awareness; stealth.

Cougar: philosopher; power; spiritual leadership.

Coyote: adaptability; humor; Nature; trickster.

Crab: tenacious; commitment; seclusion.

Crane: knowledge, arcane wisdom; vigilance, balance.

Crow: ancient wisdom; bold; diviner; magic.

Deer: grace; beauty; innocence.

Dog: loyalty; tenacity; community.

Dragonfly: agility; dreams.

Duck: trustworthy; social; unassuming.

Dolphin: community; harmony; joy; love; peace; playfulness.

Eagle: courage; healing; Divine messenger.

Elephant: [trunk up] longevity; remover of obstacles; good fortune.

Elk: endurance; explorer; roamer; strength.

Fox: adaptability; awareness; cunning; skill; wily.

Frog: love; transformation; healing; vocal.

Goat: virile; agile; stubborn; determined.

Goose: protector; reliable; territorial; safe return.

Hare: Nature wisdom; powers of observation; complexity.

Hawk: spirit world messenger.

Horse: endurance; friend; independence, travel.

Hummingbird: energy; wonder; swift action.

Leopard: retribution; shape-shifting; magic work.

Lion: courage; health; nobility.

Lizard: renewal; transformation; ancient energy.

Loon: serenity; faithfulness; dreams realized.

Lynx: inner knowledge; occultism; secrets.

Moose: confident; headstrong; arrogant.

Mouse: family unity; spirit communication .

Orca: creation; power of song; family unit.

Otter: compatibility; sharing; friendly; enjoyment of life; play.

Owl: between the worlds; divination; truth; visions; wisdom.

Panther: hunter; stealth; solitary.

Pelican: storage; readiness; renewed buoyancy.

Penguin: family dedication; self-sacrifice; groups [unlucky].

Pig: expressive; intelligence; sincerity.

Rabbit: alert; abundance; organization; unity.

Raven: altered states; battlefield; espionage; mystery; secrets.

Rhinoceros: ancient wisdom; aggressive defense.

Roadrunner: agile; quick-witted; clever.

Salmon: ancient wisdom; determination; courage.

Scorpion: defensive; powerful fighter; nimble.

Seahorse: grace; partnership; responsibility, magic.

Shark: survivor; fearsome; predatory; hungry; powerful.

Skunk: self-protective; fearless; self-esteem.

Snail: perseverance; determined; self-contained; graceful.

Snake: cycles; rebirth; regeneration; renewal; wisdom; wholeness.

Spider: creativity; dreams; fate; weaver; storyteller; dark powers.

Squirrel: resourceful; prankster; trusty; playful.

Swan: commitment; loyalty; majesty; protective.

Toad: prosperity; messenger.

Turkey: shared blessings; originality; artistic; harvest; bounty.

Turtle: Earthy; grounded; longevity; protection; shelter; steady.

Whale: creative; inspiration; intelligence life-enhancer.

Wolf: family bonds; unity; Earth wisdom.

LIST OF STONES & CRYSTALS [ELIXIR BENEFITS]

Stones may be dropped into a burning candle {pillar or votive} to add the energy of the stone to spell work; they may be included in herbal pouches or dream pillows, carried loose or in a small cloth bag, placed somewhere {house, car, etc.}, or made into jewelry to add their energy as desired; to make an elixir: soak a gem, crystal, or stone in a cup of spring water and set for an hour in the light of the Full or Dark Moon, remove the stone, consecrate the water and store away from the light, adding if desired a drop of whiskey or brandy to *hold* the energies, and drink by teaspoon as needed for the benefit imbued by the stone's energy, indicated by brackets in listing.

Agate: health, good fortune, eloquence, vitality/energy, self-confidence, bursts of mental/physical energy, balance emotions, calm body/mind/emotions.

Banded: relieve stress.

Blue-Lace: calm, third eye, self-expression, neutralize anger; [encourage trust and friendliness].

White with Blue/Black Spots: travel.

Eye Formation: bodily protection, travel.

Mossy: healing, cleansing, abundance, self-confidence, harmony, release anger/frustration, strength, earth-energies connection.

Milky with Red: visualization skills, gain goals.

Alexandrite: balance the nervous system, color therapy.

Amazonite: good fortune, female power, soothe nervous system, improve thought process, regulate metabolism; [social ability].

Amber (fossilized tree resin): strengthen/break spell: a Witch stone, increase, success, health, healing, love, absorb negative energy, manifestation, good luck; [relief from despair].

Amethyst: spirituality, protection from negativity through transformation, intuition, dreams, relieve tension, meditation, cleansing/energizing, protect against psychic manipulation; [help in compromise].

Apache Tear: protection from directed negative energies, grounding energies, spiritual meditation.

Apatite: strengthen muscles, coordination.

Aqua-Aura: meditation, release of emotional tension.

Aquamarine: psychological influence, inspire thought process, good luck in tests, positive interviews; [calms; relieves tension].

Auricalcite: calm, clear away tension, neutralize anger.

Aventurine: creativity, luck in physical activities, courage, calm, sleep, leadership, decision-making; [soothe eyes; gain an open mind; curb pride/aloofness].

Azurite: Blended Blues and Greens: psychic development; meditation; facing fears, healing, visions; [help in controlling own reality].

Beryl: intellect, willpower, aid heart/digestive system; [build self-esteem].

Bloodstone or Heliotrope: remove obstacles, vitality, enhance talents, balance, health/healing, ward injury, purify the blood, courage, strength, integrity; [curb obsessive affection].

Boji Stone: usually paired with one smooth/other bumpy with projections; strengthen chakras, healing, regenerative, balance energy fields.

Calcite: Gold: healing, cheerfulness; [reach for new goals/emotional contacts].

Green: soothe fears, calm, aid intuition, transitions.

Orange: physical energy, expand awareness, intuition.

Carnelian: career success, fast action, shield thoughts, good health, protection, grounding, motivation, personal power.

Chalcedony: optimism, spiritual/artistic creativity.

Chalcopyrite or **Peacock Stone:** alleviate worry, focus for prosperity, happiness, protect from negativity.

Chrysocolla: balance, cleanse negativity, contentment, healing, prosperity, good luck, clears mind; [open a path away from daily routine].

Chrysoprase: peace, meditation, clairvoyance, gain incentive; [temper egotism].

Citrine: success, clear thinking, protection, direction, induce dreams, improve self-image/confidence, prosperity, manifest personal power, initiative, creativity, endurance.

Coral: calm, relaxation, protect from illness, ward unwanted thought energies.

Diamond: protection, avert unseen danger, emotional healer, power, purity, strength.

Dioptase: relaxation, relieve stress, overcome emotional loss.

Dolomite: avert fear of failure; [focus on success/gain resourcefulness].

Emerald: artistic talent, memory, truth, visions, business success, peace, love, psychic insight, tranquillity.

Fluorite: meditation, Fairy Realms, dreams, past lives, aids intellect, heals energy drains in the aura, ground/balance/focus energy, absorb/alter negative energy; discernment, aid concentration.

Garnet: swift movement, balance energies, revitalization, self-esteem/confidence, dreamwork, energy/courage, love/bonding, devotion.

Geodes: freedom of spirit, linking with the cosmic dance.

Hematite: communication skills, astral projection, balance/focus energy, clear calm reasoning, draw good relationships; [diminish defenselessness].

Herkimer Diamond: relieve stress, power booster for crystals/bojis, dream interpretation, psychic attunement; [gain goals, freer expression of love].

Iron Pyrite: attract success, health/wealth/happiness, intellect, creativity, psychic development, channeling, memory.

Jacinth: spiritual insight.

Jade: peace, cleansing, harmony, friendship, good luck, protection, safe travel, wisdom, long life, dream focus/content; [realistic/practical ideals].

Jasper: strengthen energy flow, relieve stress, gather energy for directing, nurturing, protection, grounding, safe astral travel.

Red: returns negativity to sender; defensive magics.

Brown: grounding and stability; soothes nerves.

Green: healing and fertility.

Jet (fossilized pinewood): bind energy to a goal: a Witch stone, calm fears, protection.

Kunzite: meditation, balance negative emotions, purification, Divine connection.

Kyanite: meditation, past lives recall, channeling, vivid dreams, visualization, altered states, serenity, manifestation of thought into reality.

Lapis Lazuli: authority, power booster, aura cleanser, psychic development, mental balance, self-awareness, inner truths/wisdom, access universal knowledge.

Larimar: transmute negative energies like anger/greed/frustration, bring excessive energies into balance.

Lazurite: visions.

Magnetite or **Howlite:** meditation, tranquillity, calm fear/anger, honesty.

Malachite: business success, protection, vision quest, meditation, prosperity, hope, health, happiness, avert confusion/apathy, manifest desires; [ease focus for controlling reality].

Moldavite: Green Glassy Meteorite: transformation, star communication, heal longing, find life purpose, energizing, dimensional travel; [decision making, confidence, re-focusing].

Moonstone: psychic ability, divination, love, comfort, peace, long life, friends, inspiration, draw attachment/sensitivity, wish granting, new start; [eased surroundings, curb spending].

Morion Crystal: nearly black crystal used for grounding energies.

Obsidian: Black: protection, scrying, Dark Aspect meditation, Otherworld contact, Shadowland contact, banish grief, benevolence, healing.

 Green: protection of income; open financial opportunities.

 Snowflake: grounding, responsibility, purification, change, growth, deflect negative energy.

Onyx: equilibrium, end worry, justice, concentration, devotion, guidance through dreams/meditation, balance of duality.

 Black: deal with emotions/frustration.

Opal: psychic power, astral travel, meditation, calm, direct thoughts inward, reflect what is sent, shape-shifting, invisibility; best used by people born in October [relaxation, calmative].

Pearl: astral projection, dreams; [ease fears, calm the nerves].

Peridot: soulmates, clairvoyance, solar power, attract occult power, inner vision, open awareness, ward negativity, body tonic.

Petrified Wood: past lives recall, physical energy, preservation of strength, firmness of stance, serenity, balance, grounding, vitality.

Pumice: power, manifestation.

Quartz Crystal: psychic power, vision quest, protection, energy, divination, projection, attain goals, cleanse aura, meditation, intuition, store, focus, direct, transmit energy; [protection].

 Blue: release emotional tension, soothe.

Rock Crystal: scrying; energizing; water magics.

 Rose: peace, love, comfort, companionship; [self-discipline, responsibility].

 Rutilated: increase strength of will; [control self-indulgence].

 Smoky: generate energy, protection, purify energies, Fairy connection, disperse negative/draw positive energy; [personal interactions].

 Snow: meditation, serenity, peace, contemplation.

Rhodochrosite: generate energy, physical/emotional balance, heal trauma, union of male/female aspects; [regain emotional energy after frustrations].

Rhodinite: self-esteem, physical energy, self-actualization, service; [ease physical fatigue, negate fear of criticism].

Ruby: protect health/wealth, increase energy/creativity, self-confidence, intuition, contentment, courage, spiritual wisdom, generate heat.

Sapphire: wisdom, material gains, attract good influences, peace of mind, hope.

Sardonyx: draw troubles then toss stone into the sea, self-protection.

Selenite: calming for meditation/visualization, clarify thoughts, healing; [overcome guilt, let go of negativity, curb over-active fantasizing].

Sodalite: meditation, enhance memory, relieve stress, aid sleep, enhance logical thought, stimulate intellect; [control rage, curb negative behavior].

Staurolite or **Fairy Cross:** good luck, protection, security, manifesting higher self on Earth plane, astral connection, confidence.

Sugilite: logic, business expertise, astral travel, manifestation, self-healing.

Sunstone: energy, healing, success.

Tiger Eye: good luck, objectivity, truth, self-confidence, protection from ill will of others, harmony, grounding, stability, instinctive/psychic ability, wisdom, healing; [builds self-confidence].

Topaz: Blue: psychic insight, spiritual growth, leadership, concentration, clarity of thought.

Yellow: stress, deep sleep, psychic ability, calm body/mind, fulfillment of dreams/wishes by focusing into the facets, intentional creation, healing, prosperity, other realms, revitalize bodily energies; [commitment to action, building willpower and decisiveness].

Tourmaline: beauty, freshness, joy, friendship, grounding, protection, calm, attract goodwill, self-confidence, discernment, inspiration; [elixir by type].

Black: redirect restlessness into productivity.

Blue: clear speech, unblock mind/emotion, rubbing generates an electrical charge to direct energy

Green/Black: prosperity/deflect negative energies.

Green: setting reasonable goals.

Pink: encourage creativity, free personality.

Watermelon: encourage practical approach to manifesting ideas.

Watermelon/Pink: self-understanding.

Turquoise: verbal communication, putting thoughts into words, protect the spirit, health, love, joy, social life, meditation, intuition, unify spiritual/physical; [open awareness, find creative solutions to problems, curb fear of the dark].

Unikite: grounding, balance, stability.

Viviante: Rare: rebirth, clear sightedness, enlightenment.

Zircon: spiritual sight, spiritual understanding.

ELEMENTAL ASPECTS OF STONES & CRYSTALS

Add stones to spells or charms with desired Elemental alignment; some are versatile.

▽ EARTH

agate [not blue-lace]
apache tear
apatite
aventurine
boji stone
calcite [orange]
carnelian
diamond
flourite
granite
iron pyrite
jade
jasper [not red]
jet
malachite
morion crystal
onyx [not black]
petrified wood
rutilated quartz
rhodinite
ruby
staurolite
sugilite
tiger eye
tourmaline
  [black/green]
unikite

△ AIR

amethyst
aquamarine
azurite
beryl
blue lace agate
carnelian
chalcopyrite
chrysocolla
chrysoprase
citrine
diamond
flourite
hemitite
kyanite
lazurite
moldivite
opal
pearl
snow quartz
sapphire
silver
sodalite
topaz [blue]
tourmaline [blue]
turquoise [blue]
vivianite

△ FIRE

amber
beryl
bloodstone
calcite [gold]
carnelian
citrine
coal
diamond
flint
geodes
gold
jasper [red]
lorimar
obsidian
peridot
pumice
quartz [smoky]
rhodochrosite
rhodinite
sunstone
topaz [yellow]

▽ WATER

alexandrite
aqua-aura
auricalcite
beryl
calcite [green, orange]
chalcedony
diamond
dioptase
emerald
jacinth
jade
jet
kunzite
lapis-lazuli
magnetite
moonstone
obsidian
onyx [black]
opal
peridot
quartz [rose]
river rock
rock crystal
sardonyx
topaz (blue)
tourmaline
  [pink, watermelon]
turquoise [green]
zircon

AMULETS

Inscribe image on stone, carry a small image, carry the item; incorporate into spells.

Acorn: immortality, fertility.

Anise Seed: protection against poverty.

Apple Seed: draw love.

Ash Tree Leaves: bless or curse.

Bay Leaf: protection against spells and evil.

Buckeye: protection, draw money.

Buckthorn: wishes come true.

Caraway Seed: protect child from illness.

Cat [Whisker/claw]: magical power, luck.

Clove: call a lover.

Corn Husk Doll: good harvest, luck.

Corn Kernels: draw money.

Crab [Claw]: love, fertility.

Dove [Feather]: peace.

Deer [Antler]: fertility, quick gains, success.

Dragon [Image]: life, power, wisdom.

Feather: mind, wealth, prosperity in work.

Egg [Shell]: cosmos, creation, fertility.

Elk [Tooth]: swiftness, vitality.

Fish [Image]: prosperity, plenty, fertility.

Foxtail: cleverness, swiftness.

Garlic Clove: repel evil.

Grasshopper: cheer, wealth, plenty.

Horn [Cow/Sheep/Ram]: ward evil eye, virility, plenty.

Horseshoe [U-Shaped]: success, good luck, ward evil.

Lady Bug: good luck, wealth, success.

Lucky Hand Root: return evil to sender.

Nutmeg [Nut]: good luck in gambling.

Mustard Seed: good luck, protection.

Onion Bulb: absorb evil.

Peacock [Feather]: protects from evil eye, wisdom, alertness.

Pine Cone: health, longevity.

Rabbit Foot: fertility, good luck.

Rattlesnake: regeneration, fertility, health; tail-in-mouth = eternity.

Rice [Uncooked]: fertility, money.

Scarab: ward evil, eternal life.

Spider: good luck, protection from enemies, wisdom, work success, money.

Tonka Bean: good luck, wealth.

Unicorn: fertility, pureness, sexuality.

Wishbone: wishes granted, good luck.

CANDLE MAGIC SPELL CHART

Choose a candle from the color list or suggestions here [may also use candles with multiple colors or multiple candles of different colors}; choose desired shape for a goal; dress with oil {*see Oils List*}; inscribe with any or all of the planetary symbols for influence; burn one hour according to the selected planetary hour; at the appropriate Moon Phase.

Candle types: for spell work: votive or pillar; for ritual: taper; for meditation and divination: votive, pillar or taper; for general aura/atmosphere: votive, pillar, or contained in glass jar; for specified spell work—votive, pillar, figure [man/woman], animal [see Animal List], skull [mind], and other shapes; 5- to 7-day spells use a knobby, pillar, or glass container candle and burn 1 portion each day until end of spell]

Key to Candle Styles for Spells

C = Cat	G = Glass	P = Pillar	T = Taper
D = Dragon	K = Knobby	Sk = Skull	V = Votive
F = Figure	O = Owl	Sn = Snake	

Planets for Inscriptions, Days, and Hours of Spells

☉ = Sun	♀ = Venus	♄ = Saturn	♅ = Uranus
☽ = Moon	♂ = Mars	♆ = Neptune	
☿ = Mercury	♃ = Jupiter	♇ = Pluto	

Moon Phases for Spells

☽ = Waxing Moon	○ = Full Moon	☾ = Waning Moon	● = Dark (New) Moon

Goal:	Plan. Infl. /Hour	Moon	Color	Shape
Abundance	☿ ♀ ♃	○	green/copper/gold	G, K, P, V
Animal blessing	♀ ☿ ☽ ☉	○	brown/white/orange	C, G, P, Sn, V
Astral travel	☿ ♆	☽	blue/purple/indigo	G, O, P, T, V
Balance	☉ ♄	☽	rainbow/silver/brown	G, P, T, V
Banish negativity	♇ ♄	○/☾	black/white/purple	G, P, T, V
Binding	♇ ♄ ♆	☽	red/black/indigo	G, P, T, V
Blessing	♄ ☉ ♃	☽	white/lavender/lt. blue	G, P, V
Business success	♄ ☿ ♃	○	purple/red/copper	G, K, P, V
Change	☉ ☿ ♅	☽	dark blue/yellow	G, K, P, V
Communication	☿ ☉ ♃	☽	yellow/white	G, P, V
Confidence	☉ ♂	☽	orange/red/yellow	G, P, V
Creativity	♆ ☉ ☽ ☿	☽	orange/yellow	G, P, Sk, T, V
Defense	♅ ♄ ♇	●	black/purple/white	D, P, V

236

Goal:	Plan. Infl. /Hour	Moon	Color	Shape
Divinations	☿ ♆ ☽ ♅	☾	yellow/black/lavender	P, Sk, Sn, T, V
Drawing love	♀ ☽	☽	pink/white/red	F, G, P, V
Drawing power	☉ ☽ ☿ ♂	○	red/orange/gold	C, D, P, V
Dreams	☽ ♅ ☿	☽	silver/purple/dk. blue	G, P, Sk, Sn, V
Employment	☉ ♃ ☿	○	orange/brown	G, K, P, V
Energy	☉ ♂	○	gold/red	D, F, G, P, V
Energy centers	☉ ♃	☽	rainbow/purple	G, P, V
Enlightenment	☿ ♅ ☽	☽	rainbow/white/yellow	C, O, P, Sn, V
Exorcism	♄ ♅ ♆ ☉ ☽	☾	black/indigo/purple	P, Sk, Sn, T, V
Fearlessness	♂ ☉	☽	red/orange	D, P, V
Fertility	☉ ☿ ♀	☽	green/brown	F, G, K, P, V
Friendship	♃ ♀ ☽	○	gold/pink/brown	G, P, T, V
Garden blessing	♀ ☿ ☽ ☉	○	brown/green	P, T, V
Gossip halted	♄ ♅ ♀	☾	black/indigo/white	C, F, Sn, P, V
Guardian Spirits	☽ ♄ ♆ ♀	☽	purple/black/indigo	C, G, P, Sn, T, V
Happiness	☉ ♀	☽	yellow/pink/gold	G, K, P, T, V
Health	♃ ♀ ☉	○	lt. blue/pink/green	F, K, P, V
Inner vision	☽ ♆ ♀	☽	silver/gray/lavender/black	G, O, T, V
Inspiration	☿ ☽ ♀ ♅	☽	yellow/orange/rainbow	G, P, V
Legal matters	♃ ☉ ♄	☽	black/orange/purple	G, O, P, V
Love	♀ ♂ ☿ ☽	○	pink/green/red	F, K, P, V
Luck	♀ ♇ ♅	☽	orange/silver/gold	C, G, P, V
Meditation	☽ ☿ ♆	○	white/silver/dk. blue/indigo	O, Sk, T, V
Memory	☿ ♄ ☉	☽	yellow/black/violet	C, G, Sk, Sn, T, V
Mental clarity	☿ ♅ ☉	☽	yellow/orange	C, G, P, Sk, T, V
Money	♃ ♀	☽	green/gold/red	G, K, P, V
New love	♀ ☿ ☽	☽	pink/green	F, G, P, V
Opportunity	♃ ☉ ♄	☽	lt. blue/orange/purple	F, G, K, P, V
Otherworld	♅ ☽ ♆	○	lavender/gray	G, O, P, Sk, V
Peace	♄ ♃ ♀	○	white/black/pink	F, G, P, V
Power	☉ ♂	☽	gold/orange/red	D, G, P, V
Promotion	☉ ♄ ♃	☽	orange/purple/yellow	F, G, K, P, V
Protection	☉ ☽	☽	white/black/purple	C, D, P, Sn, V
Releasing past	♄ ♇	☾	black/violet/purple	F, G, P, V
Return-to-Sender	♄ ♇ ♂ ☽	●	indigo/black/white	F, G, K, P, V
Ritual purification	☉ ♀ ♃	☽	white/purple	F, G, P, T, V
Self-cleansing	♄ ☉	○	rainbow/black/white	F, G, P, T, V
Sleeplessness	☽ ♆ ♀	☾	black/dk. blue/white	G, O, P, V

Goal	Plan. Infl. /Hour	Moon	Color	Shape
Spirit communion	☿ ♆ ☽ ♅	☽	purple/indigo/yellow	P, Sk, T, V
Spirit guide	☿ ♆ ☽ ♅	☽	purple/indigo/black	C, Sn, P, T, V
Stability	♆ ♃	☾	black/brown	D, G, K, P, V
Strength	☉ ♂	○	red/orange/gold	D, G, P, V
Success	☉ ♃	☽ /○	orange/gold/violet	F, G, K, P, V
Sudden change	♄ ♅ ☿ ☉	☽ /☾	rainbow/indigo/gold	F, G, K, P, V
Thwart negativity	♀ ♄ ☿	☾	purple/black/gray	G, V, P, D
Underworld	♄ ☿ ♆	●	indigo/black/purple	G, P, Sk, Sn, V
Victory	☉ ♂	☽	red/orange	G, P, V, T
Ward evil	♂ ☉ ♀ ♆	●	indigo/black/gray	C, G, P, Sk, V
Wisdom	♃ ☽ ♅ ☿	☽	purple/indigo/yellow	G, K, O, P, T, V
Ward negative energy	☽ ♅ ♄	☾	white/black/indigo	G, Sn, P, V

QUICK SPELL CHART

GOAL	Abundance	Astral Travel	Balance	Bless/Conscrte	Cleansing
MOON	Waxing, Full	Waxing	Waxing	Waxing, Full	Full
COLOR	Green	Slvr,Blk,Purple	White,Slvr,Grn	White	White
ELEMENT	Earth	Air,Water	Earth,Air	Water,Fire	Water,Earth
DAY	Thur,Sun	Mon,Wed,Sun	Wed,Sat	Sun,Wed,Fri	Sun,Sat,Wed
PLANET	Sun,Jupiter	Pluto,Neptune	Sun,Saturn	Sun,Saturn	Saturn,Sun
NUMBER	1–3	7–8–9	2–4	8	2–3–5
OGHAM	Ur,Huath	Saille,Muin,Ur	Tinne,Ruis	Beth,Ngtl,Nion	Luis,Beith
RUNE	Beorc,Feoh, Ethel,Gera	As,Daeg, Eoh,Lagu,Rad	Gefu,Eh,Rad Ken	Daeg,Osa,Sigel, Eoh,Thrn,Beorc	Eoh,Ken,Beorc Wyn,Sigel
HERB	allspce,benzoin brgmot,coriandr trefoil,pecan, mustard,oak	acacia, rue, jasmine,mgwrt, cinquefoil, woodrff,dittany	basil,nettle, mullein,comfry, oak,woodruff	acacia,anise, mgwrt,basil,clvr, vervain,hyssop, elder,rue,birch	lavender,pine bnzoin,hyssop betony/rsmary thyme/burdock
INCENSE	patchouli,jsmin	benzoin	frnkncnse,wdrff	frnkncns,rsmry	mugwort,clove
STONE	agate,citrine amazonite	sugilite, opal jaspr,hematite	bloodstone, rhodochrosite	quartz crystal, amethyst	mossy agate amthyst, jade

GOAL	Changes	Divination	Empower	Fertility	Fortune
MOON	Waning	Drk,Full,Wning	Waxing	Waxing	Waxing
COLOR	DrkBlu,Ylw,Wh	Gold,Lvndr,Ylw	Red,Yellow	Green,Brown	Green,White
ELEMENT	Fire,Water	Air, Water	Fire,Earth	Earth,Water	Earth,Fire
DAY	St,Sn,T,Wd,Th	Wed,Mon,Sun	Tue,Sun,Sat	Mon,Tue,Fri	Thur,Wed,Sun
PLANET	Uranus,Pluto	Urnus,Nep,Mrc	Sun,Mars	Venus,Moon	Sun,Jupiter
NUMBER	1–6–7–9	7–8	1–3–9	1–3–4–6	3–4–5–8
OGHAM	Iodho,Onn,	Coll,Saille	Ailm,Duir	Beithe,Quert	Fearn,Ur
RUNE	Perth,Beorc, Eh,Daeg,Rad	Lagu,Eoh, As,Daeg	Tyr,Uruz, Ken,Ethel	Beorc,Ing, Gera	Osa,Feoh, Gera,Tyr
HERB	sunflower, woodruff,linden purple heather, elder	mugwort,anise, orris,cinqfoil, damiana, wdruff,vervain	cinquefoil, St.Johnswort, borage,elder, vervain,wdruff	hawthorn,ivy, mustard,oak, mstltoe,nuts, cones,wheat	bay,bergamot, cinquefoil, lemonbalm, star anise
INCENSE	drgnbld,wdruff	jasmine	dragonsblood	patchouli	frankincense
STONE	snowflake obsedian	moonstone quartz crystal	amber quartz crystal	green jasper	agate amzonite

QUICK SPELL CHART

GOAL	Happiness	Healing	Manifesting	Money	Meditation	Protection
MOON	Waxing,Full	Waxing	Full	Waxing	Dark,Full	Waxing
COLOR	Gld,Yllw,Pink	Lt.Blue,Yellw	Grn,Rd,Gld,Or	Grn,Slvr,Gld	Indg,Wh,Slvr	Blk,Wht,Blue
ELEMENT	Water,Air	Earth,Water	Earth,Fire	Earth	Water,Air	Fire,Earth
DAY	Thur,Fri,Sun	Thur,Sat,Sun	Thur,Sun	Thur,Sun	Mon,Wed,St	Sat,Sun,Tue
PLANET	Sun,Ven,Jup	Jupiter,Sun	Urnus,Sun,Jup	Vn,Jp,Sn,St	Moon,Np,Plt	Strn,Jup,Sun
NUMBER	1-4-5-6-8	1-3-9	1-3-4-5-9	3-4-6-8	2--5-7-8	1-4-8-9
OGHAM	Huath,Nion	Quert,Eadha,	Beithe,Nion	Ur,Onn	Muin,Luis	Duir,Eadha
RUNE	Wyn,Gefu, Osa,Tyr	Sigel,Uruz, Ken,Beorc	Tyr,Osa,Ken Gera,Eh,Ethel	Ing,Feoh,Osa Gera,Ethel	As,Mannaz, Eoh,Lagu	Thorn,Nyd, Tyr,Eolh
HERB	loosestrife, yarrow,tansy rsmry,fennel, vervain,vine	cmfry,cnqfoil, skullcap,tnsy, thyme,rsmry, coriander,cinn	linden,mgwort, prple heather, St.Johnswort, wdruf,hwthorn	basil,bergmot, chamomile, gngr,clv,mint, nutmg,vetivert	acacia, benzoin, woodruff, chamomile	betony,fennl, marjoram, mullein, rsmry,wdruff
INCENSE	lavender	sage	rsemary, pine	patchouli,pine	frnkns,sndlw	frankincnse
STONE	malachite, chrysacolla	sugilite,agate, selenite,azrite	pumce,sugilte, amber,kyanite	malachite pyrite,trmline	florite,sodlite, snw qrtz	malachite, dolomite

GOAL	PsychicPower	ReleaseNegatvty	Sealings	Transfrmation	Spirit Contact
MOON	Full,Drk	Drk,Waning,Full	Waxing,Drk	Waxing	Drk, Full
COLOR	Prpl,Blk,Wh,Lvn	Blk,Slvr,Wht,Prp	Black,Red	White,Orange	Blk,Indg,Prp,Lvn
ELEMENT	Air,Water,Fire	Water,Fire,Air	Fire	Water,Air,Fire	Air
DAY	Mon,Wed,Sun	Sat,Sun,Thr,Mn	Sat,Wed,Sun	M,Tu,Wd,Sn,St	Mn,Wed,Sun
PLANET	Nept,Moon,Plt	Strn,Mn,Npt,Plt	Saturn,Mars	Plt,Mn,Urnus	Pl,Nep,Strn,Mrc
NUMBER	4-5-7-8	2-7-8-9	9	3-7-8-9	7-9
OGHAM	Saille,Muin	Eadh,Huath,Strf	Straif	Iodho,Ngtl,Onn	Saille,Idho,Qurt
RUNE	Daeg,Ken,Eoh, Lagu,Perth,Tyr	Nyd,Is,Haegl, Beorc,Tyr,Thorn	Is,Haegl, Nyd	Kn,Sigl,Eh,Eoh Mannaz,Thorn	Eoh,Daeg,As, Lagu,Rad
HERB	mace,mugwort, vervain,anise, bay,betony burdock,dittany	agrimony,fennel, holly,rue,hyssop, yarrow,vetivert, vervain,rowan	agrimony, wormwood, St.Johnswort anglica,cnqfoil	hyssop,lilac linden,wdruff, purple heather, reed, yew	orris root,dittny, mace,clove, elder,apple, lavender,lilac,
INCENSE	mugwort,copal	sndlwood,myrrh	drgnbld,myrrh	frnkcns,drgnbld	frnkcns,sage,
STONE	quartz crystal, selenite,zircon	Apache tear, selenite,chrysclla	crnelian,jet,red jasper,srdonox	amethyst, moldavite	amethyst,zircon blk obsidian

QUICK SPELL CHART

GOAL	Strength	Success	Victory	Ward Evil	Wisdom
MOON	Waxing	Waxing, Full	Waxing	Waning, Dark	Waxing
COLOR	Rd,Gld,Ornge	Gld,Ornge,Grn	Rd,Gld,Violet	Indgo,Blck,Gry	Prpl,Ing, Blck,Wht
ELEMENT	Earth,Fire	Earth, Fire	Fire, Earth	Fire, Air, Water	Air
DAY	Tue,Sun	Tue,Thurs,Sun	Tues,Thrs,Sn	Wed, Sat	Wd,St,Sn
PLANET	Mrs,Urans,Sun	Sn,Mrc,Jp,Sat	Sun,Mars,Juptr	Mrs,Sn,Plt,Np	Jp,Sn,St, Mn,Mc
NUMBER	1–4–9	3–4–9	1–3–8–9	7–8–9	3–4–5–7
OGHAM	Duir,Fearn	Ailm,Eadha,Ur	Ur,Eadha	Huath,Strf,Edha	Onn,Coll
RUNE	Uruz,Tyr, Sigel,Ing	Osa,Gera,Tyr, Ken,Wyn,Feoh	Tyr,Feoh, Gera,Uruz	Haegle,Nyd,Is	As,Daeg,Eoh, Sigel
HERB	rsemary,bay, St.Johnswrt, dianthus, mastic,vervain	fennel,vervain, rosemary, yarrow	bergmot,clover, ginger,cinnamn, lemonbalm, wdruff,heather	agrimony,rue, mullein, nettle	elder,bay,fern, willow,iris, gorse, hazel, oak
INCENSE	drgnbld,frnkncn	bay,cdar,cinn	drgnsbld,rsmry	clv,drgbld,bybry	copl,sage,pine
STONE	bldstn,diamnd, mossy agate	carnlian,citrne, mlchte,avntrne	ambr,crnelian, citrine,emerald	Apache tear, jet coral, amber	tgr eye,ruby, jade,lapis,saphr

DEITY IMAGES

Mother Hulda: [also Holly, Holda, Halo, and Holy] Goddess of snow and rain; rides with the Wild Hunt to gather infant and child dead to aid in their rebirth; shakes her feather mattress in Underworld for it to snow on the Earth; washes her veil and it rains; Witches who ride with her are called Snow Wives who go Holle-riding. Mother Hulda's sprites are Holden [friendly underground spirits who help people, from where the word "beholden" comes]; Her mountain folk are the Hudrefolk; She is Lady Winter with white gown and crown, beautiful features, and She is Dark Lady Winter with big teeth, pointed hat, and typical *Witchy* appearance. She Rules Underworld, is Queen of the land of Elves and Fairies; She rides through the night with Her hounds in front; the holly and the halo around the Moon are dedicated to Her.

Mother Earth: Bona Dea, the Good Goddess; nurturer.

Green Man: spirit of wildlife and Spring, vigorous Earth, wild consciousness.

Hecate: Dark Moon Goddess; Queen of the Night; Ruler of Heaven, Earth, and Underworld; Queen of Witches [from Thrace, may be evolved from Bendidia/Bendis].

Herne, the Hunter: Earth Father; God of Nature; Spirit of the ancient woodlands and all growing things; the Greenman; Lord of Animals; Hu Gadarn, the Horned God of Fertility; Guardian of the Gates to Otherworld; Cernunnos; strong and awful if his domain is violated, but joyful and full of lifeforce if reverent and quiet in his domain; invoked by Hibernians with chanting circle dances with stag horns, leaves, and vines sewn into their clothes; sacred animals are stag, bull, goat, and bear.

Horned God: Hunter; God of Nature; son and lover of Mother Earth; collector of souls with the Wild Hunt; fertility and rebirth.

Lady of the Night: dreams and secrets revealed.

Lady of the Woods: Goddess of wild places, vegetation, animal mother, tree spirit.

Queen of the Stars: Goddess as the Milky Way; Goddess of the Sacred Milk.

Wildman: Greenman image; spirit of wild animals; Nature within all creatures, fertility, fecundity, abandon; ecstasy; the God Pan.

DEITY NAMES OF POWER

Adraste: Goddess of Destiny.

Amemet: Goddess of the Land of the West.

Artraea: Goddess of Justice.

Bast: Goddess of Nurturing Sun; cats; joy.

Benu: Phoenix/heron.

Cronus: God of Time.

Dedwen: God of Incense.

Diti: Goddess Who Grants Wishes.

Fjorgyn: Divine Androgyne.

Ganesha: God Who Opens the Way; Prosperity.

Gerda: Goddess of Light.

Harmonia: Goddess of Warrior Women.

Ishtar: Goddess of the Morning Star.

Lakshmi: Goddess of Fortune.

Maat: Goddess of Truth and Balance.

Mimis: God of Fresh Water and Wisdom.

Min: God of Fecundity; Roads; Travel.

Namtar: Negative Fate.

Nemontana: Goddess of Sacred Grove/Shrines.

Nixes: Water Spirits.

Nun: God/Goddess of Primordial Waters.

Ran: Sea Goddess.

Sin: Fairy Woman with Magical Warriors.

Skadia: Mountain Goddess.

Ullur: God of Justice; Archery; and Skiing.

Uraeus: Goddess of the Solar Eye.

Uto: Snake Goddess of Regeneration and Fertility.

GEOMANTIC CHARACTERS

The following geomantic figures, planetary squares, and planetary seals may be drawn on talismans, charms, candles and spell materials:

Characters of the Moon

From the Way: From the People:

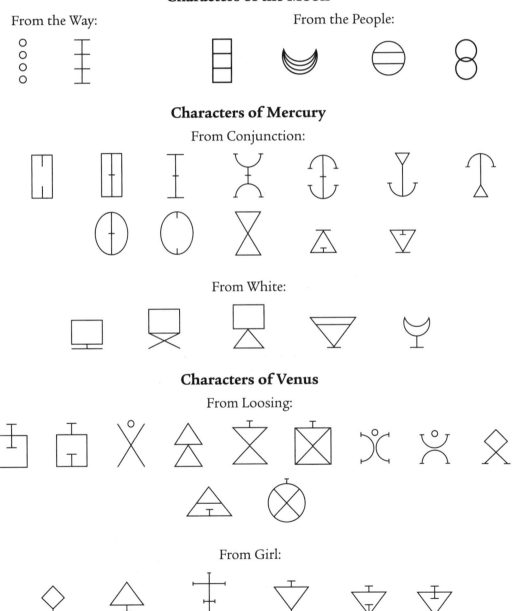

Characters of Mercury

From Conjunction:

From White:

Characters of Venus

From Loosing:

From Girl:

Characters of the Sun

From a Greater Fortune:

From a Lesser Fortune:

Characters of Mars

From Red:

From a Boy:

Characters of Jupiter

From Obtaining:

From Joyfulness:

Characters of Saturn

From a Prison:

From Sadness:

Characters of the Dragon

From the Head:

From the Tail:

Characters of the Fixed Stars

Head of Algol: Pleiades: Aldebaran: Goat Star:

 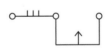

Greater Dog Star [Sirius]:   Lesser Dog Star [Canis Minor]:   Heart of the Lion:

Tail of the Bear: Wing of the Crow: Spica:

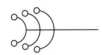 

Arturus:

Elpheia [Lucida Corone]: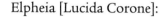

Heart of the Scorpion: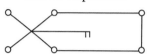

Vulture Falling:

Tail of Capricorn:

GEOMANTIC FIGURES

For divination, close eyes, make four lines of one or two dots on paper; interpret by figures.

Way,
Journey
▽ ☽ ♌

People,
Congregation
▽ ☽ ♑

Conjunction,
Assembled
△ ☿ ♍

Prison,
Bound
▽ ♄ ♓

Great Fortune/
Aid/Safe Entry
▽ ☉ ♒

Lesser Fortune/
Aid/Safe Exit
△ ☉ ♉

Obtaining,
Aware W/in
△ ♃ ♈

Loss,
Aware W/out
△ ♀ ♎

Joy, Laughing,
Health, Bearded
△ ♃ ♉

Sadness,
Cursed, Angry
▽ ♄ ♏

A Girl,
Beautiful
▽ ♀ ♎

A Boy, Yellow,
Beardless, Generous
△ ♂ ♈

White, Shining
Fair, Emptiness
▽ ☿ ♋

Reddish
Red, Danger
△ ♂ ♊

Head, Enter Threshold
Upper Threshold
▽ ☊ ♍

Tail, Exit Threshold,
Lower Threshold
△ ☋ ♐

PLANETARY SQUARES

Place Planetary Square and Sigil on back of a magical Circle containing Planetary Sigil, its Seal, and its Intelligence Symbol for Talismanic Magic.

4	9	2
3	5	7
8	1	6

Square of Saturn

4	14	15	1
9	7	6	12
5	11	10	8
16	2	3	13

Square of Jupiter

6	32	3	34	35	1
7	11	27	28	8	30
19	14	16	15	23	24
18	20	22	21	17	13
25	29	10	9	26	12
36	5	33	4	2	31

Square of the Sun

8	58	59	5	4	62	63	1
49	15	14	52	53	11	10	56
41	23	22	44	45	19	18	48
32	34	35	29	28	38	39	25
40	26	27	37	36	30	31	33
17	47	46	20	21	43	42	24
9	55	54	12	13	51	50	16
64	2	3	61	60	6	7	57

Square of Mercury

37	78	29	70	21	62	13	54	5
6	38	79	30	71	22	63	14	46
47	7	39	80	31	72	23	55	15
16	48	8	40	81	32	64	24	56
57	17	49	9	41	73	33	65	25
26	58	18	50	1	42	74	34	66
67	27	59	10	51	2	43	75	35
36	68	19	60	11	52	3	44	76
77	28	69	20	61	12	53	4	45

Square of the Moon

22	47	16	41	10	35	4
5	23	48	17	42	11	29
30	6	24	49	18	36	12
13	31	7	25	43	19	37
38	14	32	1	26	44	20
21	39	8	33	2	27	45
46	15	40	9	34	3	28

Square of Venus

11	24	7	20	3
4	12	25	8	16
17	5	13	21	9
10	18	1	14	22
23	6	19	2	15

Square of Mars

PLANETARY SEALS

Make double-ringed circle, place Seal at center top, Intelligence beneath, and Planet symbol to one side/between or below as appears balanced: Lead for Saturn, Silver for Jupiter, Iron for Mars, Gold for Sun, Copper for Venus, Silver and Tin for Mercury. *Note: Intelligence is Benevolent, while Spirit is Malevolent, hence only Seal and Intelligence are used in Ceremonial Magical circles.*

Seal of Saturn
Omeliel, Anachiel

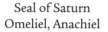

Intelligence of Saturn
Agiel

Spirit of Saturn
Zazel

Seal of Jupiter
Netoniel, Aba

Intelligence of Jupiter
Johphiel

Spirit of Jupiter
Hismael

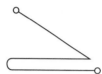

Seal of Mars
Ithuriel, He, Adonai

Intelligence of Mars
Graphiel

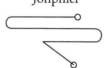

Spirit of Mars
Barzabel

Seal of the Sun
Shadiel, Vau, Eloh

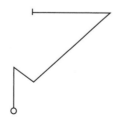

Intelligence of the Sun
Nachiel

Spirit of the Sun
Sorath

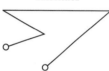

Seal of Venus
Habondia

Intelligence of Venus
Hagiel

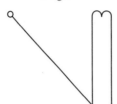

Spirit of Venus
Kedemel

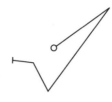

Intelligences of Venus
Aeliel, Bne Seraphim

Seal of Mercury
Vehiel, Asboga, Din, Doni

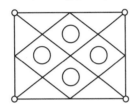

Intelligence of Mercury
Tiriel

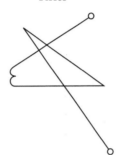

Spirit of Mercury
Cassiel, Taphthartharath

Seal of the Moon
Azarel, Hod, Elim

Spirit of the Moon
Hasmodai

Spirit of Spirits of the Moon
Ichadeil, Malcah,
Schedbarsemoth, Schartatham

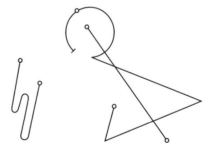

Intelligence of the Intelligences of the Moon
Yashiel, Malcha betharsithimhed beruah schehakim

SPELL CRAFTING ENTERED BY:

_____

9
Basic Spells

Spellcasting Reminders
Daily Blessing
Blessed Water
Cleansings
Protection Spells
Money Spells
Health Spells
Fertility Spells
Various Spells
Spell Crafts

☉	☾	☿	♀	♂	♃	♆	♄	♇	♅
Sun	Moon	Mercury	Venus	Mars	Jupiter	Neptune	Saturn	Pluto	Uranus

Waxing Moon [Maiden]	Full Moon [Mother]	Waning Moon [Crone]	Dark (New) Moon [Hidden Face/Mystery]

SPELL CASTING REMINDERS

MOON SIGNS

Waxing ☽ ◑ —Maiden Moon moving from Dark to Full phase

   —used for magics of increase

Full ○ —Mother Moon fully illuminated

   —influence felt three days before and three days after

   —magics of completion, success, gains, accomplishment

Waning ◑ ☾ —Crone Moon moving from Full to Dark phase

   —used for magics of decrease

New ☾ ● —Crone Moon at last sliver of crescent to Dark

   —used for magics of banishing, exorcism, cleansings

Dark ● —Crone as Mystery Moon totally non-illuminated

   —used for divinations and meditations

   —used for Dark Power Magics

   —Hidden Face of the Goddess as the One Who Transforms

   —the Womb as the Tomb, hence, passage to Rebirth

Moon Void-of-Course—passing from one Sign and entering into another [look in a Magical, Lunar, or Farmer's Almanac].

   —can be between one to four hours

   —holds the influence of both signs in balance

   —*unfavorable* for magical activities

     —activities begun rarely are completed

     —activities begun may end, but not as expected/desired

   —Rule of Thumb, influence of a Moon phase lasts three days

Ground and Center before all Magical Work: to avoid depleting personal energy levels by augmenting internal energies.

Ground again after all Magical Work: to avoid overload of personal energy levels by draining out the excess energies.

Change another's Spell slightly so it is Yours: to make the energy generated recognize it connects to work with you specifically.

Goal or Purpose of Magic

Drawing: to bring something [money; love; health; new job; etc.].

Repelling/Banishing/Exorcising: to cast something away [something unwanted; repel negative energies; banish poverty; unemployment; exorcise depression-inducing energies; aid spirits to pass on to next world].

Containment/Deflection/Reflection: to place limitations.

—shielding: to protect from incoming negativity.

—confining: to restrict negativity to its source.

—dispersing: to dissipate incoming negative energies.

—turning: to return to sender deliberate negative energy.

Retain the Rules of Conduct or the Witches' Rede:

—never initiate negative magic towards another.

—self-defense is acceptable as prevention, disbursement, or returning, for people are responsible for their own actions.

Types of Magic [per Family Tradition]

Sympathetic Magic: "This *IS* That."
—one object is seen as being another, thus, the energy directed into the magical object is directed into another object [poppets, sigils, candle-burning spells].

Comparative Magic: "This *REPRESENTS* That."
—relationship established between magical object and other object usually with the word "as," thus energy directed also enters the other [charms, connections, growth spells]

Directive Magic: "This *AFFECTS* That." [most common]
—magical energy is raised, focused on a goal, directed into an object, and released for accomplishment [candle spells, herbal pouches, stones and crystals].

Transference Magic: "This *ENTERS* That."
—negative energy is moved from affected object into another [onion or garlic braid, garlic clove, salt].

—[rare] deadly energy moved into willing host [it could die] [plant at hospital room, willing animal pet/familiar].

—willingness determined by intuitive communication.

—*Retain the Rules of Conduct:* otherwise,

1. You will draw the energy to yourself.

2. You will draw the hostility of the recipient to yourself.

3. Your auric field will be diminished doubly if intended recipient forgives you, trebly if intended recipient does not forgive you.

4. Magical goal may also fail.

Moving Energy

Magic Performed: raise, focus, direct, and send energy.

Powers of Nature: work *through* you, as the energies and spirits of the Earth, the Elementals [emanations of the Divine], and the Divine.

—There is a difference between *spirit* and *psychic* energies:

—spirit energy is the Divine essence of a being

—psychic energy used by beings, their communicative/receptive powers

—energy is cyclic, and once used, returns to the Earth for redistribution

—The Craft is both *animistic* and *pantheistic,* with everything seen as alive and respect shown to all.

—*awareness* is a deliberate activity of opening the intuitive and cognizant senses, conscious, and subconscious to receive information from animate surroundings

—*manipulating* energies requires alertness to their presence, willingness to communicate, and permission of the entity for the magical process

—*train* the extension of awareness by talking to plants, animals, birds, insects, rocks, etc.; *response* will come from in-dwelling spirits as a personal new alertness to things previously unnoticed and heightened intuitive perception of how these things feel and react

—Things of Nature that may be incorporated into spellwork include herbs, feathers, rocks, shells, crystals, minerals, *spring water* [purity], *rain water* [energy], *storm water* [power], *sea water* [cleansing], animal hair, fur, whiskers, claw sheaths [naturally shed] can be used in association with characteristics of the animal, soil may be used for seed and growth-related spells.

Circle: may be cast or not depending on the circumstances and spell—follow intuition.

Ritual: may be as simple or as complex as desired—rituals are a means of focus for the Practitioner, not for the Power.

Lists of Correspondences: bring energies together that are related to the goal.

—Communication with plants, rocks, etc. necessary before taking anything for spellwork.

—State what is needed, ask permission to take a portion of a plant, etc., and express gratitude.

—Always **give a Gift to receive a Gift** such as:

>—offering [milk, grain, beverage, coffee grounds, crushed eggshells, coin, etc.]

>—circle of protection drawn around the plant

>—blessing

>—pentagram drawn on plant around it or ground in front of it

—Inscribing items with sigils and *bindrunes* [monograms of two to three runic letters invoking their combined magical meanings] requires drawing up energy from the Earth or breathing on them to energize or enliven.

Construct Spell: determined by what is wanted, what will be written, said, steps taken, timing, and approach consistent with the goal and method.

—Spells are the vehicles of magical workings, so any ritual, brew, charm, chant, prayer, amulet, talisman, or crafted item created for magical purpose, utilizing the movement of energy, the speaking of a word or formula, in the generating of intent into manifestation is a spell.

—May inscribe a candle near the top so that as the symbol melts, the magic is released.

—May use pin to designate an accomplishment point in a candle spell [stick pin into candle near top, saying that when the candle melts to this point, the spell is sent into action, then chant, shake a rattle, meditate, etc., as desired while the candle burns to the pin].

—May write down goal and burn in candle flame during spell casting, seeing the spell as sent on its way.

—May burn herbs in candle flame, stating herb and purpose, seeing energy released to perform the task assigned.

—May use a photo, but be very careful about this so as not to go against the Rules of Conduct—it is wrong to try and force someone into an unwanted action—but may be used in healings, etc. [may be burned, torn, wrapped, buried, etc. as the spell requires].

—May combine items into pouches to place somewhere or carry.

—Learn to trust your intuition, focus on the desired outcome and see what method comes to mind as you flip through the Lists of Correspondences.

Stay Focused: to raise and send energy to accomplish goal; no drugs or alcohol needed for altered state of awareness, use meditation, breathing, chanting, dancing, etc.

—Only raise energy when spell item is completely prepared and ready for empowerment/ activation.

—Gathered energy needs to be released in one quick jolt once a peak is reached [delaying will dissipate the energy].

—*Raise* energy, *Focus* it on the intent of the spell, *Direct* it into the spell materials, and *Send* it on its way to accomplish the task.

—May address **Elemental Winds** by raising the completed spell materials to each Quarter to energize spell:

—North wind for physical actions

—East wind for new beginnings and mental actions

—South wind for power and vigorous actions

—West wind for cleansings and emotional actions

See Goal as Accomplished: at end of spell; use an ending phrase as: *So Mote It Be!*, or *It Is Done!*

—Visualize the raised energy as released to perform its task, so it is no longer hovering about.

—Ground excess energy by touching palms to floor/Earth.

Hands: tools for beseeching, invoking, blessing, unification, drawing energy inward, extending inner energies outward to share.

—Palms absorb and release energy.

—Hands gather energies called upon and direct these into spell materials.

—both hands focus raised energy into a palpable ball

—both hands push the energy into the spell object

—both hands push [send] the energy in the general direction needed for the spell to work or upward into the Universe for action

—Hands move energy, alone or with wand or athame in hand.

—Right hand draws in Elemental Fire for energizing and empowering.

—Left hand draws in Elemental Water to soothe, protect, and urge matters to completion.

—Both hands invoke, unite, receive, and bless.

—Dancing around the Circle, with arms raised and palms open gathers in energy.

—Coven dancing with hands held or opened raises a cone of energy at the center of the group for directing by the leader.

Gestures: in Sabbat rituals:

—Indicate the Goddess with palms up, arms open and raised.

—Indicate the God with arms crossed against the chest and palms inward [for Solar phases of passages: Lughnassadh, Mabon, Samhain].

—Express unity during invocation with palms outward, gathering in energy from the air as the hands are turned with palms inward, and palms are drawn to the chest, blending external and internal energies at the heart, then thrust hands back outward in front of the body with the heel of the palms down, fingertips up, and pushing outward [to return excess energy].

   —use once for unity

   —use twice for balance

   —use thrice for completion

   —may be used in calling the Quarters as well as

   —invocation of the Lady and the Lord

—Draw Divine blessings and energy with palms inward/against the chest followed by arms extended with hands motioned away with palms down then moved outward to release excessive energies.

—Access Universal energy [for an invocation, cleansing, balancing of internal energies].

   —raise arms and hands into a teepee position overhead [heel of palms nearly touch, center of palms angled back, fingers bent inward—like a blossom or bowl]

   —then bring hands down on either side of the head, with palms up, until level with the shoulders [draws Divine energy into balance with personal energy of third eye and crown to augment receptivity]

—Hold position through invocation.

—Then move to the hands against the chest and motioned outward to complete the cycle.

Feet: raise energy during dance.

—Left foot draws up strength and power of Elemental Earth to be utilized in workings.

—Right foot gathers the spiritual, mental and psychic energies of Elemental Air to be transmuted into physical manifestation through magical work

Breathing: to raise energy.

—*Chanting* with a growing crescendo [may use own with a simple rhyme to give rhythm or may use the Witch's Rune].

—*Altering* breathing pattern [sharp short intakes of breath, one large intake, hold, then release as focused and directed energy—too much will cause fainting].

—*Sweeping* intake, right to left and back again creates the loop of the cosmic lemniscate while gathering in energy; rapidly exhale directly onto the spell object for *enlivening*.

—*Breath of life* energy sends gathered energies off with a gentle power that is not rushed or distracted.

Dancing: to raise energy.

    —Deosil [clockwise] around the Circle for positive energy.

        —increasing energy drawn from the Earth

    —Widdershins [counterclockwise]around the circle to use negative energy.

        —gathering and compressing existing energy

DAILY BLESSING

Perform during: morning or evening on any day as desired.

Materials: sage and sweetgrass incense bundle [tiny ones are available]; incense holder [shell, dish, or cauldron]; matches.

Spell casting: Ground & Center, clearing out any static or chaotic energy within.

Light sage and sweetgrass bundle. Move bundle through air to make the sigil of the Solar Cross and the Lunar Spiral.

Make the sigil of the pentagram in the air with the smoke at the North, then at the East, at the South, and at the West.

Set incense bundle in holder:

> I call upon the Lord and the Lady of Sun and Moon,
> To cleanse and bless this day and room.

Envision the smoke reaching out to all corners of the home, blanketing the energies therein with soothing gentleness:

> Let this day be free from strife and fear:
> Let only joy and love come near.
> With blessings given and received,
> I walk in peace in word and deed.

SPELLS

BLESSED WATER RECIPE

Perform during: Full Moon Esbat; hour of Moon, Mercury, Mars, or Sun.

Materials: water in a cup or pitcher, bowl, rose [petals, water, extract, or oil—the latter is flammable], salt, small mirror [compact style] [make sufficient amount to store for use in spell workings between Esbats].

Spell casting:

Raise arms under Moonlight:

> I call upon Thee Great Lady of the Night, to bless this water I pour in Thy Light.

Pour water into bowl, add rose petal and hold bowl up in Moonlight:

> In this water doth shine Thy light, that it be consecrated in Thy sight. Cleansed and purified on this Esbat night, this water is blessed by Thy sacred rite.

Lift the salt in the Moonlight:

> Through the Lady hast all things their form, taking salt in the waters and lands of the Earth. Through Thy bright light, I consecrate this salt to aid in my work.

Add 3 pinches of salt to the water; stir 3 times; then use the mirror if needed to reflect the Full Moon onto the water in the bowl:

> By the light of the Moon, through the power in Thy Tides, a portion of Thy power now herein resides, that blessed be this water. By 3 times 3 this spell I bind, that it be cast with the power of nine. For as I will, *So Mote It Be!*

Set down the mirror and the bowl and turn the bowl 9 times deosil in the Moonlight:

> With power gathered and sent within, this spell is sealed 9 times again, that adds together 9 once more, that with these 3 is 9 the core. *So Mote It Be!*

Place water in bottle with lid and store away from light, to use as needed as blessed water.

SACRED SPACE PURIFICATION SPELL

Perform during: Waxing to Full Moon; day of Moon or Sun; hour of Moon, Saturn, or Mars.

Materials: small cook pot or aroma therapy bowl, blessed water, 1 star anise, 1 bay leaf, 1 tsp. sage, burner or tealight heat source; frankincense.

Spell casting: Consecrate an aromatherapy bowl or small cooking pot by passing through the smoke of frankincense and sprinkling with blessed water:

> I consecrate this container to aid in my Craft, that the spell I now weave will take hold and last.

Heat spring water in the bowl over a tealight or in the pot on a burner. When the water is hot, add star anise:

> Let all negativity be deflected from this place.

Add bay leaf:

> As the scent of this leaf moves through this place, may purification enter into this space.

Add sage:

> Through sage I now make this spell manifest, that with peace and protection this space will be blessed. For as I will, *So Mote It Be!*

Let scent move through area for an hour, then dispose of contents and wash out container.

NEW HOUSE PURIFICATION SPELL

Performed during: Waning Moon; hour of Mars [prior to occupancy].

Materials: two red candles, mortar and pestle, herbs: bay leaf, yarrow flowers, rosemary leaves, St. Johnswort leaves, Basil leaves, juniper berries, mullein leaves; charcoal block; handled cauldron; peeled garlic cloves [one for each room]; plastic baggie with twist tie.

Spell casting: Open all windows. Set red candles on either side of cauldron on kitchen counter and light. Light a charcoal block and place inside cauldron.

Grind in mortar equal parts of bay leaf, yarrow flowers, rosemary leaves, St. Johnswort leaves, basil leaves, juniper berries, and mullein. Add herbs to the glowing charcoal:

> I call upon ye herbs to drive out negativity and chaos, bringing thy blessings of peace and concord in their place.

Peel garlic cloves and place one in the center of each room:

> I call upon ye garlic to gather into yourselves the negativity and chaos that lingers, to draw into yourselves all malefic vapors and energies.

Carry the cauldron from room to room, censing each room widdershins. Return cauldron to the countertop between the candles.

Vacate the house for thirteen minutes. Return and gather the garlic cloves into a plastic bag without touching them, fasten, and put outside in the trash.

Close the windows. Let the candles burn another hour, then snuff. Scatter the cooled incense remains out of doors; bury candle remains or toss out in trash [to be buried in landfill].

ROOM CLEANSING SPELL

Perform during: Waning Moon; day of Moon or Saturn; hour of Mars or Sun.

Materials: tray with: 1 sprig white heather; 1 lit white candle in a holder; lit frankincense in a holder; bowl of blessed water.

Spell casting: take the candle and the incense and walk around the interior of the room:

> By fire and flame, by smoke and scent;
> I drive from this room all chaos and dissent.

Asperge the room using the sprig and water, sprinkling the baseboards, walls, cornices, and floor:

> By water and salt, by herb and flower;
> Peace and contentment return in this hour.

Take the tray out of doors:

> Follow the light, follow the scent.
> Into the Earth and into the Air,
> Energies gathered here I now vent.

Blow out the candle, bury the incense, lay the sprig over this, and pour out the water on top. Bury candle or toss out with trash [to be buried in landfill].

HOME PROTECTION SPELL

Perform during: Waxing to Full Moon; day of Moon, Mars or Saturn; hour of Mars or Saturn

Materials: a few stems of any combination of the following herbs: dill, fennel, marjoram, mint, mustard, mullein, mustard, rosemary, rue, white heather, woodruff, and yarrow, and red thread.

Spell casting: tie small bundles of herbs together with red thread and place on altar. Touch with ritual knife, saying:

> I conjure thee, protective herbs, on this day of [the Moon] and in this hour of [Mars], to be a protection and safeguard against all adversity and evil. Protect well this house and all who dwell within. As I will, *So Mote It Be!*

Hang one bundle in each room. Replace in one year, tossing out to scatter in the wind or putting in the trash [to be buried in the landfill].

PROTECTION POUCH

Perform during: Waning to New Moon; day of Saturn; hour of Mars, Saturn, or Sun.

Materials: black cloth; needle and red thread; tsp. of agrimony, clove, blackthorn; cauldron; wand; athame; pentacle.

Spell casting: sew a small pouch with black cloth and red thread. Place herbs into cauldron:

> Agrimony to return negative energies to the sender.
> Blackthorn to deflect negative energies away from me.
> Clove to exorcise harmful energies from my presence.

Stir with the tip of athame:

> Three herbs I call to work for me; harnessing negative energy; take and bind and send away; harmful forces in my way.

Stuff the herbs into the little pouch, then sew it up and set it on the pentacle. Wave wand over pouch, then touch to pouch:

> Earth and Air, Fire and Water! Emanations of the Lady and the Lord! I call upon thy grace and love to seal protection in this ward!

Carry in a pocket, purse, briefcase, etc. as desired.

HOME PROTECTION POUCH

Perform during: Waxing to Full Moon; day of Saturn or Moon; hour of Moon or Sun

Materials: athame; black cotton bag; 1 black candle, 1 white candle, bay leaves; garlic clove; fennel seed; dandelion root; fennel root or mandrake; rosemary oil; frankincense oil; frankincense incense; cotton ball; small piece of iron; blessed water; salt

Spell casting: rub rosemary oil on each candle. Inscribe white candle with ᚃ :

> Fearn for strength and solid foundation;

and with ⟩:

Thorn for protection and defense;

Inscribe black candle with ⟨:

Ethel for home and possessions;

and ᛗ:

Osa for good fortune and favorable outcome.

Light incense; then light white candle:

This flame burns for a solid, well-protected home!

Light black candle:

This flame burns for good fortune to smile upon my home and my possessions!

Put items into red bag as follows:

Bay for my desires; garlic for protection power; fennel seed for protection and deflecting negative energies; dandelion root for grounding; fennel root [inscribe with ᛗ or ⟨] **to be a protective watcher; iron for strength in defense of this home; and frankincense oil** [dab oil onto cotton ball] **for protection and power, that as I will, *So Mote It Be!***

Sew shut the bag:

Herbs and oil and iron strong; protect this house; that no harm come by day or night! In a quiet place is where you'll lay, keeping negativity far away, for as I will, *So Mote It Be!*

Consecrate by passing through the symbols of the Elementals:

Lord and Lady, bless this charm of protection made for your child, [Name]. Be thou empowered charm of mine, to protect my home, by Elemental Earth [sprinkle with salt]; **by Elemental Air** [pass through incense smoke]; **by Elemental Fire** [pass through candle flames]; **and by Elemental Water** [sprinkle with blessed water] **are you charged, that as I will, *So Mote It Be!*** [Place near entry to home.]

Bury candle remains or toss out with trash [to be buried in landfill].

PROTECTION FROM ACCIDENT OR DANGER

Perform during: Waxing to Full Moon; day of Saturn; hour of Moon or Sun.

Materials: one personal item; anise seeds; comfrey; mullein; heather; rosemary oil; frankincense oil; cotton ball; small black cotton pouch; red thread; needle; 1 white candle; 1 black candle; 2 lodestones; dragon's blood or frankincense incense; blessed water; salt.

Spell casting: rub rosemary oil on the two candles. Inscribe white candle with ᚦ :

> Thorn for protection.

Inscribe black candle with ᛖ :

> Eh for safe journey.

Light incense; then light white candle:

> This flame burns for protection from accident or danger!

Light black candle:

> This flame burns for safety, warding accident or danger!

Put items into pouch as follows:

> Anise for protection; comfrey for safety; mullein for protection; heather for protection; 2 lodestones of balance to draw favorable energies and repel unfavorable energies; [add frankincense oil to cotton ball] and frankincense to bind them all that as I will, *So Mote It Be!*

Sew shut the pouch:

> Herbs and lodestones work with me; protect me with thy energy! Keep me safe from any harm or accident; for as I will, *So Mote It Be!*

Pass the pouch through the symbols of the Elementals:

> Be thou empowered by Elemental Earth [sprinkle with salt], by Elemental Air [pass through incense smoke], by Elemental Fire [pass quickly through both candle flames], and by Elemental Water [sprinkle with blessed water] to protect me from accident and danger. *So Mote It Be!*

Keep in purse, briefcase, car glove compartment, pocket, or where else desired. Bury candles or toss out with trash [to be buried in landfill].

CAR PROTECTION SPELL

Perform during: Waxing to Full Moon; day of Jupiter, Saturn, or Sun; hour of Jupiter, Saturn, or Sun.

Materials: square of light-blue cotton cloth; pinch of betony, mustard seed, fennel seed, and St. Johnswort; red string; white feathers; 9 silver and black beads; dragon's blood, frankincense, or patchouli incense; red candle; cauldron; blessed water, salt.

Spell casting: Light incense. Inscribe red candle with: ᚦ ᚾ ᛏ ᛁ ᛉ ᛒ ᛗ ☉ ⊠ .

Set candle in cauldron and light. On cloth square place betony and mustard seed:

> **Betony and Mustard Seed for their protective energies!**

Add fennel seed and St. Johnswort:

> **Fennel and St. Johnswort for their power and strength!**

Tie ends of cloth together with red string:

> **Red for might!**

Pass through the symbols of the Elementals:

> **I call upon thee Elementals to charge this spell and bring forth the Power to work with me as I have cast! Be thou charged pouch of protection, by Elemental Earth** [sprinkle with salt], **by Elemental Air** [pass thru incense smoke], **by Elemental Fire** [pass thru center candle flame], **and by Elemental Water** [sprinkle with blessed or spring water].

Decorate with feathers:

> **I call upon thee Wind for thy blessing of this charm!**

Decorate with beads:

> **I call upon thee Earth for thy blessings of this charm!**

Open Circle and take pouch to the car. Walk around the car, touching the pouch to the front, back, and sides of the car:

> **Let the protective powers within this pouch bring safe travel, power, and strength to this vehicle!**

Place the pouch in the glove compartment, under the front seat or hang it from the rearview mirror for protection of the car. Bury candle remains or toss out in trash [to be buried in landfill].

ANTI-HURRICANE SPELL

Perform during: anytime there is threat of a hurricane.

Materials: a sharp knife [not athame].

Spell casting: take knife in hand and go outdoors, facing the direction from which the wind is blowing. Wave the knife overhead three times in a great circle while saying:

> I call upon thee, Elementals Air and Water!
> Go wherever ye please,
> But stay thou far away from me!
> Throughout the oceans ye may roam!
> But nowhere near to my own home!
> For kith and kin are thee to me,
> That As I Will, *So Mote It Be!*

Thrust the knife into the ground while envisioning that the winds will be "split" and not come near. After the danger has passed, retrieve the knife and rinse it off.

ANTI-LIGHTNING SPELL

Perform during: threat of lightning, Waning to Dark Moon, Saturday, hour of Saturn.

Materials: brown cloth, a few hawthorn berries, crumbled bay leaf, elderflowers, 3 peppercorns, silver ribbon or cord.

Spell casting: in the center of a square of brown cloth, place hawthorn berries:

> With hawthorn do I draw protection to this house.

Crumbled bay leaf:

> With bay is this spell strengthened.

Elderflowers:

> With elderflowers is danger deflected from this house.

Three peppercorns:

> With peppercorns is power infused into this spell.

Gather cloth and tie with silver cord or ribbon:

> Tied together with this cord, that lightning from this house is ward.

Knot three times:

> Knotted once, and twice, and thrice around.

Tie the last one three times:

> Three times more is this spell bound.

Tie one knot in each string, then knot those ends together:

> By knots of three times three, is lightning deflected into the ground.

Hang someplace high in the house.

MONEY SPELL

Perform during: Waxing to Full Moon of each Quarter [Dec, Mar, Jun, Sept]; day of Jupiter; hour of Saturn.

Materials: a dollar bill, silver and gold candles for the Goddess and God; green working candle; patchouli oil; cauldron to hold melted wax of votive and burn dollar in, lid or covering to snuff flame.

Spell casting: light silver and gold candles. Rub patchouli oil on green candle and inscribe with: ♭ ⊨ $ ♄ ♃ ☽ ☉ .

Set green candle in cauldron and light. Burn a dollar bill in the candle while rotating the cauldron nine times:

> With Saturn, Jupiter, and the Sun;
> As Lunar cycles spin endlessly;
> God of gold, laughing and free;
> Lady of silver, dancing with me;
> Bring me thy power, fill up my bower,
> Bring me this Quarter, abundance of money!

Bury candle remains or toss out in trash [to be buried in landfill].

MONEY CANDLE SPELL

Perform during: Waxing to Full Moon; day of Mercury, Jupiter, or Sun; hour of Mercury or Jupiter.

Materials: patchouli incense, green votive candle, cauldron to hold green candle and melted wax deity candles [blue, white, and orange], wand, athame, bowl to mix herbs, herbs: [pinch each] allspice, bergamot, comfrey, chamomile, cinquefoil, whole cloves, 1 nutmeg [crushed], mint, marjoram; may use a simmering pot pourri of water instead of candle and cauldron.

Spell casting: empower herbs by mixing in bowl with athame, then pass bowl thru the symbols of the Elementals:

I call upon thee Elementals to charge these herbs and bring forth their powers to work with me in the spell I cast! Be thou charged by Elemental Earth [sprinkle with salt], **by Elemental Air** [pass thru incense smoke], **by Elemental Fire** [pass thru center candle flame], **and by Elemental Water** [sprinkle with blessed or spring water].

Set cauldron or pot pourri on pentacle. Rub green candle with bergamot oil and inscribe with symbols: ᛒ ᛉ ↑ ᛈ ᚠ ᛩ and ᛪ.

Drop herbs into candle flame or simmering pot pourri:

With the power of Air is the spell carried; with the power of Fire is the magic released; with the power of Water is the will spread [sprinkle water]; and with the power of Earth is the goal brought into being [add athame tip of salt].

Move wand widdershins 3 times over votive or pot:

As this spell spreads through the air; nothing may my work impair! Bring success and wealth to me; for as this I spell, *So Mote It Be!*

Let burn one hour; snuff; scry for signs; bury candle wax or toss out in trash [to be buried in landfill]; if used, wash out pot pourri container.

MONEY DRAW POUCH SPELL

Perform during: Waxing to Full Moon; day of Jupiter or Sun; hour of Jupiter of the Moon.

Materials: small green cotton bag; green thread; needle; a coin [silver or gold is best]; 1 three-leaf clover; 1 green candle; 1 silver and 1 gold candle; 2 lodestones; clove oil; pine or patchouli oil; sweetgrass incense; cinquefoil; blessed water; salt.

Spell casting: rub clove oil on the green candle:

With clove are you enhanced to draw money by this spell.

Rub pine oil on silver and gold candles:

With pine are you enhanced with prosperity and energy for action.

Inscribe green candle with ᛪ:

Gera for rewards for my work and a fruitful harvest!

Inscribe silver candle with ᚠ:

Feoh for fulfillment, material wealth, and ambition satisfied!

Inscribe gold candle with ♢ :

Ethel for acquisitions and possessions!

Light the sweetgrass incense. Then light the silver candle:

This candle draws to me the blessing of Bendidia, the Lady of the Moon, whose twig in hand points the way to the treasures of Underworld.

Raise candle:

Bring prosperity and much money into my life through this spell!

Light the gold candle:

This candle draws to me the blessing of Dis, the Lord of the Underworld, Guardian of the treasures of the Earth.

Raise candle:

Bring the manifestation of the Earth's wealth into my life through this spell!

Light the green candle:

This candle shows the money coming to me through the blessings of She and He, to fulfill the will of Their child, [name]! *So Mote It Be!*

Put coin, clover, cinquefoil, and 2 lodestones into pouch and sew shut:

Money drawn to me, bring me more than I might need, that with this wealth content shall I be. With no harm to others wrung, be my wealth a blessed sum. This spell is sealed and it is done, for as I will, *So Mote It Be!*

Consecrate by passing through the symbols of the Elementals:

Be thou empowered by Elemental Earth [sprinkle pouch with salt], by Elemental Air [pass it through incense smoke], by Elemental Fire [pass it through the flames of the 3 candles], and by Elemental Water [sprinkle with blessed water] to bring me wealth and put money in my hand! For as I will, *So Mote It Be!*

Place in purse, pocket, wallet, or other location associated with money. Bury candle remains or toss out in trash [to be buried in landfill].

STRENGTH FOR SURGERY SPELL

Perform during: Waxing to Full Moon; day of Mars or Sun; hour of Saturn.

Materials: 2 light blue votive candles, cypress oil, St. Johnswort and rosemary leaves.

Spell casting: raise open arms:

> On this day of great energy, in this hour of self-preservation, I call upon the ruling Powers and the Elementals to aid me in this spell.

Anoint two light blue votive candles with cypress essential oil. Inscribe ᛒ on one and ᚠ on the other; set candles on Altar and light:

> I call upon the Lady and the Lord to stand by me. Let the Power of thy love and thy protection surround me, that this surgery be successful and I gain good health.

Drop in the flames rosemary and St. Johnswort leaves:

> By the power of the Lady and the Lord, by herb and by light, let ill health take flight! *So Mote It Be!*

Let the candles burn down. Bury the remains or toss out in trash [to be buried in landfill].

HEALTH SPELL

Perform during: Waxing to Full Moon; day of Mars, Jupiter, or Sun; hour of Jupiter.

Materials: peppermint oil, 1 blue votive candle, cauldron, herbs: 2 tsp. lavender flower and 1 tsp. each of thyme, allspice, coriander seed, and willow leaf.

Spell casting: grind the herbs:

> I charge you by the Sun and the Moon, on this day of high energy and hour of healing, to release your powers into my work!

Rub peppermint oil on a blue votive candle. Inscribe with ▽ △ △ , a word for the ailment, then add these symbols while saying:

> Jupiter [♃] for health, Beorc [ᛒ] for the Goddess, Water [▽] for fluids, Tyr [↑] for victory, Osa [ᛗ] for the God, and Sigel [ᚼ] to direct the healing energy.

Set candle in cauldron and light:

> I call upon thee Great Goddess to hasten my healing. Through this candle dedicated to Health, inscribed with the symbols of the God and the Goddess; Healing Energy and Victory over the Watery confusion in my body, and with the herbs of healing whose energy may be released to my aid do I call upon Thee. Cast aside my sickly imbalance I bid Thee, that as I will, *So Mote It Be!*

Add the herbal mixture, saying:

> With the protective cleansing power of lavender; with the healing strength
> of thyme, allspice, and coriander seed, and with the protective and healing
> power of the willow do I infuse this spell with the power to work my will.
> *So Mote It Be!*

Burn one hour, snuff, scry the wax for images indicating the response time, then bury the remains or toss out in trash [to be buried in landfill].

HEALTH SPELL II

Perform during: Waxing to Full Moon; day of Mars, Jupiter, or Sun; hour of Jupiter.

Materials: sandalwood incense, Goddess and God candles; 2 yellow votive candles; 2 containers for votives that will hold melted wax; rue oil; salt; blessed water; pinch each of ash bark, St. Johnswort, tansy, woodruff, and an herb that relates to the illness [*see Herbal Lists of Correspondences*].

Spell crafting: anoint yellow votives with rue oil:

> These candles are dedicated to the healing of [Name], in the Names of the
> Lady and the Lord [Names].

Pass each yellow votive through symbols of the Elementals:

> I consecrate thee through the power of Elemental Earth [sprinkle with salt],
> through the power of Elemental Air [pass through incense smoke], through the
> power of Elemental Fire [pass through the flames of both Deity candles], and
> through the power of Elemental Water [sprinkle with blessed water].

Inscribe both yellow candles with ᛒ ᚠ ᚺ ᚦ ↑ ⊠ ᛖ ᚾ ᚲ ᚦ; and ᚷ. Light one votive candle from the Goddess candle and one from the God candle.

Add the following herbs into the flames of each votive candle:

> Ash bark for health and protection; St. Johnswort for health, protection, and
> strength; tansy for health and the love of the Goddess; woodruff for victory and
> the love of the God; [ailment herb] for the healing of [name/type of ailment].

Let the votive candles burn until reduced nearly to the bottom of the container. Snuff out; scry the wax; Open the Circle; bury remains of wax or toss out in trash [to be buried in landfill].

HEALTH POUCH SPELL

Perform during: Waxing to Full Moon; day of Jupiter; hour of Sun or Jupiter.

Materials: small yellow cotton bag; red thread; needle; 1 personal item; rosemary leaves; St. Johnswort; thyme; coriander seeds; 1 white candle; 1 red candle; dragon's blood ink; pen; sage incense; vetivert oil; blessed water; salt.

Spell casting: rub oil on the candles. Inscribe the white candle with ▷ :

> Thorn for protection.

Inscribe the red candle with ᐸ :

> Ken for opening energy and transformation.

With pen and ink, draw on outside of yellow bag ᚾ :

> Uruz for physical health.

Light incense; light white candle:

> This flame doth burn to bring good health.

Light red candle:

> And this flame doth burn to bring energy and strength.

Put items into yellow bag:

> Rosemary to hold health; thyme to ward illness; St. Johnswort and coriander seeds keep me [add personal item] strong! For as I will, *So Mote It Be!*

Sew shut the bag:

> Health is mine to have and hold! Energy and strength are mine forevermore! For as I will, *So Mote It Be!*

Consecrate by passing pouch through the symbols of the Elementals:

> Be thou empowered by Elemental Earth [sprinkle with salt], by Elemental Air [pass through incense smoke], by Elemental Fire [pass through candle flames], and by Elemental Water [sprinkle with blessed water] to protect my health and keep me well and strong! This pouch keeps good health with me! For as I will, *So Mote It Be!*

Bury candle remains or toss out in trash [to be buried in landfill]. Carry pouch in pocket, purse, etc.

FERTILITY AND PREGNANCY SPELL

Perform during: Waxing to 1 day prior to Full Moon; day of the Moon or day before Full Moon; hour of the Moon.

Deity image/focus: Artemis, the High Fruitful Mother.

Have: offerings of milk and corn.

Materials: pale green votive candle for spell; clover; cassia, cinquefoil, verbena, carnation petal, woodruff; rose oil; damiana tea.

Spell casting: set up altar, cast Circle, call Elementals, light votive; sprinkle the clover on the altar/sacred space:

> This space is consecrated by Earth and Moon, that I may call upon Thee, Great Bountiful Mother of All!

Rub the votive candle with rose oil, inscribe runes: fruitful harvest ⟨ , joy ⟩ , victory ↑ , and light the candle:

> Here is the sign of that which I seek: the bountiful harvest, brings joy and victory with the fruit of my womb!

Hold up the bowls of corn and milk:

> Accept my gifts, High Fruitful Mother and Harvest Father! Bring unto me Thy gifts of life and milk!

Combine the herbs and drop into votive candle flame :

> Cassia for fertility; verbena for love; carnation petal, for the Goddess; woodruff for the God; cinquefoil for Motherhood: for as thou hast thine, grant that I have mine. Great Artemis, you have your child, now grant me mine, for I call upon you to bless me with thy bounty.

Let the candle and herbs burn down; snuff the candle:

> Through thy Power, Great Lady, do I bind all power within this circle into this spell. *So Mote It Be!*

Farewell the Elementals, open Circle, leave offerings overnight on Altar and discard in morning. Bury candle remains when cooled, or toss out in trash [to be buried in landfill].

Drink damiana tea on night of planned conception.

LOVE SPELL TO PUSH SOMEONE INTO ACTION

Perform during: Waxing Moon to Full Moon; day of Venus; hour of Venus.

Materials: 1 red votive candle, red paper, pen & ink [dove's blood or black]; small piece of parchment or red paper; cauldron or other container for candle that can hold melted wax and not break with heat; ½ tsp. marjoram, ½ tsp. yarrow, pinch of pine needles, marigold flower; stick or cone incense [jasmine, rose, or musk]; small bit of something that has belonged to the intended or a photo [will create a good size fire, so be prepared to put it out if necessary] or write the person's name [and birthdate if available] on the parchment paper.

Spell casting: on paper draw a mandala [circle] with a double ring around the edge for writing words within and with a dot between the words, as follows: at the top: -HABONDIA- at the bottom: -PHUL- at the left side: -ADONIS- at the right side: -HAGITH- [or fill in space with "Love-Conquers-All-So-Mote-It-Be" written in Runic symbols].

Draw a pentagram within the center of the circle so the tips of the star points touch the inner rim of the double ring border of the circle.

Fill in the mandala now as follows: **Hagith** sigil in the center, symbol ♀ in the top [head] of star, symbol ☽ in the left leg of star, symbol ☉ in right leg of star, [arms of star are empty], **Och** sigil in space under left arm of star, **Phul** sigil in space under right arm of star, zodiac sign symbol of desired person in space above left arm of star, planetary ruler symbol of zodiac sign of desired person in space above right arm of star, seeker's own zodiac sign symbol and planetary ruler symbol of zodiac sign in space between the legs of the star.

Inscribe the red votive candle with: ᚦ ↑ ᛒ ᚼ ᚦ ᚠ and ✕.

Place cauldron on top of paper pentagram, which is now a pentacle, add red candle, light:

> Red candle burn bright as [name] is possessed by burning love for [me].
> Let [his/her] desire burn for me as nothing has been so desired before. Let [him/her] burn with love for me.

Drop something [if you have] of the intended's into flame or use parchment paper with name [and birthdate if you have]:

> This IS [name] burning with love for me!

Add to candle flame: pinch pine needles, marigold flower :

> Bring [name] to [me], that [name] love only me, and may the essence of these herbs incite [name] to love only me, and to come to me! *So Mote It Be!*

Let the candle burn down [one hour] while scrying for signs. Snuff, cool, remove wax, and bury in ground:

Here goes the seed into the fertile soil. Let the spell grow with naught to foil.
So Mote It Be!

RETURN A WANDERING LOVER

Perform during: Waxing Moon; day of Venus; hour of Venus or Moon.

Materials: small piece of white paper; needle [*not* a pin] or black or dragon's blood ink; red votive candle; cauldron to hold candle and melting wax.

Spell casting: Inscribe red candle with: ᛒ ↑ ᛒ ᛉ ᛈ ᛊ and ✕ ; zodiac signs of intended and of self.

Light candle. If writing in own blood, heat tip of needle in flame, prick thumb of power hand [one used in writing] with needle. Write with ink or own blood your own name and that of lover so it forms a circle.

Draw two circles around the names, then fold paper toward self and touch to the candle:

> **The Blood speaks clearly! What does it say? Bring back my lover within one day! For as I will, *So Mote It Be!***

Drop all of paper into candle flame, then let burn for one hour. Bury remains or toss out in trash [to be buried in landfill].

STONE POWER SPELL

Perform during: Full Moon; day of Mars; hour of Sun.

Materials: bowl, spring water, 1 stone of aventurine, carnelian, smoky quartz.

Spell casting: place stones in bowl of spring water. Set outside so that the moon is reflected in the water.

> **Here on the day of Mars, in the hour of the Sun, I call down the Moon to charge and energize these stones!**

With wand in hand and arms raised, dance around the bowl chanting:

> **Power of Luna, Power of Sol; Power of Aries, Power I call!**

When the energy level is highest, grasp the wand in both hands and point the wand at the bowl:

> **Empowered Be!**

Drain out the water into a jar and store for use as a success and power elixir or water. Remove the stones, wrap in black cloths, and put away until needed for an extra power kick in spells and charms.

GOOD HUNTING SPELL

Perform during: hour of Mars day before hunting.

Materials: 1 red candle; patchouli incense; herbs: 1 star anise, bergamot leaves, artemesia leaves, red dianthus petals.

Spell casting: Inscribe candle with ᚱ ᚦ ᚤ and ♀ , then light. Light incense:

> Let this earthy scent attune me with Herne the Hunter, the bounty of the Earth, and the natural forces of life's cycles.

Drop herbs into the candle: first, star anise:

> I call upon the spirits of hunter ancestors to aid me in my hunt tomorrow.

Bergamot leaves:

> I call upon the power of bergamot to bring me success in my endeavors tomorrow.

Artemesia leaves:

> I call upon the Lady of the Hunt to bring me success in my endeavors tomorrow.

Red dianthus (carnation) petals:

> I honor the blood of the animal I seek; life unto life, I hunt what I eat. The cycles we share flow ever eternal; Hunters and hunted, revered and fraternal.

WARRIOR'S SPELL

Perform during: Waxing to Full Moon at the hour of Mars on a Tuesday.

Materials: mandrake root or fennel root, incense, red candle, blessed water, salt, red cotton yarn.

Spell casting: take root and pass through incense smoke, candle flame; sprinkle with water and salt:

> I consecrate this root by the powers of the Elementals that it may be cleansed and purified to aid in my work.

Set it on a pentacle:

> Little man, listen to me.
> I will dress thee and keep thee, blessed in my company,
> That thou turn aside harm from my fighting man.
> That he return safely as soon as he can.

Wrap the root in red cotton yarn. Raise energy and direct it into the rootman, saying:

> In the eye of Mars, by the fires of fury, let my warrior be steadfast, safe-kept, and victorious.

Wrap the root in a red cloth and hide in a safe place. Keep it there until the warrior returns, then unbind the root and bury it.

> You have served me well, now I unbind this spell.

Bury candle remains or toss out with trash [to be buried in landfill].

ENHANCING COURAGE SPELL

Perform during: Waxing to Full Moon, Sunday or Tuesday, hour of Mars.

Materials: red candle, rosemary oil, wand.

Spell casting: Rub candle with oil. Inscribe the candle with runic symbols:

> Feoh for energy, ᚠ
> Thorn for protection and willpower, ᚦ
> Mannaz for self-improvement, ᛉ
> Ken for opening of positive energy, ᚲ
> Ur for personal strength. ᚢ
> Daeg for a fresh start, ᛗ
> Sigel for achievement and self-confidence, ᛋ
> and Tyr for victory, courage, and success. ↑
> Be these directed to me [own zodiac and ruling planet signs].

Light the candle and wave wand above it:

> I call upon the Powers of Earth, Air, Fire, and Water; the energies of the ancient runes; the spirits of the hoary planets! As this candle melts, may these qualities I seek enter into me, that as I will, *So Mote It Be!*

Let the candle burn down, then bury the remains or toss out with trash [to be buried in landfill].

WIN AT SPORTS SPELL

Perform during: Waxing to Full Moon, hour of the Sun.

Materials: wand, bright yellow candle, dragon's blood incense & burner, herbs: orris root, woodruff leaves, bergamot leaves.

Spell casting: inscribe candle with ᚱ ᚲ ↑ ᚢ , then light dragon's blood incense:

I call upon the power and energy of dragon's blood that I may be victorious in [name of sport or contest] on [when it will occur]!

Drop orris root into the candle flame:

Let my competition not exceed me!

Drop woodruff leaves into the candle flame:

I call upon the energies of woodruff that I may overcome all obstacles in [sport/contest]!

Drop bergamot leaves into the candle flame:

May the power of bergamot enhance my success!

Raise energy chanting with wand in hand:

By root and by herb, by resin and light;
The victory I seek shall be mine by right!
This spell is bond and the rhyme complete;

Then direct the energy with wand into the candle flame:

That as this I will, *So Mote It Be!*

Let candle burn one hour; then snuff; scry the wax; bury when cools or toss out with trash [to be buried in landfill].

CALLING THE WIND TO AID A SPELL

Perform during: as required by spell being energized.

Materials: completed spell item to be energized.

Spell casting: upon completed preparations for any spell for which special energy is sought.
Raise spell item at each Quarter while addressing the winds:

Winds of the East, dazzling and bright, initiate the action of this spell!
Winds of the South, fiery and radiant, infuse this spell with power and energy!
Winds of the West, gentle and buoyant, make this spell satisfy my needs!
Winds of the North, rushing and mighty, bring this spell into manifested form!

Set the spell item on the altar:

Four Winds carry this spell that no obstacle may impede my will! *So Mote It Be!*

Bless and farewell each Wind.

RAIN SPELL

Perform during: whenever there is need for rain.

Materials: none.

Spell casting: stand outdoors with arms raised; call out to the sky:

> I call upon thee, Elemental Water, Elemental Fire,
> Elemental Air, and Elemental Earth!
> Come together in this place,
> Wind come round, and Lightning clash,
> Rain pour down onto the Ground!
> All are kin, and heed this call, for
> Earth and those upon do thirst.

Visualize the Elementals coming together:

> Elemental Air, bring cooling breezes!
> Elemental Fire, bring lightning flashes!
> Elemental Water, bring rain to fall!
> Elemental Earth, reach up to receive them all!

With hands, gather the energy in the air and motion this toward the ground. Place hands palms down, in a gesture of blessing:

> With blessings given and blessings received, I chant this spell that as I will, *So Mote It Be!*

TAROT SPELL

Perform during: Waxing to Full Moon; day of Mercury or Moon; hour of the Moon, Sun, or Mercury; after Consecration of a Tool Ritual.

Materials: 2 white votive candles, pentacle; frankincense or lavender incense; black thread.

Spell casting: set cards on pentacle; place white candles on either side of pentacle; light incense and place in front of pentacle. Pick up cards and wrap a black thread around the deck:

> This tarot is mine, consecrated to my use, bound by the thread that ties it to me. I charge that no unwanted influence hold sway over these cards by Air [pass through incense smoke], **by Fire,** [pass quickly through candle flame], **by Water** [sprinkle quickly with blessed water and wipe dry, or give a quick breath with open mouth over the cards], **and by Earth** [set the cards on the pentacle].

Remove thread from cards; store the thread to wrap the deck whenever needed. Bury candle remains or toss out with trash [to be buried in landfill].

Travel on Time Spell

Perform during: whenever needed to avoid arriving late at destination.

Materials: none.

Spell casting: Envision the vehicle covered from back to front in a protective, shiny material upon which the passing scenery is reflected, rendering the car invisible, but imprinted as an obstacle so to be unconsciously seen by other drivers. While not speeding, Time will not be registered on the vehicle. If flying, envision the clouds reflected on the plane so the plane seems to disappear in them. While doing the envisionment of this change:

> Great Lady, Great Lord, make all time slow down. I pass through the moments between the beats of time, that I arrive early at [name of destination].

Know that you will be on time, and travel with a peaceful heart.

Attracting Fairies Spell

Perform during: Full Moon; day of Venus, Mercury or the Moon; hour of the Moon or Venus.

Materials: decorations of choice to create a grotto or shrine area to attract Fairies [may use a flagstone base, add potted or planted herbs or shamrocks, and hang near it delicate wind chimes that tinkle]; spring water; lavender incense; pale lavender votive or small pillar candle; muffin [whole grain or cornmeal are best] in offering dish; wine in a shallow bowl.

Spell casting: set up grotto or shrine to attract Fairies. Light lavender incense and lavender candle. Sprinkle grotto with spring water. Hold up in front of grotto the offering of muffin and wine:

> I call upon thee, Fair Ones, with gifts of cake and wine,
> I offer blessings unto thee, and bid thee dance and dine.
> Come dwell at hand and share this land,
> That by thee my home shall blessed be.

Set the offerings in the grotto or shrine. When the incense is burned out, extinguish the candle and leave the grotto or shrine. Light candle occasionally as desired, and when it is used up, toss out remaining wax with trash [to be buried in landfill] and replace with new candle. Burn incense occasionally as desired.

Tend the grotto regularly, leaving tokens, and offerings of milk and grain or muffin. On special occasions, leave wine or whiskey instead of milk.

DIVINATION SPELL

Perform during: Waxing to Full Moon; day of Moon or Mercury; hour of Mercury.

Materials: lavender incense; lavender votive or small pillar candle; tea made from mugwort and lemonbalm; libation bowl; tea cup.

Spell casting: light incense and candle. Pour some of the tea into libation bowl, then drink a cup of tea, letting the rest cool. Look into candle and envision the psychic pathways clearing and opening.

Wash hands and face in the cooled tea, then wash any divination tools that are appropriate for this [crystal ball, mirror]:

> Great Lord of the Sun, Great Lady of the Moon;
> I call upon thee both to grant my boon!
> Open the way for my psychic sight,
> Let the symbols of divination come to my knowing,
> That I may understand the visions from the Shadow Paths,
> And communicate between the worlds.
> I ask this as thy child [name] with blessings given and
> received, that as I will, *So Mote It Be!*

Bury candle remains or toss out with trash [to be buried in landfill]. Pour tea remains on ground or down sink and rinse out with cold water.

CHARGING STORM WATER

Perform during: approaching rain storm; then Full Moon Esbat.

Materials: large bowl; white cloth; silver candle; cauldron; tsp. mugwort; feather; clean dark bottles with lids.

Spell casting: set bowl outside as powerful rain storm approaches and leave where it can collect rainwater without interference from overhanging roofs, trees, or other obstacles. When enough water collects, bring bowl indoors; cover with white cloth and set on Altar.

At the Full Moon Esbat, remove cloth so moonlight will touch the water. Light silver candle, drop mugwort into flame, and waft the smoke with the feather over the water:

> By Thunder and Lightning,
> By Mugwort and Moon!
> This water is charged to work any boon!

Do Blessed Water Spell to use as such. Burn candle for 1 hour. Pour the water into clean bottles for storage in a dark area until needed to boost the power of any spellwork. Bury candle remains or toss out with trash [to be buried in landfill].

Meditation Spell

Perform during: Waxing to Full Moon; day of Sun, Moon, or Mercury; hour of Mercury or Sun.

Materials: light blue candle; sandalwood incense; seating pillow or chair.

Spell casting: light incense and candle prior to beginning meditation. Ground and center.

Move power hand in a direct line from the top of the head to the center of the abdomen, turning the hand as proceed so as to set lightly upon the other hand as it rests palm up in the lap. For two counts each, breathe in, hold, release through the mouth, and hold. Repeat 2 more times, cleansing the lungs. Envision a shimmering white light radiating from the crown of the head.

I call upon the Powers of the Universe to aid me in my meditation.

Begin intended meditation. If there is a lot of candle remaining, let cool, then wrap in blue cloth and store to light again at next meditation session. Otherwise, bury candle remains or toss out with trash [to be buried in landfill].

Stang Rune Spell

Perform during: Waxing to Full Moon, Sunday, Monday, Wednesday, or Friday, hour of Sun, Moon, Mercury, or Venus.

Materials: the staff or stang [2–3 prong staff that acts as a portable Altar]; rock salt; lavender incense; orange candle; blessed water; vetivert or pine oil; wood burning material or something else to inscribe or paint runes on the wood.

Spell casting: rub candle with oil. Inscribe candle with ᛟ, flanked by ᛒ and ᚨ. Pass stang/staff through the symbols of the Elementals.

I consecrate thee through the power of Elemental Earth [sprinkle with salt], **through the power of Elemental Air** [pass through incense smoke], **through the power of Elemental Fire** [pass through the candle flame], **and through the power of Elemental Water** [sprinkle with blessed water].

Engrave, burn, or paint down the stang/staff ᚨ ᛏ ᚹ ᚠ ᛝ and ᛋ:

For ancient wisdom; success; joy; prosperity; creativity; and empowerment;

Add ᚷ ᛒ ᚨ ᚹ:

In partnership with the Goddess and the God, under Their protection;

Add ᛟ:

I name this my possession.

Beneath this, create a monogram of your Craft Name:

I, who am [name], **name this my Craft tool.**

Add ↓ :

Through Eoh, are we connected, I to them and they to me, and this Stang to us.

Add a sigil of Moon ◎ and Sun ⊕:

Through the Lady and the Lord, is this stang blessed and protected. *So Mote It Be!*

Let staff or stang stand with incense smoke and candle burning near the base for an hour. Bury candle remains or toss out with trash [to be buried in landfill].

PASSING THE MIDHES

Perform during: Full Moon or Sidhe Moon Ritual; Sunday or Monday, hour of the Moon or Mercury for ease at reading Ogham fews in castings.

Materials: green Altar cloth, Altar aligned North; 3 pillar candles in a horizontal line across the Altar [black-red-white]; athame, wand, candle snuffer, small cauldron, pentacle, incense burner and charcoal disk, acacia herb, lavender flowers or incense stick, spring water, anointing oil, matches, food and beverage, burdock root, calendula, mullein, ogham fews, 3x5 piece of paper or parchment, pen, dragon's blood ink, three 12-inch lengths of thread in red, purple, and green, black mirror, small black pouch, and a purple or lavender votive candle in container at Goddess side of Altar.

Spell Casting: take bath scented with lavender or vervain prior to spell. Cast Circle as with Sidhe Moon, calling upon the Elementals to aid and watch over your travels.

Inscribe on purple candle the symbols for the Lady))O((and the Lord ☿ , travel ᚏ and between the worlds ᛗ .

Place black mirror at the center of Altar with ogham fews behind it, and the three pillar candles across in front. Light incense and purple candle. If using a charcoal diskette, light it and place some of the acacia on it to smolder.

Focus on the intersecting points to Otherworld and Underworld, which are coll ᚉ and duir ᚇ ,and how coll, the hazel, connects the power of wisdom with the wand and the practitioner, and how duir, the oak, links the power of courage with the seeking of truth.

Take the red candle and light it from the purple one, then set it on top of the pentacle in front of the black mirror:

Here I stand in the center of my world, passionate of life and physical of form.

Drop some of the burdock into the red candle flame:

> The Middleworld of challenge, knowledge, prosperity, and contentment bring me joy.

Draw ≣ on the upper right top edge of the paper for traveling to Otherworld and focus on the properties of this tree as the Witches' tree, the tree of wicce ["wich'che"], or wisdom, creativity, and perception:

> I call upon the spirit of the hazel to be my guide and open the path to me to Otherworld.

Crease the paper, pass it through the incense smoke, sprinkle it lightly with the blessed water; pass it quickly through the red candle flame:

> By Earth and by Air; by Water and by Fire, I call upon the power of coll to guide me. I have the passage of hazel in my hand!

Snap shut the section of paper with the few on it and fold the paper over tightly. Hold paper with one hand and with the other, light the white candle from the red one:

> With coll do I pass the midhe from Middleworld to Otherworld.

Move the red candle to the right side and place the white candle in front of the black mirror. Gaze into the mirror past the flame and envision the path to Otherworld blocked by hazel branches. Lightly tap the mirror with the folded paper:

> Open the midhe, for I have coll in my hand.

See the branches part. See the path that lies ahead and the paper transformed into a wand of hazel. Drop some of the marigold into the white candle flame:

> I give the gift of calendula to receive the gift of sight in Otherworld. Let this herb open the way as an offering to the People of this fair world.

Move along the path, through a woodland, and enter into a broad plain to stand where the edges of four realms converge and spread outward:

> Here I stand in the center of Otherworld, filled with the wonder of eternity, and spiritual in form.

Point the hazel wand in each quarter, one at a time:

> I move with coll in the North,

See what is shown of age and wisdom, then:

> I move with coll in the West,

See what is shown of light and and gentleness, then:

> I move with coll in the East,

See what is shown of abundance, then:

> I move with coll in the South,

See what is shown of happiness. Return now to the midhe:

> I take the passage of coll back to Middleworld.

Set white candle back at the right side and place the red candle before the mirror. Envision walking back along the path through the woods and back to the altar.

With the paper still folded over the few of coll, write now ᛞ in the upper left space to travel to Underworld. Think about the properties of the oak as power, endurance, truth, and strength. Then say:

> I call upon the spirit of the oak to be my guide and open the path to me to Underworld.

Crease the paper and pass it through the symbols of the Elementals:

> By Earth and by Air; by Water and by Fire, I call upon the power of duir to guide me. I have the passage of oak in my hand!

Snap shut the section of paper and fold tightly over once more. Hold onto this with one hand and with the other, light the black candle from the red one:

> With duir do I pass the midhe from Middleworld to Underworld.

Move red candle to the right side and place the black candle in front of the black mirror. Gaze into the mirror past the flame and envision the path to Underworld blocked by low-spreading branches of river oaks. Lightly tap the mirror with the folded paper:

> Open the midhe, for I have duir in my hand.

See the branches part. See the dark river that lies ahead and the paper transformed into a wand of oak. Drop some of the mullein into the black candle flame:

> I give the gift of mullein to receive the gift of sight in Underworld. Let this herb open the way as an offering to the people of this shadow world.

Envision stepping into a small flatboat and moving across the placid river to land upon the opposite shadowy shore. Step out of the boat and enter into the place on the plain in which four realms converge, spreading outward from that point. Say:

> Here I stand in the center of Underworld, Serene with love and transformation, fleeting of form.

Point the oak wand in each quarter, one at a time:

I move with duir in the North [see what is shown of death and transformation],

Then:

I move with duir in the West [see what is shown of cleansing and positive changes],

Then:

I move with duir in the East [see what is shown of introspection, growth, and fruition],

Then:

I move with duir in the South [see what is shown of energy, new beginnings, and hidden powers].

Return now to the midhe:

I take the passage of duir back to Middleworld.

Set black candle to left side and return the red candle before the mirror. Envision moving back to the river, boarding the boat and crossing the dark river back to the altar. Look into the mirror past the flame of the red candle. Bend the folded paper so both ends point forward, and see two wands in your hand, one of hazel and one of oak. Say:

The midhes stand open, for I have coll and duir, Wisdom and Strength, in my hand.

Drop some of the burdock into the red candle flame:

I give the gift of burdock to receive the gift of sight in Middleworld. Let this herb open the way as an offering to the powers of this land.

Enter onto the plain where the four realms of Middleworld converge, spreading outward from that point.

**Here I stand once more, in the center of my world,
Passionate of life and physical of form.**

Point the double wand to each quarter, one at a time:

I move with Wisdom and Strength in the North, to learn from challenges and overcome obstacles [see what is shown of gateways to success and self-expression].

288

Then:

I move with Wisdom and Strength in the West, to gain in knowledge and learning [see what is shown of tests to come, balance, and decisions to be made].

Then:

I move with Wisdom and Strength in the East, to achieve prosperity and harvest [see what is shown of inner transformations and development for harmony].

Then:

I move with Wisdom and Strength in the South, to know contentment with the strength to enjoy life [see what is shown of inner strength, awareness, and confidence].

CREATING THE MIDHE CHARM

Hold the doubled paper folded tightly together:

Here have I the paths opened from Middleworld to Otherworld and Underworld that I move between the worlds with ease of passage.

Wrap the red thread around the paper:

Let the power of red enhance the strength of the oak.

Wrap the purple thread around the paper:

Let the power of purple enhance the wisdom of the hazel.

Wrap the green thread around the paper:

Let the power of green enhance this tool with the herbal blessing of Nature.

Place the wrapped paper into a small black pouch and close, then pass through the symbols of the Elementals:

My wand of coll and duir I keep close to me, Passed through the Elementals, warded in black from negativity and knotted thrice: [tie each knot as spoken]: once for Otherworld, once for Underworld, and once for Middleworld. The passing of the Midhes lies in my hands.

Put the ogham fews on top of the pentacle and lay the pouch on top of the fews, then snuff the white, black, and red candles. Leave the pouch on the altar one hour, then put the charm in the ogham bag.

Proceed to the Simple Feast and opening of the Circle. Bury candle remains or toss out with trash [to be buried in landfill].

OGHAM SPELL

Perform during: Full or Sidhe Moon Esbat [this short version of Passing the Midhes, may be used as a refresher].

Materials: lavender incense, purple candle, paper, pen and dragon's blood or red ink, calendula, mullein, ogham fews in a bag, lengths of thread in purple, red, and green.

Spell casting: light incense.

Inscribe candle with Ur, ≢ , Saille, ⫣ , and Beithe, ⊢ , and light. Draw a large X on a square of paper. On top edge, draw Coll, ⫤ :

> I stand with Coll at the gateway to Otherworld,

Drop some calendula into the candle flame:

> I give the gift of calendula to receive that of Other sight. I travel through the realms of Otherworld and return unto my own.

On bottom edge of paper, draw Duir ⊣ :

> I stand with Duir at the gateway to Underworld.

Drop some mullein into the candle flame:

> I give the gift of mullein to receive that of sight in Underworld. I travel through the realms of Underworld and return unto my own.

Fold paper, wrap with purple, red, and green thread, and place in the ogham bag. Bury candle remains or toss out with trash [to be buried in landfill].

CRAFTS

FAIRY HERBAL POUCH

Function: to establish or maintain an energy connection with the Other People, create the pillow and hang from a tree in the yard, a fence post, or place somewhere indoors:

a. to attract Fairies to dwell in yard and/or home

b. to seek Fairie aid in magic and/or divination

c. to gain Fairy companionship

d. to receive aid in travels to Fairy Realms

e. for dreams of Faerie

f. for Fairie protection of yard/home

Perform during: a Friday, Midsummer Eve, or November 11, Waxing to Full Moon

Materials: select desired herbs, material color, crystals/stones, decorative objects, ribbon color, etc. from Lists of Correspondences.

Create the Item:

a. select the color of cloth, herbs, and stones suitable to purpose

b. sew up the cloth in thread of the chosen color, leaving an opening for the contents

c. stuff the pillow with the herb, stones, etc., then sew the rest shut

Consecrate the Item: have pentacle, blessed water, sea salt or burdock root, floral incense, heather sprig [optional], and wand.

a. light a lavender or light gray candle

b. pass the pillow through the Elementals

> I call upon the Powers of the Elementals to enliven the magic and stir the energies into this charm that it may call Fair Ones to me! By Earth [sprinkle with salt/root], Air [pass through incense smoke], Fire [pass through candle flame], and Water [sprinkle with blessed water using heather sprig], I consecrate this pillow [or pouch] to my use. *So Mote It Be!*

c. set the pillow on the pentacle, wave the wand [or power hand] overhead in a circle:

> I gather thy energies to work this spell and do my will. *So Mote It Be!*

d. touch the pillow with the wand/power hand:

> Be thou charged, pouch [or pillow] of Fairy [name purpose of pillow or pouch]! It is done! *So Mote It Be!*

Activate the item:

    a. store in a dark place until Full Moon

    b. place the pillow in the light of the Full Moon:

> Come to me Fair Ones,
> By the light of thy Faerie Moon!
> Bless this charm and grant my boon,
> With this pillow, [purpose/intent] comes,
> May ye ever abide in friendship with me,
> That As I Will, *So Mote It Be!*

    c. let the pillow stay in the moonlight one hour, then place where desired

CORN WHEEL

Function: to be a home or outdoor representation of the Sabbats of the Wheel of the Year

    a. based on Sun phases

    b. tell the story of the God and his relationship with the Goddess as the Wheel turns through each of the Sabbats

    c. provides a visual reminder of the spiritual path:

        1. acts as a family-centered teaching tool for the Sabbats

        2. is a family project that children enjoy making

    d. acts as a charm:

        1. consecrated and hung over the doorway on Hogmanay [New Year's Day]

        2. invokes the protection of the God and the Goddess throughout the upcoming year

Perform during: Waxing to Full Moon.

Materials: 8 small ears of colorful Indian corn with husks; a willow wreath, metal circle, or wicker doily; wire, ribbon and/or hot glue gun and glue sticks.

Create the Item:

    a. lay flat a circular frame, such as with the wicker doily

    b. arrange eight ears of corn on the doily so they all touch at the center of the circle

    c. secure ears of corn in place with wire or hot glue, then tie with ribbons

1. use colors that evoke a Sabbats for each ear of corn, or

2. use colors that evoke the difference between Quarters and Cross-Quarters

3. decorate the center portion where the tips meet with husk, or other decorations [scallop shell, silk sunflower, etc.]

4. *gently* fan out the husks of each ear of corn for a more decorative appearance

d. if using a metal rim for the ears of corn,

1. *carefully* wrap one portion of the husk from either side of each ear of corn around the rim closest to it

2. make a small circle of cardboard to fit under the tips of the ears of corn

3. hot glue the tips in place

4. hot glue a decoration over the center if desired

Consecrate the Item: with the Basic Consecration Ritual, then hang it up as a reminder of the God's protection:

a. indoors over a door or next to the entrance

b. over an altar area

c. from a tree in the yard

SOLAR CROSS

Function: to be a home or outdoor representation of the Solar Quarters and the Sun God:

a. when consecrated and hung over a doorway or in a tree, invokes the Sun God for protection and prosperity:

1. resurrection aspect with use of vine or frond wheel

2. a visual reminder of the transition of the God through the Goddess in the passage of life, death, and rebirth

3. with vine wheel, is a symbol of the spreading branches of a fruitful relationship with the God and the Goddess

b. makes a fun project for children

c. acts as a teaching tool for understanding the role of the Sun in the four seasons:

1. two equinoxes [Spring and Fall]

2. two solstices [Summer and Winter]

3. demonstrates the symbol of the Sun ⊕ .

Performed during: Waxing to Full Moon

Materials: vine, willow, or palm twisted into a thin circle, holey stone or one that is drilled or wrapped so it can hang from the wreath to represent Earth, drilled or wrapped so will hang scallop or similar shell to represent Water; yellow feather to represent Air; small pouch of ashes, a candle, pumice, or other item to represent Fire; wire, ribbon, and/or hot glue gun and glue sticks; two equal length sticks with a diameter slightly longer than the wreath circle; yellow ribbon; wire

Creating the Item:

a. wind palm or vine into a circle while twisting it then wrapping one end around the loop to hold in place

b. place 1 stick across the back of the circle horizontally

c. place the 2nd stick vertically crossing in back of the horizontal stick and coming forward to the front of the circle, thus securing both sticks in place

d. secure to rim, or hang with ribbon or wire, at each point the Elemental symbol, with Earth at the top, Fire at the bottom, Air at the right side, and Water at the left side

e. fashion a loop from ribbon or wire at the top for hanging up the wheel

f. cut four lengths of yellow ribbon and tie to hang loose from the

bottom of the wreath

Consecrate the Item: with the Basic Consecration Ritual, then hang it up as a reminder of the God's protection:

a. indoors over a door or next to the entrance

b. over an altar area

c. from a tree branch in the yard

SOLAR CORN WHEEL

Variation of Solar Cross using 4 ears of Indian corn instead of 2 sticks, and using a wicker doily or vine wreath:

a. form the Solar Cross emblem of the God with the corn

b. tie with ribbons or wire, or glue into place

c. decorate with the symbols of the Elementals

1. at the points if using a wire or vine frame

2. between the ears of corn if using a wicker doily

ONION OR GARLIC BRAID CHARM

Function: to absorb negative energies and so protect the house.

Perform during: Full Moon of August or Waning Moon; day of Saturn; hour of Saturn.

Materials: yard of twine; 13 onions with stems or garlic bulbs with stems.

Spell casting: Double the yard of twine and tie a knot for a loop to hang the finished braid. Lay twine on table top with loose ends toward you. Lay an onion/garlic with bulb up and stem down; crisscross twine twice; and add next onion/garlic. Continue until end of twine; knot; and hang in the house or wrap and set aside until New Year's Eve:

> Charm of Onions [garlics], charm of string;
> Evil to thy own self bring!
> Charm of Onions [garlics] and of twine;
> Protector of this house and mine!
> I give my blessing unto you;
> For this selfless work you do!

FOLKLORE USES FOR GARLIC

- Add a clove of garlic to spell pouches or charms to strengthen the spell and ward off weakening external energies

- Tuck garlic cloves into the corners of the threshold of entry doors to keep out negative energies and wards unwanted visitors:

> Clove of garlic, entry guardian! Evil thou away shalt fling! Protect this house of me and mine. And take my blessing unto thee for this selfless work you do for me!

- On Hogmanay Eve [New Year's Eve] braid or string thirteen garlic bulbs and hang in the kitchen to absorb undesired

energies, throwing out the ones from the passing year [Onion or Garlic Braid Charm]

- Cutting a garlic clove and wiping the juice on a knife empowers it to deflect negative energies

- Wipe fresh cut garlic clove on a paring knife and stick it in the ground to deflect bad weather from coming to the house

- Roasting and eating garlic with supper aids digestion and keeps the skin young

SPELLS ENTERED BY:

_____

10
Teas, Oils & Baths

Herbal Tea Notes
Herbal Tea Recipes
Herbal Pot Teas
Magical Oils Recipes
Bath Recipes

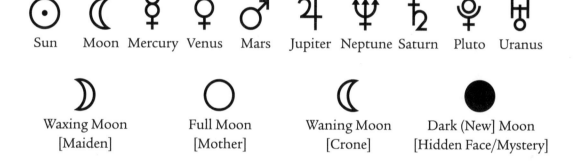

Sun	Moon	Mercury	Venus	Mars	Jupiter	Neptune	Saturn	Pluto	Uranus

Waxing Moon	Full Moon	Waning Moon	Dark (New) Moon
[Maiden]	[Mother]	[Crone]	[Hidden Face/Mystery]

HERBAL TEA NOTES

HERBS FOR MAGICAL TEAS

Drink 1–2 cups—and only for the spell event.

Alfalfa Leaf: home protection; money draw; prosperity; security.
Bergamot: money draw; success.
Black Cohosh: relaxation; turn worries aside.
Boneset: call upon devas; divination; protection; ward negativity.
Burdock Root: protection; purification; ward negativity.
Chamomile: calmness; meditation; prosperity; purification.
Chickweed: Crone wisdom; divination; honesty; love; trust.
Comfrey: health; money draw; safety.
Damiana Leaf: attraction; divination; love.
Dandelion Root: divination; Fairies; good luck; honor/invoke devas; psychic power.
Echinacea: body's self-defense; empowerment; invoke healing devas.
Elder Flower: Fairie blessing; honor/invoke the Goddess; healing; prosperity; rest.
Eyebright: mental sharpness; psychic awareness.
Fennel: healing; honor/invoke Horned God; protection; purification.
Fenugreek Seed: attract money; skill in verbal communication.
Feverfew: health; protection; purification; ward sickness.
Goldenseal: healing; honor/invoke the God; joy; prosperity; success.
Hops: comfort; good health; relaxation; well-being.
Hyssop: purification; ward negativity.
Irish Moss: invoke Fairies; luck; money draw; protection.
Lemon Balm: health; love; success.
Linden (Tila): love; luck; Otherworld; protection; rest.
Mint: Devas; money; protection; prosperity.
Mugwort: Hecate; divination; inspiration.
Mullein: between the worlds travel; courage; divination; health; protection.
Nettle: healing; love; protection; ward negativity.
Orange Peel: divination; love; luck.
Parsley: purification; protection.
Raspberry Leaf: Fairie blessings; health; love; protection.
Rose Hips: divination; love; protection; psychic healing.
Rosemary: blessing; consecration; Elves; protection; ward negativity.
Skullcap: healing (esp. headaches); hidden knowledge; Lord of Shadows; protection; wisdom.
Slippery Elm Bark: clear communications; persuasive speech; protection from envy, gossip, and slander.

Uva Ursa: divination; honor/invoke Artemis; purification; psychic awareness.
Valerian Root: Crone magics; love; protection; purification; rest; sleep.
White Oak Bark: fertility; honor/invoke the Green Man; health; protection.
Wild Cherry Bark: creativity; divination; love.
Willow Bark: health; mental acuity; reduce headache pain.

MAKING A GOOD POT OF TEA

Boil fresh cold water in tea kettle; warm china/ceramic tea pot with hot water, pour out, add loose tea or in teaball in china/ceramic pot; add boiling water over leaves. Steep 3–5 minutes; pour tea through strainer into tea cup or strain into fresh, warmed tea pot and serve with milk, sweetener, lemon to taste. Cover tea pot with cozy to keep tea warm; drink only 2–4 cups per day as tea in general acts as a diuretic and some herbs are not healthy in large doses.

TO READ TEA LEAVES

Do not strain tea, but focus on question, drink all but a scant amount, swirl leaves, overturn cup onto saucer (handle at 6 P.M.), turn three times, return cup upright, read symbols in cup clockwise with timing for the soonest events being closest to the handle [*see Symbols Listing*].

HERBAL TEA RECIPES

- Words printed to right of ingredients are to be said as herbs are added to the pot.

- Words printed following the ingredients are to be said before drinking the tea.

STRESS TEA

1	tsp. English Breakfast tea	**Black is for strength, boosting the power herein,**
1	tsp. Chamomile	**Yellow is for health and calming the nervous within;**
1	tsp. Elder flower	**White is for purifying with healing and rest,**
2	tsp. Hops	**Beige is for gentleness and feeling my best;**
2	tsp. Rose hips	**Red is for energy to overcome stress,**
1	tsp. Valerian root	**Root is for steady protection made manifest.**

Chase away pain and stress; chase away all duress; chase away the negative; open up the positive.

FRUSTRATION TEA

2 tsp. English Breakfast
1 tsp. chamomile
1 tsp. hyssop
1 tsp. raspberry leaf

May add: skullcap; betony; rosemary

TEA FOR HEALTH [SPELLS]

1 tsp. black tea
1 tsp. elder flower
2 tsp. fennel
2 tsp. hops
1 tsp. mint
1 tsp. mullein
2 tsp. rose hips
1 tsp. white oak

TEA FOR DIVINATION

1 tsp. China/English/Irish Breakfast
1 tsp. eyebright [optional]
1 tsp. mugwort
2 tsp. lemon balm
1 tbs. rose hips

TEA FOR PROTECTION

[7 Herbal Powers]

1 tbs. Irish/English Breakfast
2 tsp. burdock root
1 tsp. comfrey
2 tsp. elder flower
1 tsp. hyssop
1 tsp. linden flower [tila]
2 tsp. rose hips
1 tsp. valerian

TEA FOR LOVE [SPELLS]

1 tbs. China Black/Breakfast tea
1 tsp. raspberry leaves
2 tsp. rose hips
2 tsp. chamomile
1 tsp. damiana
1 tbs. mullein

TEA FOR PSYCHIC HEALING

1 tbs. black tea
2 tsp. burdock root
1 tsp. elder flower
2 tsp. mullein
1 tsp. nettle
2 tsp. rose hips

TEA FOR RELAXATION

1 tbs. English Breakfast
1 tsp. chamomile
1 tsp. elder flower
2 tsp. hops
2 tsp. rose hips
1 tsp. valerian

4 TEAS FOR EARTH CENTERING

Equal Parts:
1) English Breakfast; rose hips; hyssop
2) Linden flower; chamomile
3) China Black; chamomile; rose hips
4) English Breakfast; elder flower; hops; rose hips

Tea for Purification

1 tbs. black tea
1 tsp. chamomile
2 tsp. fennel
2 tsp. hyssop
1 tsp. valerian

Clairvoyance Tea

1 tsp. mugwort
1 tsp. thyme
1 tsp rosemary *or*
1 tsp. yarrow
1 tsp. black tea [optional]

Tea for Meditation

1 tbs. China Black/English Breakfast
2 tsp. chamomile
2 tsp. elder flower
1 tsp. rose hips

Goddess & God Centering

1 tbs. English Breakfast
½ tsp. chamomile
1 tsp. comfrey
¼ tsp. elder flower
1 tsp. rose hips

Earth Devas Tea

1 tsp. English Breakfast
1 tsp. Irish moss
1 tsp. dandelion root
1 tsp. rose hips
2 tsp. hops

Fairy Tea

3 tsp. black tea
1 tsp. chamomile
2 tsp. dandelion root
1 tsp. elder flower
1 tsp. hops
2 tsp. mullein
2 tsp. raspberry leaf
2 tsp. rose hips

Black for strength;
Then apple of night;
Wild grown root;
And Lady's blessing.
Hops for joy;
Then between the worlds;
Tangle of bramble and fairy knots,
Kissed with love,
Brewed to invite the Fair Folk to Tea.

SIPPING TEAS

Good with a book, friend, or family:

Note: any of the black teas can be substituted with a preferred type, such as Yorkshire and Irish or Scottish Breakfast, etc.

1. 3 tsp. China Rose; 1 tsp. chamomile

2. 3 tsp. English Teatime; 1 tsp. chamomile; 2 tsp. rose hips

3. 3 tsp. Earl Grey; 2 tsp. rose hips

4. 3 tsp. linden; 2 tsp. chamomile

5. 2 tsp. English Teatime; ½ tsp. chamomile; 1 tsp. comfrey; ¼ tsp. elder flower; 1 tsp. rose hips

6. 3 tsp. English Breakfast; 1 tsp. hyssop; 2 tsp. rose hips

7. 3 tsp. English Breakfast; 1 tsp. elder flower; 1 tsp. hops; 2 tsp. rose hips

8. Same as 7.), adding 1 tsp. chamomile

9. 3 tsp. Black tea; 1 tsp. hops; 1 tsp. hyssop; 1 tsp. mullein; 2 tsp. rose hips

10. 1 tsp. English Teatime; 2 tsp. China Rose; 1 tsp. chamomile; 2 tsp. dandelion root; 1 tsp. elder flower; 1 tsp. hops; 1 tsp. rose hips

TEAS FOR SICKIES

To drink a cup when feeling under the weather:

SICKIES TEA #1

2 tsp. black tea
2 tsp. burdock root
1 tsp. chamomile
2 tsp. dandelion root
1 tsp. mint
1 tsp. raspberry leaf
1 tsp. rose hips
1 tsp. wild cherry bark

SICKIES TEA #2

3 tsp. Earl Grey
2 tsp. English Teatime
2 tsp. burdock root
1 tsp. chamomile
2 tsp. dandelion root
1 tsp. mint
1 tsp. raspberry leaf

FEVER TEA #1

4 tsp. bayberry
2 tsp. ginger
1 tsp white pine
1 tsp. thyme

FEVER TEA #2

2 tsp. black tea
1 tsp. cinnamon
1 tsp. marjoram
1 tsp. thyme

COLDS TEA #1

2 tsp. black tea
1 tsp. elder flower
1 tsp. peppermint
1 tsp. yarrow

COLDS TEA #2

2 tsp. black tea
1 tsp. chamomile
1 tsp. elder flower
½ tsp. hyssop
½ tsp. lemon balm
1½ tsp. rose hips

COLDS TEA #3

2 tsp. black tea
⅛ tsp. ginger
1 tsp. yarrow
1 tsp. mint

SUN TEA

3 bags English Teatime
1 tbs. ea. rose hips and dandelion root

Set in clear glass jug in the sunlight to brew naturally; drink as ice tea.

Note: Sun Tea can be made with fruit flavors as well.

TEA TIME #1

3 tsp. English Teatime
3 chamomile flowers
1 tsp. dandelion root
2 tsp. elder flower
2 tsp. hops
2 tsp. rose hips

TEA TIME #2

2 tsp. English Teatime
¼ tsp. chamomile
2 tsp. elder flower
1 tsp. hops
½ tsp. lemon balm
½ tsp. mint leaves/stems
2 tsp. mugwort
1 tsp. rose hips

BISCUIT TEA

3 tsp. black tea
½ tsp. chamomile
1 tsp. dandelion root
1 tsp. mint
1 tsp. mullein
1 tsp. raspberry leaves
1 tsp. rose hips

Fairy Cakes [Biscuits]

1 cup Bisquick
⅛ cup quick oats
⅛ cup cornmeal
⅛ cup flour
⅛ tsp. almond extract
2 tsp. sugar
½ cup milk

Stir all together; knead in bowl to form ball; form into 1 inch balls; bake 10 min at 425° on ungreased cookie sheet; makes 1 dozen.

Chest Cold Tea

1 tsp. black tea
2 tsp. elder flower
2 tsp. feverfew
1 tsp. peppermint
1 tsp. rose hips
1 tsp. yarrow

Bad Cold Tea

3 tsp. English Teatime
1 tsp. horehound
1 tsp. mint
1 tsp. rose hips
1 tsp. verbena
1 tsp. yarrow

Head Cold Tea

1 tsp. black tea
1 tsp. boneset
1 tsp. fenugreek seed
1 tsp. mullein
1 tsp. rose hips

Sore Throat Tea

1 tsp. black tea
1 tsp. mullein flower
1 tsp. raspberry leaf

Sore Throat & Fever Tea

1 tsp. China Black
1 tsp. comfrey
1 tsp. elderberries
1 tsp. raspberry leaf

Upset Tummy Tea

1 tsp. black tea
2 tsp. peppermint
½ tsp. rose hips

Cramps Tea

1 tsp. black tea
½ tsp. chamomile
⅛ tsp. ginger
1 tsp. raspberry leaves
1½ tsp. valerian

Steep 5 minutes

Induce Menses Tea

2 tsp. black tea
1 tsp. cassias augustinofolios
1 tsp. hops
2 tsp. rose hips

[*1 cup only;* follow next day with:

3 tsp. black tea
1 tsp. rose hips
1 tsp. chamomile]

HERBAL POT TEAS

MEDICINE TEAPOT

Equally: spearmint
               wood betony
               rosemary
               eucalyptus

Add: 1 tsp. Ginseng
        1 tsp. Gota Kola
        2 tsp. Black tea

ENERGY TEAPOT

Equally: rose hips
               orange peel
               rosemary

Add: 1 tsp. orange pekoe
        1 tsp. ginger
        1 tsp. coriander
        1 tsp. star anise
        1 tsp. cinnamon

SUMMER UPLIFT TEAPOT

Equally: wild cherry bark
               rose hips
               orange peel
               spearmint
               lemon grass
               hibiscus flower

Add: 1 tsp. black tea

REFRESHING TEAPOT

Equally: blackberry leaf
               rose hips
               juniper berry
               strawberry leaf
               black tea

DREAM WELL TEAPOT

Equally: peppermint
               chamomile
               catnip
               valerian root
               skullcap
               passion flower
               strawberry leaf

Add: 1 tsp. black tea

GENTLE MOODS TEAPOT

Equally: white oak bark
               ginger root
               damiana
               rosemary
               angelica root
               marjoram

Add: 1 tsp. celery seed
        1 tsp. ginseng leaf

MAGICAL OILS RECIPES

Making Oils: add ground herbs and drops of essential oils to base of spring water/oils: olive, sunflower, safflower, mineral; bottle with tight lid and store in dark place.

ALTAR OIL

½ tsp. rue
½ tsp. thyme
½ tsp. vervain
3 drops citronella oil
1 drop fir oil
1 drop rue oil
2 drops sandalwood oil
¼ cup spring water

Asperge with white heather sprig.

ANOINTING OIL

1 star anise
¼ tsp. basil
¼ tsp. hyssop
½ tsp. rosemary
3 drops acacia oil
2 drops balsam of Peru oil
1 drop benzoin oil
2 drops rose oil
¼ cup base oil

BLESSING OIL

1 tsp. lavender
½ tsp. rosemary
1 tsp. St. Johnswort
2 drops juniper berry oil
2 drops rose oil
2 drops balsam of Peru oil
3 drops vetiver oil
¼ cup base oil

CLEANSING OIL

1 tsp. basil
2 tsp. rosemary
1 tsp. valerian
1 tsp. mugwort
2 drops benzoin oil
1 drop fir oil
2 drops lavender oil
4 drops rue oil
¼ cup base oil

CONSECRATION OIL

1 tsp. fennel
1 tsp. tansy
1 tsp. rue
1 tsp. wormwood
½ tsp. yarrow
2 drops fir oil
3 drops rue oil
2 drops sandalwood oil
¼ cup base oil

ASTRAL PROJECTION OIL

[Dab: all pulse points; forehead; soles]

1 tsp. jasmine
1 tsp. cinquefoil
2 tsp. mugwort
1 tsp. woodruff
2 drops acacia oil
4 drops benzoin oil
3 drops rue oil
1 drop sandalwood oil
¼ cup base oil

HERBAL BATHS

BATH HERBS

Bergamot, Calendula, Chamomile, Dianthus, Elder Flower, Heather, Hops, Lavender, Lemon Balm, Marjoram, Mint, Mugwort, Peppermint, Rosemary, Rose Petals, Rose Hips, Sage, Savory, Spearmint, Thyme, Vervain, Verbena, Yarrow.

For Comforting

Calendula (Marigold), Chamomile, Lavender, Mint, Raspberry Leaves, Rosemary.

For Energy

Heather, Lemon Balm, Rosemary, Savory.

For Peace

Chamomile, Hops, Lavender, Peppermint, Rose.

For Relaxation

Chamomile, Dianthus, Heather, Jasmine Flower, Lemon Balm.

Soothing

Calendula, Chamomile, Lavender, Mint, Rosemary.

Stress Relief

Chamomile, Dianthus, Lemon Balm.

RECIPES ENTERED BY:

_____

11
Divinations

Symbolism for Divination
Tea Leaf Reading
Tarot
Black Mirror Scrying
Crystal Ball & Other Stone Scrying
Pendulum
Rune Casting
Ogham Casting
Palmistry

| Sun | Moon | Mercury | Venus | Mars | Jupiter | Neptune | Saturn | Pluto | Uranus |

Waxing Moon
[Maiden]

Full Moon
[Mother]

Waning Moon
[Crone]

Dark (New) Moon
[Hidden Face/Mystery]

SYMBOLISM FOR DIVINATION

Acorn: youth, strength, man, small start for large accomplishment.
Airplane: travel, new projects.
Anchor: voyage, rest, problem solved.
Arrow: news, disagreements, direct action.
Basket: gift, security, comfort.
Baby: new interests, security, new beginnings.
Bees [hive, comb]**:** fertility, industry, community, self-sacrifice.
Bell: celebrations, news (good or bad depending on other indicators).
Bird: psychic power, flight, luck, friendship end, communication.
Boat: discoveries, travel, companionship.
Book: wisdom, learning.
Bottle: celebration, success.
Broom: Goddess, purification, healing, end of a problem, changes.
Bridge: crossing to new endeavors, transition, partnership, travel.
Butterfly: the soul, spiritual contact, frivolity, insincerity.
Castle: financial gain, security, inheritance, life of bounty.
Cage: isolation, restriction, imprisonment, containment.
Camel: long journey, need to conserve energy or goods, relocation.
Cat: wisdom, spiritual access, female friend, domestic strife.
Car: local travel, movement in business affairs, overcome obstacles.
Cauldron: Goddess, transformation, endings/new beginnings, vitality.
Candle: illumination, innovation, inspiration.
Clock: time indicated for a spell's completion, change.
Chair: relaxation, pause, comfort, entertainment.
Clouds: mental activity, thoughtfulness, problems, hidden obstacles.
Coffin: end of a matter, lengthy but not serious illness.
Clover: good fortune, success, rural location.
Cow: money, property, comfort, tranquillity.
Cradle: newcomers, beginning of a new idea or project.
Crescent: Goddess, wish granted, newness, freshness.
Cornucopia: Goddess, abundance, fertility, prosperity, protection.
Cross: [Solar] God, nature works with power [Roman]; suffering, conflict.
Cup: love, harmony, close friendship, gift.
Dagger: complications, dangers, power, skill.
Death/dying: birth, marriage, long life, prosperity.
Distaff: creativity, changes, sexuality.
Dog: fidelity, friendship, companionship, faithfulness.
Duck: plenty, wealth, success.
Elephant: advice needed, obstacles overcome, good luck.

Egg: increase, fertility, luck, creativity, new start, hoarding.

Eye: introspection, awareness, evaluation, spirit.

Fan: indiscretion, disloyalty, things hidden, inflammations.

Fish: riches, luck, sexuality, productivity.

Flag: warning, defensiveness, identification with group/ideals.

Flame, fire: purification, change, domination of the will.

Flower: marriage, unhappy love affair, passing joy.

Glove: protection, luck, aloofness, nobility, challenge.

Gate: opportunity, advancement, change, new directions.

Gun [any type]: power to gain goals, discord, slander, infidelity.

Hammer: hard work rewarded, building, creativity, fortitude.

Hat: honors, rivalry, independence, self-assertion.

Hound: advice, help given, companionship, trust.

Heart: love, pleasure, confidence, strength of will.

Harp: contentment, spirituality.

Horns: God, fertility, spirituality, forces of nature.

Horse: travel, strength, work, grace, power, success, prosperity.

Horseshoe: protection, luck, start of a new enterprise.

Hourglass: caution, passage of time.

House: security, authority, success, comfort.

Key: understanding, mysteries, opportunity, gain, security.

Kite: warning for caution, new ideas, plans made public.

Knot: restrictions, marriage, bindings.

Knife: duplicity, misunderstanding, direct action.

Ladder: initiation, rise or fall in status, connections.

Lion: power, strength, influence, ferocity, pride, domination.

Lock: protection, concealment, security, obstacles, sealed.

Man: visitor, helpful stranger.

Mirror: reversal, knowledge, Karma.

Moon: the Goddess, intuitive wisdom, guidance.

Mountain: hindrance, challenge, obstacle, journey, steadfastness.

Mouse: poverty, theft, frugality, inconspicuousness.

Mushroom: shelter, food, business complications, Fairy contact.

Nail: labor, construction, pain, unity.

Owl: wisdom, spiritual communication.

Palm tree: respite, relief, security, protection, blessings.

Parrot: gossip, ostentatiousness.

Peacock: luxury, vanity, arrogance: all with little foundation.

Pineapple: hospitality, good things hidden by harsh exterior.

Pipe: truth obscured, concentration, comfort, ease.

Purse: monetary gain, possessions kept close.

Ring: eternity, containment, wheel of life/year, wedding.
Rose: love, lost or past love, fullness of life, healing, caring.
Salt: purity, stability, cleansing, grounding.
Scales: balance, justice, careful evaluation.
Scissors: duplicity, arguments, separation, division, strife.
Shell: Goddess, emotional stability, luck, artistic ability.
Ship: travel, news, material gains, romance.
Skull: consolation, comfort, personal hurts, endings and a new life.
Snake: God and Goddess, wisdom, immortality, knowledge, prophecy.
Spider: good luck, industry, entrapments, secrecy, cunning.
Spoon: luck, sustenance, the basic needs of life secured.
Sun: the God, success, energy, power.
Star: good luck, divine protection, opportunity, success, destiny.
Swan: good luck, love, evolving beauty, noble spirit.
Sword: power, strife, conflict, overcoming adversity.
Tree: blessings of Nature, good fortune, stability, power, security.
Turtle: fertility, security, defense against obstacles, slow gains.
Umbrella: temporary shelter, limited protection.
Unicorn: purity, nature, Fairy blessings, Otherworld intervention.
Well: blessing from the Goddess, inspiration, spirituality, health.
Wheel: completion, eternity, season/life cycles, rebirth, gains.
Windmill: business dealings, factors working together for one goal.

TEA LEAF READING

1. Querant drinks almost all of the tea in a teacup while focusing on a question or information being sought, leaving tea leaves.

2. Querant swirls remnant tea and leaves in cup 3 times.

3. Querant turns cup upside down on saucer and hands to reader.

4. Reader turns cup 3 times deosil.

5. Reader sets cup upright, with handle at the reader's 6:00 position.

6. Reader examines leaves for symbols [*see above listing*].

7. Reading goes deosil from handle, with the closest timing being at the left side of the handle.

8. Items closest to the rim are read as locations that are further from the querant, while those closest to the bottom are nearest to the reader.

Variation: after Querant drinks tea, the Reader swirls the tea, upends the cup, turns the cup, rights the cup, and does the reading.

TAROT

- See Consecration of a Tool Ritual for tarot deck; then wrap in cloth of desired color, according to meaning of color [black, green, red are most commonly used]

- Normally upright in readings, but may vary according to intuition; tool of mediumship bringing contact with Universal Energy to address a particular question or problem, or to simply offer guidance and comfort

- If a vision or sense of a strong association for a card occurs that is not described, follow the intuitive interpretation

- Contains Major Arcana of archetype cards and Minor Arcana of mundane cards

- **Pathworking:** meditating on a tarot card to encounter the beings or images represented on each card to understand the card by walking with them for awhile in their setting, and listening to what they may speak or indicate through gesture and action

- **Pentacles [Disks, Coins, Diamonds]:** Earth [North, Winter, Midnight, Green/Brown, Mineral, Body] suit of: Finances, Money, Business, Physical and Material Matters, and Comfort

- **Swords [Knives, Daggers, Spades]:** Air [East, Spring, Sunrise, Yellow/White, Spirit, Intellect, Breath] suit of: Strength, Power, Conflicts, Worries, Mental Processes, and Intellect

- **Wands [Rods, Staves, Clubs]:** Fire [South, Summer, Noon, Orange/Red, Plant, Insight, Life-force] suit of: Career, Study, Creative Ventures, Work, Self, and Spirit

- **Cups [Bowls, Cauldrons, Hearts]:** Water [West, Autumn, Sunset, Blue/Indigo, Animal, Blood] suit of: Emotions, Intuition, Psychic Power, Love, Friendship, and Feelings

MAJOR ARCANA

Craft-oriented pairs of Similarity or Polarity:

1. *The Greenman [Fool] and the Witch [Magician]:* Earth powers of Nature.

2. *Drawing Down the Moon [High Priestess] and Drawing Down the Sun [Hierophant]:* Communion with the Goddess and with the God.

3. *Mother Earth [Empress] and the Horned God [Emperor]:* complimentary emblems of fertility, creativity, nurturing, responsibility, and authority.

4. *Lord and Lady of the Wild Wood [Lovers] and the Battle Wagon [Chariot]:* balance from partnership and balance from personal power.

5. *The Crone [Strength] and the Holly King [Hermit/Sage]:* wisdom and power by self-control and by self-guidance.

313

6. *The Wheel of the Year [Wheel of Fortune] and the Standing Stone [Justice]:* rewards from external influences and from internal influences.

Craft-oriented pairs of Progression:

7. *The Oak King [Hanged Man] and the Wild Hunt [Tower]:* movement from meditative inaction into sudden enlightenment.

8. *The Sidhe [Temperance] and the Star:* harmonious balances of blending rational and intuitive and inspiration and manifestation.

9. *Nature [Devil] and the Lord of Shadows [Death]:* life passage with decisions and with transformations.

Ultimate of the two sets of Pairings:

10. *Moon and Sun:* similarity and polarity symbols of Intuitive and Rational; Goddess and God; Night and Day/also necessary as united for seasons of Earth.

11. *Harvest [Judgement] and the World Tree [Universe/World]:* finalize the parings of progression; reap what is sown and the end of a cycle begins a new one.

12. *World Tree and Greenman:* final capping of all, since conclusion creates the new beginning.

Major Arcana Meanings

0—The Greenman [The Fool]: Ostara Awakening of the Earth: *Meaning:* Awakening, fearlessness, courage, joy of life, enthusiasm, a new beginning, hidden potential about to be revealed, creativity, fertility, open minded, innovation, fresh ideas, playfulness, recreation, originality, primal energy; *Reverse:* Indecisive, fearful, naive, inconsiderate, unfocused energy, reckless, entering a period of inactivity, tending a started project through to completion; *Key Words:* Spontaneity, courageous, fresh start, excitement, carefree.

1—The Witch [The Magician]: Practicing magic through the Elementals: *Meaning:* Control over personal destiny, proficiency, communication skills, influence, diplomacy, dexterity, creativity, new opportunities, able to create changes, practical use of knowledge, originality, solving problems; *Reverse:* Banal articulation, blocked expression, lack of self-confidence, guile; *Key Words:* Communication, creativity, skill, astuteness, adaptability.

2—Drawing Down the Moon [High Priestess]: the Esbats: *Meaning:* Secrets may soon be revealed, perception, insight, hidden knowledge understood, Divine inspiration, good judgment, trusting own intuition, learning the meanings of mysteries, innate wisdom, occult studies, psychic dreams/power; *Reverse:* Comprehension is less than desired, clouded insight, not heeding valuable intuition, delusion, shortsighted, superstitious, understanding needed; *Key Words:* Secrets, intuition, esoteric wisdom, developing psychic abilities.

3—Earth Mother [The Empress]: Litha: *Meaning:* Abundance, inspiration, emotional fulfillment, communion with Nature, nurturing a project to fruition, using folk magics, growth, fertility, creativity, robust health, intellect influences action taken, understanding, protection, sensitivity, beauty, pleasure, domestic joy, pregnancy; *Reverse:* Potential unrecognized, slow progress, vacillation, blocked creativity;

Key Words: Bounty, growth, fruitfulness, inspiration, creativity, security.

4—The Horned God [The Emperor]: Litha: *Meaning:* Authority, leadership skills, acceptance of innate personal power, self confidence, determined, initiating plans, creating, building, accomplishing goals, experienced, attainment, protecting what is created, accepting responsibility, ownership with accountability, husbandry, satisfaction with efforts, reason as power, forceful but ethical; *Reverse:* Bureaucratic, inflexible, petty, ineffectiveness, indecisive, timid; *Key Words:* Builder, responsibility, stability, empowerment, productivity.

5—Drawing Down the Sun [Hierophant]: writing a Book of Shadows: *Meaning:* Transmitting teachings, gentle mentorship, scholarship, philosophical intellect, spiritual energy, inspiration, organizing personal spirituality, finding a teacher, patience, working within social/cultural custom, conventional, security; *Reverse:* Social/cultural conformity, dominance, overly traditional, spirituality as ritualism, rigid attitudes, manipulation of spiritual truths, magics of formulae; *Key Words:* Organizing spirituality, inspiration, teacher, tradition, ritual.

6—The Lady and the Lord of the Wild Wood [The Lovers]: Beltane union of Goddess and God: *Meaning:* Partnership, trust, balance between opposites, camaraderie, choice requires careful consideration, love despite differences, intense feelings, need for a decision, harmony, collaboration, commitment, importance of truth, loyalty; *Reverse:* Irresponsibility, obsessiveness, insensitivity, procrastination, worry; *Key Words:* Choices, decision making, balance, partnership, trust.

7—The Battle Wagon [The Chariot]: directing energy through the Athame: *Meaning:* Self-confident, success through willpower/control/dominance, goal-focused, conquest, personal achievement, merit recognized, leadership, business travel, military service, career advancement/relocation, starting new projects, good health, swift results from efforts, consolidation of power; *Reverse:* Inaction, impatience, collapse of plans, unrealistic, incomplete work; *Key Words:* Victory, merit recognized, control, dominance, fast action, travel.

8—The Crone [Strength]: Casting and Opening the Circle: *Meaning:* Fortitude, courage, power to achieve goals, control over situations, overcoming obstacles, power used wisely, perseverance, self-discipline, will; *Reverse:* Blame placing, emotionalism, short-sighted, unconfident, sentimentality, boasting, compromises; *Key Words:* Courage, fortitude, power, defeating obstacles.

9—The Holly King [The Hermit]: Yule birth of Oak King: *Meaning:* Seeking personal enlightenment, patience is required, guiding others by example, wisdom, forging a new path, old ways yield to new ways, progress, personal growth, prudence, introspection, contemplation and evaluation; *Reverse:* Shallow knowledge, imprudence, being mislead, change needed; *Key Words:* Wisdom, seeker, guide, personal growth, changing times.

10—Wheel of the Year [Wheel of Fortune]: celebrating the Sabbats: *Meaning:* Sudden change for the better, stroke of good luck, success, progress, wisdom replaces folly, try new ideas, fate, destiny, help comes, a happy surprise; *Reverse:* Short-term success, small gains, new goals replace old ones; *Key Words:* Fortunes improve, success, opportunity, progress.

11—The Standing Stone [Justice]: Rules of Conduct or Witches' Rede: *Meaning:* Objectivity, impartiality, fairness, balance, truth, virtue, honor, law, win in a legal matter, equilibrium, an agent working on your behalf, consideration, advice, conscience, impartiality, equity, reward and retribution for the aggrieved; *Reverse:* Retribution, misrepresentation, bias, intolerance, legal action delayed, complications, gossip, false accusation, tedious bureaucracy, cloudy perception; *Key Words:* Objective, balanced, fair, ethical, prevail in legal matter.

12—The Oak King [The Hanged Man]: setting spell items on the Pentacle: *Meaning:* Period of transition, paused activity, contemplation, letting matters evolve without interference, meditating for answers, inner peace, patience, discretion, turning point coming soon, giving up some things to gain others; *Reverse:* Action decided, decision forced, fear of change, missed opportunity; *Key Words:* Suspended activity, transition, meditation, vision questing.

13—The Lord of Shadows [Death]: tomb and womb of Samhain: *Meaning:* Change, transformation, an ending and new beginning, clearing away negative conditions, a turning point in life, optimism, removal of opposition, renewal, sweeping aside resistance, movement, creating positive changes; *Reverse:* Resistance to change, immobility, prompting change in others, self-evaluation needed, impediment, stagnation, slow change; *Key Words:* Change, transformation, turning point, optimistic new start.

14—The Sidhe [Temperance]: beverage of the Chalice: *Meaning:* Fusion, invigoration, blending ideas, inspiration, harmony of rational and intuitive, difficulties overcome, reconciliation, infusion of power, diplomacy; *Reverse:* Disharmony, attitude of no compromise, imbalance, stagnation; *Key Words:* Harmony of mental and psychic states, blend of ideas, inspiration.

15—Nature [The Devil]: the Cord knotted with the person's measurements: *Meaning:* Natural course, decisions, powerful forces, attraction, freedom, sense of humor, release, following inclinations, potential unleashed, conquer obstacles; *Reverse:* Energy/potential restricted, discontent, inhibited, timid, self-limiting; *Key Words:* Freedom, choosing what appeals, following instincts.

16—The Wild Hunt [The Tower]: meditation work with the Black Mirror: *Meaning:* Enlightenment, secret/truth revealed, shocking event, unexpected major change, darkness before the light of truth, release from oppression, hope restored, beliefs overthrown, life-altering shock, inner spirit freed, situation ends; *Reverse:* Self-deception, ineffective communication, isolation; *Key Words:* Shocking event, sudden change from enlightenment, illusions go.

17—The Star [The Star]: the Wand gathering/directing energy: *Meaning:* Wishes and dreams can be manifested, hopes are attainable, clear vision, inspiration, creativity, opportunity, bright prospects, following a dream, talent recognized by others, help from unexpected places, positive energy; *Reverse:* Letting opportunities pass, insecurity, need for peace and release of past, tensions, doubting own abilities, distrust of others, letting opportunities pass; *Key Words:* Opportunity, wishes granted, hopes obtainable, inspiration.

18—The Moon [The Moon]: the Cauldron of the Esbat: *Meaning:* Heed instincts, following intuition, manifesting the subconscious, exposing deception, seeing the hidden truths, introspection, psychic visions or dreams, creative cycle, union of spiritual and physical, learning magics; *Reverse:* Illusion, unmanifested dreams, facades, moody, deception, limited imagination, vision obscured, suspicion, impractical ideas, socially inhibited; *Key Words:* Trust instincts, subconscious manifested, creativity, psychic.

19—The Sun [The Sun]: grain of life harvest of Lughnassadh: *Meaning:* Success, contentment, mental/spiritual growth, good health, children, material happiness, satisfying achievements, joy, revitalization, accomplishment, harmony, recognition, individuality, optimism, new beginning, joy, marriage; *Reverse:* Delay, temporary setback, lack of communication, over-extended; *Key Words:* Happiness, success, achievement, satisfaction.

20—Harvest [Judgement]: wine or life harvest of Mabon: *Meaning:* Rewards, harvest, good choices made, rebirth, accountability, good health restored, self-evaluation, a new awakening, making a major decision, discretion is necessary, potential fulfilled, conflict concluded, renewed energy; *Reverse:* Hesitancy, learning from past mistakes, disappointment, indecision, taking stock of one's past with the desire for improvement; *Key Words:* Efforts rewarded, self-evaluation, transformation, renewal.

21—The World Tree [The Universe]: cleansing of Imbolc: *Meaning:* Wholeness, totality, spiritual unity, good conclusion to effort or matter, objectives attained, honors, perfection, completion, end of an era, success, joy, advancement, achievement, promotion, reward, fulfillment, recognition; *Reverse:* Unresolved situation, unfinished project, lack of foresight, striving for greatness, seeking attainment, time of transition, success creates new burdens; *Key Words:* Completion, achievement, success, joy, conclusion and beginning.

Minor Arcana Meanings

Pentacles

Ace: [Timing upright is December; reverse is January to February]: *Meaning:* Prosperity, big commercial success, favorable period of financial security, attainment, well-being, a new money-making venture, new job, good earnings, growth, promotion, business sense, acquisition of material goods, beneficial financial news, business or financial opportunity, doorway opening, comfort with work and creations, good use of resources, productivity, happiness; *Reverse:* Opportunity not fully utilized, unsatisfied with prosperity, financial immobility; *Key Words:* Commercial success, prosperity, material attainment, promotion.

Two: *Meaning:* Employment opportunity, agility with money, learning new skills to replace old ones, tension from job training, two areas of financial action, job relocation, learning stage will pass leading to rewards, weighing work choices, weighing options for business decision, energy/determination for gaining goals; *Reverse:* Extra effort needed to complete a project, difficult situation requires careful balance, weakness/lack of enthusiasm where required for success, need for a balanced budget; *Key Words:* New skills learned, balancing money, business decision, new job.

Three: *Meaning:* Celebrity in a field, artistic ability, renown, powerful support, work rewarded, skill in craft, dedication in work, work is fun and profitable, disciplined methods of work, clear priorities, goods acquired, contract, working to make plans a reality, business opportunity, fruition of training, possibly a pregnancy; *Reverse:* Lack of skill, indifference, greed, hoarding possessions, dissatisfaction with abilities, desiring more, withholding talent; *Key Words:* Celebrity, prestige, commitments, work rewarded, craftsmanship.

Four: *Meaning:* Budgeting money, financial security, controlling personal access, a small gift, endurance, gentle power, savings, accumulated wealth, pay raise, productive harvest, income directed to private enjoyment of beauty, influence, withdrawn, joy expressed with a quiet reserve, able to achieve new desires; *Reverse:* Materialism, greed, pent-up creative energies, miserly, coming into a legacy, gain from a loss, delays, uncertainties, fortunes reversed, suspiciousness, further gains difficult, blockage in financial endeavors; *Key Words:* Financial security, private, budget, self-contained, withdrawn.

Five: *Meaning:* Prosperity/rewards lie ahead, unexpected expenses, temporary material instability, negative trend will be reversed in time, hidden opportunities, feeling isolated, obstacles, financial worries, over-extended, bound by enforced restrictions, new interests arriving soon, dissatisfaction with status quo, keeping occupied while awaiting improvement in situation; *Reverse:* Relief comes, courage to find hidden opportunities, temporary difficulties, overcoming troubles in a relationship; *Key Words:* Financial worries, delayed income, unexpected expenses.

Six: *Meaning:* Generosity, careful donations, gift or money coming, sharing talent, self-confidence, gratification, sharing prosperity, rewards, bonus, good fortune, sincerity, material increase, beneficiary of another's bounty, appreciated; *Reverse:* Overspending, avarice, loss through negligence or theft, debts, unpaid loans, money owed to others, others envious of your success; *Key Words:* Gift or bonus, tempered generosity, financially self-confident.

Seven: *Meaning:* Perseverance brings rewards, anticipated gains, progress, wealth comes, impatient for rewards, goals achieved in due time, ongoing productivity, hard work pays off, nurturing a project or plan, business recovery, gathering resources for a business start, working hard to acquire what is desired, expertise and skill in job will be rewarded, work decision needs careful consideration; *Reverse:* Wasted efforts, minimal rewards, imprudent action, lack of achievement, poor investment, unwilling to expend effort for rewards; *Key Words:* Gain by perseverance, nurturing a project, impatient for results.

Eight: *Meaning:* Talent/artistic skills applied to commercial gains, meeting deadlines, increase through own effort, business venture, commercial ability, work rewarded, career change, pay raise or bonus, individuality appreciated, developing new skills or hobbies, demonstrated abilities bring increase; *Reverse:* lack of ambition, vision limited by minutiae, vanity, conceit, need care with money, hypocrisy, all talk no action; *Key Words:* Commercial ability, enthusiasm with work, personal effort and skill.

Nine: *Meaning:* Accomplishment, good self-esteem, well-being, sudden luck, large financial gain, money from unexpected sources, comfort, growth, security, prudence, discretion, love of nature, discernment, gift, awareness of self-worth; *Reverse:* Discontent, insecurity, lack of confidence, self-depreciative, growth impaired, health cares, possible health cares or loss of a valued possession; *Key Words:* Accomplishment, self-esteem, good fortune, surprise gift.

Ten: *Meaning:* Prosperity, joy, stability, expansion, earnings, favorable placement, good investment planning, sense of alignment in life, things falling into place, security, family heritage/heirlooms/traditions, creating family heritage; *Reverses:* Disruptions, family quarrels, problems with a legacy, need for a change, money worries, loss of inheritance, frittering away income, gambling; *Key Words:* Prosperity, family heritage, stability, joy.

Page: *Meaning:* Diligence, scholarship, study, application to work, money coming, business ideas or deals, completion, news from child, new lifestyle or identity, practical developmental skills, seeking more responsibility, seeking a new job, going to school or furthering education for future employment; *Reverse:* Energy dissipated, indolence, unrealistic goals, dissatisfaction with work or career choice, need for more study, reluctance to see a job through, not thinking through a process before beginning work; *Key Words:* Turning an interest into a career, diligence in work, study.

Knight: *Meaning:* Auspicious occasion, useful person, responsible, competent, mature, stable, reliable, practical application of talent and potential, hard worker, persistence, goals gained, beginning a new stage of work or training, career development, able, methodical, gentle, careful preparation, diligent service, self-reliant, consistent effort applied to tasks, shrewd business sense; *Reverse:* Recklessness, foolhardy, moving too quickly, complacent, idleness; *Key Words:* Propitious occasion, competence, reliable, hard worker.

Queen: *Meaning:* Plans realized, organized, fruitfulness, comfort, independent work is rewarded, dignity, culture, stability, practical ambitions, attainment of physical goals, freedom, able to provide for self and others, desire for social position/success/security; *Reverse:* Self-indulgence, lacking in understanding, negligence, spend thrift; *Key Words:* Plans realized, realistic ambitions, financial independence.

King: *Meaning:* Economic power, steadfast, ideas manifested, able to generate or create wealth, real estate transactions, sensible, methodical financial planning, dealing with the material world, meeting challenges head on, strong business energy, worldliness, successful leader, attaining the top of profession or career; *Reverse:* Speculation, traditionalist, dullness, narrow views, tyrannical, vicious old man, inability to see ideas through to completion, overly materialistic, unable to accept or make necessary changes; *Key Words:* Economic power, business/career success, ideas manifested.

Swords

Ace [Timing upright is March; reverse is April to May]: *Meaning:* Triumph, victory, power to achieve goals, strength, breakthrough, success, wisdom, clarity of mind, intellectual power, conquest, mental agility, strong mind and great determination, strength of will, taking determined action, conquest, enlightenment, truth; *Reverse:* Obstacles, inaction, embarrassment, tyranny, hindrance, plans delayed; *Key Words:* Victory, strength, power, determination, truth.

Two: *Meaning:* Balance opposing forces, truce, cold analysis in decision-making, harmony of power, tensions ease, temporarily solutions, emotions repressed for decision, stalemate, armed truce, tensions beneath the calm, diplomacy; *Reverse:* Duplicity, indecision, tentative peace, misguided/malicious advice, lies, treachery, false friends, frustrated efforts to resolve a situation; *Key Words:* Tensions ease, balance of opposites, vital decision, diplomacy.

Three: *Meaning:* Striking out on a new path, unfinished business, absence, separation, conflict/ talks clears the air/resolves problem, new path requires courage, consider options before acting, lack of communication brings sorrow, disappointment; *Reverse:* Fear of loss, confusion, imposition of own ideas, regrets, treachery results in loss and suffering, beware of malice nearby; *Key Words:* New path to unknown, separation, unfinished business, conflicts.

Four: *Meaning:* Tensions ease, gathering thoughts and strength in solitude, rest from stress/period of struggle, introspection, fatigue, recuperation from illness, repose, replenishment, patience, security through readiness, negotiation, orderly peace, conflict temporarily resolved, energy grounded, not the time to make definite plans, period of self-cleansing and releasing the emotional burdens of others; *Reverse:* Discretion needed, enforced seclusion, illness, excluded from former associates, care in renewed activity, taking precautions; *Key Words:* Rest, vigilance, orderly peace, recuperation, cleansing, patience.

Five: *Meaning:* Injured self-esteem, overcoming challenges, assimilating ideas, force used for good, overwhelming obligations, courage, positive attitude turns around a negative situation, reprioritize for success, face own limitations, blaming others for failures, parting due to ideas, struggles, antagonisms reveal personal courage; *Reverse:* Fear of defeat, vacillation, spite, power dissipated, empty gains; *Key Words:* Injured self-esteem, forcefulness gains goals, honorable struggle.

Six: *Meaning:* Leaving troubles behind, overcoming difficulties, journey, success after worry, making a decision ends worries, long-term planning, starting a new life, focused mind, new ideas open new opportunities, new knowledge alleviates limitations, success from self-sacrifices; *Reverse:* Turmoil, displacement, problems ignored, hindered, self-sabotage; *Key Words:* Journey, leaving troubles behind, overcoming difficulties.

Seven: *Meaning:* Strategy, success through perseverance, diplomacy and tact, new plans, creative action, confidence, fortitude, hope, interactive communication, able to defend oneself in a difficult situation, confidence, taking easy solutions; *Reverse:* Deceit, plans postponed, frustration, inadequate diplomacy, betrayal, indecision, poor advice, quarrels; *Key Words:* Strategy, perseverance, tricky situation, clever approach, careful decisions.

Eight: *Meaning:* Feeling entrapped, stay the course, patience needed, goals only temporarily obstructed, feeling hurt by criticism, scholarship dispels rumor and gossip, discovery of truth, untrustworthy gossip and rumor, indecision, distractions, difficult choice or dilemma needs time for resolution, frustration, possible illness; *Reverse:* Temporary relief through distancing rather than solutions, fears end, new options, improved health, self-imposed restrictions; *Key Words:* Dilemma, stay the course, patience needed, ignore rumor.

Nine: *Meaning:* Anxiety, plans about to be realized despite worries, understanding alleviates worries, issue needs resolution, actions need to be based on clear thinking, fears out of proportion to reality, feeling isolated, patience needed; *Reverse:* Doubt, deception, feeling oppressed by troubles, opposition to ideas raise self-doubts, impaired communications; *Key Words:* Anxieties, unfounded worries, plans about to be realized.

Ten: *Meaning:* Difficulties end, abilities proven after a struggle, wisdom gained, end of present troubles, worst is over, making a fresh start, honest assessment of situation, troubles conquered, exhaustion, sadness, able to finish a difficult task; *Reverse:* Ideas not workable, be wary of the plans and actions of others, going along with what cannot be changed, disappointment; *Key Words:* End of present troubles, proven ability to defend ideas, fresh start.

Page: *Meaning:* Vigilance, insight through careful observation, scrupulous preparation, learning a skill with practice, knowing what is wanted, discretion, news that brings understanding, practicing language skills, beginnings of independent thinking, perception, ready to take action or resolve an issue; *Reverse:* Cunning, deceitfulness, spying, unfinished projects, lack of preparation, taking inappropriate shortcuts, obstructions to learning, unforeseen events, change of plans; *Key Words:* Insightful, readiness for action, communication skills, vigilance.

Knight: *Meaning:* Sudden changes, self-assurance, incisive career activity, courage, conflict between old and new, intelligence, strong balance of power between ideas and implementation, bravery, skill, capable, heroic action, temporary chaos resulting from changes, action has begun, no more delays to accomplishing goals, penetrating mind and ideas, goal-focused; *Reverse:* Headstrong, impractical ideas, conceit, unprincipled action to achieve goals, deception, quick-tempered, adventurer; *Key Words:* Swift action, sudden changes, ability and courage, self-assured.

Queen: *Meaning:* Keenly perceptive, quick-witted, independent, intellect expressed through language, taking action, a determined and focused mind, thoughts manifested, breaking free from restrictions, self-determined, self-protective; *Reverse:* Impractical, suspicious, spiteful, isolated, negative, ill-tempered; *Key*

Words: Independent, insightful, perceptive, determined, language skills.

King: *Meaning:* Authority, legal action, judicial power, professionalism, decisions made and ideas implemented, will, determination, application of scientific method and thought, alert intellect, shrewdness, career satisfaction, objectivity; *Reverse:* Indecision, tyranny, domineering and willful, plans and ideas resisted, impractical, selfishness, a malicious person; *Key Words:* Authority, legal action, implementing decisions, determination.

Wands

Ace: [Timing upright is June; reverse is July to August]: *Meaning:* Creative energy, new career start or gains, invention, new ideas applied to work, start of an enterprise, new beginning, creative success, journey for career or artistic work, new initiative, taking action, adventure, birth of a baby; *Reverse:* Stagnation, plans canceled, goals unrealized, career delays, burdens postpone decisions; *Key Words:* Career start, creative awakening, new beginning, invention.

Two: *Meaning:* Business venture, attainment of goals, energizing new ideas, financial success, fulfillment, earned success, forceful personality brings goals to fruition, heeding good advice, careful planning of new goals, spiritual journey or growth, good use of potential, beginning studies or a course of action to gain goals; *Reverse:* Lack of growth, unfocused ideas or plans, gains less than desired, unsatisfying success, feeling unworthy, suffering or sadness while awaiting confirmation of success of venture; *Key Words:* Boldness, fulfillment, earned success, seeking a new challenge.

Three: *Meaning:* Good career news, enterprise about to succeed, gains in commerce, trade, unity for success, negotiation and flexibility, planning, power of creativity, sense of strength/independence, certitude, celebrating initial stages of success, activity nearly complete, accepting advice from others; *Reverse:* Promising

venture fails, pride interferes with goals, more facts needed, ulterior motives of others create difficulties; *Key Words:* Good career news, negotiations, practical knowledge, teamwork.

Four: *Meaning:* Celebration of work completed, job satisfaction, camaraderie with coworkers, working toward a common goal, unexpected occasion, teamwork, strong career foundation laid, stability of venture, romance, new home, sense of security and serenity, fruits of labor, completion, reaping rewards from project, demands in relationship ease, harmony, content with life and home; *Reverse:* Small rewards, disorganization, work dissatisfaction, delays in finishing a project, romance fades, minor disruptions at home; *Key Words:* Efforts rewarded, promotion, harmony, rejoicing, romance.

Five: *Meaning:* Tests and competition, struggle to gain goals, disagreements, challenges, overcoming obstacles through cooperation, renewal, exerting more effort, conflict brings change, formalizing rituals for growth, need for grounding to realize plans, caught off balance, hold fast to own resolve, rise in status; *Reverse:* Complex problems, contradictions, provoking arguments, indecisive; *Key Words:* Competition and tests, struggle, teamwork needed.

Six: *Meaning:* Victory, acknowledgment, public recognition, honors, good news, gains, advancement, goals realized triumph after difficulties, self-expression, success after hard work, lots of creative energy, understanding, ideas made reality, others receptive to ideas, career goals gained, gains from own efforts; *Reverse:* Vanity, overestimation of own abilities, disloyalty, insurmountable odds, need to focus on home and family, consider plans of others; *Key Words:* Victory, public acclaim, triumph over obstacles.

Seven: *Meaning:* Surmounting the odds, success, advantage, writer/student/teacher, creative flow, obstacles overcome, trust intuition, enterprise completed, keeping problems under control by methodical approach, pushing for own ideas, not giving up, handling problems as they appear, facing and managing issues; *Reverse:* Letting problems build up, energy dissipated, self-doubts, attention diverted from problems, opportunity lost through hesitancy, embarrassment, may need to accept offered assistance; *Key Words:* Advantage, defending a position, writer/student/teacher, courage.

Eight: *Meaning:* New or letter coming soon from a distance, swift action, travel, rapid but not permanent progress, taking control, taking action on ideas, ending a period of inactivity or of waiting, events gain speed, tensions resolved, plans allowed to proceed; *Reverse:* Deception, journey canceled, creative tensions, self-analysis stalls progress, hastily made decision or foolish impulse has far-reaching consequence, discord, delays, family quarrels interfere with career, travel plans delayed; *Key Words:* News from a distance, swift action, travel.

Nine: *Meaning:* Readiness, productivity, secure position, pause in work, anticipating difficulties, regroup thoughts before continuing, deeper awareness, strength in adversity, career strength, perseverance, disciplined and orderly approach needed, satisfaction with current situation, prepared to meet possible challenges, seizing opportunities, taking responsibility for own success and defense; *Reverse:* Impracticality, need for help from others, overly protective, obstinate, difficulties to overcome, uncertainties; *Key Words:* Strength, readiness, security, project nears completion.

Ten: *Meaning:* Promotion, culmination of creative venture, determination to achieve goals, problems resolved, stress, work pressures, carrying the burden of others, need to delegate duties, cooperation brings unity, pride for work well done; *Reverse:* Overcommitted, plans halted, oppression, difficulties, success becomes a burden, envy of others detracts from satisfaction, malicious gossip; *Key Words:*

Stress of success, overcommitted, need for delegation, tenacity.

Page: *Meaning:* Important news, new ideas need to be useable, emissary with message, consistent person, completion, energy, new cooperations and ideas, reliable friend, independent action, self-reliance, creative potential, good intentions, looking for direction in life, creating long-term plans, eager to apply learning, travel, ambition, resourcefulness; *Reverse:* Impatience, petty rivalries, uncertainty, flattery from false friend, easily influenced, used to achieve another's goals, lack of forethought; *Key Words:* Restlessness, resourceful, reliable, ambitious, important news.

Knight: *Meaning:* Enterprising new experience, journey, departure, energetic ambition, creativity, physical activity in learning process, time of action and adventure, new experiences, change of residence, imminent opportunities, setting out to explore the unknown, rapid action and dynamic energy; *Reverse:* Discord, activity interrupted, plans change, achievements belittled by those who are envious; *Key Words:* Looking for new adventure, enterprising activity, fearless explorer.

Queen: *Meaning:* Practical, meaningful expression, cleverness, self-confident, sincere, insightful, self-knowledge and self-mastery, friendly confidant, trusting others to do their part in a job, sustaining a vision, nurturing the spirit, independence, creativity, warmth, strong willed, loyal, imaginative, concept formed, gracious, willing to help others, ideas need continuous cultivation, leadership, good planner; *Reverse:* Irritability, seeking durable relationships, jealousy, poorly laid plans, accusatory, domineering, deceitful and distrustful, difficulty expressing ideas; *Key Words:* Practical, optimistic, joyful, creative, imaginative, kindness.

King: *Meaning:* Able to bring ideas to fruition, honest, following good council, good relations, conscientious professional, direct action taken, spiritual attainment, seeing things as they really are, living the ideal of truth and enlightenment, plans are possible, educated and refined, respected teacher, self-assured; *Reverse:* Austerity, critical, deliberations, action impeded by criticism, autocrat, slow changes, dogmatic, disapproving of ideas differing from own, thoughtless actions; *Key Words:* Professional cooperation, good counsel, conscientious, honesty.

Cups

Ace [Timing upright is September; reverse is October to November]: *Meaning:* Abundance, joy, emotional fulfillment, inspiration, productive, perfection, fount of life, inspiration, important relationship, positive change, contentment, pure and noble feelings, love, overflowing happiness; *Reverse:* Emotional upset, change, delays, unrequited love; *Key Words:* Abundance, joy, love, inspiration, emotional fulfillment.

Two: *Meaning:* Harmony, partnership, reconciliation, cooperation, intuition may be manifested, emotional balance, love, affinity, affection, trust, a happy surprise, engagement or marriage, union, synthesis, making peace, new relationship or a new phase in developing in one, strong intuition, agreements; *Reverse:* Emotional misunderstandings, disagreements, self delusion, self indulgence, lack of appreciation for another, ending of a relationship; *Key Words:* Harmony, partnership, affection, marriage.

Three: *Meaning:* Celebration, emotional fulfillment, satisfactory result, problem resolved, good work relations, flexibility and compromise, good news received, vitality, happy conclusion, relief, good luck, intuition takes form, creativity/unity with another, communication, consummation of a relationship, reunion with friends, wedding, birth; *Reverse:* Excesses, overindulgence, unappreciative, prestige dimin-

ished; *Key Words:* Celebration, good news, problems resolved, wedding, birth.

Four: *Meaning:* Discontent, reassessment, stationary period, new approach to old problem, success brings desire for new challenges, satiation, new friendships, faithfulness, new creative partnership, new possibilities; *Reverse:* Boredom, apathy, aversion, seeking distractions; *Key Words:* Reassessment, new possibilities, unidentified longings.

Five: *Meaning:* Partial loss, useless regrets, disillusioned, difficulties with a legacy, stressful relationships, anxiety, delayed inheritance, shallow friendships, sharing bounty, wasting a legacy, imperfections, avoiding a decision, dwelling on a loss; *Reverse:* Difficulties are overcome, hopeful outlook, unexpected lifestyle change, new alliances, sharing abundance; *Key Words:* Useless regrets, disillusionment, partial loss, troubled legacy.

Six: *Meaning:* Longings, nostalgia, happy memories, renewal, shared energy, harmony with others, reunions with friends from the past, able to manifest past expectations, serenity, spiritual communication, loving acceptance; *Reverse:* Living in the past, resisting change; *Key Words:* Nostalgia, manifesting past expectations, reunions.

Seven: *Meaning:* Many choices available, daydreams, bright ideas, dreams may be manifested, prioritize options, determination, truth revealed, imaginings, seeing order through the chaos, willpower needed to achieve goals, opportunity; *Reverse:* Fear of failure or wrong choices, unable to decide, delusion, gifts rejected, improbable ideas, false promises, self-deception, confusion; *Key Words:* Choices, materialize dreams, truth revealed, evaluate plans.

Eight: *Meaning:* Turning point in life, abandoning plans, seeking a new path, reason takes over, release inconsequential matters, moderation, seeking deeper meanings, scholarship sets one apart from colleagues;. *Reverse:* changes forced, dissatisfaction, reckless abandonment; *Key Words:* Turning point, new path, new direction in life, moderation.

Nine: *Meaning:* Wishes gained, satisfaction, difficulties surmounted, material and emotional attainment, victory, prosperity, happy future, contentment, empathy and understanding, fulfillment of a dream, good health, happiness, able to assimilate learning, self-satisfaction, enjoyment of life, intuition is accurate, serendipitous events lead to fulfillment of dreams, enjoying the kindness of others; *Reverse:* Imperfect impressions, unwarranted self-satisfaction, tied to the past, irresponsibility, selfishness, self-indulgence, vanity, complacency; *Key Words:* Wishes fulfilled, efforts rewarded, contentment, happy future.

Ten: *Meaning:* Happiness, esteem, recognition, reputation, gains in love, rest, enjoyment of family and friends, family heritage, reaping rewards of efforts, long-lasting achievement, success, contentment in home and family, satisfying emotional commitments, well-earned self-esteem; *Reverse:* Loss of friendship, family instability, no future planning, quarrel, only casual friendships, interrupted peace, family disputes, reputation endangered; *Key Words:* Contentment, recognition, esteem, good reputation, security.

Page: *Meaning:* Invitation or offer, a loyal friend, a trustworthy worker, practical use of artistic talents, creative thoughts, emotions satisfied, artistic or other creative expression, intention determined and linked with planning for emotional changes, emotional realization, perception and awareness, new social contacts, period of withdrawal for introspection, reflective mood; *Reverse:* Indiscretion, lack of fulfillment, newness, superficial love notes, flattery, distraction, susceptibility to a smooth talker; *Key Words:* Practical use of talents, creative inspiration, emotions satisfied.

Knight: *Meaning:* Artistic ability/inspiration, a proposition, opportunity, invitation coming, advancement, close friend, relaxations, filling own needs as well as those of others, love, emotional breakthrough, inducement, emotionally sensitive man, making use of opportunities when they arise, possibly a romantic proposal; *Reverse:* Deception, unworkable ideas, opportunistic cooperation, conniving, sly, fraudulent schemes, swindler; *Key Words:* Opportunity, invitation, artistic expression, breakthrough, young man of sensitivity.

Queen: *Meaning:* Being true to feelings, devotion, honesty, gift of vision, psychic, intellectual, artistic, creative, intuitive, fair and just, romanticism, nurturing, emotional support in difficult situations, loving and loved, serenely confident, authenticity of emotions; *Reverse:* Ambivalent feelings, emotional changes, unreliable, dishonesty, moody, self-centered; *Key Words:* Emotional truth, sensitive, psychic, nurturing, artistic.

King: *Meaning:* Responsibility, creativity, interest in the arts and sciences, reliable, considerate, a counselor, intuitive, a professional person in business, law, or medicine, community spirited, ready for talks and giving advice, loyalty and commitment to others; *Reverse:* Self-promoting, obstructionist, immobility, changeable, crafty, shifty, self-serving, unjust; *Key Words:* Responsible, reliable, counselor, creative, arts and sciences.

KEY WORD TAROT CHART

Major Arcana

	Card	Keyword
0	The Greenman	Spontaneity
1	The Witch	Communication
2	Drawing Down the Moon	Secrets
3	Earth Mother	Abundance
4	The Horned God	Builder
5	Drawing Down the sun	Tradition
6	Lady and Lord of the Wild Wood	Decisions
7	The Battle Wagon	Victory
8	The Crone	Fortitude
9	The Holly King	Wisdom
10	The Wheel of the Year	Progress
11	The Standing Stone	Objectivity
12	The Oak King	Transition
13	The Lord of Shadows	Change
14	The Sidhe	Harmony
15	Nature	Freedom
16	The Wild Hunt	Shocking Event
17	The Star	Hopes Obtainable
18	The Moon	Trust Instincts
19	The Sun	Happiness
20	Harvest	Reward/Renewal
21	The World Tree	Completion

KEY WORD TAROT CHART

Minor Arcana

Card	Pentacles	Swords	Wands	Cups
Ace	Prosperity	Victory	Creativity	Fulfillment
Two	Changes	Tensions Ease	New Venture	Partnership/Love
Three	Celebrity	Unknown/ Separation	Career News	Celebration
Four	Security	Recuperation	Rewards	Reassessment
Five	Financial Worries	Lessons Learned	Competition/ Strife	Useless Regrets
Six	Generosity/Gift	Leaving Troubles	Public Acclaim	Nostalgia/ Pleasure
Seven	Impatience	Strategy/Cunning	Valor/Advantage	Many Choices
Eight	Commercial Skills	Dilemma/Patience	News Coming Fast	Turning Point
Nine	Accomplishment	Anxieties/Worries	Strength/ Readiness	Wishes Fulfilled
Ten	Wealth/Stability	Turning From Trouble	Stress/Oppression	Recognition/ Joyful
Page	Diligent Work/ Study	Ready For Action	Restless/ Resourceful	Creative Inspiration
Knight	Propitious Occasion	Swift Action	Seeking Adventure	Opportunity
Queen	Plans Realized	Perceptive	Practical/ Optimistic	True To Own Feelings
King	Business Leader	Legal Authority	Professional Helper	Reliable Arts/ Sciences

Black Mirror Scrying

- The Black Mirror is an excellent divination tool, used like a crystal ball for scrying or used as a ritual tool in meditations, especially Dark Aspect meditations, through which you align with the Hunter and Crone aspects of the Divine

- Ground and center before use; decide what you want to explore; light candles and incense as desired

- Gaze into the mirror, do not lose focus—blink as necessary, allow the mirror to fog over, then project the thought into the mirror of what you want to see [future events, specific events, past lives, ancestors, etc.]

- The blackness of the reflection opens the way to other worlds and realms with ease, and may have many uses, including for Ancestor Meditations, Past Lives Meditations, and travels to Otherworld and Underworld

- When travel is finished cover mirror with black cloth; ground excess energy and take some refreshment

- Mirror may be made so as to prop up or set on a stand for the purpose of travel or rituals involving Otherworld and Underworld, or small enough to hold in the palm of the hand

- The double triad of the bindrune used will allow passage between the worlds and balance; offering magical protection, clear sight, power and balance, and power and success

- The herbs maintain grounding through Elemental Earth for divinations, meditations, and astral travel from a solid foundation.

How to Make a Black Mirror

A mirror is only a piece of glass with one side coated or painted to keep light rays from passing through, which is then reflected back to the viewer. Take a piece of circular glass and wash it with spring water. Dry it and let it sit in the moonlight during a full moon and then during a dark moon. Next, paint the back of the glass with black enamel and let it dry. Cut out a piece of black felt to fit the back of the mirror and glue it into place. A small photo frame with glass can be used for this same purpose. Another method of construction is to paint a circle of black enamel in the center of a circle of silver aluminum foil. While the paint is still tacky, but not "wet," add a clear glue to the foil rim. Lay the painted foil against the clean glass and carefully press it onto the glass. This leaves a silvery edge around the mirror. After this dries, glue the black felt to the back of the mirror to avoid scratching or scraping the foil and paint. Use the *Consecration of a Tool Ritual* to energize the mirror.

The mirror may be set in a decorative frame or on a support frame or easel such as used to display plates or small pictures. Keep mirror covered with a black cloth when not in use. To retain the focus of the energies, only use the mirror in magical workings. Imbolc is a good time to cleanse and rededicate all tools, including this one.

Bindrune and Incantation

Draw the runes so they form one image on the backing to be laid against the mirror or on a piece of parchment to be laid on the mirror before gluing a felt backing on, stating while doing:

ᛞ   *Daeg* for working between the worlds
ᛋ   *Sigel* for wholeness and vitality
ᚲ   *Ken* for opening energy
ᛏ   *Tyr* for success
ᚦ   *Thorn* for protection
ᛇ   *Eoh* for channel opened and sigil bound

Herbs and Incantation

When paint is dry and bindrune is ready, add a pinch of herbs to back of mirror as it lies in the frame:

> I bless thee mugwort for divination, thou elderflower for blessing me,
> lavender for Otherworld and working with the Sidhe, with blessings given
> and received, this mirror now empowered be!

Immediately cover the mirror with inscribed backing from picture frame, or place paper on mirror back and cover with selected backing.

CRYSTAL BALL & OTHER STONE SCRYING

1. **Wash** crystal ball or other scrying tool in cooled mugwort tea.
2. **Consecrate** with Consecration Ritual; and if small, with the Crystal Consecration and Dedication Rituals.
3. **Cover** with a cloth when not in use: black, green, or purple are best.
4. **Familiarize yourself** with the energy or spirit of the crystal to work productively together.
5. **Ground and center** before use, ground after use, take refreshment.

What to Use

Any size crystal ball of natural quartz crystal, man made lead crystal, glassy obsidian, fluorite, labradorite, amethyst, or any other stone for which there is an attraction and willingness to work is suitable. May have bubbles or other flaws, which may be an aid to focusing, or may be clear.

How to Use

1. Focus on bubble, flaw, or center of clear crystal.

2. Do not let vision blur; blink as necessary to stay focused.

3. Think about what you want to see.

4. Object will appear to become cloudy or smoky, but stay focused and let this happen.

5. Let the vision come to you.

6. Vision will be clear, unfolding within the area of focus, moving like a motion picture in color.

PENDULUM

1. May be made of anything with a little weight to it, but quartz, amethyst, lapis lazuli, and gold are most popular, and a string or chain not longer than your forearm to hold it so it does not touch the table top when suspended.

2. Rest bent elbow on table top, with pendulum string or chain held between thumb and forefinger so pendulum falls free.

3. Focus into the center of the pendulum and mentally project into it the word "Stop" and it should stop all movement. Do this between questions to end motion and prepare the pendulum for the next answer.

4. Ask a yes or no question to which you know the answer ["Did I drink coffee this morning?"] and watch to see in which direction the pendulum moves: circles or lines—one means yes, the other means no, but this will vary with the scryer, so establish which one is correct for you.

5. May use a pendulum board with other answer options on it, but the pendulum needs to be swung over these options and informed as to what they mean, which is called programming.

RUNE CASTING

1. **Draw, paint, or inscribe** runes on small stones, clay tiles, slivers of wood, pebbles, small crystals, etc.

2. **Consecrate** runes according to Consecration of a Tool Ritual and store in dark-colored pouch.

3. **Handle** bag of runes while focusing on a question.

4. **Open bag**, pull out the number of runes needed for a rune spread, laying them out face-up as they arrive as upright or reversed runes.

RUNE SPREADS

1. Lay out 1–2–3 = all upright means yes, all reverse means no; partial is iffy

2. Lay out 1 = overview of situation

  2 = challenge

  3 = course of action needed

  4 = options and choices

  5 = evolved situation or outcome

3. Lay out 1–2–3: 1 = present; 2 = action needed or likely; 3 = result

4. Lay out 1–2–3: 1 = background; 2 = present; 3 = future

5. Lay out

	6		1 = past
	5		2 = present
3		1	3 = future
	2		4 = foundation or heart of the matter
	4		5 = obstacles or challenges
			6 = outcome or new developing situation

RUNE MEANINGS

Name	Sign	Meanings and [R] Reverse Meanings
Osa	ᚢ	The God; good fortune; favorable outcome [R] Delays, outcome uncertain
As	ᚨ	Ancestor; signs; gain ancient wisdom; occult messages; new awareness [R] Inhibited energy; feeling a sense of futility
Beorc	ᛒ	Goddess; fertility; growth; new beginnings; family; manifesting ideas; gentle but pervasive action; evolving as a flow into new forms [R] Need to renew impetus or start over to achieve desired results
Daeg	ᛞ	Daybreak; between the worlds; breakthrough; catalyst; invisibility; transformation; fresh start; growth; passage concluded; fruitful communications [R] No reverse meaning
Eh	ᛗ	Movement; safe journey; progress; changes; new project; swift changes; security in position requires growth and progress [R] Movement is blocked; resistance to change or development

Name	Sign	Meanings and [R] Reverse Meanings
Feoh	ᚠ	Material wealth; fulfillment; ambition satisfied; prosperity; good fortune; good luck [R] Frustrations; situations are doubtful; lessons learned by experience
Gefu	ᚷ	Union; partnership; love; gifts; self-confidence; freedom; individuality [R] No reverse meaning
Eoh	ᛇ	A channel; action; Otherworld communication; dynamic action; go-ahead given; obstacles removed through foresight and planning [R] No reverse meaning
Haegl	ᚻ	Hail; limits/disruptions; awakening; upheaval; need to release restrictive ideas and thoughts; desire for freedom and change; releasing negativity opens way to a positive new reality to be revealed [R] No reverse meaning
Is	ᛁ	Ice; immobility; rest period; focus; energy drain; action not favorable; halt negative forces; stop slander [R] No reverse meaning
Gera	ᛄ	Year; harvest; rewards; tangible results from work; good outcome to projects or endeavors; all things come in due time; cannot hurry events [R] No reverse meaning
Ken	ᚲ	Transforming fire; opening energy; fresh start; positive attitude; sense of well-being; negativity is dispelled; ready to receive positive energies [R] Evolution; the old is swept away by growth and change
Lagu	ᛚ	Fluidity; water; psychic power; intuition; vitality; re-evaluation for success; movement; emotions [R] Heed instincts; efforts hindered by being over-extended
Mannaz	ᛗ	Self; self-improvement; cooperation; meditation; no excesses, [R] Blocking own progress; need to get rid of bad old habits
Nyd	ᚾ	Constraint; self-control; overcome obstacles; goals achieved [R] Cleansing needed to regain freedom; release from restraints needed
Ing	ᛝ	The Horned God; fertility; family; completion; potential; new life/path; power to achieve goals; new freedom from constraints [R] No reverse meaning
Ethel	ᛟ	Possession; home; social status; acquisitions/benefits; seeking new path [R] Need to depart from old ways of doing things/old way of life
Perth	ᛈ	Destiny; hidden forces; unexpected luck; initiation; opportunity; good fortune; secrets revealed [R] Bound to the past; conventional; traditionalist; unwilling to change

Name	Sign	Meanings and [R] Reverse Meanings
Rad	ᚱ	Travel; quest; find what is sought; attunement; safe journey; justice; communication; attunement; be rational rather than instinctive; action now brings good results [R] Need to act with care in relationships
Sigel	ᛋ	Sun wheel; wholeness; healing; vital energy; power; victory; success; life-force; self-confidence; regeneration; achievement; honor and honors [R] No reverse meaning
Tyr	↑	Victory; success; courage; favorable outcome to actions [R] Timing not right for action; need to question motives of self/others
Thorn	ᚦ	Protection; gateway; foes neutralized; defense; safe from evil; release the past for a new beginning; door and passage to new start [R] Hasty action is detrimental; pause and re-evaluate prior to acting
Uruz	ᚢ	Strength; determination; manifesting physical health; courage; promotion; change and passage from a loss [R] Not being aware of opportunities; need to look outward not inward
Wyn	ᚹ	Joy; comfort; happiness; harmony; love; well-being; wisdom through understanding; success; material gain [R] Slow realization of plans; tests and difficulties to be overcome
Eolh	ᛉ	Elk; protection; friendship; going unnoticed; victory; optimism; help comes; opportunities; aspirations [R] Temperate nature needed; choose associates with care
Wyrd	[ ]	unknowable fate; destiny; cosmic influence; total trust; endings and new beginnings; nothing is predestined or unchangeable [R] No reverse meaning

OGHAM CASTING SYSTEM

THE THREE WORLDS

[[X]] - Otherworld [spiritual]
[[X]] - Middleworld [physical]
[[X]] - Underworld [transformational]

The X continues through two subsequently larger squares, but beyond is outside the reading. Innermost square shows the most influential fews, second square is less. Create a Casting Cloth by cutting a large square from material; drawing an X from the corners to cross in the center, and drawing another inner square to form two squares, as shown in the diagram.

THE FOUR REALMS

The three worlds are arranged in Quarters, called Realms, with each one aspected to the Queens of the North, West, and East, and the King of the South: *The Three Queens and Their King* of Sumerian, Mycenea, and Celtic tradition. See as three large, quartered squares, with the top segment being North, the bottom South, the left West, and the right East. They all meet at the intersection of the X at the center, or *Midhe*—called the *Fifths*.

THE PATH FEWS

From the Midhe of Middleworld, there are four paths to Otherworld and four path fews to Underworld, traveled with the casting to give a three-dimensional reading, with each few influenced by its location. The path fews move in both directions and are read in both the worlds they connect, with the reading continuing in the new world.

Reading the Casting of the Fews

Ask a question, toss the Ogham fews, then remove and set aside those that are outside the outer square and those that are backside up. Readings begin at the centermost few, in Middleworld, then continue in a deosil spiral through the rest of the cast fews. Form a coherent answer sentence with these fews.

Natural Alignment of the Fews

Otherworld [OW]:
N = Age and Wisdom— ≢ Iodha [I]
W = Silver Light and Gentleness— ≣ Quert [Q]
E = Abundance and Delight— ≣ Nion [N]
S = Wonder and Happiness— ⦚ Ruis [R]
1. ≡ Eadha [E]
Paths}
2. ≣ Saille [S]
3. ⦚ Coll [C]
4. ≡ Straif [Z]

Middleworld [MW]
[X of casting cloth]:
N = [Cath ⚹] Challenge and Resistance— ≢ Ur [U]
W = [Fis コ] Knowledge and Recent Influences— ≣ Tinne [T]
E = [Blath ▥] Prosperity and Manifestation— ⊫ Fearn [F]
S = [Seis ◈] Contentment and Past— ⦚ Ngetal [Ng]
1. ⊹ Onn [O]
Paths}
2. ⊣ Duir [D]
3. ⊨ Luis [L]
4. ⦚ Gort [G]

Underworld [UW]:
N = Endings and Death— ⊹ Ailm [A]
W = Love and the Lady— ⊣ Huath [H]
E = Growth and Youth— ⊦ Beithe [B]
S = Energy and Life Vitality— ⦚ Muin [M]
Blank:
Unknowable Fate or Cosmic Destiny—| WYRD [ ]

252 OGHAM PLACE MEANINGS

1. Iodho [Yew] ≣ [I/Y]-Realm [O]-Transformation/Death/Immortality
OWN: Ending through Age or wisdom; transformation; immortality
OWW: Changed by light of inspiration or by gentleness
OWE: Ending of bounty or transformation into abundance
OWS: Ending of one kind of happiness; change in what brings joy
MWN: Challenge motivates a change; brings immortality
MWW: Transformed by new knowledge
MWE: Reaping a small harvest; change in prosperity
MWS: Contentment/harmony ends and interests change
UWN: Period of significant endings and changes
UWW: Transformation of love to immortality; end of a love
UWE: Youthfulness transformed by growth
UWS: Life changes; end of era; transformed by new energy & vitality

2. Quert [Apple] ≣ [Q]-Realm [O]-Regeneration/Eternity/Life
OWN: Age or wisdom brings a regeneration or a new Life
OWW: New calmness in life; perfection in peacefulness
OWE: Renewal of abundance
OWS: Happiness from a new life; enjoyment of beauty
MWN: Challenge leads to regeneration or a new life
MWW: Renewal/perfecting of knowledge
MWE: Return of prosperity; upturn in fortune; reap rewards
MWS: Contentment from beauty/perfection; harmony in life
UWN: Ending brings regeneration; perfection ideal changes
UWW: Love renewed; love of life, beauty, the arts
UWE: Growth brings new youthfulness; eternally young
UWS: Energy and life revitalized

3. Nion [Ash] ≣ [N]-Realm [O]-Awakening/Rebirth/Peace/Emergence
OWN: Awakening/communication of wisdom; age/longevity/tenure gain influence
OWW: Peace emphasized; inspiration and rebirth; hope
OWE: Abundance brings peace; fruitful communications; reward
OWS: Happiness communicated; new joy in life
MWN: Challenges open awareness; communication/influence soothes friction; renew efforts
MWW: New awareness through learning; communicating knowledge; old knowledge reborn
MWE: Prosperity through communication; peaceful harvest
MWS: New influence leads to harmony/contentment; awakening to the things that matter
UWN: Endings become beginnings through awakening/rebirth; creating transformation
UWW: Love/pleasure rediscovered; love as a new influence; peace in relationships through communication

UWE: Rebirth of youth; growing process starts; communication/new influence with youths

UWS: revitalization; re-energized; vital communications; dynamic renewal of efforts

4. Ruis [Elder] ╲ [R]-Realm [O]-Change/Evolution

OWN: Wisdom leads to new path; old ways decay; evolve into new forms

OWW: Lack of contentment inspires search for a new path; peace comes from releasing what is outmoded

OWE: Change in bounty; deterioration of delight pushes for a new path

OWS: Old forms of happiness replaced with new ones

MWN: Challenge to old ways leads to new forms

MWW: Learning brings changes; knowledge results in evolution

MWE: Gains deteriorate/disappointing; need new methods for success

MWS: Contentment/harmony comes in due course; that which brings satisfaction is in a state of change; seeking new goals

UWN: Old patterns give way to new ideas; need to adjust to changes

UWW: New love coming; seeking new friends

UWE: Evolution and growth emphasized to maintain youthful outlook

UWS: New insight revitalizes old ways; change comes through energy

5. Eadha [Aspen] ≢ [E]-Path [O]-Intuition/Overcoming Obstacles

OWN: Sensitive to elders; wisdom gained through intuition

OWW: Inspiration by intuition; peace gained through perseverance

OWE: Obstacles overcome to gain abundance; willing sharing of bounty

OWS: Kindliness leads to happiness; follow instincts for bliss

MWN: Challenges overcome; intuition is accurate

MWW: Knowledge comes intuitively; overcome learning obstacles; use knowledge with sensitivity

MWE: Overcoming obstacles for prosperity; rewards from the care of others

MWS: Intuition/sensitivity leads to harmony/contentment; obstacles to harmony overcome

UWN: Transformed by intuition; obstacles end

UWW: Sensitivity to others increases love/pleasure; follow intuition in matters of the heart

UWE: Enjoyment of youth; intuition leads to growth

UWS: Energy to overcome obstacles; strong intuition

6. Coll [Hazel] ≣ [C]-Path [O]-Wisdom/Creativity/Perception

OWN: Strong wisdom; career in science/writing/creativity; mental power; understanding is accurate

OWW: Inspirational turn of mind; spiritual writing; perceptions for peacefulness

OWE: Bounty and abundance from wisdom and creative expression

OWS: Understanding brings happiness; joy in writing/science

MWN: Wisdom/understanding challenged; friction in creativity

MWW: Educational writing; knowledge increased by perceptive ability; participation in learning

MWE: Prosperity from creativity/understanding

MWS: Wisdom leads to harmony; contentment from creativity

UWN: Wisdom transformed; misunderstanding; perceptions change

UWW: Love of learning; pleasure in creative efforts

UWE: Wisdom grows; youthful audience; writing for young people; science endeavors beginning to grow; creativity and understanding increases

UWS: Energy to pursue interests

7. Saille [Willow] ≣ [S]-Path [O]-Intuition/Flexibility/Psychic

OWN: Wisdom enhanced by psychic power; liberation in age

OWW: Flexibility for peace; intuition leads to inspiration

OWE: Abundance gives liberation; bounty through intuition

OWS: Happiness from flexibility; intuition/psychic power brings bliss

MWN: Challenge to use psychic power wisely; flexibility eases friction

MWW: Flexibility in learning and knowledge; wide variety of interests; intuitive learning; liberation through knowledge

MWE: Prosperity from intuition and psychic power; what is sent returns

MWS: Use of intuition to find contentment; in harmony with psychic power; contentment from adaptability

UWN: Psychic power is transforming; end of restrictions

UWW: Love is intuitive; adaptability in finding love/enjoyment; psychic power enhances love; liberation in love

UWE: Growth of intuition and psychic power

UWS: Psychic energy; vitality of freedom; keenly intuitive; life vitality enhanced by flexibility

8. Straif [Blackthorn] ⦚ [Z]-Path [O]-Coercion/Control/Forcefulness

OWN: Wisdom controlled by others; obstacles of age turned to benefits

OWW: Inspiration muted; peace enforced by others; dissatisfaction

OWE: Abundance lacking; bounty dissipated

OWS: Happiness muted by others; own joy lies in the hands of others

MWN: Challenged to seize control of own life; destructive power used against obstacles

MWW: Learning is a difficult process; knowledge controlled/constricted; need to explore new ideas

MWE: Prosperity controlled by others; need to overcome obstacles to goals for independence and success

MWS: Disharmony; discontent; contentment comes when freed from constraints

UWN: Destructive power turned against obstacles; ending of coercion; transformation of negative forces into positive ones

UWW: Forbearance in love; false pleasure; pretense of love; dominance in love can be destructive; resigned to will of others in love/pleasure

UWE: Growth inhibited; control of youth

UWS: Energy controlled by others; vitality dependent on others

9. Ur [Heather] ⟊ [U]-Realm [M]-Fervor/Gateway/Success/Prosperity

OWN: Wisdom provides a gateway to strong self-expression/gains

OWW: Inspirational fervor; peace from success

OWE: Success brings abundance

OWS: Happiness through strong self-expression; success brings bliss

MWN: Friction leads to strong self-expression; challenge brings success

MWW: Gains in knowledge/learning; self-expression in knowledge; philosopher; education is a gateway to success

MWE: Highly successful; many gains; fervor and self-expression reaps successful harvest

MWS: Harmony from successes; strong self-expression harmonized for contentment and gains

UWN: Self-expression is a gateway to transformation; gains dwindle and new forms for success need to be found

UWW: Enjoyment of self-expression; pleasure from success; ardent in pursuit of love and pleasure

UWE: Success is a gateway to growth; youthful self-expression

UWS: Energy and fervor invigorate self-expression and gains

10. Tinne [Holly] ⟊ [T]-Rlm [M]-Balance/Retribution/Tests/Challenges

OWN: Age and wisdom bring new challenges for balance

OWW: Peace through balance

OWE: Balance needed in decisions affecting bounty

OWS: Choices to be made for happiness

MWN: Challenges to balance mounting; retribution/justice; care needed in making decisions in time of friction

MWW: Learning determined by conscious decisions; balanced education; tests of knowledge

MWE: Balance needed for prosperity; choices determine the harvest

MWS: Contentment from balance; harmony affected by decisions

UWN: Endings from retribution; transformation to balance by decisions

UWW: Balance in love and pleasure; love a matter of decisions rather than emotion; pleasure/love test balance; retribution in love

UWE: Balanced growth; tests in youth; decisions/choices affect growth

UWS: Energy to maintain balance; vitality to overcome tests; choices approached with vigor

11. Fearn [Alder] ⟊ [F]-Realm [M]-Inner Strength/Foundations

OWN: Wisdom emphasized as awareness ends doubts; inner strength through wisdom/age

OWW: Inspiration to inner strength; peace through end of doubt

OWE: Foundation of abundance; awareness/appreciation of bounty; generosity

OWS: Foundation of happiness; bliss from awareness/end of doubts; satisfaction

MWN: Friction leads to end of doubts; challenge brings inner strength

MWW: Learning ends doubts; foundation of knowledge brings inner strength

MWE: Prosperity from determination

MWS: Contentment from awareness and end of doubts; harmony from inner strength

UWN: Awareness is transformative; ending of doubts emphasized; inner strength develops

UWW: Love faced with full awareness; inner strength brings pleasure; doubt-free love

UWE: Growth of awareness to overcome doubts; youthful foundation of inner strength

UWS: Vitality of inner strength; energy to open awareness

12. Ngetal [Reed] ⊼ [NG]-Realm [M]-Harmony/Inner Transformation

OWN: Age/wisdom brings internal transformation/development

OWW: Harmony from inspiration; peacefulness within

OWE: Abundance comes from inner development

OWS: Happiness lies in internal transformation

MWN: Harmony difficult to maintain; inner development challenged; friction leads to internal transformation

MWW: Knowledge/learning has a profound, transformative effect

MWE: Balance is harvest of inner development

MWS: Harmony/contentment emphasized through internal transformation

UWN: Transformation emphasized through internal development and harmony; end of harmony through internal transformation

UWW: Inner transformation/development through love; harmony in pleasure

UWE: Growth of harmony; youthful inner transformation; emphasis on inner development

UWS: Energy for internal transformation/development; vitality for harmony

13. Onn [Gorse] ⊹ [O]-Path [U]-Opportunity/Wisdom/Life Changes

OWN: Wisdom emphasized through opportunity; life changes due to age and wisdom gathered

OWW: Positive changes from gathered wisdom lead to peace; inspiration generates life changes

OWE: Opportunity for abundance; bountiful wisdom

OWS: Happiness from opportunity & wisdom used to create life changes

MWN: Challenge causes positive changes; friction in life changes overcome through gathered wisdom

MWW: Increased knowledge emphasized resulting in opportunities and positive changes or new life

MWE: Wisdom harvested; prosperity from knowledge; opportunity for gains from education/learning

MWS: Contentment from gathered knowledge and positive changes; harmony in life changes

UWN: Ending of harmony; transformation through gathered knowledge and wisdom emphasized; rapid changes for the better

UWW: Knowledge increases capacity for love/pleasure; wisdom in love; opportunity in love; positive changes in love/pleasure

UWE: Growth of opportunity; increase in positive changes; youthful approach to life

UWS: Energy to implement life changes; vitality of knowledge and wisdom; energetic changes

14. Duir [Oak] ⊣ D]-Path [U]-Truth/Endurance/Strength/Courage

OWN: Endurance of wisdom; longevity

OWW: Inspiration of truth; willpower brings peace

OWE: Abundance through strength/willpower

OWS: Happiness found in truth/inner strength

MWN: Able to endure challenges; overcome obstacles

MWW: Learning truth; overcome obstacles to learning; strength in knowledge

MWE: Endurance/willpower beings results; prosperity in truth; solid achievements

MWS: Contentment from overcoming obstacles; harmony in truth; creating own contentment through willpower

UWN: Positive force applied to create transformation; obstacles end; truth revealed

UWW: Use of determination secures love; truth in love; love conquers all

UWE: Ability to overcome obstacles leads to growth; growth through willpower; youthful strength

UWS: Vitality of truth; energy to overcome obstacles; energy enhances strength; vitality of willpower

15. Luis [Rowan] ⊨ [L]-Path [U]-Insight/Foreknowledge/Enlivening

OWN: Insight in age; ability in foreknowledge enhanced

OWW: Healing; inspiration enhances creativity

OWE: Abundance of insight; power of healing; great activity

OWS: Happiness in creativity; able to find own bliss; relief; using insight to bring happiness; joyfully active

MWN: Challenge leads to increase in activity; argument clears the air; friction in creativity; insight leads to friction

MWW: Learning healing; knowledge of healing; insightfulness; creative learning

MWE: Prosperity from insight/healing; foreknowledge used wisely; successful creativity; fruitful activity

MWS: Contentment in creativity; insight brings contentment; harmonious activity

UWN: Transformation from insight; endings/new beginnings brought about through healing; new activities

UWW: Healing love; insightfulness in love; creativity brings pleasure

UWE: Youthful activities; growth of insight; creativity enhanced

UWS: Energy for activities; vitality of insight; healing energy

16. Gort [Ivy] ↘ [G]-Path [U]-Developing Skills/Learning/Resistance

OWN: Gains in due time; increasing wisdom

OWW: Peace comes through tenacity; inspired to learning; new skills discovered

OWE: Abundance by persistence; developing skills lead to favorable results; learning brings gains

OWS: Joy of learning; happiness is attained by tenacity

MWN: Challenge in persistence; friction leads to new skills developed; difficult studies

MWW: Learning emphasized; learning involves new skills; gains in knowledge through hard work/tenacity

MWE: Prosperity from new skills; gains from persistence

MWS: Contentment found in new skills/learning; harmony comes with effort and persistence

UWN: Hard work pays off; persistence transforms into tangible gains; transformation through learning

UWW: Pleasure in a new skill/learning; persistence in love succeeds

UWE: Growth by learning; growth of skills; youthful persistence works

UWS: Energy to gain goals through tenacity; vitality of learning; energy to develop skills

17. Ailm [Fir] ⼗ [A]-Realm [U]-Autonomy/Discretion/Objectivity

OWN: Discretion in wisdom; vigor in age; secret wisdom

OWW: Secret inspiration; discretion in peace

OWE: Discrete use of bounty; vigorous abundance

OWS: Discretion ensures happiness; happiness in rulership; vigor in bliss

MWN: Autonomy challenged; vigorous response; friction from secrecy

MWW: Learning discretion; secret knowledge; aptitude for learning; leader in education

MWE: Prosperous rulership; gains from discretion/secrecy; vitality in prosperity

MWS: Harmony from discretion; contentment in autonomy/rulership

UWN: Secrecy leads to transformation; new openness; transformation of rulership/autonomy

UWW: Secret love; discretion in pleasure; vigorous love; dominance in love

UWE: Growth of autonomy/discretion/secrecy; youthful vigor

UWS: Vigor emphasized; energy for rulership/autonomy

18. Huath [Hawthorn] ⊣ [H]-Realm [U]-Pleasure/Misfortune/Cleansing

OWN: Pleasure in wisdom; comfortable old age; positive changes in age

OWW: Inspirational cleansing; stimulating peace; positivity

OWE: Enjoyment of abundance

OWS: Cleansing brings happiness

MWN: Challenge/friction may lead to misfortune or positive changes

MWW: Knowledge leads to positive changes; pleasure in learning

MWE: Harvest what is sown as either pleasure or misfortune; prosperity from positive changes/cleansing

MWS: Harmony emphasized; contentment from cleansing

UWN: Endings bring a positive change; transformation through cleansing

UWW: Pleasure emphasized; enjoyment of love; care needed to avoid misfortune in love

UWE: Growth of pleasure; youthful pleasures; growth brings cleansing

UWS: Energy for positive changes; vitality for pleasure

19. Beithe [Birch] ⊢ [B]-Realm [U]-Beginnings/Energy/Vitality

OWN: Beginnings of wisdom; energetic age

OWW: Beginnings of inspiration; unseen forces lead to inspiration and peace

OWE: Abundant energy; auspicious beginnings

OWS: Happiness from new beginning; energy for bliss

MWN: Challenge pushes for new beginning; energy from friction

MWW: Beginning of learning/knowledge; energy for learning; subtle growth of knowledge

MWE: Beginning of period of prosperity; energy to bring matters to fruition

MWS: Contentment from new beginnings; harmony with the unseen forces of growth

UWN: Ending leads to a new beginning; transformative energy; transformed by growth

UWW: Beginning of love/pleasure; unseen forces of growth at work in love; energy for love/pleasure

UWE: Growth emphasized; youthful energy; growth leads to new beginning

UWS: Energy emphasized; vitality in new beginning; vitality of quiet growth

20. Muin [Vine] ⅄ [M]-Realm [U]-Introspection/Other Sight/Renewal

OWN: Introspection in age; introspective wisdom

OWW: Inspiration from introspection; peace through reflection

OWE: Bounty from other sight; introspection leads to abundance

OWS: Happiness from looking inward

MWN: Challenge in self-analysis; friction leads to introspection

MWW: Learning through introspection/reflection; knowledge comes from within/from other sight

MWE: Rewards reaped from reflection/introspection

MWS: Contentment found by introspection; harmony based on reflection

UWN: Transformed by introspection/other sight

UWW: Introspective approach to love

UWE: Growth from looking inward

UWS: Energy turned to introspection; reflective youth

21. Blank [Mistletoe] |-Wyrd [X]-Hidden Cosmic Influence/Destiny/Fate

OWN: destiny/cosmic influence in age/wisdom

OWW: destiny/cosmic influence in light/gentleness/inspiration

OWE: destiny/cosmic influence in abundance

OWS: destiny/cosmic influence in happiness

MWN: destiny/cosmic influence in conflict/resistance/challenge

MWW: destiny/cosmic influence in learning/knowledge

MWE: destiny/cosmic influence in prosperity/harvest

MWS: destiny/cosmic influence in harmony/contentment

MWM: destiny/cosmic influence in the central focus

UWN: destiny/cosmic influence in endings/transformation

UWW: destiny/cosmic influence in love

UWE: destiny/cosmic influence in growth

UWS: destiny/cosmic influence in vitality/energy

PALMISTRY

WHAT TO READ

Palmistry is holistic—read the lines in both hands as well as their shape, finger placement, palm shape and appearance, presence and thickness of mounds, length of fingers, and flexibility of thumb. Not all possible features are in any given palm.

Lines can change if a person works at developing areas of limitations. Be discrete when reading a palm and look at the entire hand. *Know what you are looking at, and be careful what you do.* The *Rules of Conduct* apply.

- **Left Hand**—"birth hand"—shows innate aspects and life's potentials
- **Right Hand**—shows how potential is being used
- **Power Hand**—most often read—favored hand
- **Ambidextrous**—a flow between both hands

Hand Types

Air: Long fingers, square palm, many fine lines in palm; expressive, emotionally stable, intellectually curious; writers, teachers, public people, communications.

Earth: Short fingers, square palm, deeply lined palm; serious, practical, active; manual labors like farming, carpentry, machine operator, business, office, sales.

Water: Long fingers, rectangular palm, many clear lines in palm; sensitive, creative, quiet studious careers and low pressure occupations like research.

Fire: Short fingers, rectangular palm, shallow, thin lines; creative, energetic, assertive; artists, customer service.

Finger Shapes

Conic: Sensitive, impulsive, intuitive, could be eccentric or nervous.

Round: Balanced disposition, adapts easily to changes.

Square: Likes order and regularity, confident, clear-thinking, could be dull.

Spatulate: Independent, energetic, action-loving, could be devious and cruel.

Mixed: Versatility, adaptable, can excel in various occupations.

Fingers & Their Lengths

Little [Mercury]: Communications, business, science, relationships; *long:* shrewd and clever; *short:* difficulty with self-expression.

Ring [Sun]: Art, personality, creativity, success, talents; *long:* imaginative, dreamer, takes chances; *short:* easily frustrated, prefers solid reality.

Middle [Saturn]: Responsibility, self-direction, introspection, wisdom; *long:* careful and meticulous in duties; *short:* holds back on abilities.

Index [Jupiter]: Ambition, self-confidence, sociability, leadership, religion; *long:* self-assured, a leader; *short:* is under-confident, insecurity.

Thumb [Earth/Human]: *First joint* is will, *second joint* is logic; *third joint* is the rhythm of life; *long overall:* is enterprising; *short overall:* is practical and loyal; *longest joint:* most influential; *equals:* balanced.

Mound Locations & Descriptions

Mound of Mercury: Beneath little finger; *none:* lack of business skills, unable to communicate well; *well-developed:* talent for self-expression, liveliness; *highly developed:* talkative, garrulous.

Mound of Sun: Beneath ring finger; *none:* low energy levels, lack of aesthetic interests or creative pursuits; *well-developed:* artistic ability, love of beauty, fine arts, culinary arts, etc.; *highly developed:* extravagant, materialistic, vanity, self-indulgent.

Mound of Saturn: Beneath middle finger; *none:* indecisiveness, pessimism, humorlessness; *well- developed:* independent nature, enjoys solitude as well as companionship, self-awareness, emotional balance, fidelity, prudence; *highly developed:* self-absorbed in sense of preferring isolation.

Mound of Jupiter: Beneath the index finger; *none:* low self-esteem, idleness, dislike of authority; *well-developed:* even temper, assertive, self-assured; *highly developed:* can be a strong leader or overbearing, vain, self-absorbed in sense of insistence of rightness of own way.

Mound of Venus: Beneath the thumb—everyone will have this one; *weak:* delicate health, lack of exuberance and sensitivity; *firm and round:* love of outdoors, compassionate, successful, vitality; *highly developed:* physical energy, sexuality, enjoys eating and drinking.

Mound of Moon: Opposite of Mound of Venus—balance of imagination and reality, subconscious, peace, harmony: *weak or none:* totally realistic, no fantasizing; *well-developed:* good intuition and imagination, strong nurturer; *highly developed:* restlessness, active imagination, creativity.

Mound of Mars [+]: Between Mound of Jupiter and Mound of Venus—ability to overcome obstacles and assertiveness: *weak:* quiet and passive nature; *well-developed:* average courage and aggressiveness; *highly developed:* hot-tempered, passionate.

Mound of Mars [-]: Between Mound of Mercury and Mound of Moon shows determination, resistance; *weak:* not assertive; *well-developed:* self-reliance, courage, somewhat stubborn; *highly developed:* inflexibility, tendency to cruelty or violence.

Plain of Mars: Hollow of the center of the palm; *shallow:* person tends to be confident; *average:* person tends to careful; *deep:* person tends to be more timid.

Lines of the Hand

Life: Around thumb into palm from Mound of Mars [+]: *wide arc:* warm and responsive person; *shallow:* aloof and inhibited; *curve ends at Mound of Venus:* enjoyment of domestic life; *curve ends at Mound of Moon:* love of adventure and travel; *long, unbroken line:* long, healthy life; *short, unbroken line:* shorter, but healthy life; *breaks in line:* illnesses or life changes; *broken toward the end of line:* old age of 85+; *inner arc line:* protection/spirit guide; *"M" in hand:* the clearer it is the longer the life.

Heart: From edge of palm under Mound of Mercury across upper palm—shows affection: *clean and strong:* has a loving nature; *chains:* indecision; *breaks:* a disappointment in love; *goes through a circle:* temporary separation from a loved one; *upswing:* instinctive sexuality, physical is important in love; *straight:* romantic imagery important in love; *2–3 branches at end:* physical, emotional, intellectual balance; *chained:* freely emotional; may be frequently hurt due to sensitivity; *island (especially by Mound of Jupiter):* disappointments; possible divorce.

Head: From edge of palm under Mound of Jupiter across mid-palm—shows intelligence and interests: *clear and strong:* so is the mind; *straight across the palm:* logical thinker; *slight downward curve:* likes math or science; *sharp downward curve:* artistic mind; *joined with Life Line:* close ties to family; *reaches the Mound of the Moon:* highly imaginative; *two-thirds of way across palm:* has average intelligence, influenced by lines touching it; *long line:* keen insight, range of intellectual interests; *wide gap at Life*

Line: impulsive and impatient; *narrow gap at Life Line:* tentativeness.

Heart and Head: *Close together:* cautiousness, introverted; *wide apart:* independent, high-spirited, extrovert; *longest line:* rules in love; *equal:* balance of both.

Destiny/Fate: Vertical base of palm to mounds beneath the fingers—shows career information [not everyone has this]: *long:* active throughout life; *unbroken:* lots of success; *crossed/breaks in line:* a setback or change in direction; *islands:* temporary obstacles; *fades at base of palm:* career tends to fade with age; *small triangle at base of palm:* quiet, uneventful life; *starts high in palm:* late career; *starts at Mound of Moon:* several careers; people involved; *starts at Mound of Venus:* family important in career; *second vertical line:* second career; *ending:* location influences career ending.

Health: Vertical from base of palm toward Mound of Mercury—shows the state of health (not everyone has this); *presence of line:* anxieties and nerves; *absence of line:* general good health.

Uranus: Vertical along or within the Mound of Moon—show psychic power [not everyone has this]: *presence of line:* highly intuitive, psychic, perceptive, eccentricity is a form of expressiveness; *absence of line:* normal intuitive powers.

Bracelets: A long wrist below palm—shows luck/longevity by clarity and length of lines: *first line by thumb:* health; *second line:* wealth; *third line:* happiness; *for women:* each line is also a week in a month; *complete ones:* high energy weeks in a month; *incomplete ones:* low energy weeks in a month.

Little Lines

Neptune: Arc at base of palm—shows health; *presence of line:* tendency to allergies or addictions [smoking, drinking, overeating, etc.); *absence of line:* non-allergic and not prone to addictions.

Children: Vertical beneath little finger: *number:* shows probable children.

Relationships: Horizontal lines beneath the little finger; *number:* deep friendships or mates; *age 35:* midway between base of little finger and heart line.

Healer: Set of vertical lines beneath area between little finger and ring finger: *three lines together:* healer or caregiver (nurse, doctor, etc.).

Travel: Horizontal lines at end of palm by Mound of Moon: *deep lines:* significant travels; *faint lines:* lesser travels; *no lines:* travels minimal or are not significantly important (vacations).

Circles & Rings

Circle of Venus: Arc beneath Mounds of Sun and Saturn: *presence:* artistic flair, sensitivity.

Ring of Saturn: Arc beneath Mound of Saturn: *presence:* conservative, sober, enjoys solitude.

Mystic Ring: Arch beneath Mound of Jupiter: *presence:* wisdom, able to teach, spiritual discernment and authority.

Other Marks

Asterisks or triangles: good luck; *cross-hatches on a line:* complications; *line breaks and begins:* above or below the former line indicates change; *dots on a line:* interruptions; *linked islands on a line:* recovering from a crisis; *grid on a line:* diffusion of energy; *line ends in a split:* adaptability.

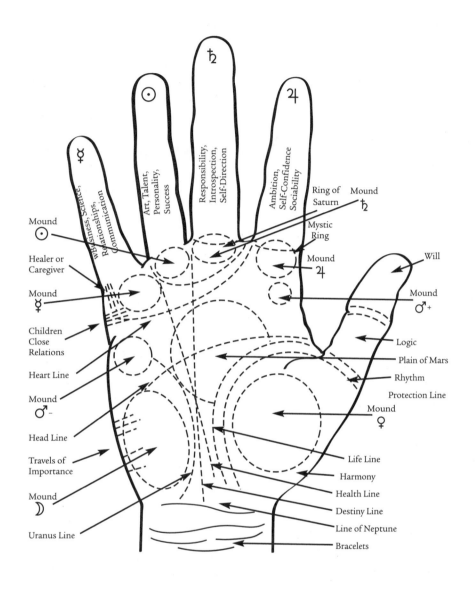

Responsibility,
Introspection,
Self-Direction

Art, Talent,
Personality,
Success

Business, Science,
Relationships,
Communication

Ambition,
Self-Confidence
Sociability

Ring of
Saturn

Mound
♄

Mystic
Ring

Mound   Will

Mound
☉

Healer or
Caregiver

Mound
☿

Mound
♃

Mound
♂+

Children
Close
Relations

Logic

Plain of Mars

Rhythm

Heart Line

Protection Line

Mound
♂-

Mound
♀

Head Line

Life Line

Travels of
Importance

Harmony

Health Line

Mound
☽

Destiny Line

Line of Neptune

Uranus Line

Bracelets

Key to Lines of the Hand

☉	Sun	☿	Mercury	♂	Mars	♄	Saturn
☽	Moon	♀	Venus	♃	Jupiter	○	Mounds

DIVINATION ENTERED BY:

_____

Divination Entered By:

_____

TO WRITE TO THE AUTHOR

If you wish to contact the author or would like more information about this book, please write to the author in care of Llewellyn Worldwide and we will forward your request. Llewellyn Worldwide cannot guarantee that every letter written to the author can be answered, but all will be forwarded. Write to:

Ann Moura
℅ Llewellyn Worldwide
2143 Wooddale Drive
Woodbury, MN 55125-2989

Please enclose a self-addressed stamped envelope for reply, or $1.00 to cover costs.
If outside U.S.A., enclose international postal reply coupon.

Many of Llewellyn's authors have websites with additional information and resources.
For more information, please visit our website at http://www.llewellyn.com.